Come, Let's Play

Springer-Verlag Berlin Heidelberg GmbH

David Harel   Rami Marelly

Come, Let's Play:

Scenario-Based Programming
Using LSCs and the Play-Engine

With 185 Figures and CD-ROM

 Springer

David Harel
Rami Marelly

The Weizmann Institute of Science
Faculty of Mathematics and Computer Science
Rehovot 76100, Israel

Library of Congress Cataloging-in-Publication Data
Harel, David, 1950–
Come, let's play: scenario-based programming using LSCs and the play-engine/
David Harel, Rami Marelly.
  p.cm.
  ISBN 978-3-540-00787-6   ISBN 978-3-642-19029-2 (eBook)
  DOI 10.1007/978-3-642-19029-2
  1. Software engineering. 2. System design. 3. Object-oriented programming (Computer
  science) 4. Visual programming languages (Computer science) I. Marelly, Rami, 1967–
  II. Title
QA76.758.H365 2003
005.1–dc21   2003045546

ACM Computing Classification (1998): D.2, C.2.0, B.4.0, D.0, D.1.5,
D.3, I.6.5, I.6.8

http://www.springer.de

© Springer-Verlag Berlin Heidelberg 2003
Originally published by Springer-Verlag Berlin Heidelberg New York in 2003

Cover design: KünkelLopka, Heidelberg
Typesetting: Camera-ready by authors
Printed on acid-free paper   45/3142 GF– 5 4 3 2 1 0

Preface

This book does not tell a story. Instead, it is *about* stories. Or rather, in technical terms, it is about scenarios. Scenarios of system behavior. It concentrates on **reactive systems**, be they software or hardware, or combined computer-embedded systems, including distributed and real-time systems.

We propose a different way to program such systems, centered on inter-object scenario-based behavior. The book describes a language, two techniques, and a supporting tool. The language is a rather broad extension of **live sequence charts** (**LSCs**), the original version of which was proposed in 1998 by W. Damm and the first-listed author of this book. The first of the two techniques, called **play-in**, is a convenient way to 'play in' scenario-based behavior directly from the system's graphical user interface (GUI). The second technique, **play-out**, makes it possible to execute, or 'play out', the behavior on the GUI as if it were programmed in a conventional intra-object state-based fashion. All this is implemented in full in our tool, the **Play-Engine**.

The book can be viewed as offering improvements in some of the phases of known system development life cycles, e.g., requirements capture and analysis, prototyping, and testing. However, there is a more radical way to view the book, namely, as proposing an alternative way to program reactivity, which, being based on inter-object scenarios, is a lot closer to how people think about systems and their behavior.

We are excited by the apparent potential of this work. However, whether or not it is adopted and becomes really useful, what kinds of systems are the ideas most fitting for, and how we should develop methodologies for large-scale applications, all remain to a large extent open questions. Whatever the case, we hope that the book triggers further research and experimentation.

David Harel and Rami Marelly
Rehovot, February 2003

Note on the Software

The Play-Engine tool is available with the book for free, and the attached CD contains most of the files needed for using the software. However, some of the ideas behind the play-in and play-out methods are patent-pending, and both the relevant intellectual property and the Play-Engine software itself are owned by the Weizmann Institute of Science. In order to obtain the remaining parts of the software, please visit the book's website, `www.wisdom.weizmann.ac.il/~playbook`, where you will be asked to sign an appropriate license agreement and to register your details.

A reservation is in order here: the Play-Engine is not a commercial product (at least at the time of writing), and should be regarded as a research-level tool. Thus, its reliability and ease of use are less than what would be expected from professional software, and we cannot be held responsible for its performance. Nevertheless, we will make an effort to correct bugs and to otherwise improve and modify the tool, posting periodical updates on the website. In fact, we have already made some slight changes in the software since the text of the book was finalized a few weeks ago; these are all documented in the User Guide that is attached to the software. We would be very grateful if readers would use the appropriate locations on the website to report any errors, both in the software and in the text of the book.

So, please do come and visit the site, sign in, download, play, and enjoy...

Acknowledgments

Our first thanks go to Werner Damm from the University of Oldenburg. His 1997–98 collaboration with the first-listed author — to which he brought both the scientist's skill and the pragmatist's insight — yielded the original version of the LSCs language, which turned out to be the crucial prerequisite of our work.

A very special thanks goes to Hillel Kugler and Na'aman Kam for being such demanding, yet tolerant users of the Play-Engine. Many of their comments and suggestions have found their way into the material presented here. Hillel's work on smart play-out (cosupervised by Amir Pnueli) is the most promising follow-up research project related to the topic of this book, and we would like to further thank him for his help in our research on symbolic instances, and for his dedication in the effort of writing Chap. 18. Na'aman also supplied the examples from the C. elegans nematode model given in that chapter.

We received helpful suggestions and insightful comments from several other people during our work. They include Liran Carmel, Sol Efroni, Yael Kfir, Jochen Klose, Yehuda Koren, Anat Maoz, David Peleg, Amir Pnueli, Ehud Shapiro, Gera Weiss and an anonymous referee.

Thanks go to Dan Barak for his work on connecting multiple Play-Engines (the SEC project) and for helping with the implementation of external objects. Evgeniy Bart and Maksim Frenkel helped develop an early version of GUIEdit.

The first-listed author would also like to thank the Verimag research center in Grenoble, and its director, Joseph Sifakis, for a generous part-time visiting position in 2002, during which parts of the book were written.

The second-listed author would like to thank Orna Grumberg and Moti Kehat for helping him make the right choices at the right times.

Contents

Part III. Basic Behavior

Part I

Prelude

1. Introduction

1.1 What Are We Talking About?

What kinds of systems are we interested in? Well, first and foremost, we have in mind computerized and computer embedded systems, mainly those that are reactive in nature. For these **reactive systems**, as they are called, the complexity we have to deal with does not stem from complex computations or complex data, but from intricate to-and-from interaction — between the system and its environment and between parts of the system itself.

Interestingly, reactivity is not an exclusive characteristic of man-made computerized systems. It occurs also in biological systems, which, despite being a lot smaller than us humans and our homemade artifacts, can also be a lot *more* complicated, and it also occurs in economic and social systems, which are a lot larger than a single human. Being able to fully understand and analyze these kinds of systems, and possibly to predict their future behavior, involves the same kind of thinking required for computerized reactive systems.

When people think about reactive systems, their thoughts fall very naturally into the realm of **scenarios of behavior**. You do not find too many people saying things like "Well, the controller of my ATM can be in waiting-for-user-input mode or in connecting-to-bank-computer mode or in delivering-money mode; in the first case, here are the possible inputs and the ATM's reactions, ...; in the second case, here is what happens, ..., etc.". Rather, you find them saying things like "If I insert my card, and then press this button and type in my PIN, then the following shows up on the display, and by pressing this other button my account balance will show". In other words, it has always been a lot more natural to describe and discuss the reactive behavior of a system by the scenarios it enables rather than by the state-based reactivity of each of its components. This is particularly true of some of the early and late stages of the system development process — e.g., during requirements capture and analysis, and during testing and maintenance — and is in fact what underlies the early stage use case approach. On the other hand, it seems that in order to *implement* the system, as opposed to stating its required behavior or preparing test suites, **state-based modeling** is needed, whereby we must specify for each component the complete array of possibilities for incoming events and changes and the component's reactions to them.

This is, in fact, an interesting and subtle duality. On the one hand, we have scenario-based behavioral descriptions, which cut across the boundaries of the components (or objects) of the system, in order to provide coherent and comprehensive descriptions of scenarios of behavior. A sort of **inter-object**, 'one story for all relevant objects' approach. On the other hand, we have state-based behavioral descriptions, which remain within the component, or object, and are based on providing a complete description of the reactivity of each one. A sort of **intra-object**, 'all pieces of stories for one object' approach. The former is more intuitive and natural for humans to grasp and is therefore fitting in the requirements and testing stages. The second approach, however, has always been the one needed for implementation; after all, implementing a system requires that each of the components or objects is supplied with its complete reactivity, so that it can actually run, or execute. You can't capture the entire desired behavior of a complex system by a bunch of scenarios. And even if you could, it wouldn't be at all clear how you could execute such a seemingly unrelated collection of behaviors in an orderly fashion. Figure 1.1 visualizes these two approaches.

This duality can also be explained in day-to-day terms. It is like the difference between describing the game of soccer by specifying the complete reactivity of each player, of the ball, of the goal's wooden posts, etc., vs. specifying the possible scenarios of play that the game supports. As another example, suppose we wanted to describe the 'behavior' of some company office. It would be a lot more natural to describe the inter-object scenarios, such as how an employee mails off 50 copies of a document (this could involve the employee, the secretary, the copy machine, the mail room, etc.), how the boss arranges a conference call with the project managers, or how information on vacation days and sick leave is organized and forwarded to the payroll office. Contrast this with the intra-object style, whereby we would have to provide complete information on the modes of operation and reactivity of the boss, the secretary, the employees, the copy machine, the mail room, etc.

We are not claiming that scenario-based behavior is technically superior in some global sense, only that it is a lot more *natural*. In fact, now is a good time to mention that mere isolated scenarios of behavior that the system can possibly give rise to are far from adequate. In order to get significant mileage out of scenario-based behavior, we need to be able to attach various modalities to the scenarios we are specifying. We would like to distinguish between scenarios that *may* occur and those that *must*, between those that occur spontaneously and those that need some trigger to cause them to occur.

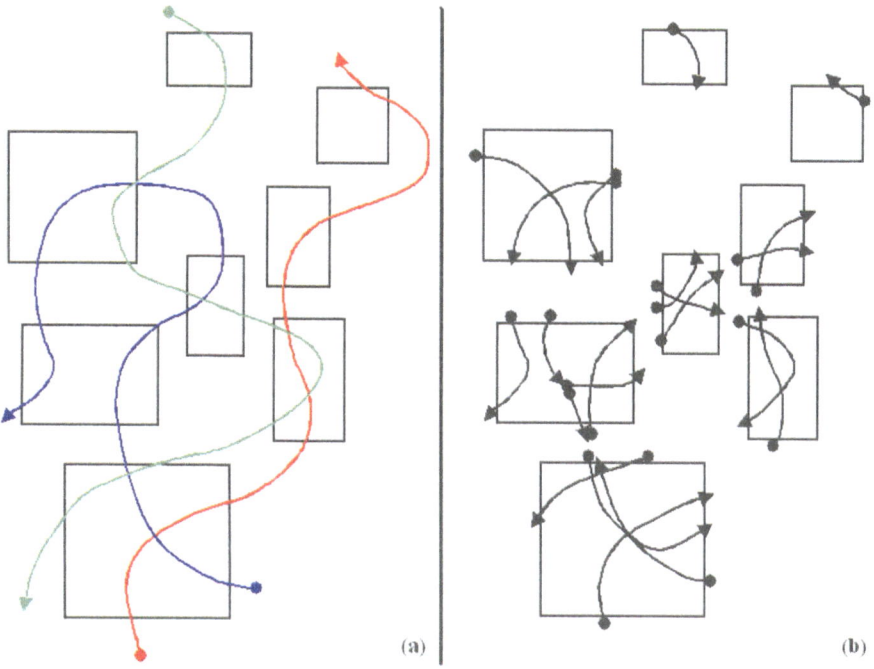

Fig. 1.1. Inter-object vs. intra-object behavior

We would like to be able to specify multiple scenarios that combine with each other, or even with themselves, in subtle sequential and/or concurrent ways. We want generic scenarios that can be instantiated by different objects of the same class, we want to be able to use variables to store and retrieve values, and we want means for specifying time. Significantly, we would also like to be able to specify **anti-scenarios**, i.e., ones that are forbidden, in the sense that if they occur there is something very wrong: either something in the specification is not as we wanted, or else the implementation does not correctly satisfy the specification.

Obviously, it would also be very nice if we could actually 'see' scenario-based behavior in operation, before (or instead of?) spending lots of time, energy and money on intra-object state-based modeling that leads to the implementation. In other words, we could do with an approach to inter-object behavior that is expressive, natural and executable.

This is what the book is about.

1.2 What Are We Trying to Do?

We propose a powerful setup, within which one can conveniently capture scenario-based behavior, and then execute it and simulate the system under development exactly as if it were specified in the conventional state-based fashion. Our work involves a language, two techniques with detailed underlying algorithms, and a tool. The entire approach is made possible by the language of **live sequence charts**, or **LSCs**, which is extended here in a number of ways, resulting in a highly expressive medium for scenario-based behavior. The first of our two techniques involves a user-friendly and natural way to **play in** scenario-based behavior directly from the system's GUI (or some abstract version thereof, such as an object-model diagram), during which LSCs are generated automatically. The second technique, which we consider to be the technical highlight of our work, makes it possible to **play out** the behavior, that is, to execute the system as constrained by the grand sum of the scenario-based information. These ideas are supported in full by our tool — the **Play-Engine**.

There are essentially two ways to view this book. The first — the more conservative one — is to view it as offering improvements to the various stages of accepted life-cycles for system development: a more convenient way to capture behavioral requirements, the ability to express more powerful scenario-based behavior, a fully worked-out formalization of use cases, a means for executing use cases and their instantiations, tools for the dynamic testing of requirements prior to building the actual system model or implementation, a highly expressive medium for preparing test suites, and a means for testing systems by dynamic and run-time comparison of two dual-view executables.

The second way to view our work is less conservative. It calls for considering the possibility of an alternative way of programming the behavior of a reactive system, which is totally scenario-based and inter-object in nature. Basic to this is the idea that LSCs can actually constitute the implementation of a system, with the play-out algorithms and the Play-Engine being a sort of 'universal reactive mechanism' that executes the LSCs as if they constituted a conventional implementation. If one adopts this view, behavioral specification of a reactive system would not have to involve any intra-object modeling (e.g., in languages like statecharts) or code.

This of course is a more outlandish idea, and still requires that a number of things be assessed and worked out in more detail for it to actually be feasible in large-scale systems. Mainly, it requires that a large amount of experience and modeling wisdom be accumulated around this new way of specifying executable behavior. Still, we see no reason why this ambitious possibility should not be considered as it is now. Scenario-based behavior is what people use when they think about their systems, and our work shows that it is possible to capture a rich spectrum of such behavior conveniently, and to execute it directly, resulting in a runnable artifact that is as powerful as an intra-object model. From the point of view of the user, executing such behavior looks no different from executing any system model. Moreover, it is hard to underestimate the advantages of having the behavior structured according to the way the engineers invent and design it and the users comprehend it (for example, in the testing, maintenance and modifications stages, in sharing the specification process with less technically oriented people, etc.).

In any case, the book concentrates on describing and illustrating the ideas and technicalities themselves, and not on trying to convince the reader of this or that usage thereof. How, in what role, and to what extent these ideas will indeed become useful are things that remain to be seen.

1.3 What's in the Book?

Besides this brief introductory chapter, Part I of the book, the Prelude, contains a chapter providing the background and context for the rest of the book, followed by a high-level overview of the entire approach, from which the reader can get a pretty good idea of what we are doing.

Part II, Foundations, describes the underlying basics of the object model, the LSCs language and the Play-Engine tool.

Parts III, IV and V treat in more detail the constructs of the enriched language of LSCs, and the way they are played in and played out. Almost every chapter in these three parts contains a section named "And a Bit More Formally ...", which provides the syntax and operational semantics for the constructs described in the chapter. As we progress from chapter to chapter, we use a blue/black type convention to highlight the additions to, and modifications of, this formal description. (Appendix A contains the fully accumulated syntax and semantics.)

Part VI describes extensions and enhancements, with chapters on the innards of the Play-Engine tool, particularly the play-out algorithms, on the GUI editor we have built to support the construction of application GUIs, on the smart play-out module, which uses formal verification techniques to drive parts of the execution, and on future research and development directions.

Part VII contains several technical appendices, one of which is the full formal definition of the enriched LSCs language.

2. Setting the Stage

In this chapter we set the stage for the rest of the book, by describing some of the main ideas in systems and software engineering research that lead to the material developed later. We discuss visual formalisms and modeling languages, model execution and code generation, the connection between structure and behavior, and the difference between implementable behavior and behavioral requirements. We then go on to describe in somewhat more detail some of the basic concepts we shall be expanding upon, such as the inter-/intra-object dichotomy, MSCs vs. LSCs, the play-in and play-out techniques, and the way all these fit into our global view of the system development process.

2.1 Modeling and Code Generation

Over the years, the main approaches to high-level system modeling have been **structured-analysis and structured-design** (SA/SD), and **object-oriented analysis and design** (OOAD). The two are about a decade apart in initial conception and evolution. Over the years, both approaches have yielded **visual formalisms** for capturing the various parts of a system model, most notably its structure and behavior. A recent book, [120], nicely surveys and discusses some of these approaches.

SA/SD, which started in the late 1970s, is based on raising classic procedural programming concepts to the modeling level and using diagrams for modeling system structure. Structural models are based on **functional decomposition** and the flow of information, and are depicted using hierarchical dataflow diagrams. Many methodologists were instrumental in setting the ground for the SA/SD paradigm, by devising the functional decomposition and dataflow diagram framework, including DeMarco [31], and Constantine and Yourdon [25]. Parnas's work over the years was very influential too.

In the mid-1980s, several methodology teams enriched this basic SA/SD model by providing a way to add state-based behavior to these efforts, using state diagrams or the richer language of **statecharts** (see Harel [42]).

These teams were Ward and Mellor [117], Hatley and Pirbhai [54], and the Statemate team [48]. A state diagram or statechart is associated with each function or activity, describing its behavior. Several nontrivial issues had to be worked out to properly connect structure with behavior, enabling the modeler to construct a comprehensive and semantically rigorous model of the system; it is not enough to simply decide on a behavioral language and then associate each function or activity with a behavioral description.[1] The three teams struggled with this issue, and their decisions on how to link structure with behavior ended up being very similar. Careful behavioral modeling and its close linking with system structure are especially crucial for **reactive systems** [52, 93], of which real-time systems are a special case.

The first commercial tool to enable **model execution** and full **code generation** from high-level models was Statemate, built by I-Logix and released in 1987 [48, 60]. (Incidentally, the code generated need not necessarily result in software; it could be code in a hardware description language, leading to hardware.) A detailed summary of the SA/SD languages for structure and behavior, their relationships and the way they are embedded in the Statemate tool appears in [53].

Of course, modelers need not adopt state machines or statecharts to describe behavior. There are many other possible choices, and these can also be linked with the SA/SD functional decomposition. They include such visual formalisms as **Petri nets** [101] or **SDL diagrams** [110], more algebraic ones like **CSP** [59] or **CCS** [88], and ones that are closer in appearance to programming languages, like **Esterel** [14] and **Lustre** [41]. Clearly, if one does not want to use any such high-level formalisms, code in an appropriate conventional programming language could be written directly in order to specify the behavior of a function in an SA/SD decomposition.

The late 1980s saw the first proposals for object-oriented analysis and design (OOAD). Just like in the SA/SD approach, here too the basic idea in modeling system structure was to lift concepts up from the programming level — in this case object-oriented programming — to the modeling level and to use visual formalisms. Inspired by **entity-relationship (ER) diagrams** [21], several methodology teams recommended various forms of **class diagrams** and **object model diagrams** for modeling system structure [16, 26, 105, 111]. To model behavior, most object-oriented modeling approaches also adopted statecharts [42]. Each class is 'programmed' using a statechart, which then serves to describe the behavior of any instance object of that class; see, e.g., [105, 16, 44].

---

[1] This would be like saying that when you build a car all you need are the structural things — body, chassis, wheels, etc. — and an engine, and you then merely stick the engine under the hood and you are done.

In the OOAD world, the issue of connecting structure and behavior is subtler and a lot more complicated than in the SA/SD one. Classes represent dynamically changing collections of concrete objects. Behavioral modeling must thus address issues related to object creation and destruction, message delegation, relationship modification and maintenance, aggregation, inheritance, and so on. The links between behavior and structure must be defined in sufficient detail and with enough rigor to support the construction of tools that enable model execution and full code generation. See Fig. 2.1.

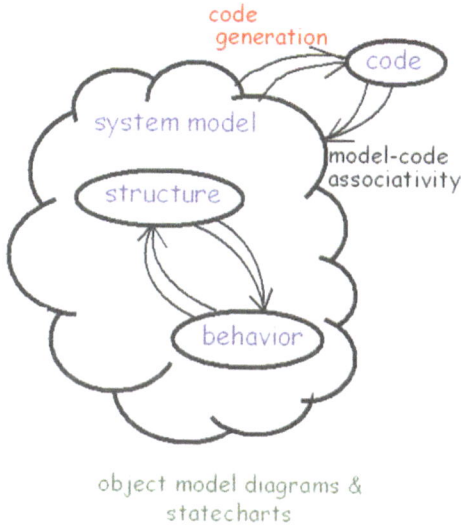

Fig. 2.1. Object-oriented system modeling with code generation

Obviously, if we have the ability to generate full code, we would eventually want that code to serve as the basis for the final implementation. In the OOAD world, a few tools have been able to do this. One is Rhapsody, also from I-Logix [60], which is based on the work of Harel and Gery in [44] on executable object modeling with statecharts. Another is ObjectTime, which is based on the ROOM method of Selic et al. [111], and is now part of the Rose RealTime tool from Rational [100]. There is no doubt that techniques for this kind of 'super-compilation' from high-level visual formalisms down to programming languages will improve in time. Providing higher levels of abstraction with automated downward transformations has always been the way to go, as long as the abstractions are ones with which the engineers who do the actual work are happy.

In 1997, the Object Management Group (OMG) adopted as a standard the **unified modeling language** (UML), put together by a large team led by Booch, Rumbaugh and Jacobson; see [115, 106]. The class/object diagrams, adapted from the Booch method [16] and the OMT (object modeling technique) method [105], and driven by statecharts for behavior [44], constitute that part of the UML that specifies unambiguous, executable (and therefore implementable) models. It has been termed XUML, for **executable UML**. The UML also has several means for specifying more elaborate aspects of system structure and architecture (for example, packages and components). Large amounts of further information on the UML can be found in OMG's website [115].

2.2 Requirements

So much for modeling systems in the SA/SD and OO worlds. However, the importance of executable models lies not only in their ability to help lead to a final implementation, but also in testing and debugging, the basis of which are the **requirements**. These constitute the constraints, desires, dreams and hopes we entertain concerning the behavior of the system under development. We want to make sure, both during development and when we feel development is over, that the system does, or will do, what we intend or hope for it to do.

Requirements can be formal (rigorously and precisely defined) or informal (written, say, in natural language or pseudocode). An interesting way to describe high-level behavioral requirements is the idea of **use cases**; see Jacobson [62]. A use case is an informal description of a collection of possible scenarios involving the system under discussion and its external actors. Use cases describe the observable reactions of a system to events triggered by its users. Usually, the description of a use case is divided into the main, most frequently used scenario, and exceptional scenarios that give rise to less central behaviors branching out from the main one (e.g., possible errors, cancelling an operation before completion, etc.). However, since use cases are high-level and informal by nature, they cannot serve as the basis for formal testing and verification. To support a more complete and rigorous development cycle, use cases must be translated into fully detailed requirements written in some formal language.

Ever since the early days of high-level programming, computer science researchers have grappled with requirements; namely, with how to best state what we want of a complex program or system. Notable efforts are those embodied in the classic Floyd/Hoare **inductive assertions** method, which uses

invariants, pre- and post-conditions and termination statements [12], and in the many variants of **temporal logic** [82]. These make it possible to express different kinds of requirements that are of interest in reactive systems. They include **safety constraints**, which state that bad things will not happen; for example, this program will never terminate with the wrong answer, or this elevator door will never open between floors. They also include **liveness constraints**, which state that good things must happen. For example, this program will eventually terminate, or this elevator will open its door on the desired floor within the allotted time limit.

A more recent way to specify requirements, which is popular in the realm of object-oriented systems, is to use **message sequence charts** (**MSCs**), which are used to specify scenarios as sequences of message interactions between object instances. This visual language was adopted as a standard long ago by the International Telecommunication Union (the ITU; formerly the CCITT) [123], and it also manifests itself in the UML as the language of **sequence diagrams** (see [115]). MSCs combine nicely with use cases, since they can specify the scenarios that instantiate the use cases. Sequence charts thus capture the desired interrelationships between the processes, tasks, components or object instances — and between them and the environment — in a way that is linear or quasilinear in time.[2] In other words, the modeler uses MSCs to formally visualize the actual scenarios that the more abstract and generic use cases were intended to denote.

Objects in MSCs are represented by vertical lines, and messages between these instances are represented by horizontal (or sometimes down-slanted) arrows. Conditional guards, showing up as elongated hexagons, specify statements that are to be true when reached. The overall effect of such a chart is to specify a scenario of behavior, consisting of messages flowing between objects and things having to be true along the way.

Figure 2.2 shows a simple example of an MSC for the quick-dial feature of a cellular telephone. The sequence of messages it depicts consists of the following: the user clicks the * key, and then clicks a digit on the *Keyboard*, followed by the *Send Key*, which sends a *Sent* indication to the internal *Chip*. The *Chip*, in turn, sends the digit to the *Memory* to retrieve the telephone number associated with the clicked digit, and then sends out the number to the external *Environment* to carry out a call. A signal is then received from the environment, guarded by a condition asserting that it is not a busy signal.

---

[2] Tasks, processes and components are mentioned here too, since although the book is couched in the terminology of object-orientation, many of the ideas apply also to other ways of structuring systems.

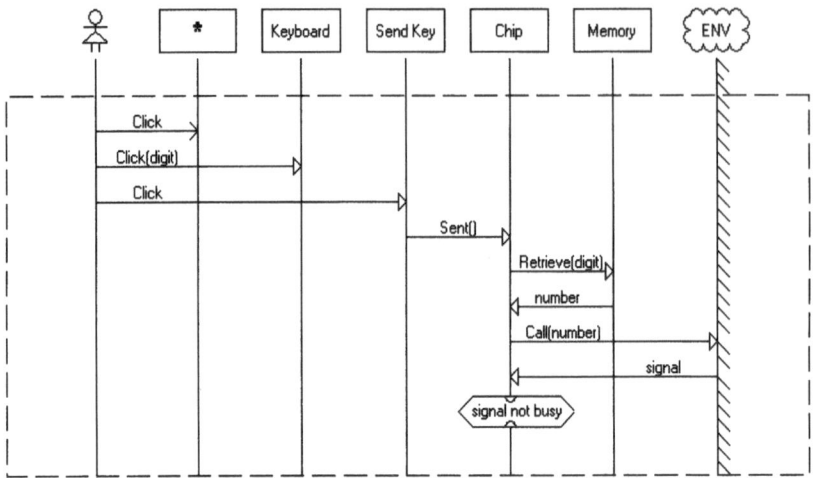

Fig. 2.2. A message sequence chart (MSC)

2.3 Inter-Object vs. Intra-Object Behavior

The style of behavior captured by sequence charts is inter-object, to be contrasted with the intra-object style of statecharts. Whereas a sequence chart captures what goes on in a scenario of behavior that takes place between and amongst the objects, a statechart captures the full behavioral specification for one of those objects (or tasks or processes). Statecharts thus provide details of an object's behavior under all possible conditions and in all the possible 'stories' described previously in the inter-object sequence charts.

Two points must now be made regarding sequence charts. The first is one of exposition: by and large, the subtle difference in the roles of sequence-based languages for behavior and component-based ones is not made clear in the literature. Again and again, one comes across articles and books (many of them related to UML) in which the very same phrases are used to introduce sequence diagrams and statecharts. At one point such a publication might say that "sequence diagrams can be used to specify behavior", and later it might say that "statecharts can be used to specify behavior". Sadly, the reader is told nothing about the fundamental difference in nature and usage between the two — that one is a medium for conveying requirements, i.e., the inter-object behavior required of a model, and the other is part of the executable model itself. This obscurity is one of the reasons many naive readers come away confused by the multitude of diagram types in the full UML standard and the lack of clear recommendations about what it means to specify the behavior of a system in a way that can be implemented and executed.

The second point is more substantial. As a requirements language, the many variants of MSCs, including the ITU standard [124] and the sequence diagrams adopted in the UML [115], as well as versions enriched with timing constraints and co-regions, and the **high-level MSCs** that make it possible to combine charts using the power of regular expressions, have very limited expressive power. Their semantics is intended to support the specification of possible scenarios of system behavior, and is therefore usually given by a set of simple constraints on the partial order of possible events in a system execution: along a vertical object line higher events precede lower ones, and the sending of a message precedes its receipt.[3] Virtually nothing can be said in such diagrams about what the system will actually do when run. They can state what might *possibly* occur, not what *must* occur. In the chart of Fig. 2.2, for example, there is nothing to indicate whether some parts of the scenario are mandatory. For example, can the *Memory* 'decide' not to send back a number in response to the request from the *Chip*? Does the guarding condition stating that the signal is not busy really *have* to be true? What happens if it is not? If one wants to be puristic, then, under most definitions of the semantics of message sequence charts, an empty system -- one that doesn't do anything in response to anything — satisfies such a chart. Hence, just sitting back and doing nothing will make your requirements happy. (Usually, however, there is a minimal, often implicit, requirement that each one of the specified sequence charts should have at least one run of the system that winds its way correctly through it.)

MSCs can be used to specify expected scenarios of behavior in the requirements stage, and can be used as test scenarios that will be later checked against the executing behavior of the final system. However, they are not enough if we want to specify the actual behavior of a reactive system in a scenario-based fashion. We would like to be able to say what may happen and what must happen, and also what is not allowed to happen. The latter gives rise to what we call **anti-scenarios**, in the sense that if they occur something is very wrong: either something in the specification is not as we wanted, or else the implementation does not correctly satisfy the specification. We would like to be able to specify **multiple scenarios** that combine with each other, or even with themselves, in subtle ways. We want to be able to specify **generic scenarios**, i.e., ones that stand for many specific scenarios, in that they can be instantiated by different objects of the same class. We want variables and means for specifying real time, and so on.

---

[3] There can also be **synchronous** messages, for which the two events are simultaneous.

2.4 Live Sequence Charts (LSCs)

In 1998 Damm and Harel addressed many of these deficiencies, resulting in an extension of MSCs, called **live sequence charts** (or **LSCs**); see [27]. The name comes from the ability to specify liveness, i.e., things that must occur. Technically, LSCs allow a distinction between possible and necessary behavior, both globally, on the level of an entire chart, and locally, when specifying events, guarding conditions, and progress over time within a chart.

LSCs have two types of charts: **universal** (enclosed within a solid borderline) and **existential** (enclosed within a dashed borderline). Universal charts are the more interesting ones, and are used to specify scenario-based behavior that applies to all possible system runs. A universal chart has two parts, turning it into a kind of if-then construct.[4] It has a **prechart** that specifies the scenario that, if satisfied, forces the system to also satisfy the actual chart body, the **main chart**. Thus, such an LSC induces an action-reaction relationship between the scenario appearing in its prechart and the one appearing in the chart body. Taken together, a collection of LSCs provides a set of action-reaction pairs of scenarios, and the universal ones must be satisfied at all times during any system run.

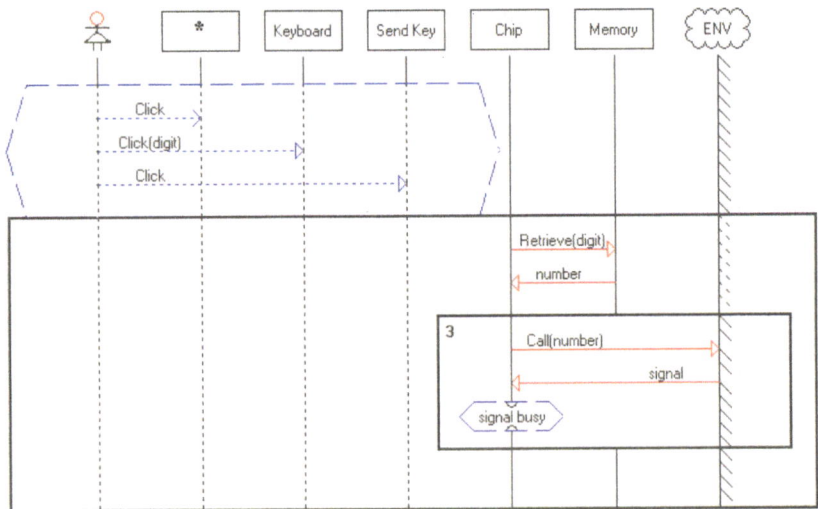

Fig. 2.3. A live sequence chart (LSC)

---

[4] This structure is actually very much like a $[\alpha]\langle\beta\rangle$**true** construct in dynamic logic, evaluated in each system run.

Within a chart, the live elements, termed **hot**, signify things that must occur, and they can be used to specify various modalities of behavior, including anti-scenarios. The other elements, termed **cold**, signify things that may occur, and they can be used to specify control structures like branching and iteration. In subsequence chapters we will see numerous examples of the expressive power of these two kinds of elements, and the subtlety of the differences between them.

Figure 2.3 shows a universal LSC that is an enriched version of the MSC in Fig. 2.2. The first three events are in the prechart, and the others are in the main chart. Hence, the LSC states that whenever the user clicks ∗, followed by a digit, followed by the *Send Key*, the rest of the scenario must be satisfied. The messages in the main chart are hot (depicted by solid red arrows, in contrast to the dashed blue ones in the prechart), as are the vertical lines. Thus progress along all lines in the main chart must occur and the messages must be sent and received in order for the chart to be satisfied. In addition, a loop has been added, within which the chip can make up to three attempts to get a non-busy signal from the environment.

The loop is controlled by the cold (blue dashed line) guarding condition, which means that as long as the signal is busy the 3-round loop continues. The semantics of a cold condition, however, is such that if it is false nothing bad has happened, and execution simply moves up one level, out of the innermost chart or subchart. In our case, if the signal is not busy the loop is exited (which means that the entire chart has been satisfied). In contrast to this, a hot condition *must* be true when reached during a system run, and if it is not the system must abort, since this is an unforgivable error. One way to specify an anti-scenario using hot conditions (e.g., an elevator door opening when it shouldn't, or a missile firing when the radar is not locked on the target) is to include the entire unwanted scenario in the prechart, followed by a main chart that contains a single false hot condition.

2.5 Testing, Verification and Synthesis

Since they are more expressive than MSCs,[5] LSCs also make it possible to have a closer look at the aforementioned dichotomy of reactive behavior, namely, the relationship between the inter-object requirements view and the intra-object implementable model view.

If we now extend Fig. 2.1, adding to it the requirements, we obtain Fig. 2.4. Its right-hand side is the implementable intra-object system model, which

---

[5] The expressive power of LSCs is actually very close to that of statecharts as embedded in the object-oriented paradigm — what we called earlier XUML.

leads to the final software or hardware, and will consist of the complete behavior coded for each object. In contrast, it is common to assume that the left-hand side, the set of requirements, is not implementable or executable. A collection of scenarios cannot be considered an implementable model of the system: How would such a system operate? What would it do under general dynamic circumstances? How would we decide what scenarios would be relevant when some event suddenly occurs out of the blue? How should we deal with the mandatory, the possible and the forbidden, during execution? And how would we know what subsequent behaviors these and other modalities of behavior might entail?

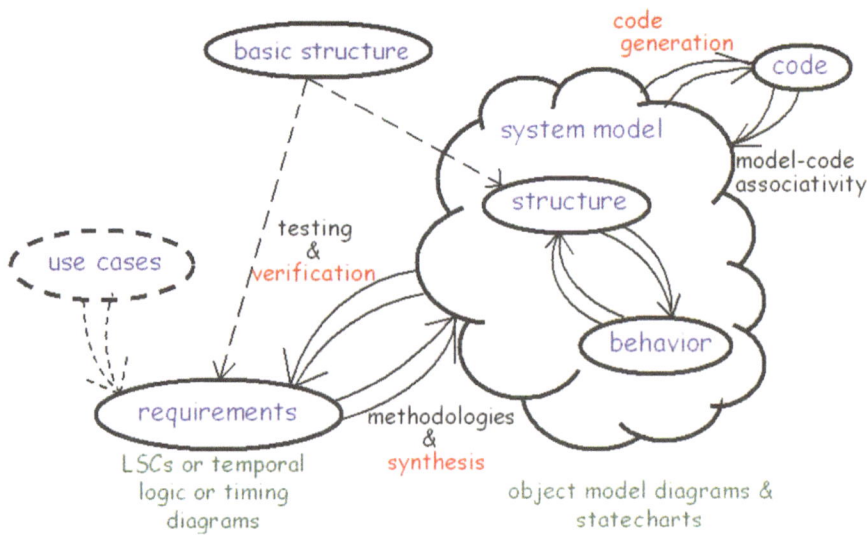

Fig. 2.4. Conventional system development

One of the main messages of this book is that this assumption is no longer valid. Scenario-based behavior need not be limited to requirements that will be specified before the real executable system is built and will then be used merely to test that system. Scenario-based behavior, we claim, can actually be executed. Furthermore, we predict that in many cases such behavior will become the implemented system itself. This will be illustrated and discussed in detail as the book progresses.

For now, let us discuss the relations and transitions between the different parts of the conventional setup of system development, as shown in Fig. 2.4. The arrow between the use cases and the requirements is dashed for a reason: it does not represent a 'hard' computerized process. Going from use cases to formal requirements is a 'soft' methodological process performed manually by system designers and engineers. It is considered an art or a craft and requires a good understanding of the target formal requirements language and a large amount of creativity.

The arrow going from the system model to the requirements depicts testing and verifying the model against the requirements. Here is a nice way to do testing using an automated tool.[6] Assume the user has specified the requirements as a set of sequence diagrams, perhaps instantiating previously prepared use cases. For simplicity, let us say that this results in a diagram called A. Later, when the executable intra-object system model has been specified, the user can execute it and ask that during execution the system should automatically construct an animated sequence diagram, call it B, on the fly. This diagram will show the dynamics of object interaction as it actually happens during execution. When this execution is completed, the tool can be asked to compare diagrams A and B, and to highlight any inconsistencies, such as contradictions in the partial order of events, or events appearing in one diagram but not in the other. In this way, the tool helps debug the behavior of the system against the requirements.

A recently developed tool, called TestConductor, which is integrated into Rhapsody [60], enables a richer kind of testing using a subset of LSCs. The test scenarios can describe scenarios of interaction between the environment and the system under development. The tool then runs the tests, and simulates the behavior of the environment by monitoring the test scenarios and sending messages to the system on behalf of the environment, when required. The tool determines the results of such a test by comparing the sequence diagrams produced by the system with those that describe the tests using visual comparison, as described above.

Note that even these powerful ways to check the behavior of a system model against our expectations are limited to those executions that we actually carry out. They thus suffer from the same drawbacks as classic testing and debugging. Since a system can have an infinite number of runs, some will always go unchecked, and it could be those that violate the requirements (in our case, by being inconsistent with diagram A). As Dijkstra famously put it years ago, "testing and debugging cannot be used to demonstrate the absence of errors, only their presence".

One remedy is to use true verification. This is not what CASE-tool people in the 1980s often called "validation and verification", which amounted to little more than checking the consistency of the model's syntax. What we have in mind is a mathematically rigorous and precise proof that the model

---

[6] Rhapsody supports this technique.

satisfies the requirements, and we want this to be done automatically by a computerized verifier. Since we would like to use highly expressive languages like LSCs (or the analogous temporal logics [82] or timing diagrams [108]) for requirements, this means far more than just executing the system model and making sure that the sequence diagrams you get from the run are consistent with those you prepared in advance. It means making sure, for example, that the things an LSC says are not allowed to happen (the anti-scenarios) will indeed never happen, and the things it says must happen (or must happen within certain time constraints) will indeed happen. These are facts that, in general, no amount of execution can fully verify.

Although general verification is a non-computable algorithmic problem, and for finite-state systems it is computationally intractable, the idea of rigorously verifying programs and systems — hardware and software — has come a long way since the pioneering work on inductive assertions in the late 1960s and the later work on temporal logic and model checking. These days we can safely say that true verification can be carried out in many, many cases, even in the slippery and complex realm of reactive real-time systems.

So much for the arrow denoting checking the model against the requirements. In the opposite direction, the transition from the requirements to a model is also a long-studied issue. Many system development methodologies provide guidelines, heuristics, and sometimes carefully worked-out step-by-step processes for this. However, as good and useful as these processes are, they are 'soft' methodological recommendations on how to proceed, not rigorous and automated methods. Here too, there is a 'hard', computerized way to go: Instead of guiding system developers in informal ways to build models according to their dreams and hopes, the idea is to automatically synthesize an implementation model directly from those dreams and hopes, if they are indeed implementable. (For the sake of the discussion, we assume that the structure — for example, the division into objects or components and their relationships — has already been determined.) This is a whole lot harder than generating code from a system model, which is really but a high-level kind of compilation. The duality between the inter-object scenario-based style (requirements) and the intra-object state-based style (modeling) in saying what a system does over time renders the synthesis of an implementable model from the requirements a truly formidable task. It is not too hard to do this for the weak MSCs, which can't say much about what we really want the system to do. It is a lot more difficult for far more realistic requirements languages, such as LSCs or temporal logic.

How can we synthesize a good first approximation of the statecharts from the LSCs? Several researchers have addressed such issues in the past, resulting in work on certain kinds of synthesis from temporal logic [98] and timing diagrams [108]. In [46], there is a first-cut attempt at algorithms for synthesizing state machines and statecharts from simple LSCs. The technique therein involves first determining whether the requirements are consistent (i.e., whether there exists any system model satisfying them), then proving that being consistent and having a model (being implementable) are equivalent notions, and then using the proof of consistency to synthesize an actual model. The process just outlined yields unacceptably large models in the worst case, so that the problem cannot yet be said to have been solved satisfactorily. We do believe, however, that synthesis will eventually end up like verification — hard in principle but not beyond a practical and useful solution in practice. This is the reason for the solid arrow in Fig. 2.4.

2.6 The Play-In/Play-Out Approach

To complete a full rigorous system development cycle we need to bridge the gap between use cases and the more formal languages used to describe the different scenarios. How should the more expressive requirements themselves be specified? One cannot hope to have a general technique for synthesizing LSCs or temporal logic from the use cases automatically, since use cases are informal and high level. This leaves us with having to construct the LSCs manually. Now, LSCs constitute a formal (albeit, visual) language, and constructing them requires the skill of working in an abstract environment, and detailed knowledge of the syntax and semantics of the language. In a world in which we would like as much automation as possible we would like to make this process more convenient and natural, and accessible to a wider spectrum of people.

This problem was addressed towards the end of [43], and a higher-level approach to the problem of specifying scenario-based behavior, termed **play-in scenarios**, was proposed and briefly sketched. The methodology, supported by a tool called the **Play-Engine** was presented in more detail by the present authors in [49]. The main idea of the play-in process is to raise the level of abstraction in requirements engineering, and to work with a look-alike version of the system under development. This enables people who are unfamiliar with LSCs, or who do not want to work with such formal languages directly, to specify the behavioral requirements of systems using a high-level, intuitive and user-friendly mechanism. These could include domain experts, application engineers, requirements engineers, and even potential end-users.

What 'play-in' means is that the system's developer (we will often call him/her a **user** — not to be confused with the eventual end-users of the system under development, which are sometimes called **actors** in the literature) first builds the GUI of the system, with no behavior built into it, with only the basic methods supported by each GUI object. This is given to the Play-Engine. In systems for which there is a meaning to the layout of hidden objects (e.g., a board of an electrical system), the user may build the graphical representation of these objects as well. In fact, for GUI-less systems, or for sets of internal objects, we simply use the object model diagram as a GUI. In any case, the user then 'plays' the incoming events on the GUI, by clicking buttons, rotating knobs and sending messages (calling functions) to hidden objects, in an intuitive drag & drop manner. (With an object model diagram as the interface, the user clicks the objects and/or the methods and the parameters.) By similarly playing the GUI, often using right-clicks, the user then describes the desired reactions of the system and the conditions that may or must hold. As this is being done, the Play-Engine does essentially two things continuously: it instructs the GUI to show its current status using the graphical features built into it, and it constructs the corresponding LSCs automatically. The engine queries the application GUI (that was built by the user) for its structure and methods, and interacts with it, thus manipulating the information entered by the user and building and exhibiting the appropriate formal version of the behavior. So much for play-in.

After playing in (a part of) the behavior, the natural thing to do is to make sure that it reflects what the user intended to say. Instead of doing this the conventional way, by building an intra-object model, or prototype implementation, and using model execution to test it, we would like to test the inter-object behavior directly. Accordingly, we extend the power of our GUI-intensive play methodology, to make it possible not only to specify and capture the required behavior but to test and validate it as well. And here is where our complementary **play-out** mechanism enters.

In play-out, which was first described in [49], the user simply plays the GUI application as he/she would have done when executing a system model, or the final system, limiting him-/herself to end-user and external environment actions. As this is going on, the Play-Engine keeps track of the actions and causes other actions and events to occur as dictated by the universal charts in the specification. Here too, the engine interacts with the GUI application and uses it to reflect the system state at any given moment. This process of the user operating the GUI application and the Play-Engine causing it to react according to the specification has the effect of working with an executable model, but with no intra-object model having to be built or synthesized.

Figure 2.5 shows an enhanced development cycle, which includes the play-in/play-out methodology inserted in the appropriate place.

We should emphasize that the behavior played out need not be merely the scenarios that were played in. The user is not just tracing previously

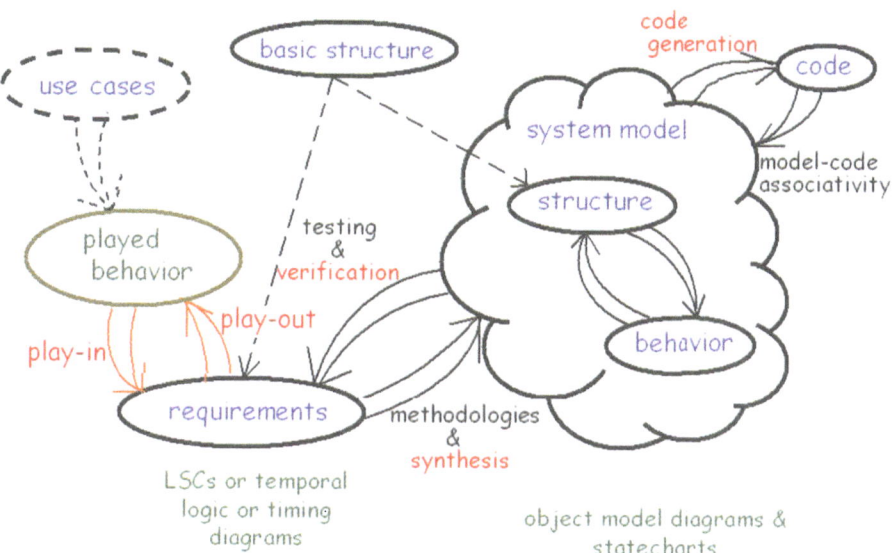

Fig. 2.5. Play-in/play-out in the system development cycle

thought-out stories, but is operating the system freely, as he/she sees fit. The algorithmic mechanism underlying play-out is nontrivial, especially when we extend LSCs with symbolic instances, time and forbidden elements, and will be described in more detail later on.

We should also remark that there is no inherent difficulty in modifying the Play-Engine so that play-in produces the formal version of the behavior in languages other than LSCs, such as appropriate variants of temporal logic [92] or timing diagrams [108]. The same applies to the play-out process, which could have been applied to carefully defined versions of such languages too.

As discussed in the previous chapter, we believe that the LSC specification, together with the play-in/play-out approach, may be considered to be not just the system's requirements but actually its final implementation. A more modest goal would be to build system prototypes by first creating the application GUI and then playing in the behavior, instead of coding it. The same holds for constructing tutorials for system usage prior to actual system development. Thus, we strongly believe there is a potential to use the Play-Engine and its underlying ideas not only for isolated parts of a development cycle, but throughout the entire cycle. Figure 2.6 shows the parts of the development cycle that could become eliminated for certain kinds of systems.

Figure 2.7 shows a futuristic development cycle, where the played-in behavior is not considered merely as requirements, but is actually used as the

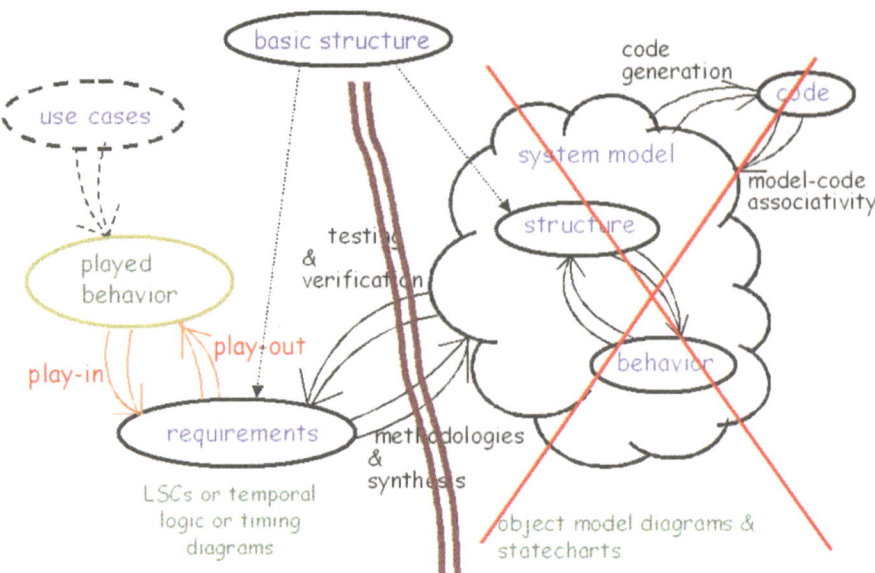

Fig. 2.6. Eliminating parts of the system development cycle

only behavior that needs to be specified for the system. We believe that the vision depicted in this figure is not as far-fetched as it might seem. Of course, we don't really mean that intra-object style will disappear; but we do believe that the behavior of complex systems will be designed in the future using a mix of ideas, with both intra-object and inter-object styles being used in tandem.

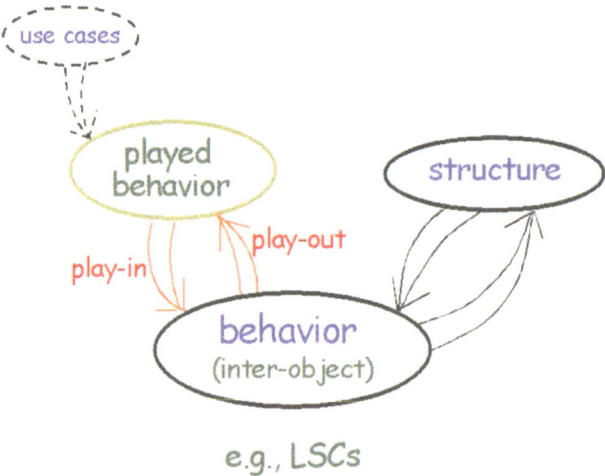

Fig. 2.7. A futuristic system development cycle

3. An Example-Driven Overview

In this chapter, we overview the main ideas and principles of our work. The purpose of the overview is to give a broad, though very high-level, view of the LSC language, the play-in methodology for specifying inter-object scenario-based behavior, and the play-out mechanism for executing such behavior. We will touch upon many issues, but will not dwell on the details of the language constructs, nor the methodology, nor the tool. The overview is presented as a guided walk-through, using a simple example of a reactive system.

3.1 The Sample System

Consider a bakery, in which different kinds of bread, cakes and cookies are baked in three ovens. Suppose Ms. B., the owner of the bakery, wants to automate the bakery by adding a bakery panel that will control and monitor the three ovens. According to the **play-in** approach, the first thing to do is to ask our user, Ms. B, to describe the desired panel. In this preliminary phase, a very high-level description, focusing on the panel's **graphical user interface** (GUI), is sufficient. The panel, coded using some rapid development language (or a special-purpose tool, as we discuss later) is shown in Fig. 3.1. The panel

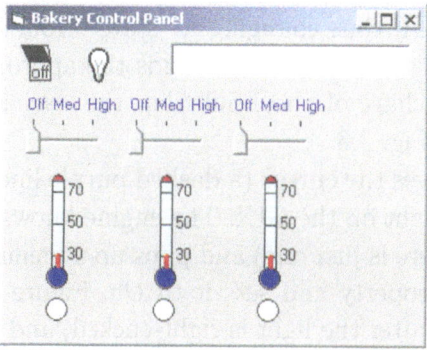

Fig. 3.1. A central panel controlling the bakery's ovens

has a main switch and a main light in its top-left corner. On the top right, there is a console display, which is used to show textual messages. The rest of the GUI contains three 3-state switches, three thermometers and three warning lights. Each set of switch, thermometer and light is used to control and monitor a different oven.

Note that this bakery panel is nothing but a graphical user interface. No behavior is programmed into it, and all it can do is interact with the Play-Engine tool in a rather trivial way. All the behavioral requirements of this panel will be defined as we go along. As we progress with the example, we may add more graphical elements to the panel and define their behavior as well.

3.2 Playing In

Having the GUI application at hand, Ms. B. is ready to specify the required behavior of the bakery panel. She wants to add a new LSC and give it a name. Figure 3.2 shows the Play-Engine with the empty LSC just added. The top blue dashed hexagon is the LSC's prechart and the bottom solid rectangle is its main chart. The prechart should contain a scenario, which, if satisfied, forces the satisfaction of the scenario given in the main chart. The relation between the prechart and the chart body can be viewed as an action-reaction; if and when the scenario in the prechart occurs, the system is obligated to satisfy the scenario in the main chart.

The first thing our user would like to specify is what happens when the bakery panel is turned on. Since this is done using a switch, the action of clicking the switch is put in the prechart, and the appropriate system reactions are put in the chart body. In our case, we want the system, as a response, to turn on the light and to change the display's color to green.

The process of specifying this behavior is very simple. First, the user clicks the switch on the GUI, thus changing its state[1] from *Off* to *On*. When the Play-Engine is notified of this event, it adds the appropriate message in the (initially empty) prechart of the LSC from the *user* instance to the *main switch* instance. See Fig. 3.3.

The user then moves the cursor (a dashed purple line) into the chart body and right-clicks the light on the GUI. The engine knows the properties of the light (in this case, there is just one) and pops up a menu, from which the user chooses the **State** property and sets it to *On*. Figure 3.4 shows the popup menu that is opened after the light is right-clicked, and the dialog that opens

---

[1] We use the word 'state' to describe a property of the switch. This should not to be confused with the term 'state' from finite state machines and statecharts.

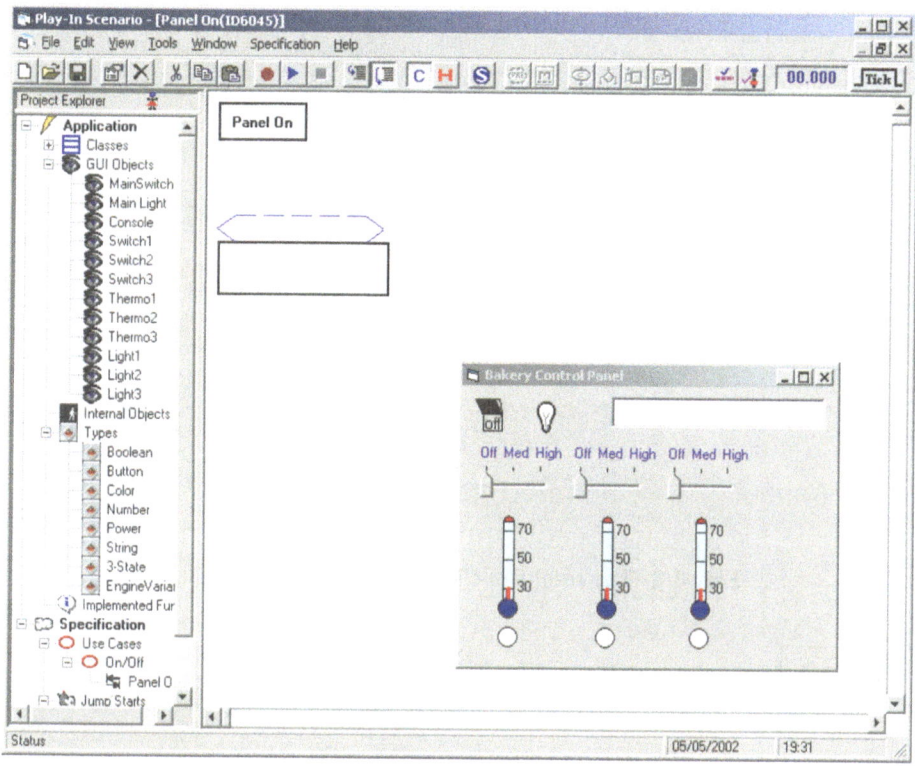

Fig. 3.2. An empty universal LSC in the Play-Engine

after the `State` property is chosen. A similar process is then carried out for the *background* property of the display. After each of these actions, the engine adds a self-message in the LSC from the instance representing the selected object, showing the change in the property. The Play-Engine also sends a message to the GUI application, telling it to change the object's property in the GUI itself so that it reflects the correct value after the actions have been taken. Thus, when this stage is finished, the GUI shows the switch on, the light on, and the display colored green. Figure 3.5 shows the resulting LSC and the status of the GUI panel.

Suppose now that the user wishes to specify what happens when the switch is turned off. In this case we want the light to turn off and the display to change its color to white and erase any displayed characters. The user may, of course, play in another scenario for this, but these two scenarios will be very similar, and they are better represented in a single LSC. This can be done using symbolic messages. We play a scenario as before, with the switch being clicked as part of the prechart, and the system's reactions being played in as the chart's body. However, this time we do it with the *symbolic* flag on.

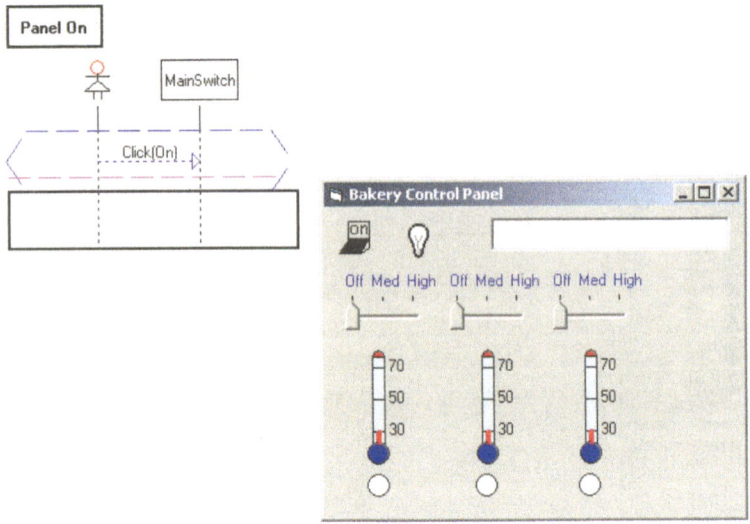

Fig. 3.3. The results of clicking the main switch to *On*

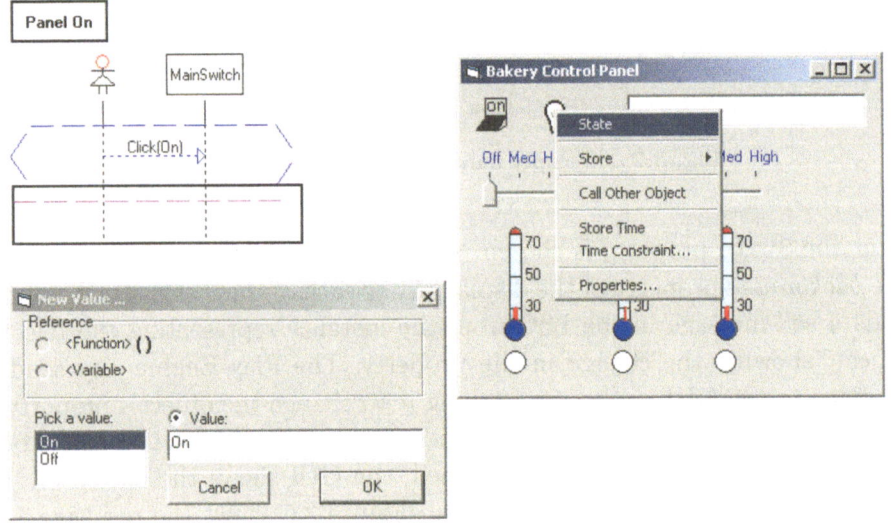

Fig. 3.4. Changing the light state to *On*

When in symbolic mode, the values shown in the labels of messages are the names of variables (or functions), rather than actual values. So the user will now not say that the light should turn on or off as a result of the prechart, but that it should take on the same state as the switch did in the prechart. The Play-Engine provides a number of ways of doing this. A variable can be selected from a table of predefined variables or, as shown in Fig. 3.6, we

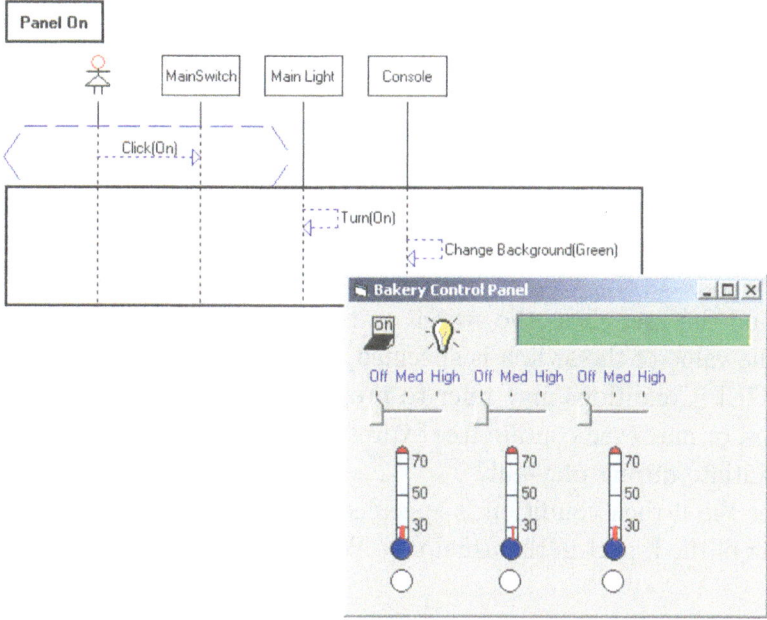

Fig. 3.5. LSC: Turning on the panel

can indicate that the value should be the same as in some message in the LSC. Here X_s is a variable. For the second option, the user simply clicks the

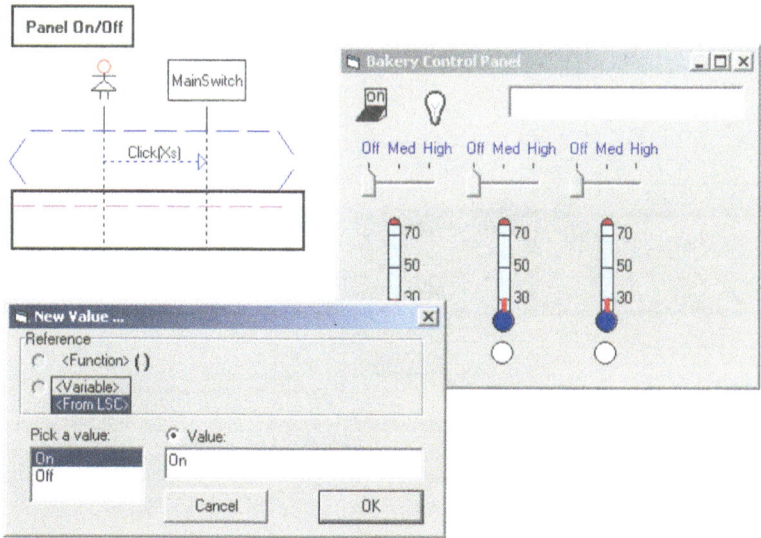

Fig. 3.6. Symbolic mode: the light takes on the same state as the switch

desired message inside the LSC and its variable will be attached to the new message as well.

This takes care of turning the light on or off. We now want to deal with the display's color. In one case it should become green and in the other white. We use an *if-then-else* construct for this. The user clicks the `If-Then` button on the toolbar and in response a wizard and a condition form are opened. Many kinds of conditions can be specified directly via the GUI, except that, in contrast to simple GUI-based actions, here several kinds of relation operators can be used (e.g., $<, \leq, >$, etc.). Figure 3.7 shows the system after the wizard opens and the user clicks the switch on the GUI. Note that in the condition form, the value of the switch is specified, and the switch itself is highlighted in the GUI. Conditions may refer to properties of GUI objects, to values of variables, or may even contain free expressions that the user will be requested to instantiate during play-out.

After the if-then condition is specified, the user continues playing in the behavior of the If part in the usual way. When this is completed, he/she clicks

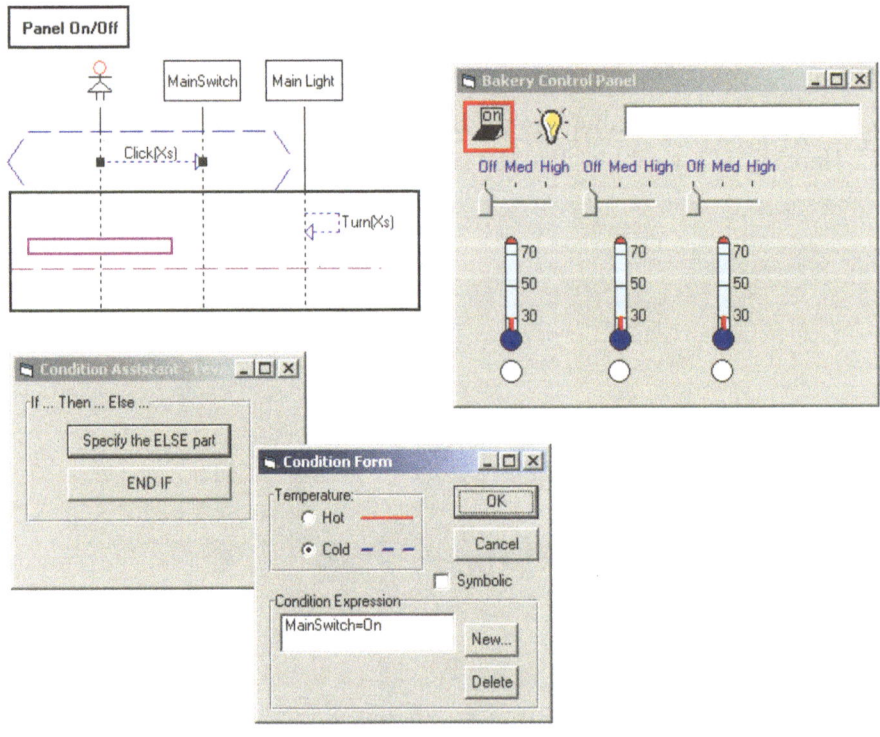

Fig. 3.7. Specifying if-then-else using a wizard

the `Specify the ELSE part` on the wizard and plays in the behavior for the Else part. The resulting LSC is shown in Fig. 3.8.

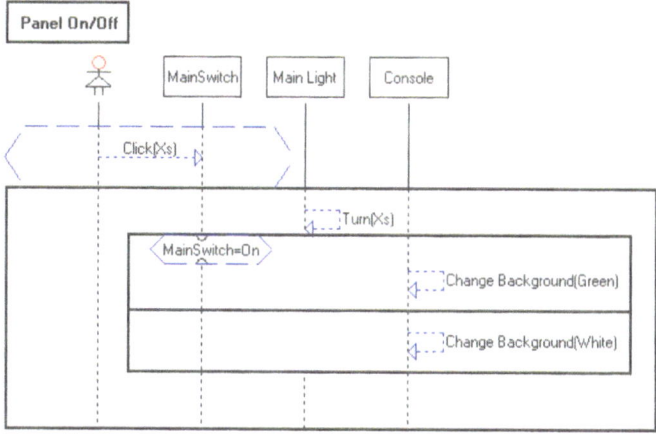

Fig. 3.8. An if-then-else construct

We could have specified in the Else part that the display should also be cleared (e.g., by asking to show an empty string). However, in order to introduce and exemplify stand-alone conditions we do it in a different way. We already saw that conditions may serve in if-then-else constructs, but they can also serve as stand-alone guards, either hot or cold. If a cold condition is *true*, the chart progresses to the location that immediately follows the condition, whereas if it is *false*, the surrounding (sub)chart is exited. A *hot* condition, on the other hand, must always be met, otherwise the requirements are violated and the system aborts. We will use a cold condition to check whether the switch is *Off*. If this is the case, the display is cleared, otherwise the chart is gracefully exited and the display's text does not change. A stand-alone condition can be inserted into the chart at any moment by clicking an appropriate button on the toolbar. After the button is clicked, the same condition dialog that was used in the if-then-else construct is opened.

An object can participate in a condition without being actually constrained. This is usually done when we want the object's progress to be synchronized with the condition's evaluation, but to have no effect on its value. Synchronizing an object with a condition (i.e., making the object a non-influential part of the condition) is done by right-clicking the object and choosing **Synchronize** from the popup menu. In our example, we want the *console* object to be synchronized with the condition but to have no effect on its value. Figure 3.9 shows how this is done.

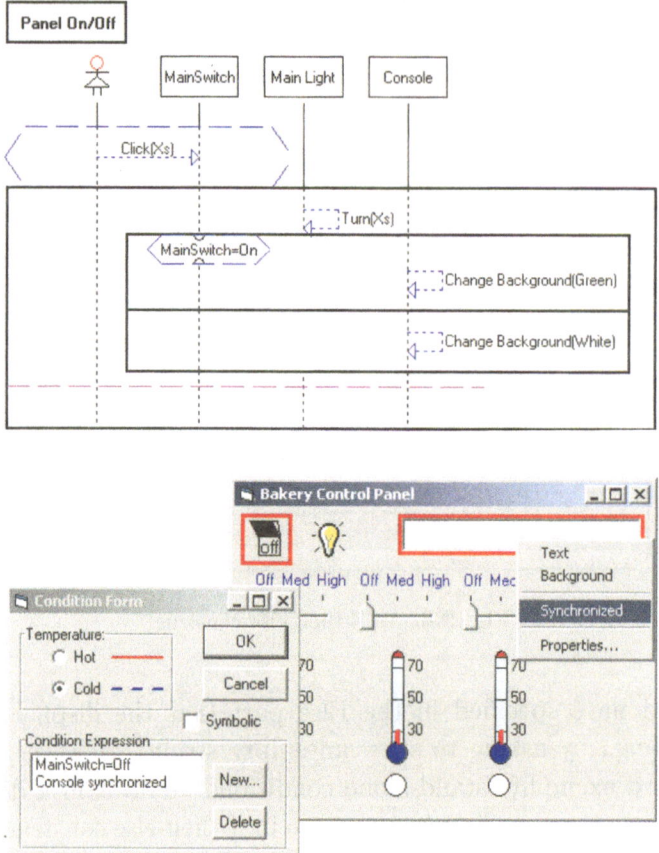

Fig. 3.9. Specifying a stand-alone condition guard

A condition hexagon will be stretched along the LSC, reaching all the instances to which it refers. To distinguish such instances from those that do not participate in the condition's definition or are not to be synchronized with it, the engine draws small semicircular connectors at the intersection points of the condition with the participating instance line. Figure 3.10 shows the final LSC and the way conditions are rendered.

One aspect of the LSC language that contributes to its flexibility is the fact that behaviors can be given in separate charts, and these can each describe a fragment of a more complex behavior. When these fragments become relevant during execution is a consequence of their precharts, and thus no explicit order is imposed on the charts (in contrast to the mechanism for combining charts in high-level MSCs, for example). So, suppose that our user has just decided that when the switch is turned on, the three warning lights should flicker (by changing colors from green to red and back) three times, termi-

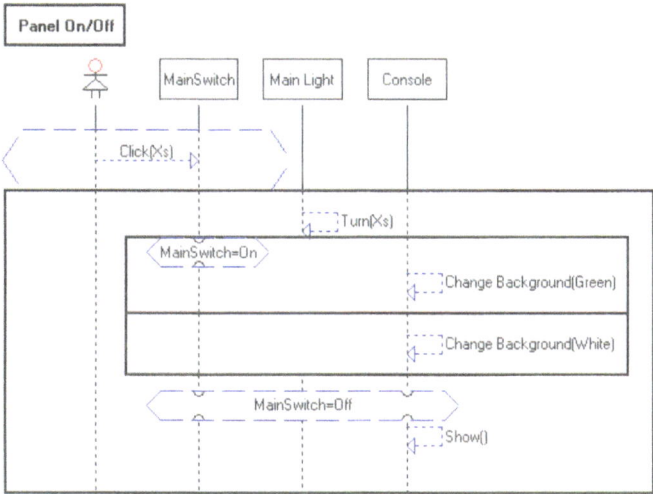

Fig. 3.10. A symbolic LSC for turning the panel on or off

nating in green. One way to capture that is to go back to the LSC shown before and add this 'piece' of behavior in its correct place (i.e., in the 'then' part of the if-then-else construct). Alternatively, we can create another LSC, which is activated only when the switch is turned *On*.

To do this, the user clicks the switch on the GUI to *On* while the cursor is in the prechart, in the same way as described earlier. We now want to specify the three-fold flickering itself. Of course, we could simply play in the six color changes for every light. It is better, however, to use the loop construct of LSCs. As with the if-then-else construct, a loop is inserted by clicking a button on the toolbar, which causes a wizard to open. Figure 3.11 shows the wizard and the LSC during the process of specifying a loop.

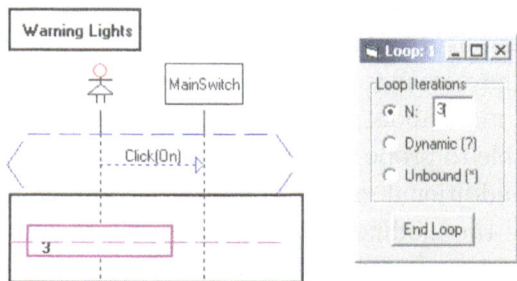

Fig. 3.11. Specifying loops in LSCs

There are three types of loops in LSCs. This one is a **fixed** loop; it is annotated by a number or a variable name, and is performed a fixed number of times.

After selecting the desired type of loop using the loop wizard, the user continues playing in the required behavior in the same way as before. The loop is ended by clicking the End Loop button in the loop wizard. Figure 3.12 shows the resulting LSC. Note the special use of a cold condition in

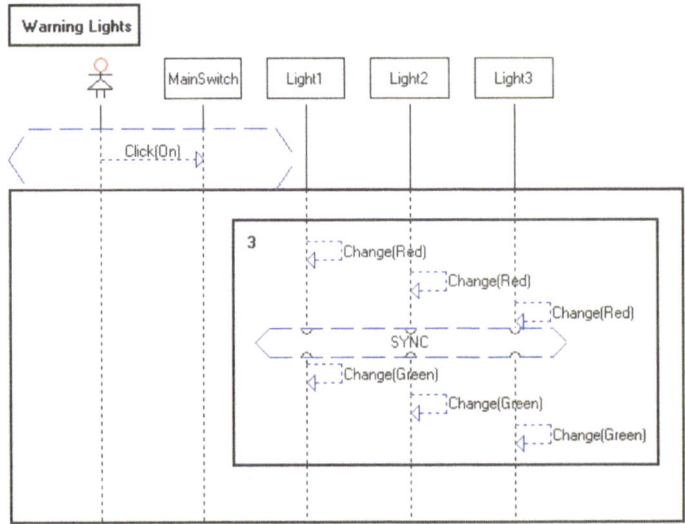

Fig. 3.12. An LSC with a fixed loop

the middle of the loop. A condition with the reserved word *SYNC* is always evaluated to *true*. (Actually, the reserved word *TRUE* could have been used instead, but SYNC reflects better the underlying intuition.) Placing such a condition where it is, and synchronizing the three lights with it has the effect of synchronizing the lights and forbidding a light to change its color to *green* before the others have changed their color to *red*.

Thinking a bit more about the bakery panel, Ms. B. now decides that she would like to be able to probe the thermometers for their exact temperature. To do that, some additional graphical objects should be added to the panel. Figure 3.13 shows the modified panel. Two selectors and one *Probe* button have been added. One selector is used to select a thermometer and the other to select the units for displaying the temperature (i.e., Celsius or Fahrenheit).

We now specify the following requirement:

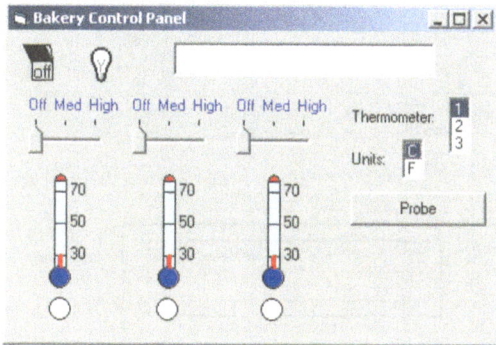

Fig. 3.13. The modified bakery panel

When the Probe button is clicked, the console should display the temperature of the thermometer selected using the thermometer selector. The temperature should be displayed in Celsius or Fahrenheit degrees, according to the units in the units selector.

The prechart is quite simple, and contains a single message denoting the event of the user clicking the *Probe* button. In the chart body, we first want to store the temperature of the selected thermometer. We do this using three if-then constructs. The temperature is stored in a variable using an assignment construct. Assignments are internal to a chart, and can be used to save values of the properties of objects, or of functions applied to variables holding such values. The assigned-to variable stores the value for later use in the LSC. The expression on the right-hand side contains either a reference to a property of some object (this is the typical usage) or a function applied to some predefined variables. It is important to note that the assignment's variable is local to the containing chart and can be used in that chart only, as opposed to the system's state variables, which may be used in several charts. Figure 3.14 shows how an object property can be stored, by right-clicking the desired object, choosing `Store` and then the desired property name. It also shows the resulting assignment, drawn as a rectangle folded in its top-right corner. Since after storing a value we might like to refer to it later, and for this a meaningful name is helpful, the Play-Engine lets the user name the assigned variable; here we use Tc (since the original temperature is given in Celsius). Figure 3.15 shows an LSC in which the variable Tc stores the required temperature.

Next, the console should display Tc according to the selected units. If Celsius is selected, then Tc should be displayed as is. If Fahrenheit is selected, the temperature should be converted. This is an example of the need to use data manipulation algorithms and functions that are applied to specified variables. Such functions cannot (and should not) be described using LSC-

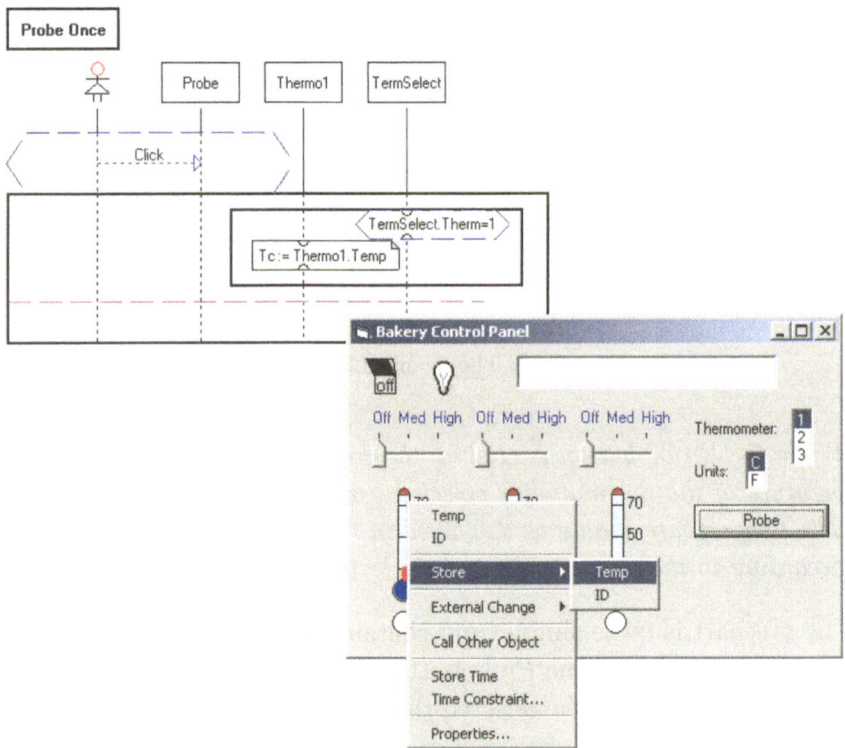

Fig. 3.14. Using assignments to store the temperature

style interactions between objects, but rather should be imported as external artifacts that have to be worked into the requirements. The Play-Engine allows the specification of an event value as a function applied to variables. These functions are user-implemented and their declarations are obtained from the GUI application. Figure 3.16 shows the final LSC. Using an if-then-else construct, which depends on the units selector value, the console displays the temperature in the correct units, using the function *Cels2Fahr* to convert Celsius to Fahrenheit.

The next requirement our user wishes to express is the following:

> *If the temperature in one of the ovens gets below* 30 *degrees Celsius, the console should display a "Cold Oven!" warning message.*

The temperature is a property of a thermometer, which is not changed by the user or by the system. It is actually changed by the *environment*. Often, a reactive system works in the presence of other elements, apart from the user who interacts with it. Such elements might include other machines, computers, sensors, and even Mother Nature. The collection of all these elements

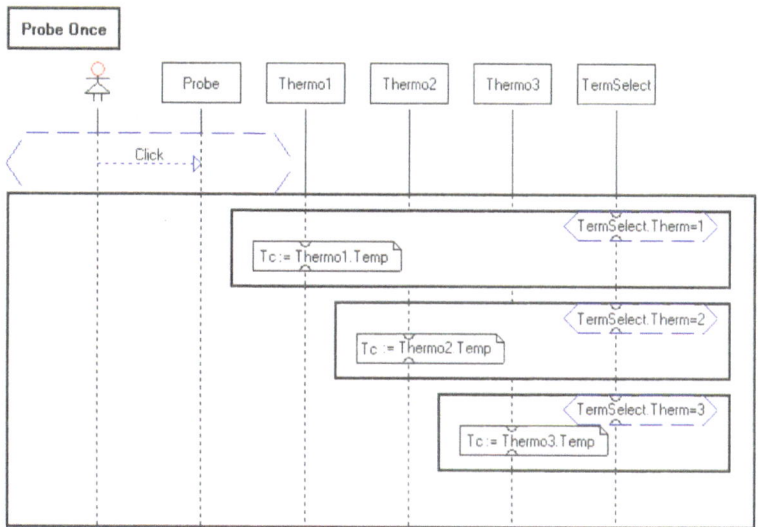

Fig. 3.15. Storing the temperature of the selected thermometer

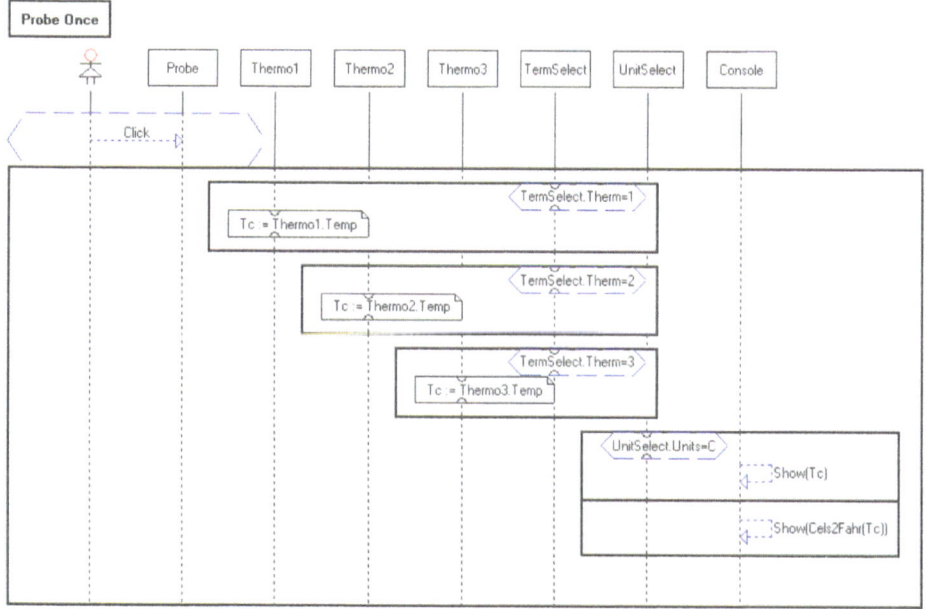

Fig. 3.16. Probing and displaying a thermometer temperature

is referred to as the system's **environment**. When playing in the required behavior of a reactive system, it is necessary to be able to express its interaction with this environment. The Play-Engine allows the user to specify how the environment reacts with the system in a way similar to the interaction with the end-user.

Figure 3.17 shows an LSC that describes the above requirement for thermometer ♯1. When the temperature of thermometer ♯1 is changed (by the

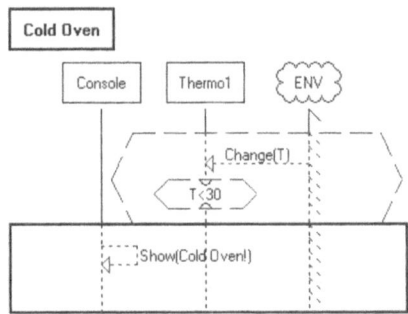

Fig. 3.17. Interacting with the external environment

environment) to some value T, and T is less than 30 degrees Celsius, then the console displays the required warning message.

We could have created two more charts for the other two thermometers, yet there is a more elegant way to do this. Many systems feature multiple objects that are instances of the same class. This is one of the central maxims of the object-oriented paradigm. For example, a communication system contains many phones, a railroad control system may have not only many trains and terminals but also many distributed controllers, etc. We would like to be able to specify behavioral requirements in a general way, on the level of classes and their parameterized instances, not necessarily restricting them to concrete objects. In our example, since the three thermometers are actually three instances of the same *thermometer* class, we would like to take the LSC shown in Fig. 3.17 and generalize it so that it deals with all the thermometers in the system. We can do this using an extension we have defined for LSCs, involving **classes** and **symbolic instances**. A symbolic instance is associated with a class rather than with an object, and may stand for any object that is an instance of the class. Figure 3.18 shows the generalized version of the LSC of Fig. 3.17. In our example, a *CTherm* class was created and all the thermometers were defined as instances thereof. In Fig. 3.18, the instance representing thermometer ♯1 was turned into a symbolic instance, and thus now represents any object that is an instance of class *CTherm*.

Symbolic instances constitute a rather complex topic, raising several interesting and non-trivial issues that we deal with later in the book.

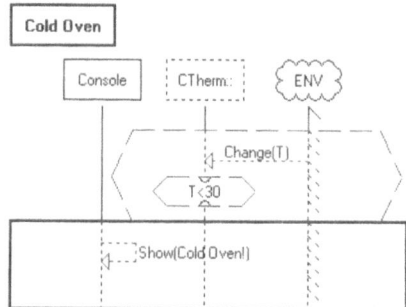

Fig. 3.18. Using symbolic instances to represent classes

3.3 Playing Out

After playing in the required behavior so far, Ms. B. is ready to check her
model, and she therefore moves to **play-out** mode. Playing out is the process
of testing the behavior of the system by providing any user actions, in any
order, and checking the system's ongoing responses. The play-out process
calls for the Play-Engine to monitor the applicable precharts of all universal
charts, and if successfully completed to then execute their bodies. As discussed earlier, the universal charts contain the system's required reactions to
other actions. By executing the events in these charts and causing the GUI
application to reflect the effect of these events on the system objects, the user
is provided with a simulation of an executable application.

Note that in order to play out scenarios, the user does not need to know
much about LSCs or even about the use cases and requirements entered so
far. All he/she has to do is to operate the GUI application as if it were a final
system and check whether it reacts according to the expectations.

We should emphasize that the possible runs of the system are not simply different orders of the same sequences of inputs, but can include totally
different runs that contain unexpected events and messages. This is doubly
true in the presence of symbolic instances, symbolic messages and unbounded
loops.

The underlying play-out mechanism can be likened to an over-obedient
citizen who walks around with the Grand Book of Rules on him at all times.[2]
He doesn't lift a finger unless some rule in the book says he has to, never does
anything if it violates some other rule, and always carries out — to the letter
— what he was asked to do, as well as anything else that doing so entails.
He constantly scans and monitors all rules at all times. Clearly, in so acting,

---

[2] Chapter 5 contains this idea applied to a female citizen too.

he might have choices to make, and could also discover inconsistencies in the rules. More about that later.

Back now to Ms. B. The first thing she would like to do is to turn on the panel. She therefore clicks the switch to *On*. The Play-Engine can react to user and environment actions in two modes: **step** and **super-step**. When in step mode, the user is prompted before each event, each condition evaluation, etc., and the next event to be carried out is marked on all relevant charts. In the super-step mode, the Play-Engine carries out as many events as possible, until it reaches a 'stable' state, in which the system can do nothing and waits for some input from the user. Figure 3.19 shows one of two charts that are

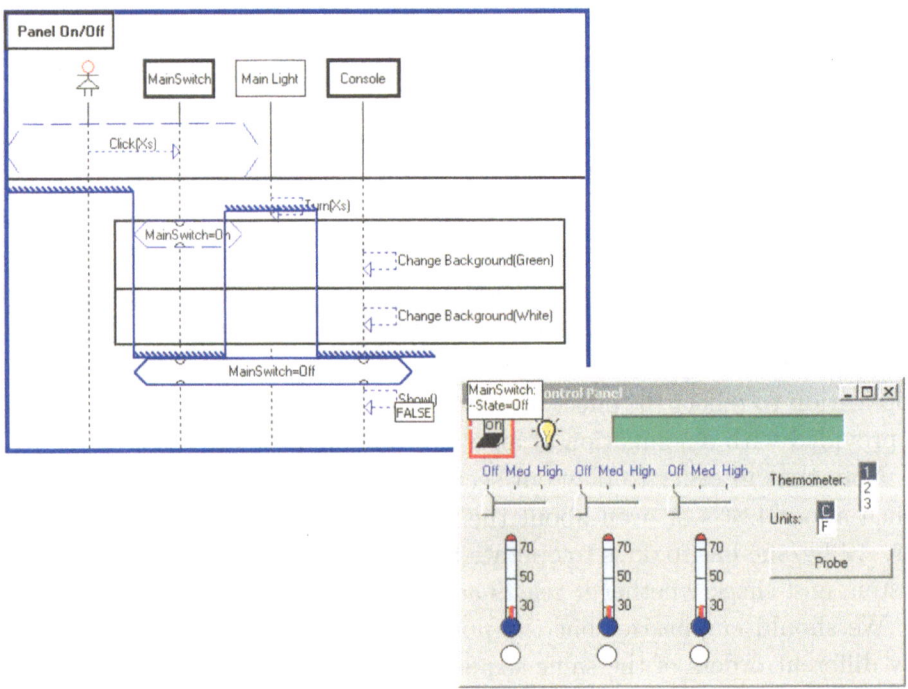

Fig. 3.19. Clicking the switch: first effect

activated by the Play-Engine as a response to the event of the user clicking the switch. In this LSC, the message in the prechart is symbolic and its variable Xs is therefore bound to the value *On*, remaining with this value until the chart completes. The Play-Engine progresses through the chart and continuously interacts with the GUI application, causing it to reflect the changes prescribed by the executed events. As this is happening, the user may examine values of assignments, conditions and message variables, by moving the mouse over them in the chart. In this example, the mouse is located over the cold condition. As a result, the condition is evaluated and a tooltip shows the valuation result (false). At the same time, the GUI objects participating in the condition are highlighted in the panel and each one displays a tooltip with its relevant constraints. Since this cold condition evaluates to false, the chart completes (denoted by the surrounding blue thick frame).

Figure 3.20 shows the second chart that is activated as a result of clicking the switch to *On*. In this figure, the Play-Engine is in *step* mode, after some

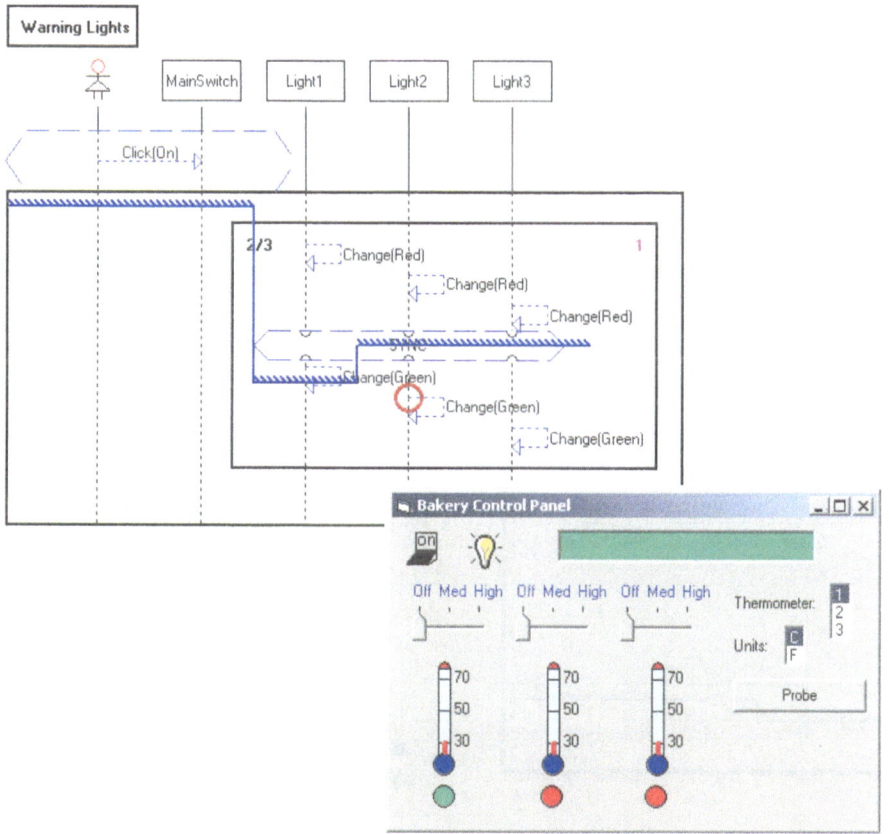

Fig. 3.20. Clicking the switch: second effect

steps have already been taken. The next step to be taken is circled in red. The number in the top-right corner of the loop shows how many iterations have already been performed; the numbers in the top-left corner denote the current and total iteration numbers. Note that in the bakery panel the first warning light has already changed to green while the other two are still red.

After turning on the panel, our user, Ms. B., wishes to test the effect of one thermometer going below 30 degrees Celsius. To do that, she has to play the role of the environment. Figure 3.21 shows how this is done. The user

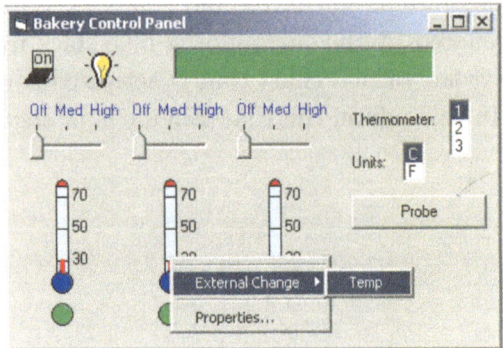

Fig. 3.21. Playing out the environment

right-clicks the desired object (in this case thermometer ♯2), selects **External Change** and then chooses the property to be changed. Here, Ms. B. chooses **Temp** and then enters a value of 20 degrees (not shown in the figure). As a result, the chart in Fig. 3.22 is activated and is completed. Recall that the

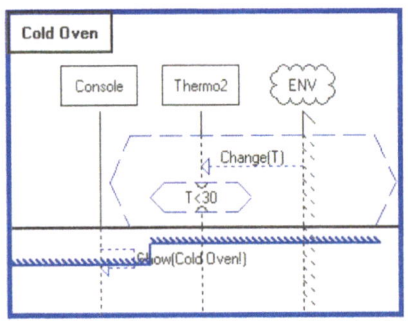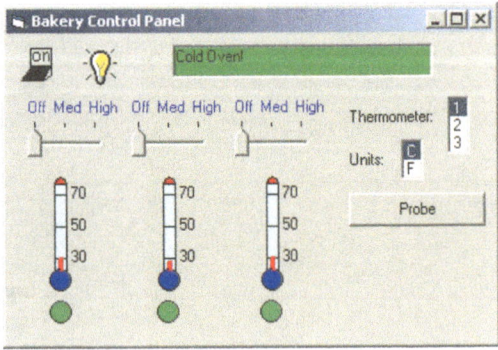

Fig. 3.22. Play-out: binding symbolic instances

scenario in this chart was played in using thermometer ♯1, and the instance representing it was turned symbolic. Now, since Ms. B. played out using thermometer ♯2, the symbolic instance is bound to this thermometer for the rest of the scenario.

Thus, as explained earlier, playing out enables the user to actually activate the specified system directly from the scenario-based inter-object behavioral specification — possible and mandatory scenarios, forbidden scenarios and other constraints — without the need to prepare statecharts, to write or generate code, or to carry out any other detailed intra-object thinking. The process is simple enough for many kinds of end-users and domain experts, and can greatly increase the chance of finding errors early on.

3.4 Using Play-Out for Testing

Universal charts 'drive' the model by their **action-reaction** nature, whereas existential charts can be used as system tests or as examples of required interactions. Rather than serving to drive the play-out, existential charts are **monitored**; that is, the Play-Engine simply tracks the events in the chart as they occur. When (and if) a traced chart reaches its end, it is highlighted, and the user is informed that it was successfully traced to completion. The user may select the charts to be monitored, thus saving the Play-Engine the need to track charts that might currently not be of interest.

Figure 3.23 shows an existential chart that was successfully traced to completion. This chart represents a test (as indicated by the "T" in the top-left corner), stating that after the switch is turned on, the light should be

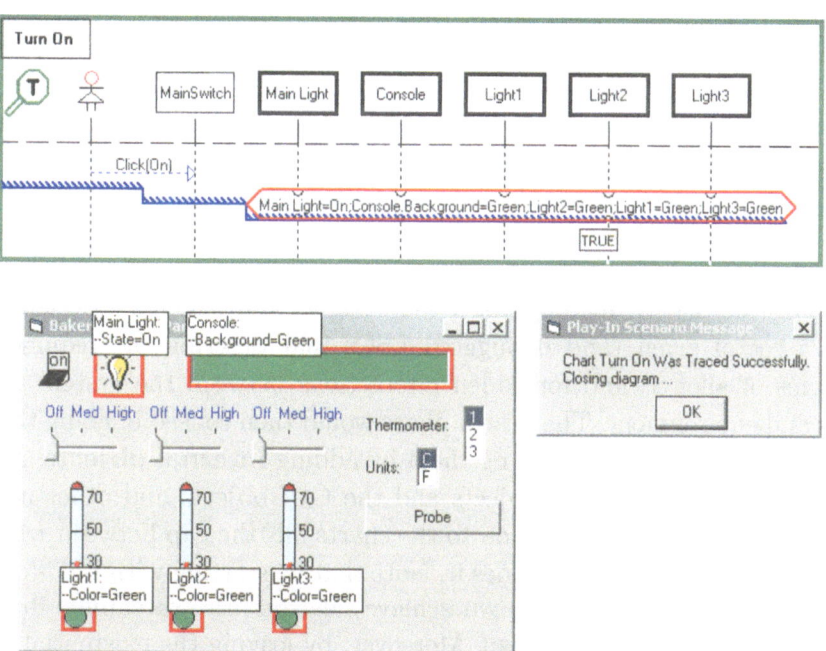

Fig. 3.23. Monitoring existential charts

on and the console and the three warning lights should all be green. As a test, this LSC is not required to explicitly show how the required result is accomplished but only that it is eventually accomplished. The required test results are specified using a hot condition, thus enabling the chart to complete only if the condition evaluates to true.

When playing out the GUI application, a run trace is produced, which includes all the user actions and the system reactions. These runs can be recorded, to provide testimonies (that can be replayed) for fulfilling existential LSCs. Recorded runs can be saved (in XML format) and then reloaded. More importantly, runs can be imported from different sources and then be replayed in the same manner. These external sources can be different implementations of the specification, either given as executable programs or as more detailed design models, (e.g., statecharts, labeled transition systems, etc.). Importing a run from an implementation and replaying it, while tracing all charts, can be used to show that the implementation is consistent with the requirements in the sense that existential charts are successfully traced and universal charts are not violated.

3.5 Transition to Design

After playing in the requirements using the GUI application, and validating them using play-out, the Play-Engine can be used to make a smooth transition into the design phase. In many development methodologies, the designer begins the design phase with a requirements specification, usually given as a text document, and then constructs scenarios (say, in some variant of sequence diagrams) to show the interaction between the objects comprising the system, and to become convinced that these scenarios satisfy the original requirements.

Using the play-in methodology, the designer can begin the design phase with a set of given (and debugged) LSCs that describe the requirements in terms of allowed and forbidden interactions between the system and its users and environment. The design phase would then consist of going through the universal charts and refining them by adding **internal objects** and the interactions between these objects and the GUI objects and other internal objects. Adding this information to the charts fills the gap between *what* the system should do and *how* it does it. Note that by starting with LSCs created by, or on behalf of, the user, we achieve near-perfect traceability between the requirements and the design. Moreover, by leaving the existential charts unmodified, the designer may prove the correctness of the modified LSCs by performing regression testing to satisfy the original existential charts.

The Play-Engine provides means for adding internal objects on the fly. It also enables the addition of properties and methods to the new objects and also to the objects exported by the GUI application. The internal objects are drawn in an **object map**, which is a kind of object model diagram. In this diagram, each object is shown with all its methods, its properties and their values.

Suppose that in our bakery panel example the designer wants to specify how the light is turned on or off after the switch is clicked. He/she decides that a new switch controller, *Sw-Ctrl*, will be used. Figure 3.24 shows an object map with the new object and an LSC that shows how the information is transferred from the switch to the light.

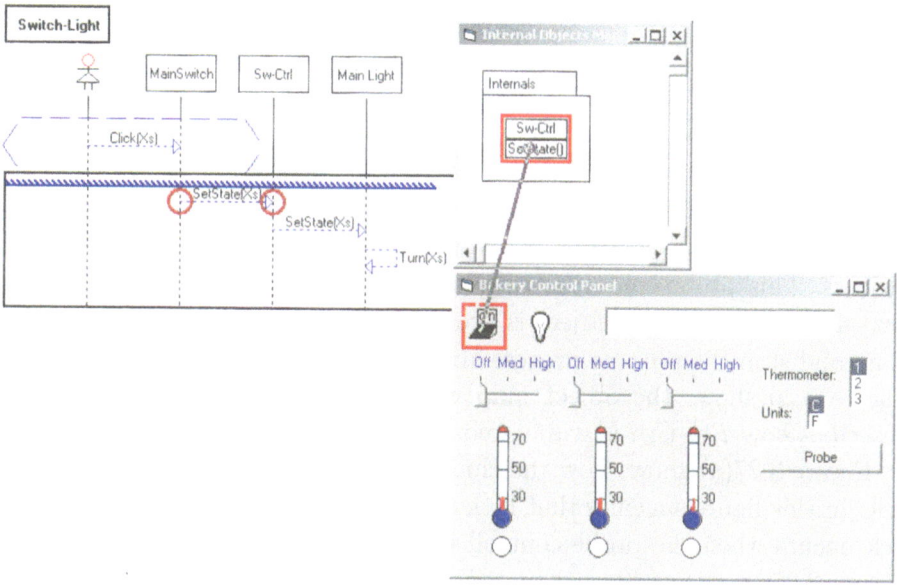

Fig. 3.24. Playing out internal objects

When LSCs containing method calls are played out, the Play-Engine animates them by drawing arrows between the involved objects and highlighting them. Thus, the play-out mechanism can be used not only to help end-users validate requirements but also as a useful tool for demonstrating, reviewing and debugging a design. Figure 3.24 shows how interaction between objects is animated in the Play-Engine. Note that the arrows are not limited to being internal to the GUI application or to the object map themselves, but can run from one to the other.

3.6 Time

Many kinds of reactive systems must explicitly refer to and react to **time**.
Suppose that Ms. B. is not satisfied with the standard way the lights have
been made to flicker as the panel is turned on (Fig. 3.25(a)), but wants them
to remain red for one second and green for two seconds.

We have extended the LSCs to handle time by adding a single *clock* object
with one property, *time*, and one method, *Tick*.

Using the clock object together with the existing constructs of LSCs, we
can specify a wide variety of timing constraints and time-driven events. Figure
3.25(b) shows an LSC that describes the modified requirement. Before the
lights change to red, the time is stored in a variable T. Before they change to
green, the hot condition $Time > T$ must first be satisfied, and this happens
only after the elapse of one second. The same goes for the change from green
to red, except that in this case the condition forces a delay of two seconds.

Reactive real-time systems are often required to react to the passage of
time and not only to refer to it when constraining the intervals between
actual events. Suppose that in our case Ms. B. wishes to continuously probe
the selected thermometer at a rate of one probe per second. For this we add
a new internal object, *Prb-Ctrl*, which will be responsible for the probing
process. This probe-controller object has one Boolean property, *IsProbing*,
that shows whether the object is probing, and two methods, *ToggleProbe* to
start and stop the probing process and *ProbeOnce* to activate a single probe.
Figure 3.26 shows the object map with the new object and an LSC that
describes how *Prb-Ctrl* is stimulated by the *Probe* button.

Figure 3.27(a) shows how the clock ticks can be referred to in LSCs. The
LSC in this figure specifies that if the probe controller is probing and a clock
tick occurs, then the probe controller calls itself to perform a single probe.
Figure 3.27(b) shows that when *Prb-Ctrl* calls its *Probe* method, it performs
a single probe as described earlier. Hence, when the probe controller is in
probing mode, each clock tick activates the *'Probe Tick'* LSC, and this in
turn activates the *'One Probe'* LSC in a chain reaction.

The play-out mechanism supports LSCs that refer to time. Specifications
can be executed in **manual clock mode**, where the user advances the clock
by clicking a `Tick` button, or in **automatic clock mode**, where the clock
ticks are performed by the Play-Engine at fixed intervals (which can be determined by the user).

3.7 Smart Play-Out

As described earlier, play-out is actually an iterative process, where after each step taken by the user, the Play-Engine computes a super-step, which

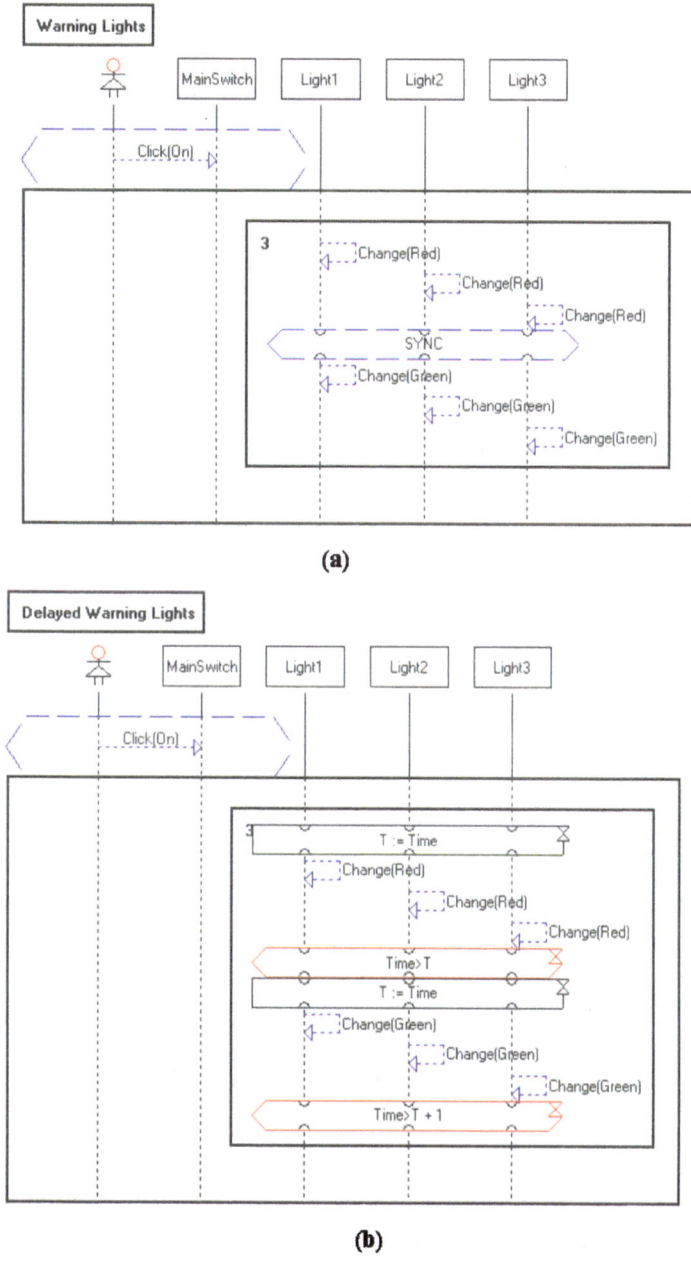

Fig. 3.25. Specifying time constraints

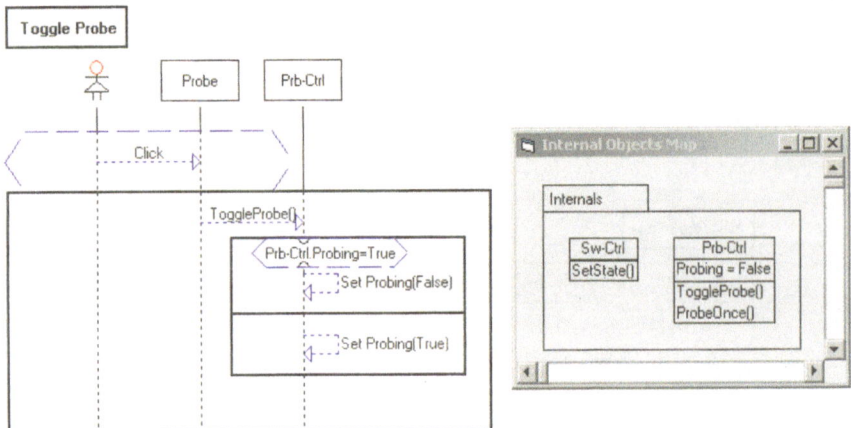

Fig. 3.26. Toggling the probe controller using the Probe button

is a sequence of events carried out by the system as the response to the event input by the user. However, the 'obedient citizen' mechanism of the play-out process is rather naive, for several reasons. For example, there can be many sequences of events possible as a response to a user event, and some of these may not constitute a 'correct' super-step. We consider a super-step to be correct if when it is executed no active universal chart is violated. By acting blindly according to the 'Grand Book' of requirements, reacting to a user-generated event with the first action it finds that is a possible reaction to that event, the naive play-out process could very well follow a sequence of events that eventually causes violation, whereas another sequence could have been chosen that would have completed successfully. The multiplicity of possible sequences of reactions to a user event is due to the fact that a declarative, inter-object behavior language, such as LSCs, enables the formulation of high-level requirements in pieces (e.g., scenario fragments), leaving open details that may depend on the implementation. The partial order semantics among events in each chart, and the ability to separate scenarios in different charts without saying explicitly how they should be composed are very useful in early requirement stages, but can cause underspecification and nondeterminism when one attempts to execute them.

Consider, for example, the two charts given in Fig. 3.28. '*LSC1*' says that when the main switch is turned on, the first warning light turns *green*, the first switch is automatically set to *Med* and the console displays the string *Switch1_Med*. Note that the LSC does not enforce any particular order on these three events, so that there are several possibilities for the order in which they execute, and the play-out mechanism will choose one, in a way that is not controllable by the user.

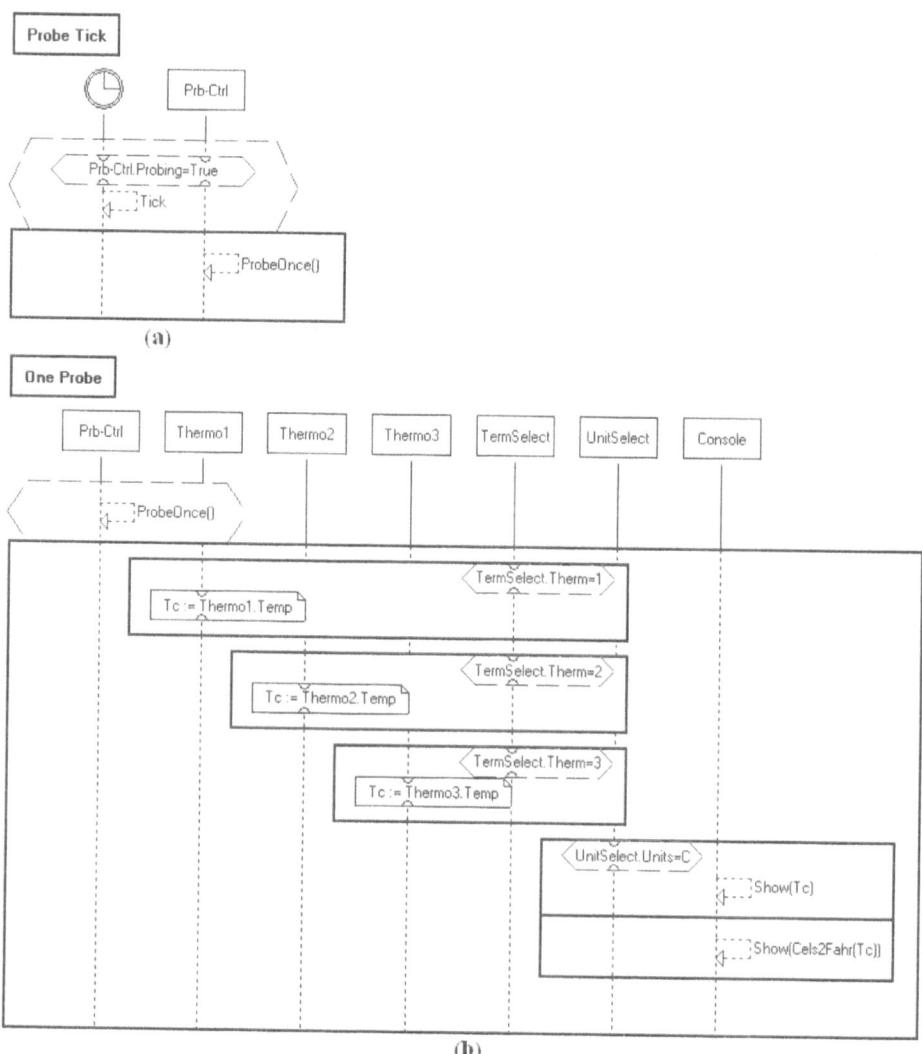

Fig. 3.27. Periodic probing

'*LSC2*' says that whenever the state of the first switch is set to *Med*, the first light should not yet be *green*. Then this light turns *green*, and only then does the console display the string *Switch1_Med*.

If these are the only two specified charts, and the user turns the switch to *On* during play-out, the play-out mechanism chooses the events in an order that results in the charts shown in Fig. 3.29. The first event to be taken is the top-most, i.e., changing the color of the first light to green. The second is setting the state of Switch1 to *Med*. As this event occurs, '*LSC2*' is activated but cannot progress, since the warning light is *green*. '*LSC1*'

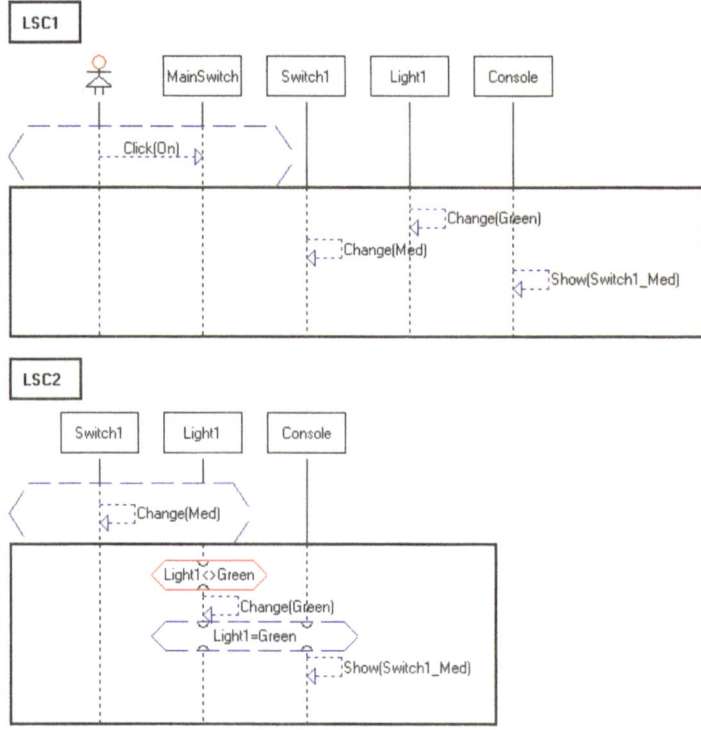

Fig. 3.28. Nondeterministic choice during play-out

is also not allowed to progress, since the event of showing *Switch1_Med* on the console violates '*LSC2*'. Therefore, no progress is allowed at all and the super-step terminates.

The **smart play-out** approach focuses on executing the behavioral requirements with the aid of formal analysis methods, mainly model-checking. The smart play-out process finds a 'correct' super-step if one exists, or proves that such a super-step does not exist. This is achieved using model-checking at the occurrence of each user event, in order to examine the different potential super-steps and to find a correct sequence of system reactions if there is one. Model-checking thus drives the execution. Another way of putting it is that the 'smartness' in smart play-out works as an aid, helping the objects in the system cooperate in fulfilling the requirements.

In our example, the result of applying the smart play-out algorithm for finding the correct super-step is shown in Fig. 3.30. In this case, the first event taken after the main switch is turned on is that of changing the state of Switch1 to *Med*. This event activates '*LSC2*', but this time the warning light is not *green* yet. The hot condition is thus evaluated to true and is

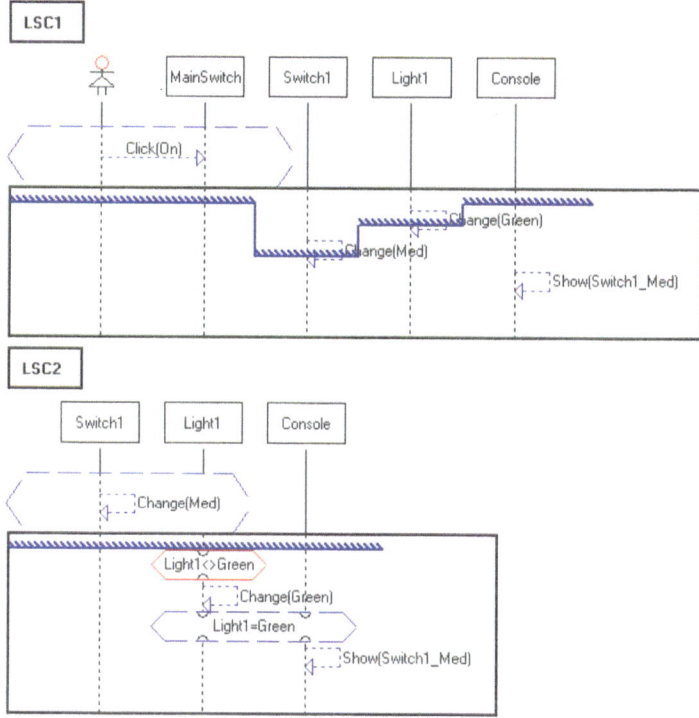

Fig. 3.29. Standard play-out

propagated. Now the event of changing the warning light to *green* can be carried out, affecting both charts. Next the cold condition is successfully passed, and again the event of showing *Switch1_Med* on the console can be performed, causing the successful completion of both charts.

Smart play-out illustrates the power of putting formal verification methods to use in early stages of the development process, with the potential of impacting the development of reactive systems. More ways of utilizing smart play-out in the Play-Engine and the details of the smart play-out algorithms are discussed in Chap. 18.

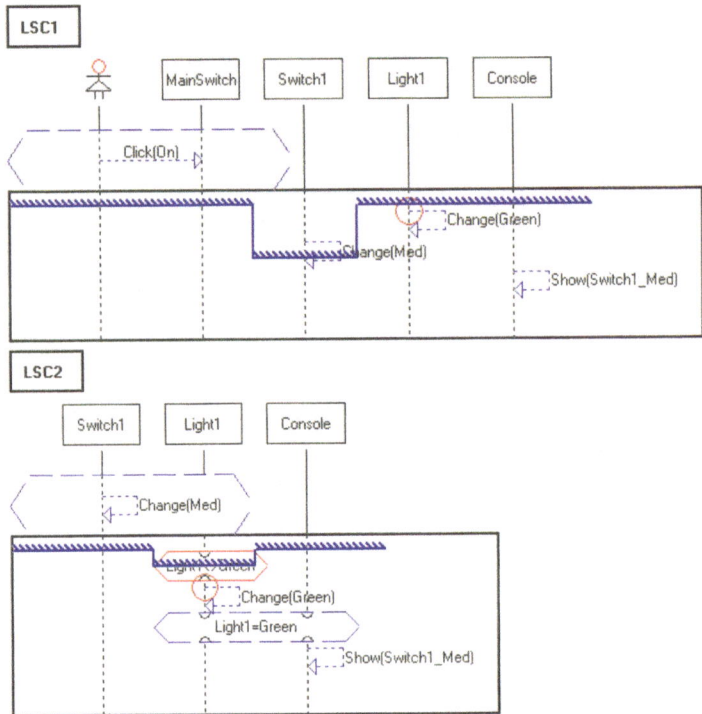

Fig. 3.30. Using smart play-out

Part II

Foundations

4. The Model: Object Systems

Scenario-based languages, such as LSCs, are not restricted to particular systems, architectures or modeling techniques. They can serve to specify the behavior of either sequential or parallel systems, based on either centralized or distributed architectures, and they can be used to describe the interaction between processes, tasks, functions and objects. The same applies to virtually all the ideas and techniques described in this book. However, it will be convenient for us to use a single system model throughout the book. Since object-orientation appears to be the most dominant development methodology today, we will use the basic OO notions and terminology in our system model as well.

To describe the structure of a reactive system within the play-in/play-out methodology and the supporting Play-Engine tool, we use **object systems**. In our setting, a system consists of an arbitrary number of **objects**, each of which embodies an arbitrary number of properties. Since the approach is not restricted to modeling applications and systems from a specific domain or field, the object's properties are based upon application types, which are also considered part of the system model. Each object may be an instance of some defined class. An object that is not explicitly associated with a class is considered to be the single object in a special singleton class having the same properties as the object itself.

In this chapter, we describe the various elements comprising a system model. As we continue our description of the more advanced elements and features of the language and the play-in/play-out approach, the system model will be extended appropriately.

4.1 Application Types

The most basic element in our models is an **application type**. When clear from the context, we will refer to application types simply as **types**. There are three kinds of types:

Enumeration type – defined by a finite set of values.

Discrete type – defined by a minimum value, a maximum value and a step (delta) that defines the interval between two consecutive values. For example, a discrete type having $0, 10$ and 1 as its minimum, maximum and delta, respectively, contains the integers between 0 and 10, inclusive.

String type – defined by a maximal length.

Each type is identified by a name and a unique ID, and may be provided with a description. Here are some examples of application types.

Color – The possible colors that can be used in an application can be described using an enumeration type that consists of the different color names (e.g., {Red, Blue, Green, White, Black, ...}). To represent a 24-bit color we could use a discrete type with integer numbers ranging from 0 to $2^{24} - 1$, with a delta of 1, thus representing all the possible RGB combinations.

Boolean – The Boolean type is defined simply as an enumeration containing the values {True, False}.

Character – Characters can be defined using a string type of length 1. An alternative way would be to use a discrete type, with the characters encoded by their ASCII codes.

Byte – A byte can be represented by a discrete type ranging from 0 to 127 with a delta of 1, or by a *string* type of length 8, which would explicitly show the bits constituting the byte.

The choice of the type for a particular application should be made so that its representation is the most convenient for the way it will be used.

4.2 Object Properties

Every object in the application is associated with a set of properties. The values of the properties for GUI objects are usually reflected in the way these objects are rendered in the application, but this is not mandatory.[1] A property has a name and is identified by a unique ID (unique within the object scope). Each property is based on a *type*, from which its values can be selected.

In order to provide an intuitive and user-friendly support for play-in and play-out, we require object properties to also have the following characteristics:

Prefix – The property prefix is a verb used to describe the action of changing the property's value (e.g., *show* a value, *turn* the light on/off, etc.). This feature is used mainly to help make the specification clear and intuitive.

---

[1] In Chap. 14 we discuss how GUI-less objects display their property values.

Is default – If a property is default, its name is not shown in the LSC messages. Let us take for example, a light object with one property, State, that can be on or off. If the property is not declared as default, then when the light is turned on the message in the chart will read "Turn State(On)", whereas if it is declared as default the message will read "Turn(On)". Again, this feature is used to make the requirements clearer by hiding redundant information in the charts.

In only – Object properties are usually changed by either operating the object (e.g., clicking a switch, moving a slider, etc.), or by right-clicking it and then choosing a property from a popup menu and specifying its new value. The first method is used to demonstrate user actions while the second is used to specify system reactions. An *in only* property can be changed only using the first of these, and therefore is not shown on the object's right-clicked popup menu (e.g., a button in a GUI is usually clicked by the user, hence there is no reason why one would want to specify that the button was clicked by the system).

Can be changed externally – This indicates that the property can be changed by the system's environment (i.e., some external element other than the end-user). When playing in behavior, changes caused by the environment are played by right-clicking an object, choosing "External Change" and then selecting the property to be changed. Only properties that can be changed externally are shown on that menu.

Affects – When the value of an object's property is changed, a message is drawn in the LSC. The value of the *Affects* flag shows how this arrow is drawn; the possibilities are User, Env and Self, and the arrow is drawn towards the user, towards the environment, or as a self arrow, respectively.

Synchronous – A message referring to a synchronous property may be propagated only if both the sender of the message and its receiver are ready. The arrowhead of a synchronous message is different too.

Examples of object properties are the *state* of a light or a switch, the *value* shown in a display, the *background color* of a display, and the *temperature* shown on a thermometer.

The current implementation of our Play-Engine calls for a GUI application to be described as an XML application description file. Appendix B gives the detailed structure of such files. This method of describing the system model is merely an implementation issue, and it can be carried out in various other ways.

4.3 And a Bit More Formally ...

An object system $\mathcal{S}ys$ is defined as

$$\mathcal{S}ys = \langle \mathcal{D}, \mathcal{C}, \mathcal{O} \rangle$$

where $\mathcal{D}$ is the set of application types (domains), $\mathcal{C}$ is the set of classes and $\mathcal{O}$ is the set of objects. We refer to the user of the system as *User* and to the external environment as *Env*.

A class C is defined as

$$C = \langle Name, \mathcal{P} \rangle$$

where *Name* is the class name and $\mathcal{P}$ is the set of class properties. An object O is an instance of some class and is therefore defined as

$$O = \langle Name, C, \mathcal{PV} \rangle$$

where *Name* is the object's name, C is its class and $\mathcal{PV} : C.\mathcal{P} \rightarrow \bigcup_i D_i$ is a function assigning a value to each of the object's properties. We define the function $class : \mathcal{O} \rightarrow \mathcal{C}$ to map each object to the class it is an instance of. We will also use the shortcut $Value(O.P) = O.\mathcal{PV}(O.C.P)$ to denote the current value of property P of object O.

An object property P is defined as

$$P = \langle Name, D, InOnly, ExtChg, \mathit{Affects}, Sync \rangle$$

where *Name* is the property name and D is the type it is based on. *InOnly*, *ExtChg* and *Sync* range over $\{true, false\}$, and *Affects* ranges over $\{User, Env, Self\}$, as explained earlier. The *IsDefault* and *Prefix* characteristics are purely cosmetic and do not affect the semantics of the model. We do not formalize the different kinds of application types, but rather view a type D as a finite set of values.

5. The Language: Live Sequence Charts (LSCs)

Message sequence charts (MSCs) were discussed in Chap. 2. They were adopted long ago by the International Telecommunication Union (the ITU, formerly the CCITT), and constitute a visual scenario-based language that is popular in the realm of object-oriented systems for capturing behavioral requirements. The language also manifests itself in the UML, somewhat modified, and is referred to there as **sequence diagrams**.

Objects in MSCs are represented by vertical lines, called instances,[1] and messages going between these instances are represented by horizontal (or sometimes down-slanted) arrows. Every instance line contains *locations*. An instance progresses from one location to the next by participating in some activity associated with the location. Such an activity could, for example, be the sending or receiving of a message. Every instance has also an initial location and a final location, in which the instance begins and terminates, respectively.

As explained in Chap. 2, the semantics of all known versions of MSCs, including the ITU standard and the UML sequence diagrams, is a set of simple constraints on the partial order of possible events in some possible system execution, i.e., a partial order among the instance locations. This partial order is determined by two simple rules. First, time is assumed to go from top to bottom, so the partial order restricts the locations along a single instance to be processed in that order. Second, for asynchronous messages (most uses of MSCs are restricted to such messages), the send event of the message precedes the receive event. For synchronous messages the two events are simultaneous. The partial order is essentially the transitive closure of these two rules. For a given chart L, we refer to the partial order it induces by $\leq_L$. Virtually nothing can be said in MSCs about what the system will actually do when run. The charts can state what might possibly occur, but not what must occur, and neither can MSCs specify **anti-scenarios**, whose occurrence we want to forbid.

---

[1] The term *instance* is given in the MSC standard to describe the vertical line representing an object, a process or a task. It should not be confused with class instances, a term used in object-oriented methods.

5.1 Constant LSCs

We now describe the basic version of **live sequence charts** (**LSCs**), proposed in 1998 by W. Damm and the first-listed author of this book. They
eliminate the above deficiencies by their ability to specify liveness, i.e., things
that must occur. This is done by allowing the distinction between possible
and necessary behavior both globally, on the level of an entire chart, and
locally, when specifying events, conditions and progress over time within a
chart.[2]

LSCs have two types of charts: **universal** (annotated with a solid borderline) and **existential** (annotated with a dashed borderline). Universal charts
are used to specify restrictions that apply to all possible system runs. Each
universal chart is associated with a **prechart** that specifies the scenario that,
if successfully executed, forces the system to satisfy the scenario given in the
actual chart body. Existential charts are more like MSCs and UML sequence
diagrams. They are used in LSCs to specify sample interactions between the
system and its environment and must be satisfied by at least one system run.
They thus do not force the application to behave in a certain way in all cases,
but rather state that there is at least one set of circumstances under which
a certain behavior occurs. Existential charts can be used to specify system
tests, or simply to illustrate longer (non-restricting) scenarios that provide a
broader picture of the behavioral possibilities to which the system gives rise.
We will see more on this later, particularly in Chaps. 12 and 18.

Figure 5.1 shows a universal chart and an existential chart. Although the
two contain the same events, their semantics are very different. The universal

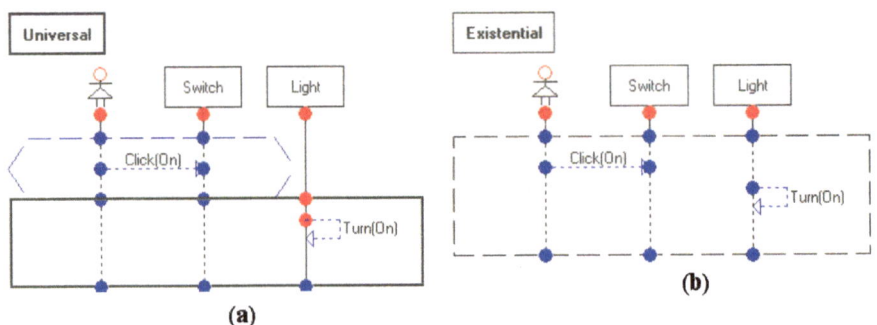

Fig. 5.1. Universal and existential charts

---

[2] Recently, there has been an attempt to adopt some of the ideas of LSCs in an extension
of UML sequence diagrams, which will feature certain constructs that specify mandatory
behavior. We are not familiar with the details of this extension, nor with the level of
rigor of its semantics, but some variant of the extension will probably become part of
the UML 2.0 standard.

chart (Fig. 5.1(a)) says that *every time* the user clicks the switch to on, the light should turn on. Hence, a universal chart induces an action-reaction relationship between the scenarios in its prechart and the scenarios in the chart body, and these action-reaction pairs must be satisfied during the entire system run. The existential chart merely says that there is at least one run of the system, and one point during that run, in which the user clicks the switch to on and the light indeed turns on. It is important to note that there is no causality between the two events in the existential chart. Actually, in this chart the events are not even restricted by the partial order, and therefore a scenario in which the light turns on and then the user clicks the switch to on also satisfies the chart.

The small circles shown in the charts are the instance locations. All instances have at least three locations: an initial location, a location associated with the beginning of the main chart, and a final location. In the universal chart, all the instances that participate in the prechart have also a location for the prechart start. The beginnings of the prechart and the main chart are synchronization points; all instances enter the prechart simultaneously, while the main chart may be entered only after all instances have successfully completed their activities in the prechart.

A location may be either **hot**, thus forcing the instance to progress, or **cold**, thus enabling the instance to remain in its location without violating the chart. A hot location is denoted by a red circle and a solid line from the location to its successor. A cold location is denoted by a blue circle and a dashed line.

As we shall see later, locations may be attached to various kinds of events, but in this chapter we restrict our discussion to LSCs that contain only the most basic events — sending and receiving constant messages.

Messages in LSCs may also be **hot** or **cold**. A hot message must be received after it is sent. A cold message may be sent and not received (which can be viewed as expressing a communication failure). Hot messages are denoted by red solid lines and cold messages are denoted by blue dashed lines.

Messages can represent **synchronous** or **asynchronous** interactions. Self messages are always synchronous, so properties that have their *Affects* attribute set to *Self* are always represented by synchronous messages. Since the user and the environment are external to the system and therefore interact with the GUI objects directly, and not by sending messages over a communication channel, most properties are defined as synchronous. When it is important to show that the interaction of the user or the environment with an object may take time from the moment the action is performed until the object notices it, asynchronous properties can be used. We use closed triangular arrowheads to denote synchronous messages, see Fig. 5.2(a), and open arrowheads for asynchronous ones, see Fig. 5.2(b).

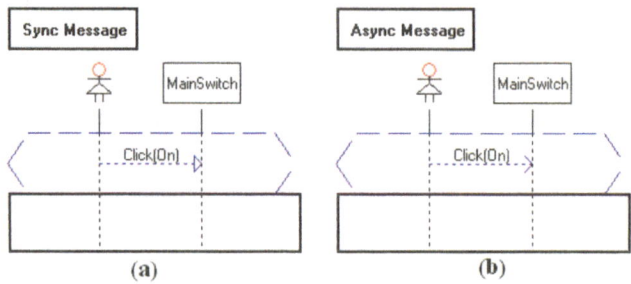

Fig. 5.2. Synchronous vs. asynchronous messages

5.2 Playing In

Messages in LSCs are used to indicate different kinds of events and interactions in the system. Here, we further restrict our discussion to messages that reflect changes in property values only. Other kinds of messages are discussed in Chap. 14.

As an example system we use the bakery panel described in Chap. 3. Suppose we wish to specify that every time the main switch is clicked to *On*, the main light should turn *On*. The LSC in Fig. 5.3 describes this requirement. The text in the small box on the right is a natural language description, generated automatically from the LSC by the Play-Engine.

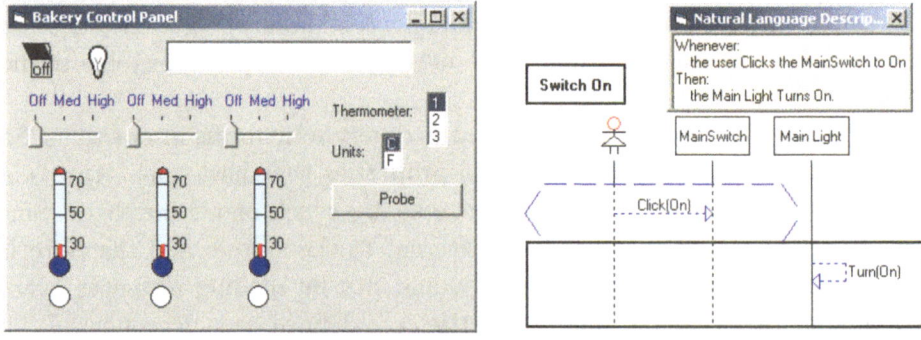

Fig. 5.3. Turning the bakery panel on

In this example, the value of the switch's *state* property is changed to *On* by the user simply clicking it as is done with a working system. In response, the *state* property of the light is also changed to *On*, this time by the system (i.e., the object itself). Note that the locations along the light's instance line are hot (denoted by solid line segments), thus forcing the light to be turned on if the prechart is successfully completed. Each of the two messages in the chart is a **constant** message (sometimes referred to as an **exact** message). A constant message is parameterless, i.e., is one for which all the information it represents — the identities of the sender and receiver and the message content — is known and fixed.

The value of an object's property can be changed by the end-user of the system (e.g., by clicking a switch, rotating a knob, typing text in a text box, etc.). When specifying behavioral requirements, these kinds of events are played in using the same actions, i.e., operating the GUI objects as is done in the final system.

Typically, the system responses are also reflected by changes in the values of object properties (e.g., a light turns on, a console displays some text, etc.). Since these kinds of objects and properties cannot be directly operated by the user to specify the desired value, the changes are specified by right-clicking the target object. The Play-Engine then shows a popup menu, which shows all the properties of the selected object according to the system model (see Fig. 5.4(a)). After selecting a property from the menu (in this example, the

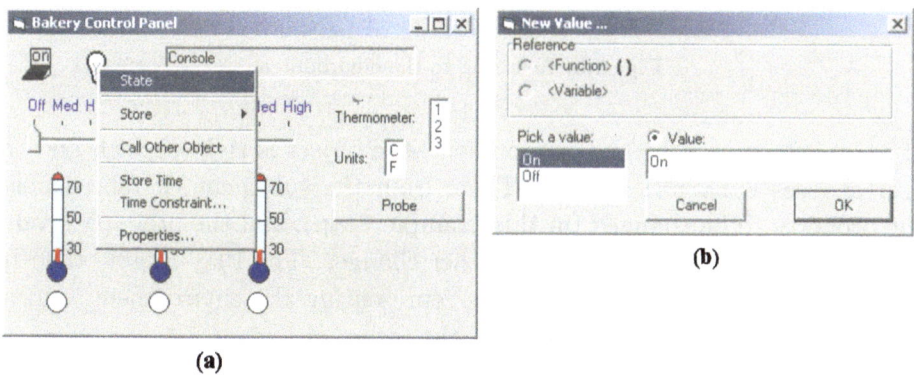

Fig. 5.4. Specifying the system's response

light has only one property — **state**), a dialog opens where the user can specify the new value. If the property is based on an *enumeration* type, the list of values is shown and the user may select a value from there (see Fig. 5.4(b)).

A property value of an object can be changed not only by the end-user or by the system but also by the system's external environment. In the bakery panel example, one may wish to specify that when the temperature of thermometer ♯1 reaches 100 degrees, the system should react in some specified way. A thermometer is a sensor that indicates the value of some property (temperature), which is controlled neither by the user nor by the system. Therefore, there should be a way to express changes in this property caused by the external environment. Figure 5.5 illustrates how this is done and shows the resulting message. In order to specify a change in one of the properties

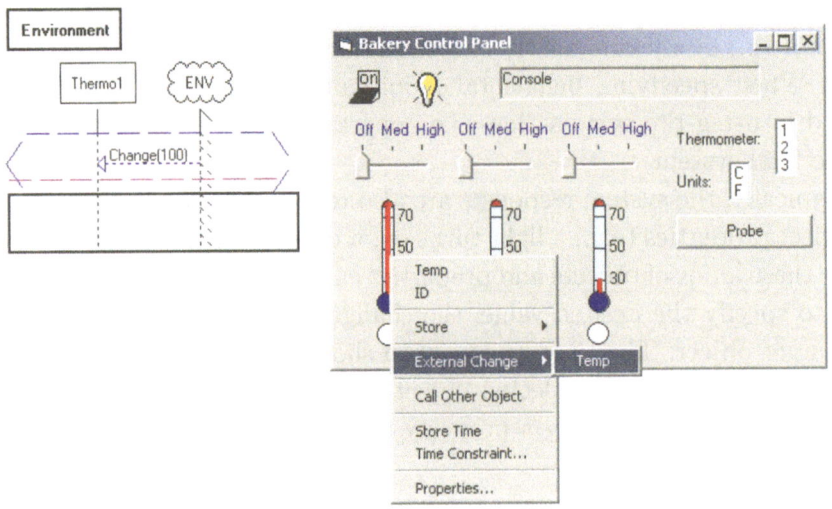

Fig. 5.5. Referring to the environment

of an object, caused by the environment, the object is right-clicked, and the user chooses **External Change**. Then, from the sub-menu, he/she chooses the property to be changed (in this example **Temp**), and the property's value is inserted in the same way as for other changes. The Play-Engine then inserts into the LSC a special instance representing the environment, and an appropriate message going from it to the target object.

When a property is changed by the user or the environment, the message indicating the change goes from the user or the environment instances to the instance representing the affected object. When specifying a system response, the resulting message originates from the changing object and arrives at one of three possible instances, determined by the *Affects* attribute of the changed property, which ranges over { *User, Self, Env* }. Typically, properties have their *Affects* property set to *Self*, since it is common to view a change in the state of an object as a local event involving no other object or entity.

However, when we wish to emphasize that the change in the property is to be seen by the user or the environment, the other options are used. Note, however, that the choice of the instance receiving the message may affect the partial order induced by the LSC.

5.3 The General Play-Out Scheme

Like MSCs and UML sequence diagrams, LSCs can be used to specify requirements that serve later in the process of testing and validating more detailed executable models or implementations. The set of events produced by a monitored system consists of property changes triggered by the user and the environment, as well as property changes triggered by the system's objects. A system event is identified by a message and an indication as to whether the message is being sent or received. The message contains the information regarding the originator, the target object, the changed property and the new value for that property. When a run is being traced, the events from the run are continuously checked against the events in the LSCs to verify that the order induced by the LSCs in the specification is not violated.

This usage of LSCs is beneficial, and the language's added expressive power makes it possible to test and validate more powerful requirements. However, while the precursors of LSCs — MSCs and UML sequence diagrams — are used essentially only in this capacity, the expressive power of LSCs opens up a new and powerful possibility: executing them directly, without the need for an intra-object model or implementation. This idea is one of the main issues this book attempts to cover in detail.

Behavioral requirements for a reactive system specify constraints on how the system reacts with respect to external stimuli such as user actions, events coming from the external environment, timing events, etc. By way of executing such behavior, we would like to enable the user to specify end-user or environment actions and for him/her to then be able to observe the system responses to these stimuli.

One must realize, however, that it is much harder to execute the behavior given in an inter-object language, such as sequence diagrams or LSCs, than it is to do so for intra-object languages such as statecharts, or for code. The latter provide clear information on each object's reactions to every possible event. Thus, executing a system whose objects are described in an intra-object fashion is easy (at least in principle). In contrast, inter-object scenario-based languages do not contain explicit instructions for the behavior of each object under any given set of circumstances. If we want to be able to execute behavior given in such a language, the instructions for each object must be figured out in runtime by considering all the relevant scenarios combined. This is the central issue that our execution mechanism has to address.

Before describing in detail how this is done, it is worth repeating verbatim (except for a gender change) the informal explanation given in the overview chapter, Chap. 3: The underlying play-out mechanism can be likened to an over-obedient citizen who walks around with the Grand Book of Rules on her at all times. She doesn't lift a finger unless some rule in the book says she has to, never does anything if it violates some other rule, and always carries out — to the letter — what she was asked to do, as well as anything else that doing so entails. She constantly scans and monitors all rules at all times.

More technically, our approach for executing LSCs can be described using the following general set of capabilities that an execution mechanism for inter-object behavior should supply:

1. Identify an external stimulus and find all the requirements that should be considered when resolving the system's response to it (e.g., identify the event of flipping a switch and find all the requirements that specify the system's responses to the switch being flipped).
2. Apply the relevant requirements to create the sequence of system reactions. This is done iteratively, and thus includes identifying additional requirements that become relevant as the system is responding and applying them too (e.g., after the switch is flipped, send a signal to the controller, which, in turn, may result in sending a signal to the light and turning it on).
3. Identify scenarios that are forbidden according to the requirements, and avoid generating them (e.g., make sure that if the requirements say that a certain signal cannot be sent to the light while it is on, it will indeed not be sent when the light is on).
4. In case a forbidden scenario actually occurs (e.g., because some other mandatory scenario forces it to, or as a result of a user action or an external action), indicate a violation.

Playing out is the process of testing the behavior of the system by providing any user or environment actions, in any order, and checking the system's ongoing responses. The play-out process calls for the Play-Engine to monitor the applicable precharts of all universal charts, and if successfully completed to then execute their bodies. By executing the events in these charts and causing the GUI application to reflect the effect of these events on the system objects, the user is provided with a simulation of an executable application.

When a universal LSC is activated, it can be in one of two **activation modes**. As long as execution is in the prechart, the mode is said to be **preactive**, and as soon as the prechart successfully completes, the mode changes to **active**. After an LSC becomes activated, in either mode, each of its instances begins at its initial location and progresses as the run continues. The mapping of each instance of an LSC L to its current location is called a **cut** of L. A cut is hot if at least one of the instances is in a hot location and cold if all the instances are in cold locations. Cuts are drawn in the diagrams as thick comb-like lines (see Fig. 5.6). Note that in executing LSCs (and also in using them for testing), a single universal chart may become activated several times during a system run. Thus, we have to cater for multiple incarnations of LSCs.

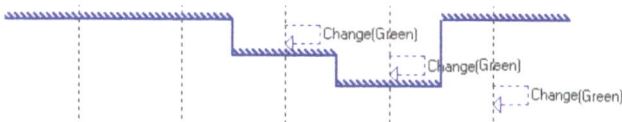

Fig. 5.6. An LSC cut

A run is **consistent with** an LSC if the events in the run occur in the order dictated by the LSC. When referring to this order, one must be precise as to when an event is allowed to happen. According to our semantics, events that do not appear in an LSC are not restricted by it and can therefore occur at any point. (This principle is modified in Chap. 17, where we extend the language with the ability to specify forbidden elements.) An event that appears in an LSC is **enabled** with respect to the current cut of the LSC if it appears immediately after the cut, that is, all the events that should have occurred prior to this event have already occurred. An event is **violating** an LSC if it appears in the LSC but is not enabled by the current cut (an alternative semantics, in which such an event is not violating, is also given in Chap. 17).

In order to correctly identify the full status of a chart, as soon as it becomes activated a copy of the chart is created, termed a **live copy**. A live copy of an LSC contains a copy of the original LSC, its activation mode and its current cut. The basic life cycle of a live copy of a universal LSC is illustrated in Fig. 5.7. (We defer the discussion of existential LSCs until later on.)

Initially, the copy does not exist. Whenever a **minimal event** (i.e., minimal in the partial order induced by the LSC) that appears in L's prechart occurs, the copy is created in preactive mode. As long as events occur in an order consistent with that of the LSC, the cut of the copy is propagated. When all locations in the prechart have been traversed, the copy moves into active mode. Here too, as long as events occur in a consistent order, the cut is propagated. If all locations in the chart are reached, the copy terminates and

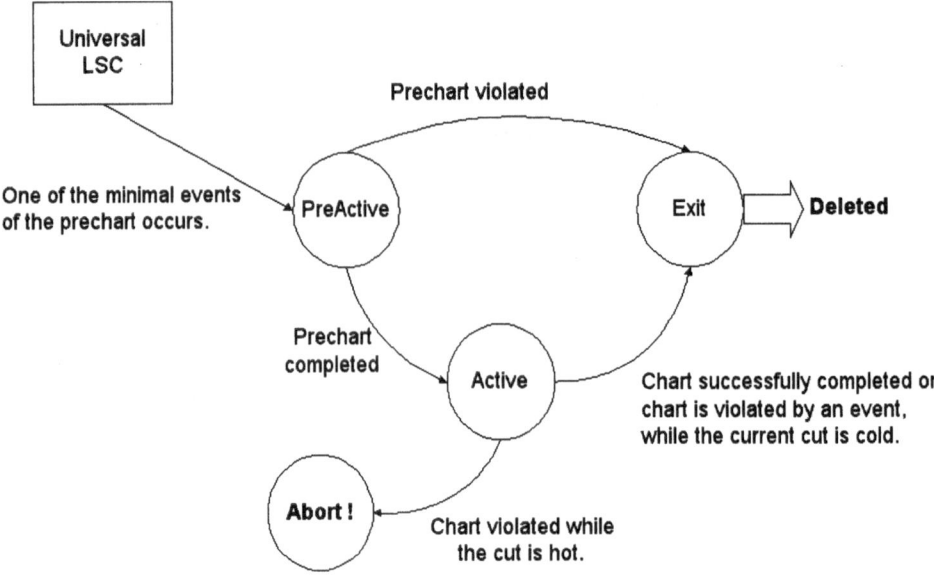

Fig. 5.7. Basic life cycle of the live copy of a universal LSC

stops existing. If the LSC is violated while its cut is still in the prechart, the copy terminates and stops existing, causing no error. Such a violation only indicates that the triggering scenario was not fully completed, and there is no longer an obligation to carry out the main chart. If the chart is violated by an event (i.e., sending or receiving a message) while its cut is in the main chart, and the temperature of the current cut is cold, the copy terminates and stops existing. This kind of termination also causes no error, since all the instances are in cold locations and are therefore not obligated to progress. If the main chart is violated by an event and the temperature of the current cut is hot, the chart aborts causing an error, since an illegal run has been identified.

The play-out execution mechanism works in iterations, each of which consists of an action, called a *step*, which is an event initiated by the user, followed by a reaction, called a *super-step*, which is a sequence of events selected from the set of enabled events that are not violating. As this is going on, minimal events are identified and new LSC copies are created. The reaction ends when there are no more enabled events that can be carried out.

5.4 Playing Out

Figure 5.8 shows what happens when the switch is turned on while the Play-Engine is in play-out mode. The event of the user clicking the switch to *On*

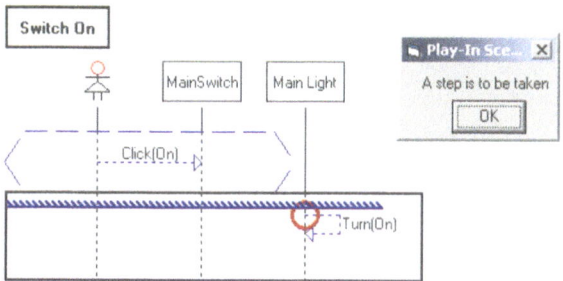

Fig. 5.8. Playing out in step mode

is sought for in all the precharts of universal charts.[3] As the event is found in the LSC *"Switch On"*, this LSC becomes activated, and a live copy of it is created in *preactive* mode. Since the message in the prechart is synchronous, the send and receive events occur simultaneously, and then, because there is only one message in the prechart, the prechart is successfully completed and the mode of the LSC copy is set to *active*. Now, the Play-Engine chooses one event from the set of currently enabled events. In this case the only event is that of the light changing its state to on. Note that although the locations of the light and the message in the main chart are cold, so that according to pure LSC semantics execution doesn't necessarily have to progress from them, in actuality the Play-Engine executes the event of turning the light to on. This is because according to our operational semantics, the Play-Engine takes a greedy approach, trying to execute as many events as it can, and it does not stop in its tracks just because elements are cold. This issue will be discussed in more detail later in the book.

The Play-Engine can be set to react to user and environment actions in two modes: *step* and *super-step*. When in step mode, the user is prompted before each event, and the next event to be carried out is marked on all relevant charts. In super-step mode, the Play-Engine carries out as many events as possible, until it reaches a 'stable' state, in which the system can do nothing but wait for some input from the user. In this example, the Play-Engine is shown running in *step* mode. The event is circled in red and the user is prompted for confirmation before it is taken.

After the user clicks OK in the popup prompt, the event is carried out. Since this is the last event in the chart, the Play-Engine realizes that the chart has successfully completed, marks it with a solid blue frame and notifies the user of its completion. Figure 5.9 shows the completed chart. Once the user

---

[3] In this chapter we deal with a single active LSC at a time. Chapter 11 discusses in detail how the Play-Engine handles multiple charts.

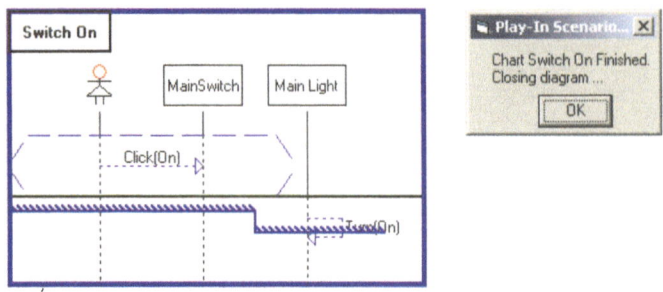

Fig. 5.9. A successfully completed LSC

confirms the popup message, the chart is closed and removed from the set of live copies.

It is quite natural to have a prechart started but not successfully completed; that is, cases where the triggering scenario does not occur in full. Consider the following requirement:

> *When the three switches are set to their Med state in reverse order (i.e., starting with switch 3 and ending with 1), the system should enter master mode and indicate it by displaying "MASTER" on the console.*

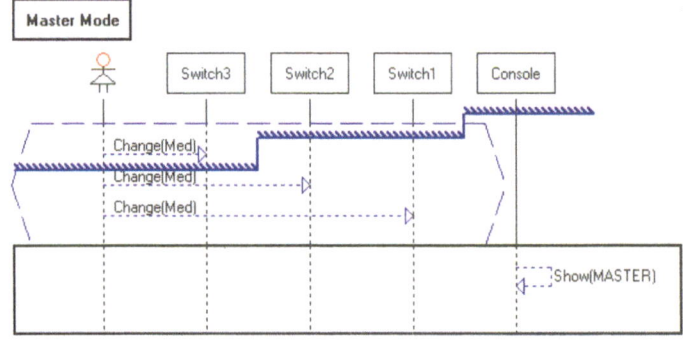

Fig. 5.10. Monitoring a chart in preactive mode

Suppose now that in play-out the user moves switch 3 to Med. The event is identified by the Play-Engine, and the LSC is activated, as shown in Fig. 5.10. At this stage, the prechart is not yet completed, so the Play-Engine awaits the next event. The user now moves switch 1 to Med. This event appears in the chart but is currently not enabled. The prechart is thus violated, but this is not a big deal since the system is not committed to any behavior dictated

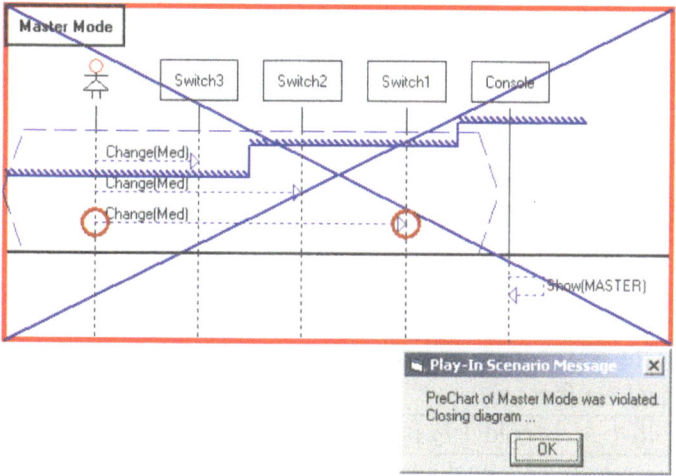

Fig. 5.11. Violating a prechart

by that main chart. Consequently, the LSC is marked by a red frame and is crossed out in blue. The violating event is circled in red, thus enabling the user to examine the reason for the violation. See Fig. 5.11. After confirming the popup message, the chart is closed and is removed from the set of live copies.

Were such a violation to occur while the LSC copy was in *active* mode and the cut was *hot*, the cross would have been *red* and the popup message would have shown that a *violation of the requirements* was detected.

5.5 Combining Locations and Messages

Consider the LSC given in Fig. 5.12, in which object O_1, being at location l_1, sends a message M to O_2, who receives the message at location l_2. As denoted by the solid lines, the message and the locations are all *hot*, meaning that O_1 must send the message, the message must arrive, and O_2 must receive it.

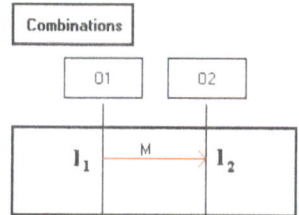

Fig. 5.12. Temperatures of messages and locations

In the following, we discuss some less trivial combinations of temperatures for messages and locations. The discussion is relevant to *asynchronous* messages only, since in the synchronous case the message is sent and received simultaneously.

There are eight different cases, each indicating a different combination of temperatures for l_1, M and l_2. We point out any conflicts they introduce, and discuss how these conflicts are handled by our proposed LSC semantics.

1. | l_1 is hot | M is hot | l_2 is hot |

   This is the case discussed above. It is rather intuitive and causes no semantical conflicts.

2. | l_1 is cold | M is cold | l_2 is hot |

   In this scenario, O_2 must progress beyond l_2, but O_1 is not obligated to send the message M, and even if it indeed sends M, M itself may not arrive. According to our semantics, an LSC cut is hot if at least one of the instances is in a hot location. In this case, as long as O_2 remains in l_2 the cut stays hot, and therefore any event not allowed by the LSC that is triggered will cause a violation of the specification. Therefore, the fact that O_2 is in a hot location implicitly forces O_1 to send the message and M to arrive. Hence, this case is semantically equivalent to the first case discussed, where the two locations and the message are all hot.

3. | l_1 is cold | M is hot | l_2 is hot |

   Since l_2 is hot, and M is hot anyway, this case is equivalent to case 2.

4. | l_1 is hot | M is cold | l_2 is hot |

   Again, O_1 must send M and O_2 must receive it. However, the message is cold and therefore may not arrive. Like in case 2, having l_2 hot affects the message and forces it to arrive. Non-arrival is therefore a violation.

5. | l_1 is cold | M is cold | l_2 is cold |

   In this scenario, O_1 is not obligated to send M. If it chooses to do so, M may or may not be received by O_2. If M does not arrive, O_2 is allowed to remain in l_2 without violating the scenario.

6. | l_1 is cold | M is hot | l_2 is cold |

   In this scenario, O_1 is not forced to send M and O_2 is not forced to receive it. However, once M is sent, the definition of a hot message forces it to be received, but this conflicts with l_2 being cold. According to our semantics, assuming that the location following l_1 in O_1 is also cold, after M is sent the cut is still cold and the chart may terminate without causing a violation. As opposed to the previous case, where the temperature of a location caused a change in the declared nature of a message, the converse — i.e., the temperature of a message changing the nature of a location — does not apply.

7. $\boxed{l_1 \text{ is hot} \mid M \text{ is cold} \mid l_2 \text{ is cold}}$

This case also conforms with the intuition underlying the formal semantics: O_1 is indeed forced to send M, but M may not arrive, and even if it does O_2 is not obligated to accept it and proceed.

8. $\boxed{l_1 \text{ is hot} \mid M \text{ is hot} \mid l_2 \text{ is cold}}$

Here, O_1 must send the message and the message must arrive. However, O_2 may decide not to receive the message. Following the same considerations as in case 6, we derive that in this case too the temperature of l_2 overrides that of M.

This eight-way analysis leads to an interesting observation. According to our semantics, the temperatures of instance locations are actually given higher priority than those of messages. This means that message temperatures really serve only to graphically emphasize communication failures; the temperature of a message has no semantic meaning and it is totally determined by the temperature of the receiving object.

We have chosen this semantics as it seems to us to be the most intuitive, but we do not rule out an alternative semantics in which the hot temperature of a message overrides the cold temperature of the receiving location. To achieve this change would merely require changing the definition of the temperature of a cut to be hot not only if one of its locations is hot but also if it "crosses" a hot message, i.e., the send event has already occurred but the receive event has not. In any case, we recommend using only the simpler and more intuitive combinations from among the eight; they should suffice for all practical purpose.

This situation is, in fact, typical of many of the semantic decisions we have taken in our work, and which we describe as we progress. As with any language, there could be several valid ways to define meanings for the various parts of our charts. In each case we adopt the one we felt to be the most practical and intuitive for use by engineers who want to build reactive systems. By no means do we say that the semantics we provide is the only one possible; nor do we claim it to be the best. As the topics unfold, we will try to justify these decisions and describe the considerations that led to them.

5.6 And a Bit More Formally ...

In this chapter we provide the operational semantics of basic LSCs. This semantics will be extended and modified in the chapters to come, and the parts repeated will be shown in blue, with the new additions being given in the regular font. The semantics here, and in each of the subsequent extensions, will be organized into three parts:

System Model and Events – This part contains definitions of the events that can be generated by the system model.

LSC Specification – This part contains definitions of the various LSC constructs.

Operational Semantics – This part contains a description of the operational semantics of LSCs with respect to the system model.

System Model and Events

Given a system model Sys, we define a system message M_s as

$$M_s = \langle Src, Dst, P, V \rangle$$

where Src is the object sending the message, Dst is the object receiving the message (which could be the same as Src), P is the property changed, and $V \in P.D$ is the new value for the property, taken from the set of values defined by the property type D.

Definition 5.6.1 (synchronous system messages). *A message M_s is synchronous if $M_s.P.Sync = true$. A self message is also synchronous.*

The alphabet of possible messages of Sys, denoted by Σ, is defined as

$$
\begin{aligned}
\Sigma &= \Sigma_{FromUser} \cup \Sigma_{ToUser} \cup \Sigma_{FromEnv} \cup \Sigma_{ToEnv} \cup \Sigma_{Self} \\
\Sigma_{FromUser} &= \{M_s \mid Src = User \wedge P \in class(Dst).\mathcal{P}\} \\
\Sigma_{ToUser} &= \{M_s \mid Dst = User \wedge P \in class(Src).\mathcal{P} \wedge P.Affects = User \\
&\qquad \wedge P.InOnly = False\} \\
\Sigma_{FromEnv} &= \{M_s \mid Src = Env \wedge P \in class(Dst).\mathcal{P} \wedge P.ExtChg = True \\
&\qquad \wedge P.InOnly = False\} \\
\Sigma_{ToEnv} &= \{M_s \mid Dst = Env \wedge P \in class(Src).\mathcal{P} \wedge P.Affects = Env \\
&\qquad \wedge P.InOnly = False\} \\
\Sigma_{Self} &= \{M_s \mid Dst = Src \wedge P \in class(Src).\mathcal{P} \wedge P.Affects = Self \\
&\qquad \wedge P.InOnly = False\}
\end{aligned}
$$

where $\Sigma_{FromUser}$ is the set of messages representing a property change in some object caused by the user, Σ_{ToUser} captures the messages representing a property change caused by the system and directed towards the user, $\Sigma_{FromEnv}$ are those messages representing a property change in some object caused by the external environment, Σ_{ToEnv} are property changes caused by the system and directed towards the environment, and, finally, Σ_{Self} is the set of messages representing a property change caused locally by the system.

The set of *system events*, $\mathcal{E}$, is defined as

$$\mathcal{E} = ((\varSigma_{FromUser} \cup \varSigma_{ToUser} \cup \varSigma_{FromEnv} \cup \varSigma_{ToEnv}) \times \{Send, Recv\})$$
$$\cup \ (\varSigma_{Self} \times \{Send\})$$

LSC Specification

Now, given a system model Sys and the possible events it may generate, an LSC specification for Sys is defined as the disjoint union

$$\mathcal{S} = \mathcal{S}_{\mathcal{U}} \cup \mathcal{S}_E$$

where $\mathcal{S}_{\mathcal{U}}$ is a set of universal charts and $\mathcal{S}_E$ is a set of existential charts.

An LSC L is defined to be:

$$L = \langle I_L, M_L, [Pch_L], evnt, temp \rangle$$

Here, I_L is the set of instances in L, M_L is the set of messages in L, Pch_L is the prechart of L (in universal charts), and $evnt$ and $temp$ are functions that will be discussed shortly.

An instance I is defined as

$$I = \langle \ell, O \rangle$$

where ℓ is the set of instance locations and $O \in \mathcal{O}$ is the object represented by I.

We denote by l_x^i the xth location of instance I_i, and by $\ell(I) = I.\ell$ the set of locations of instance I. We use $\ell(L)$ as an abbreviation for $\bigcup_{I \in L} \ell(I)$.

We define the function $AppObj$ to map each instance to the object it represents

$$AppObj : \bigcup_{L \in \mathcal{S}} I_L \to \mathcal{O}$$

and we require that a single object cannot be represented by more than one instance in an LSC

$$\forall I, I' \in I_L : \ AppObj(I') \neq AppObj(I)$$

A message $M \in M_L$ is defined as

$$M = \langle I_{Src}, I_{Dst}, M_s \rangle$$

where $I_{Src} \in I_L$ is the instance representing the sender, $I_{Dst} \in I_L$ is the instance representing the receiver, and $M_s \in \varSigma$ is the system message represented by M, so that $M_s.Src = AppObj(I_{Src})$ and $M_s.Dst = AppObj(I_{Dst})$. The message M is synchronous if and only if $M.M_s$ is synchronous.

The temperature function *temp* assigns temperatures to some of the LSC constructs:

$$temp : \ell(L) \cup M_L \rightarrow \{hot, cold\}$$

We denote by E_L the set of *LSC events* in L, which consists of two disjoint sets. An LSC event can be an actual system event of sending or receiving a message, or it can be one of the acts of entering the prechart, exiting it or reaching the end of the chart body. We will refer to the first kind of event as *visible events* and to the second as *hidden events*. The set of visible events is defined as

$$\begin{aligned}
(\{m \in M_L \mid m.M_s \in \Sigma_{FromUser} \cup \Sigma_{ToUser} \cup \Sigma_{FromEnv} \cup \Sigma_{ToEnv}\} \\
\times \{Send, Recv\}) \\
\cup (\{m \in M_L \mid m.M_s \in \Sigma_{Self}\} \times \{Send\})
\end{aligned}$$

The set of hidden events is defined as

$$(Pch_L \times \{Start, End\}) \cup \{Completed\}$$

The function $evnt : \ell(L) \rightarrow E_L$ maps a location to the event it is associated with. Its inverse, $loc : E_L \rightarrow 2^{\ell(L)} = evnt^{-1}$, maps an event to the set of locations associated with it. Note that when restricting the domain of loc to $M_L \times \{Send, Recv\}$, loc becomes single-valued.

Every LSC induces a partial order among instance locations, which is the central aspect in determining the order of execution. The partial order, $\leq_L$, induced by a chart L, is obtained by the following relations:

Instance line – The locations along a single instance line are ordered top-down, beginning with the prechart start and ending with the chart end. Thus, things higher up are carried out earlier:

$$x < y \Rightarrow l_x^i <_L l_y^i$$

Send-Receive – For an asynchronous message $m \in M_L$, the location of the $\langle m, Send \rangle$ event precedes the location of the $\langle m, Recv \rangle$ event. Thus, an asynchronous message is sent before it is received. For synchronous messages, the two events take place simultaneously:

$$\begin{aligned}
\forall m \in M_L : \\
(async(m) \Rightarrow loc(\langle m, Send \rangle) <_L loc(\langle m, Recv \rangle)) \\
\wedge (sync(m) \Rightarrow loc(\langle m, Send \rangle) =_L loc(\langle m, Recv \rangle))
\end{aligned}$$

Prechart – All the instances participating in the prechart are synchronized
at the beginning of the prechart and at its end. That is, no instance is
allowed to move into the prechart before all other instances have arrived
at their prechart entry points, and no instance is allowed to exit the
prechart (and enter the main chart) before all other instances have arrived
at their prechart exit points.

$$\forall l_x^i, l_y^j \in loc((Pch, Start)) : l_x^i =_L l_y^j$$
$$\forall l_x^i, l_y^j \in loc((Pch, End)) : l_x^i =_L l_y^j$$

Chart completion – In order for a chart to complete, all the instances must
reach their final location.

$$\forall l_x^i, l_y^j \in FinalLocations(L) : l_x^i =_L l_y^j$$

We extend the partial order $\leq_L$ to events in the following way: $e' <_L e$ if
$\exists l \in loc(e), \exists l' \in loc(e')$ such that $l' <_L l$.

Operational Semantics

In order to describe the operational semantics of LSCs, we must define the
notions of an *LSC cut*, *minimal*, *enabled* and *violating* events, and an LSC
live copy.

Definition 5.6.2 (LSC legal cut). *An* LSC cut *of L is a tuple of locations
mapping every instance of L to one of its possible locations:*

$$Cut_L \in \prod_{I \in I_L} \ell(I)$$

A set of locations S is down-closed *if*

$$l_x^i \in S \Rightarrow \forall y \leq x, l_y^i \in S$$

The down-closure *of an LSC cut C, denoted by $\downarrow C$, is the minimal down-
closed set that contains C.*

An LSC legal cut *C is an LSC cut that satisfies:*

$$\forall l \in C, \ \forall l' \leq_L l : l' \in \downarrow C$$

The top-line *of a down-closed set S, denoted by $\uparrow S$, is a set of locations
obtained by:*

$$l_x^i \in \uparrow S \iff l_x^i \in S \land \nexists l_y^i \in S \text{ s.t. } y > x$$

Note that $C = \lceil \downarrow C$. From now on we will refer only to LSC legal cuts and denote by $Cut(I)$ the location of instance I in Cut.

The following utility functions dealing with cuts are used as we continue:

- The function $InitialCut(L)$ returns a legal cut of L containing the initial location for each instance.
- The function $BeginMainCut(L)$ returns the cut containing for each instance the location associated with the beginning of the main chart.
- The function $AdvanceCut(C, e) = \lceil (\downarrow C \cup loc(e))$ is defined for a legal cut C and an event e that is enabled with respect to C, and returns a legal cut that is the result of advancing the cut C beyond e.

Definition 5.6.3 (temperature of a cut). *The temperature of a cut is hot if at least one of the instances is in a hot location and cold otherwise. We use $temp(C)$ to denote the temperature of cut C.*

Definition 5.6.4 (minimal event). *An event e is minimal in a chart L if there is no event e' in L such that $e' <_L e$.*

Definition 5.6.5 (enabled event). *An event e is enabled with respect to a cut C if $\lceil (\downarrow C \cup loc(e))$ is a legal cut; that is, if the location in C of every instance[4] participating in the event e is the one exactly prior to e, and there is no $e' <_L e$ that is not already in the down-closure of C. If $e = \langle m, Send \rangle$, m is synchronous and $e' = \langle m, Recv \rangle$, we require also that $\downarrow C \cup loc(e) \cup loc(e')$ is down-closed, thus making sure that a synchronous message will not be sent unless it can be received.*

Definition 5.6.6 (violating event). *An event e violates a chart L in a cut C if $e \in M_L \times \{Send, Recv\}$ but e is not enabled with respect to C.*

There is one point to be clarified regarding the relation between system events and LSC events. A system event e_s is defined over the set $\Sigma \times \{Send, Recv\}$. When such an event is generated by the system, it has to be matched with LSC events that are defined over the set $M_L \times \{Send, Recv\}$. As we shall see later, we also want to be able to match two LSC events (usually in different charts). These two kinds of matching are captured in the following definition.

Definition 5.6.7 ($level_0$-unification).

1. *A system event $e_s = \langle m_s, t \rangle$ and an LSC event $e_l = \langle m_l, t' \rangle$, with $t, t' \in \{Send, Recv\}$, are $level_0$-unifiable if $t = t'$, $m_l.M_s = m_s$, $AppObj(m_l.I_{Src}) = m_s.Src$, and $AppObj(m_l.I_{Dst}) = m_s.Dst$.*

---

[4] Usually, there will be only one such instance, but precharts (and other constructs, as we shall see later) may have several participating instances.

2. *Two LSC events $e = \langle m, t \rangle$ and $e' = \langle m', t' \rangle$, with $t, t' \in \{Send, Recv\}$, are level$_0$-unifiable if $t = t'$, $m.M_s = m'.M_s$, $AppObj(m.I_{Src}) = AppObj(m'.I_{Src})$, and $AppObj(m.I_{Dst}) = AppObj(m'.I_{Dst})$.*

From now on, we will use the expression $e = \langle m, t \rangle$ both for system events and for LSC visible events. Note that in the first case $m \in \Sigma$ and in the second $m \in M_L$. In both cases $t \in \{Send, Recv\}$.

Definition 5.6.8 (LSC live copy). *Given an LSC L, a live copy of L, denoted by C^L, is defined as*

$$C^L = \langle LSC, Mode, Cut \rangle,$$

where LSC is a copy of the original chart, $Mode \in \{PreActive, Active\}$ is the execution mode of this copy, and Cut is some legal cut of L representing the current location of the instances of L in this particular copy.

We can now turn to the operational semantics for an LSC specification $\mathcal{S}$. We present the semantics as a state transition system $Sem(\mathcal{S})$. As we progress through the book and more elements are added to the language, the definition of $Sem(\mathcal{S})$ will be extended and modified.

$$Sem(\mathcal{S}) = \langle \mathcal{V}, V_0, \Delta \rangle$$

where $\mathcal{V}$ is the set of possible configurations (states) of $Sem(\mathcal{S})$, V_0 is the initial configuration and $\Delta \subseteq \mathcal{V} \times (\mathcal{E} \cup \bigcup_{L \in \mathcal{S}} E_L) \times \mathcal{V}$ is the set of allowed transitions.

A state $V \in \mathcal{V}$ is defined as

$$V = \langle \mathcal{RL}, Violating \rangle$$

where $\mathcal{RL}$ is the set of currently running LSCs, that is, the set of existing live copies, and $Violating$ indicates by $True$ or $False$ whether the state is a violating one. The initial configuration is $V_0 = \langle \phi, False \rangle$.

We describe Δ as a set of rules to be applied to the $\mathcal{RL}$ and $Violating$ components of a given state V with respect to a given event e. The result is a new state V' consisting of the modified components. Given an event, all the applicable rules are applied before the next event is considered. Also, Δ handles *hidden events* with higher priority than *visible events*. Therefore, in order for a visible event to be handled, all hidden events must be processed first. Other than that, the semantics imposes no order on the particular event to be processed, and is thus nondeterministic.

- If $e = \langle M, t \rangle$ (where $t \in \{Send, Recv\}$) then:

1. If $\exists C^L \in \mathcal{RL}$ and $\exists e' \in C^L.LSC$ such that e and e' are $level_0$-unifiable and e' violates C^L, then set $\mathcal{RL} \leftarrow \mathcal{RL} \setminus \{C^L\}$. If $temp(C^L.Cut) = hot$, set $Violating \leftarrow True$.

2. For every universal LSC $L \in \mathcal{S}_\mathcal{U}$ which has in its prechart a minimal event e' that is $level_0$-unifiable with e, create a copy of L, C^L, and set $\mathcal{RL} \leftarrow \mathcal{RL} \cup \{C^L\}$. Set $C^L.Mode = PreActive$ and set its cut by $C^L.Cut \leftarrow AdvanceCut(InitialCut(L), \langle Pch_L, Start \rangle)$.

3. For every copy $C^L \in \mathcal{RL}$ which has an enabled event e' $level_0$-unifiable with e, set its cut by $C^L.Cut \leftarrow AdvanceCut(C^L.Cut, e')$. Then, if $e' = \langle M, Send \rangle$, M is synchronous and $e'' = \langle M, Recv \rangle$, set the cut by $C^L.Cut \leftarrow AdvanceCut(C^L.Cut, e'')$.

- If $e = Completed(C^L)$ for some $C^L \in \mathcal{RL}$, then set $\mathcal{RL} \leftarrow \mathcal{RL} \setminus \{C^L\}$.
- If $e = \langle Pch_L, End \rangle$ for some $C^L \in \mathcal{RL}$, then set
  $C^L.Cut \leftarrow BeginMainCut(C^L.LSC)$ and $C^L.Mode \leftarrow Active$.

Definition 5.6.9 (violating transition). *A transition in Δ is* violating *if it sets Violating to false.*

Definition 5.6.10 (run/trace). *A* run *or* trace *is a sequence of visible events.*

Definition 5.6.11 (consistent run). *A* run R *is consistent with an LSC specification $\mathcal{S}$ if, starting from V_0, the rules of Δ can be applied iteratively to the events in R, and to the hidden events generated between them, without reaching a violating transition.*

One of the main purposes of our Play-Engine is to make it possible to execute the specification directly. The engine's execution mechanism, the *play-out*, works in phases of *step* and *super-step*. The input to a *step* is a system event e. The procedure for a step phase is then simply:

---

step(e)

1. Apply $\Delta(e)$.
2. Change the property value according to the value in the message:
   a)

$$O \leftarrow \begin{cases} e.M.Src \text{ if } M \in \Sigma_{ToUser} \cup \Sigma_{ToEnv} \\ e.M.Dst \text{ otherwise} \end{cases}$$

   b) $P \leftarrow e.M.P$
   c) $Value(O.P) \leftarrow e.M.V$

In the *super-step* phase, the Play-Engine continuously executes the steps associated with internal events, i.e., those that do not originate with the user or the environment, until it reaches a 'stable' state where no further such events can be carried out. The external events are those with $Src \in \{User, Env\}$. Thus, we define:

$$External = \{\bigcup_{L \in \mathcal{S}} \langle m, Send \rangle \mid m.M_s.Src \in \{User, Env\}\}$$

A super-step phase is therefore given as:

---

super-step

1. Compute the set of enabled events:

$$Enabled \leftarrow \bigcup_{C^L \in \mathcal{RL}} \{e \in E_L \mid enabled(e)\}$$

$$Enabled \leftarrow Enabled \setminus External$$

2. If there are *hidden* enabled events in *Enabled*, then choose one, e, and propagate it:
   a) Apply $\Delta(e)$.
   b) Go back to 1.
3. If there are *visible* enabled events in *Enabled* that do not violate any copy in active mode, then choose one, e, and propagate it:
   a) $step(e)$.
   b) Go back to 1.
4. Terminate super-step.

5.7 Bibliographic Notes

The original definition of the MSC standard, published in 1996, is given in [123] and its algebraic semantics in [124]. In 1999 the MSC'96 standard was extended to MSC 2000 [91]. A detailed history of the MSC standard can be found in [102]. UML sequence diagrams and their equivalent collaboration diagrams are presented in [115, 106]. There are many other variants of sequence diagrams in the literature. Some of these are object MSCs (OMSC) [19], extended event traces (EET) [78], interworkings [85], high-level MSCs [123] and hybrid sequence charts (HySC) [39].

Symbolic timing diagrams (STD) [28] is another visual formalism for the specification of VHDL-based hardware, which is successfully used in industry [109]. STDs also utilize the notion of possible and mandatory constraints with a semantics similar to that of LSCs. The STD constraints, however, can only limit the temporal relation between events and are not used to constrain the system state.

A number of variants of temporal logic [82] are used in industry for specifying the requirements of reactive systems. Tempura [90] is an executable language consisting of statements that are actually formulas in a variant of temporal logic called interval temporal logic (ITL) [89], and it thus bridges the gap between the requirements language and the language used to define the model. A visual representation of interval logic, supported by a tool set for creating and analyzing graphical interval logic specifications, is presented in [32]. Another formalism for specifying requirements in a variant of temporal logic is the temporal logic of actions (TLA) [75], which can be used for specifying and reasoning about concurrent systems. In TLA, systems and their properties are represented in the same logic, so the assertion that a system meets its specification and the assertion that one system implements another are both expressed by logical implication.

In [71] an extensive discussion of several MSC dialects is presented, and a comparison is carried out. Another survey of scenario-based languages can be found in [11], where the formalisms are also discussed within the context of the possible transition from scenario-based languages to state-based behavioral descriptions.

The original definition of live sequence charts appears in [27]. An alternative semantics for LSCs, based on timed Büchi automata, is given in [65]. The semantics is given there for a single LSC, since it is used to monitor an LSC with respect to a given run and not to execute an LSC specification consisting of many charts. The LSC language subset described in [65] uses activation conditions for triggering universal charts, rather than the more general precharts. As mentioned in a footnote in the text, the UML 2.0 standard will probably contain an extension of UML sequence diagrams that incorporates some ideas taken from LSCs.

The idea of playing in scenarios was discussed in [43]; it was worked out and described in detail in [49]. Play-out was first described in [49].

The use of a partial order in the context of system execution was first proposed in [74]. Our formal definitions of legal cuts and enabled events are inspired by [104].

6. The Tool: The Play-Engine

In the previous two chapters we introduced two basic foundations of our approach, the system model and the language, and our goal is to use the latter to describe the behavior of the former, by playing in. The result of the play-in process is a formal specification in the language of LSCs, and this specification can then be executed and tested by playing out different scenarios and observing system responses. The link between the two foundations of language and model and the play-in/play-out methodology is provided by the **Play-Engine** tool.

We have constructed the Play-Engine in order to cater for both play-in and play-out, utilizing the system model and supporting all the LSC features that will be described in this book. The Play-Engine in its current guise does not support the process of building a GUI application as the front end to some system model. This is mainly because we did not want to restrict the methodology or the tool to work with a specific technology for building user interfaces, since such technologies constantly develop, providing increasingly faster ways of constructing ever nicer-looking applications. In Chap. 20 we describe a separate tool we have built, GUIEdit, with which one can build GUI applications that are 'aware' of the Play-Engine, in that they provide all the information required by the engine and can interact with it as needed. GUIEdit should be considered as an add-on to the Play-Engine, and as such it is not perfect. Using it is not as easy as using the Play-Engine itself, but we expect this to change as the ideas and the tool mature and evolve.

As the book progresses, we shall describe how simple and less simple LSC constructs can be played in, and we shall illustrate the different options for playing out. The purpose of the present chapter is to describe the basics of the Play-Engine itself and to give the look-and-feel of the environment in which the play-in and play-out occur.

We shall use the screen shot in Fig. 6.1 to describe the main elements involved in the Play-Engine's development environment. They are numbered here to match the numbers overlaying the figure.

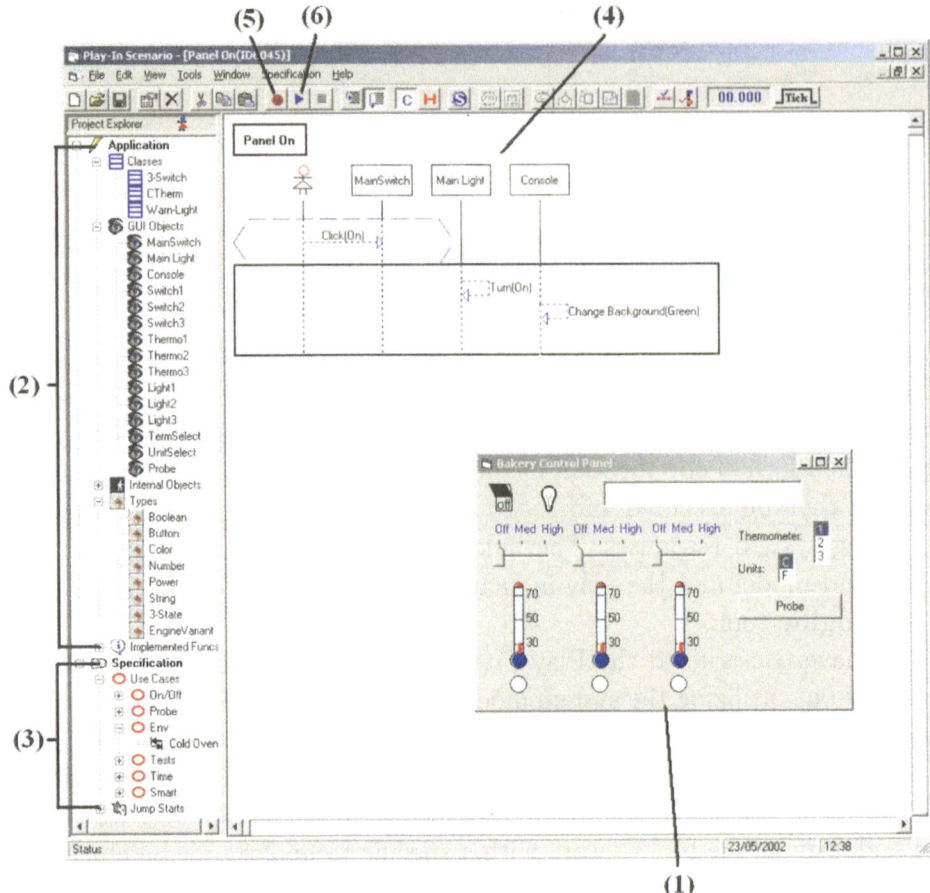

Fig. 6.1. The Play-Engine

1. **The GUI application**

   This is the GUI application (in our example, the bakery panel), which is provided by the user. It may be constructed using any means, providing it supports the interface required by the Play-Engine. Our bakery panel (as well as most of the examples shown in the book) was written in Visual Basic using the GUIEdit tool, described in Chap. 20.

2. **The application section**

   This section contains the elements defined in the system model. The information contains:

   - The classes defined in the system model (e.g., 3-Switch, CTherm, etc.).
   - The GUI objects defined in the system model (e.g., MainSwitch, Main Light, Switch3, etc.).

- The internal objects defined in the system model (this figure shows none). Internal objects are discussed in Chap. 14.
- The application types (e.g., Boolean, Button, Color, etc.).
- The functions implemented by the application (this figure shows none). Implemented functions are described in Chap. 8.

3. **The specification section**

   This section contains the behavioral elements specified by the user:

   - The use cases and LSCs. This is the main part of the requirements specification, and it consists of the LSCs (constructed by the engine as a result of the play-in), clustered into use cases. The idea is that the LSCs associated with a use case capture the behaviors that implement/instantiate it. As in many methodologies, the user starts by identifying a use case and giving it a name and a short description.
   - Jump starts. Users often describe different scenarios, assuming different initial system configurations. The Play-Engine allows the definition of jump starts, which can be used to move the system to one of its initial configurations by a single mouse click. A jump start is a set of the properties of objects that are associated with initial values.

4. **The LSCs**

   This area shows the LSC that is currently being constructed by the Play-Engine during play-in, or the LSCs that are currently being executed during play-out.

5. **Play-in button**

   This button is used to enter play-in mode. Other toolbar buttons that are used in the process of playing in behavior are introduced throughout the book as new LSC constructs are presented.

6. **Play-out button**

   This button is used to enter play-out mode. Other buttons and options used to determine the play-out configuration are described together with the play-out mechanism.

After playing in (part of) the behavioral specification of the target system, the specification can be saved into a specification file. Separating the behavioral specification from the application enables the user to create and test several specifications for a single GUI. Moreover, the same behavioral specification can be used with different GUI applications, given that they consist of the same set of objects. Actually, it will turn out that if we use classes even the set of objects need not be identical. Also, as we show later, the system model itself can be extended on the fly by adding objects, classes, properties and methods. This type of information is considered part of the system structure, rather than the behavior. However, the Play-Engine cannot override the application file since it is provided by the user. Therefore, all the extensions to the application are saved in a different *application extension* file. Combining the same GUI with different application extensions can be used, for example, to describe different designs for the similar-looking GUI applications.

Although the different combinations of GUI applications, application extensions and behavioral specifications are very useful, at any given time one usually works with a single set, consisting of an application and its extensions, and the behavior of the extended system. To simplify the process of saving and loading this combination of files, the Play-Engine uses *workspace* files. A workspace contains references to all the other files and the user's preferred values for the various Play-Engine options. A workspace file can be saved and loaded as an integrated unit, although each of its components can be opened and saved separately.

In order for a GUI application to interact with the Play-Engine, it must implement the *IUserApp* interface, and use the *IPlayEngine* interface. The former allows the Play-Engine to interact with the application (e.g., set the values of object properties, query the application for the geometric location of objects, etc.). The latter allows the application to notify the Play-Engine of different events (e.g., an object was clicked, an object value was changed by the user, etc.). Appendix C describes the *IPlayEngine* interface and Appendix D describes the *IUserApp* interface.

The first thing the Play-Engine does upon loading a GUI application is to query it for the name of its application description file. The Play-Engine then reads the file and builds the application section in the project explorer tree. The structure of the application description file is given in Appendix B.

The procedures for playing in scenarios and playing out behavioral specifications, together with some other useful features that are not in the main core of the play-in/play-out approach, have all been implemented in the Play-Engine. Chapter 19 describes the high-level architecture of the Play-Engine and the main components it is composed of. Chapter 19 also provides an overview of some of the less major features that help make the Play-Engine a user-friendly means for specifying and executing behavioral specifications.

6.1 Bibliographic Notes

The Play-Engine was first described in [49]. Short animations demonstrating some capabilities of the Play-Engine tool are available on the Web: `http://www.wisdom.weizmann.ac.il/~rami/PlayEngine`.
All the files that are saved and loaded by the Play-Engine are in XML format [122]. A detailed discussion of the advantages of XML as an interchange format is given in [113].

Part III

Basic Behavior

7. Variables and Symbolic Messages

In this chapter we present our first extension to the basic constant-message LSCs discussed in Chap. 5. It involves the simplest means LSCs have for specifying generalized scenarios, namely, variables and symbolic messages.

7.1 Symbolic Scenarios

Often it is natural to specify a small number of sample cases that represent more general scenarios. Suppose, for example, that we wish to model the behavior of a cellular phone. One of the things we require is that when the cover is opened, the antenna should automatically open too. We can describe this requirement using the LSC in Fig. 7.1.

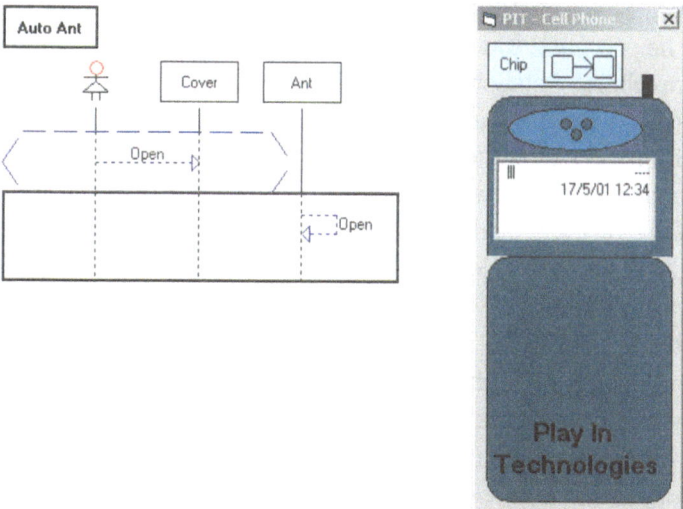

Fig. 7.1. The antenna opens automatically

This example also shows the possibility of using some of the more 'cosmetic' features that we have incorporated into the engine. The structure of a message label is of the general form *Prefix Property-Name(Value)*. The words "Open" and "Close" serve to describe the state of the cover, but they can also serve as verbs describing user actions. Since, we would like to refer to the state of the cover (e.g., in conditions), the *state* property of the cover (and the antenna) is defined over a type containing the values {*Open, Close*}. Had we used the messages in Fig. 7.1 in the standard way, the labels along the transitions would have read "Set State(Open)" and "Set State(Close)". However, the double usage of the words as states and verbs describing the actions makes it possible to specify this in a simpler way. What we did in this case was to set the *Is Default* attribute of the property (for both the cover and the antenna) to *true* and the *Prefix* attribute to the empty string. This tells the engine that since the property is a default, its name need not be explicitly stated, and also that there is no need for the "Set" prefix, thus yielding the simple label *Open*.

Suppose now that the user wishes to specify that when the cover is closed the antenna should automatically close too. This could, of course, be played in as a separate scenario, very similar to the previous one. However, the two are better represented by a single LSC, which we can specify using **symbolic messages**. We play a scenario as before, with the cover being opened as part of the prechart, and the antenna's reaction being played in as the chart's body. However, this time we do it with the *symbolic* flag on. When in symbolic mode, the values shown in message labels are names of variables rather than actual values. The user does not say that the antenna should open or close as a result of the prechart, but that it should take on the same state as the cover did in the prechart. As shown in Fig. 7.2, we do this here by indicating that the value should be the same as that of the prechart message in the LSC. The user simply clicks the desired message inside the LSC, and its variable will be attached to the new message as well. The resulting LSC is shown in Fig. 7.3. (This variable could have been selected from a list that would have popped up had the user selected <Variable> rather than <From LSC> in the menu appearing Fig. 7.2.)

A variable is local to an LSC, and therefore can be referred to only within the chart in which it is defined. An occurrence of a variable in an LSC means that it may take on any value from the variable's type, and using the same variable in different places in a chart allows the user to specify that the same value will occur in these places in a specific run (not necessarily the same value in all runs, of course). Variables can be given meaningful names; in this example the variable was named $X_{op/cl}$, to capture the fact that it can take on the values *Open* and *Close*.

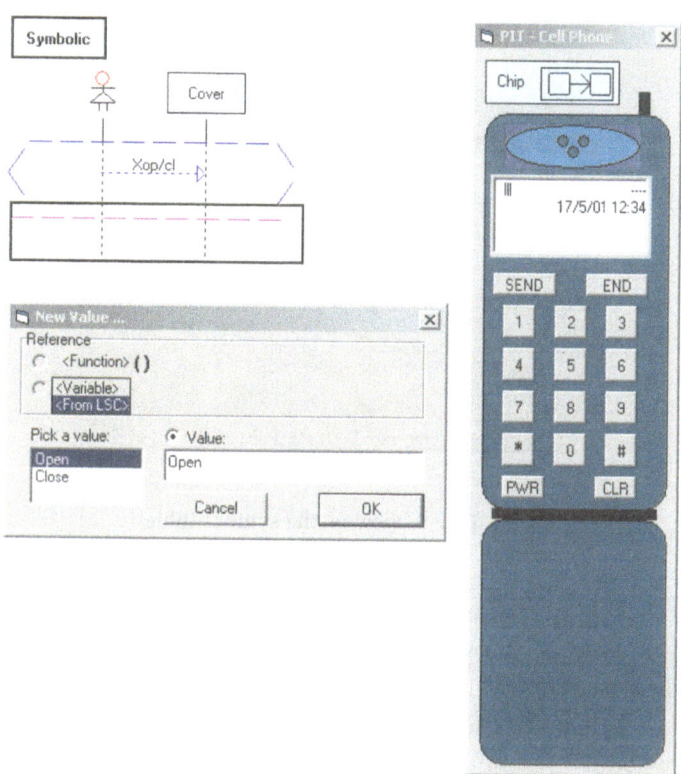

Fig. 7.2. Play-in in symbolic mode

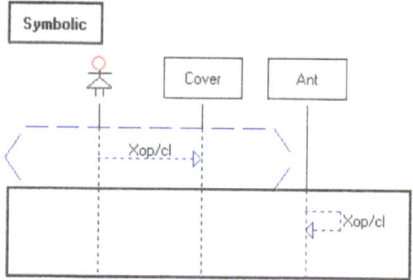

Fig. 7.3. Symbolic (generic) linking between the states of the cover and antenna

The Play-Engine's **symbol table** points to all the variables in all the LSCs of the current workspace, and can be used to view and modify the variable names and values (see Fig. 7.4).

Messages within an already generated LSC can be made **symbolic** or **exact** even after they have been played in using the opposite mode. This is done by right-clicking the message and choosing the appropriate option from

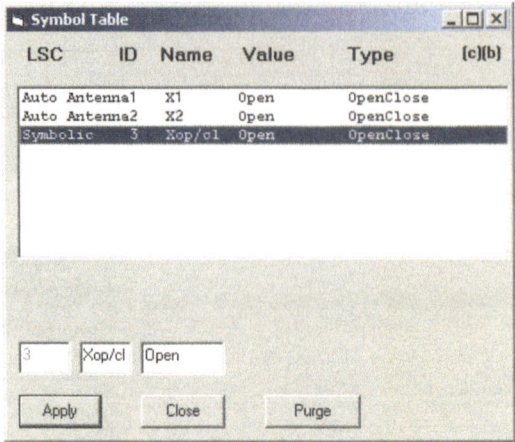

Fig. 7.4. A view of the symbol table

the popup menu, as shown in Fig. 7.5. Since a message can be either symbolic or exact, regardless of the way it was played in, we associate each message with a variable that is assigned the value that was used when the message was played in. When the message is exact we can refer only to the variable's value, and when it is symbolic we refer to the fact that the variable may be assigned other values. More about this later.

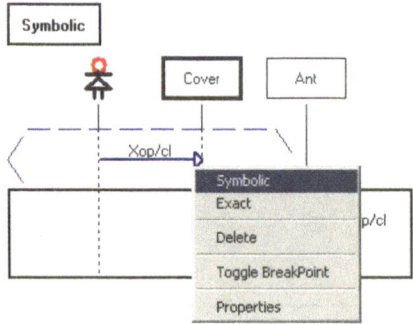

Fig. 7.5. Making a message exact/symbolic

7.2 Enriching the Partial Order

Figure 7.6(a) shows a simple example of using variables to link messages with different verbs but the same state space. We have a switch that can be clicked

On or *Off* by the user, and a light that is required to be in the same state as the switch; when one is *On*, so is the other, and the same for *Off*. In this case, the variable *Xpower* is of type *Power* which was defined as an enumeration containing the values *On* and *Off*.

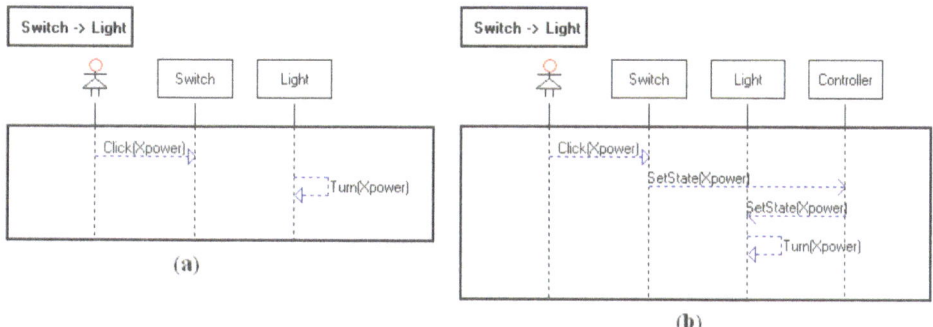

Fig. 7.6. The effects of variables on LSCs partial order

A careful look at Fig. 7.6(a) reveals an interesting issue concerning the partial order defined by the chart. There is no prechart here, but the way the chart is displayed seems to say that "the user changes the state of the switch to *On* or *Off*, and the light then changes its state to be the same as that of the switch". However, the partial order of this LSC does not restrict the clicking of the switch to only come before the light changes its state, since they are not related to some common instance. This is a problem if we really want the first to happen before the second.

We can resolve this by introducing a control object that receives the state from the switch and sends it to the light (Fig. 7.6(b)), thus restricting the partial order, as required.[1] However, we most often wish to remain on a higher, more abstract, level of specification. On the one hand we do not want to get into the details of how information about the value of the variable is actually transferred between the objects, but on the other hand we do want some initial event to be the first, and hence to determine the value of the variable, so that subsequent uses of the same variable in different places will have the same value. We make this possible by a slight extension of the partial order $<_L$ induced by an LSC L, which takes into account the vertical placing of locations that are not on the same instance line.

---

[1] Although we have not yet discussed messages going from one object to another, the given scenario should be clear. Messages representing interactions of that kind are discussed in Chap. 14.

If we imagine a vertical line T aligned with an LSC L, we may consider the ordering of locations from top to bottom, as projected on T. See Fig. 7.7, in which locations l_1 and l_2 are not ordered by $<_L$ but are vertically ordered; we may write $l_1 <_V l_2$ for this. The partial order $<_L$ is now extended to handle

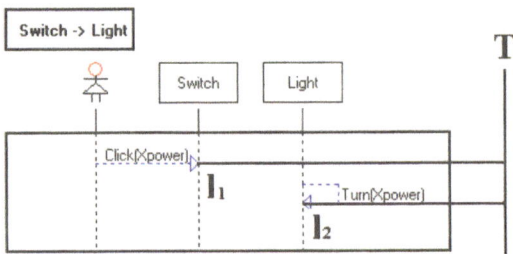

Fig. 7.7. Vertical order: $l_1 <_V l_2$

the order induced by the variables. A location is said to **affect** a variable X if it is associated with a message that has X as its variable. A location l is the **first** to affect X if it is associated with the *send* event of a message that affects X, and for every other location l' that affects X either $l <_L l'$ or $l <_V l'$. Now, for a location l that is the first in L to affect the variable X, we add the relation $l <_L l'$ to the partial order $<_L$ for every other location l' in L that affects X.

This extension thus causes the first occurrence of a variable to come before all the others, but no new order is imposed on subsequent occurrences. We have decided to do this, despite the fact that one of the basic maxims of sequence charts prescribes that the vertical order between locations on different instance lines does not influence the semantics. However, we find that it is very natural for users building LSCs to specify dependent events in the order they occur, and to cause this order to be reflected in the geometry of their LSCs. While we do not go as far as to attach significance to the entire vertical ordering, we do think that the first occurrence of each variable is a significant aspect of the way the user chose to enter the information, and that if the intention is to use the element in question as a symbolic one then the user probably meant to say "this is the first occurrence of this symbolic value, and the value given here during execution should impact later occurrences". And, incidentally, if the requirements are played in, events that are played in first will appear higher up in the generated LSC anyway, which is consistent with this philosophy.

Having said all this, we should note that this decision is not sacred, and was made for convenience. We could have required the user to specify separately which of the minimal occurrences of each variable is the dominating one for the purpose of receiving and distributing a value.

7.3 Playing Out

As we have seen, when playing out behavior, the user operates the GUI application and inserts various external events. These events are then matched with events that appear in the different LSCs and thus force the application to react. In the presence of symbolic variables, events cannot be matched simply by straightforward identification, but, rather, should be unified in a more sophisticated way.

Recall that every message is defined as having a single variable. A variable can be either **bound** or **free**. Initially, all the variables that appear in *exact* messages are bound to their initial values and all other variables are free. We say that a message is bound if its variable is bound, and an event is bound if its message is bound. The same goes for free messages and events. Now, in order for two events to be matched, it is not enough for them to be of the same type (i.e., send/recv) and to be associated with the same system message; their variables should be **unifiable**.

Here is how the unification of two variables works: If X and Y are both bound to the same value, they are successfully unified and if they are bound to different values, they cannot be unified. If X is bound and Y is free, then after the variables are unified Y will be bound to the value of X. The same applies to the case where Y is bound and X is free. If both X and Y are free, they are connected via a connection list. Later, when one of the variables in the connection list is bound to some value, all other variables in the connection list will be bound to the same value.

Figure 7.8 shows the symbolic LSC that was previously played in, as it is activated by the user opening the cover. When placing the mouse over a message, the current value of its variable is shown in a tooltip, and the figure shows this happening for the message in the prechart.

As a simple example, suppose one chart that contains an event $e = \langle m(X), Send \rangle$, where $m(X)$ is a message going from O_1 to O_2 and is associated with variable X. A second chart contains $e' = \langle m(Y), Send \rangle$, also from O_1 to O_2. Now, suppose that the event of O_1 sending $m(3)$ to O_2 has occurred. There are a number of cases to consider:

- If both e and e' are enabled in their charts, and X and Y are free, we bind X and Y to 3 and advance both charts.
- Suppose Y is already bound to the value 4. Clearly, after binding X to 3, the messages are not the same and therefore they cannot be unified. In this

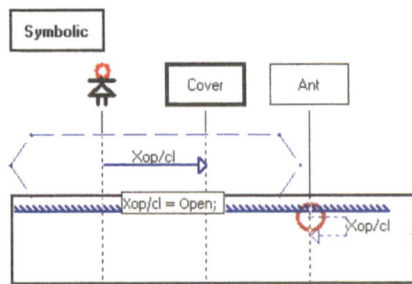

Fig. 7.8. Binding variables during play-out

case, e will be advanced and e' will neither be advanced nor be considered violating.

- The last and most interesting case is when Y is free and e' is currently not enabled. There are really two possibilities we could adopt here. The first is to succeed in unifying e and e', thus advancing the first chart and causing violation of the second, and the second possibility is to fail in the unification, thus advancing the first chart and leaving the second as is. The first approach maintains that if it is possible for an event to cause a violation it should be handled as if it indeed will, and the second says that if it is possible that an event will not cause a violation, it should be handled as if it won't.

We have to make a decision regarding the two possible approaches in this third case. Our experience with many examples shows that the second approach is significantly more practical. For example, suppose there is a system with a display that shows several warnings while running, using messages of the form "show(X_i)" where the X_i's are assigned values during the execution. These messages are spread throughout several charts and should not necessarily be synchronized with each other. If the first approach is taken, whenever the display tries to show something as dictated by one chart, it will cause a violation of other charts. This limits the specification in a way that is very difficult to overcome. Hence, we adopt the second approach.

This decision causes a distinction between **positive unification**, in which we allow variables to be bound, and **negative unification**, in which variable binding is forbidden. Positive unification is used to find minimal events in precharts that will cause the activation of new LSC copies, and also to find events in different active charts that should be propagated simultaneously. Negative unification is used to find violating events in active LSCs, so that only if a violating event is already bound to a violating value will it cause a violation. If the event is not yet bound, it means that we currently do not know that it will cause a violation, and we therefore leave it as is.

With this settled, we can now describe the relevant parts of our execution algorithm. When a user initiates an event e, this event is by its very nature bound (e.g., the user has clicked the digit 7, turned the switch *On*, etc.). The universal charts are scanned for minimal events that are unifiable with e and are then unified with it, thus (possibly) causing their variables to be bound. Once these variables are bound, new events that depend on these now definitely valued variables may become enabled (e.g., asking for the display of a 7, for a light to turn *On*, etc.). A super-step is then performed, where enabled events that are positively-unifiable are carried out simultaneously. Before triggering any event, however, the active LSC copies are scanned for events that are negatively-unifiable with this event. If such a violating event is found, the original event is not taken at all.

7.4 And a Bit More Formally ...

Following the skeleton described in Chap. 5, we show the extensions and modifications to the different parts of the semantics. Recall that the blue parts are those repeated verbatim.

System Model and Events

A variable is defined as

$$V = \langle D, \omega \rangle$$

where $D \in \mathcal{D}$ is the variable's type, and $\omega \in D \cup \{\bot\}$ is the value assigned to V. For a free variable we have $\omega = \bot$. We shall use simple predicate notation for notions like free and bound, as in $free(x)$.

A system message M_s was previously defined as

$$M_s = \langle Src, Dst, P, V \rangle$$

where $V \in P.D$ represented the value associated with the message. We now redefine a system message M_s as follows:

$$M_s = \langle Src, Dst, P, V, Symbolic \rangle$$

where *Src*, *Dst* and *P* represent the source object, destination object and property as before. V is now the variable associated with the message and *Symbolic* is a Boolean flag that indicates whether the message is symbolic.

LSC Specification

We denote by V_L the set of variables that appear in an LSC L.

$$L = \langle I_L, V_L, M_L, [Pch_L], evnt, temp \rangle$$

As shown earlier, variables have an important role in determining the partial order of the LSC. This is captured in the following definition.

Definition 7.4.1 (affecting a variable). *An LSC message $M \in M_L$ affects a variable X if $M.M_s.V = X$.*[2]

The notion of affecting a variable is extended to LSC events and locations in the natural way, and we use the predicates *affects(l, X)* and *affects(e, X)* with the appropriate meanings.

We say that l_x^i is the *first* location in L to affect the variable X if it affects X, and for any other location l_y^j that affects X either $l_x^i <_L l_y^j$ or $l_x^i <_V l_y^j$ (where $<_V$ is the vertical order in L). The predicate *first(l,X)* is true iff l is the first location that affects X. The partial order $<_L$ is now extended to handle the order induced by variables as follows:

$$\forall l, l' \in \ell(L) : first(l, X) \wedge \textit{affects}(l', X) \Rightarrow l <_L l'$$

Operational Semantics

The operational semantics remains basically the same, except that now events have to be unified taking variables into consideration. In Chap. 5 we defined $level_0$-unifiable events.

Definition 7.4.2 ($level_0$-unification).

1. *A system event $e_s = \langle m_s, t \rangle$ and an LSC event $e_l = \langle m_l, t' \rangle$, with $t, t' \in \{Send, Recv\}$, are $level_0$-unifiable if $t = t'$, $m_l.M_s = m_s$, $AppObj(m_l.I_{Src}) = m_s.Src$, and $AppObj(m_l.I_{Dst}) = m_s.Dst$.*
2. *Two LSC events $e = \langle m, t \rangle$ and $e' = \langle m', t' \rangle$, with $t, t' \in \{Send, Recv\}$, are $level_0$-unifiable if $t = t'$, $m.M_s = m'.M_s$, $AppObj(m.I_{Src}) = AppObj(m'.I_{Src})$, and $AppObj(m.I_{Dst}) = AppObj(m'.I_{Dst})$.*

This definition is now modified so that instead of checking for equality of messages, the messages are checked as to whether they can be unified.

---

[2] The symbol '=' is used here to denote the fact that the two arguments point to the same variable, rather than to the fact that two different variables have the same value.

Definition 7.4.3 (variable unification). *We say that the two variables X and Y are* positively-unifiable *if $X.\omega = Y.\omega$ or $free(X)$ or $free(Y)$. We say that X and Y are* negatively-unifiable *if $X.\omega = Y.\omega \neq \bot$.*

Definition 7.4.4 (message unification). *Two system messages $M_s = \langle Src, Dst, P, V, Symbolic \rangle$ and $M'_s = \langle Src', Dst', P', V', Symbolic' \rangle$ are Q-unifiable, where Q is 'positively' or 'negatively', if $Src = Src', Dst = Dst', P = P'$, and V and V' are Q-unifiable.*

Definition 7.4.5 (level$_1$-unification).

1. *A system event $e_s = \langle m_s, t \rangle$ and an LSC event $e_l = \langle m_l, t' \rangle$, with $t, t' \in \{Send, Recv\}$, are Q-level$_1$-unifiable (where Q is 'positively' or 'negatively') if $t = t'$, and $m_l.M_s$ and m_s are Q-unifiable.*
2. *Two LSC events $e = \langle m, t \rangle$ and $e' = \langle m', t' \rangle$, with $t, t' \in \{Send, Recv\}$, are Q-level$_1$-unifiable if $t = t'$, and $m.M_s$ and $m'.M_s$ are Q-unifiable.*

From now on, when we use the term unification without specifying whether it is positive or negative, it should be read as positive unification.

As events occur in the system, LSC events are checked to see if they can be unified, and if so their variables are actually bound to new values according to the unification process. If both variables are free, no binding occurs and the two variables are connected in a connection set, as described below. Such a set contains variables that should be assigned to the same value. The connection sets are stored in collections called *unification contexts* until they can be bound to some value. Here is how a pair of variables is added to such a context:

Connect(X, Y, Context)

1. Create a connected pair in the context:

$$S \leftarrow \{X, Y\}; \quad Context \leftarrow Context \cup \{S\}$$

2. If X or Y are already connected, join the sets:

if $\exists S_X \in Context$, s.t. $X \in S_X$, then $S \leftarrow S \cup S_X$;
$$Context \leftarrow Context \setminus \{S_X\}$$
if $\exists S_Y \in Context$, s.t. $Y \in S_Y$, then $S \leftarrow S \cup S_Y$;
$$Context \leftarrow Context \setminus \{S_Y\}$$

Binding a variable in *Context* with a given value entails binding all the variables in its connection set, and is done as follows:

Bind(X, Val, Context)

1. Let S_X be the set in $Context$ s.t. $X \in S_X$.
2. Assign values to all variables in the set:

   $$\forall U \in S_X : \ U.\omega \leftarrow Val$$

   $$Context \leftarrow Context \setminus \{S_X\}$$

With these last two definitions in mind, we now describe the unification procedure:

Unify(X, Y, Context)

1. If $X.\omega = \bot \wedge Y.\omega \neq \bot$ then set $X.\omega \leftarrow Y.\omega$.
2. If $X.\omega \neq \bot \wedge Y.\omega = \bot$ then set $Y.\omega \leftarrow X.\omega$.
3. If $X.\omega = \bot \wedge Y.\omega = \bot$ then $Connect(X, Y, Context)$.
4. If $X.\omega \neq \bot$ then $Bind(X, X.\omega, Context)$.
5. If $Y.\omega \neq \bot$ then $Bind(Y, Y.\omega, Context)$

We use $Unify(M, M', Context)$ as an abbreviation of $Unify(M.V, M'.V', Context)$, and $Unify(e, e', Context)$ as an abbreviation of $Unify(e.M, e'.M', Context)$.

Finally, the transition relation Δ is modified to consider variables and to assign values to them as a part of executing events.

- If $e = \langle M, t \rangle$ (where $t \in \{Send, Recv\}$) then:

1. Set $Context \leftarrow \emptyset$.

2. If $\exists C^L \in \mathcal{RL}$ and $\exists e' \in C^L.LSC$ such that e and e' are negatively level$_1$-unifiable and e' violates C^L, then set $\mathcal{RL} \leftarrow \mathcal{RL} \setminus \{C^L\}$. If $temp(C^L.Cut) = hot$, set $Violating \leftarrow True$.

3. For every universal LSC $L \in \mathcal{S}_\mathcal{U}$ which has in its prechart a minimal event e', positively level$_1$-unifiable with e, create a copy of L, C^L, and set $\mathcal{RL} \leftarrow \mathcal{RL} \cup \{C^L\}$. Set $C^L.Mode = PreActive$ and set its cut by $C^L.Cut \leftarrow AdvanceCut(InitialCut(L), \langle Pch_L, Start \rangle)$. Unify the variables of e and e', by $Unify(e, e', Context)$.

4. For every copy $C^L \in \mathcal{RL}$ which has an enabled event e', positively level$_1$-unifiable with e, set its cut by $C^L.Cut \leftarrow AdvanceCut(C^L.Cut, e')$. Then, if $e' = \langle M, Send \rangle$, M is synchronous and $e'' = \langle M, Recv \rangle$, set the cut by $C^L.Cut \leftarrow AdvanceCut(C^L.Cut, e'')$. Unify the variables of e and e', by $Unify(e, e', Context)$.

- If $e = Completed(C^L)$ for some $C^L \in \mathcal{RL}$, then set $\mathcal{RL} \leftarrow \mathcal{RL} \setminus \{C^L\}$.
- If $e = \langle Pch_L, End \rangle$ for some $C^L \in \mathcal{RL}$, then set $C^L.Cut \leftarrow BeginMainCut(C^L.LSC)$ and $C^L.Mode \leftarrow Active$.

7.5 Bibliographic Notes

The notion of unification was first described by Robinson in [103]. The procedures for message unification described in this chapter are somewhat similar to the unification of clauses in Prolog [23, 69, 118].

8. Assignments and Implemented Functions

We often want to use data manipulation algorithms and functions that are applied to specified variables. These algorithms and functions usually cannot (and should not) be described using LSC-style interactions between objects but are better viewed as external pieces of computation or logic to be worked into the scenarios. In this chapter we discuss these, and the assignment statements that can be used to apply them.

8.1 Using Implemented Functions

The Play-Engine allows for GUI applications to provide **implemented functions**, each of which is identified by its name, the names and types of its formal parameters and the type of the returned result. These functions are described in the application description file (see Appendix B) and are implemented in the code of the GUI application. The *IUserApp* interface, which is implemented by all GUI applications, allows the Play-Engine to query the GUI application for the result of applying a function to specified values.

Consider the following example of a pocket calculator (Fig. 8.1). Now, suppose the user would like to specify that when clicking the following se-

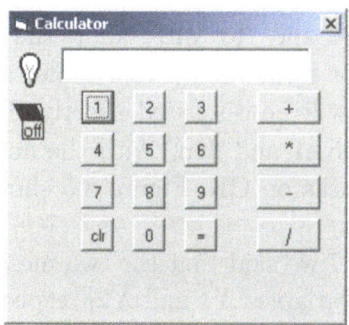

Fig. 8.1. A pocket calculator GUI

quence of keys, '$X1$', '+', '$X2$' and '=' in that order, where $X1$ and $X2$ are any digits, the display should show the value of $X1 + X2$.

The prechart is specified by entering symbolic mode and clicking the above sequence using any digits for $X1$ and $X2$. The result is shown in Fig. 8.2.

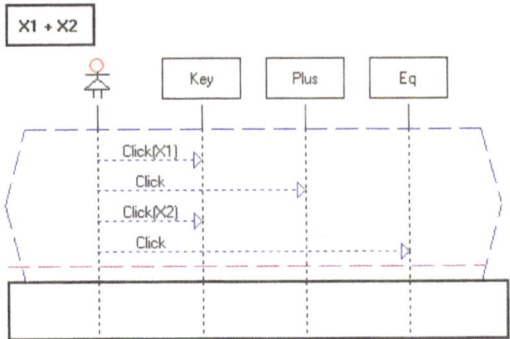

Fig. 8.2. Prechart for summing two digits

In the main chart, the user now has to specify how the display shows $X1$ + $X2$. He/she right-clicks the GUI's display and chooses the **Value** property from the popup menu. Now, instead of entering a fixed value or choosing an existing variable, the user clicks the **Function** button. As a result, a list of all the functions is shown and the user may choose one of them (see Fig. 8.3).

Continuing with our example, the user chooses the '+' function,[1] and the **Function** button is replaced with a description of the selected function, consisting of its name and formal parameters. The user now instantiates each of the formal parameters with an actual one, by placing the mouse cursor on the parameter and selecting an option from the list that appears (see Fig. 8.4).

The options **From LSC** and **Variable** allow the user to select a variable from the current LSC or from the symbol table, as described in Chap. 7. The **New Value** option will be discussed shortly. The user instantiates the two formal parameters **Num1** and **Num2** with the actual parameters $X1$ and $X2$, respectively, and clicks on OK. Figure 8.5 shows the final LSC for the summation of two digits.

Recall that in Chap. 7 we said that the two messages containing $X1$ and $X2$ were **affecting** the variables $X1$ and $X2$, respectively. In contrast to the

---

[1] Even though the summation operation is simple and could have been provided by the Play-Engine itself, we consider it, for the sake of the example, as a function taken from the application domain, which could not be provided by a general purpose tool.

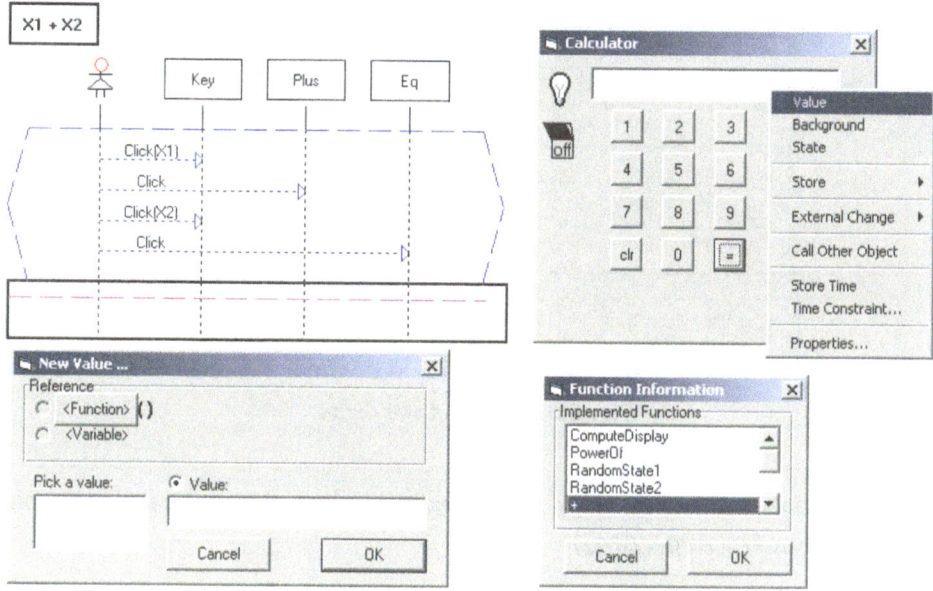

Fig. 8.3. Choosing an implemented function

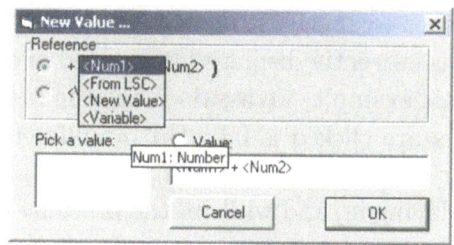

Fig. 8.4. Options for instantiating a function parameter

notion of affecting a variable, we introduce the notion of using a variable. A message is **using** a variable X if X must be bound before the message can be sent. In our example, the last message, showing $X1 + X2$ on the display, *uses* the variables $X1$ and $X2$. The difference between affecting a variable and using it is that in the first case the variable can be bound to a concrete value as the message occurs, because of unification, whereas in the second case the value has to be known for the message to take place.

Note that the label of the last message shows $X1+X2$ and not $+(X1, X2)$. An implemented function that has exactly two parameters may be referred to as a binary operation. This is done by setting an attribute — *IsBinary* — to true. This attribute has no semantical meaning and is cosmetic. Binary

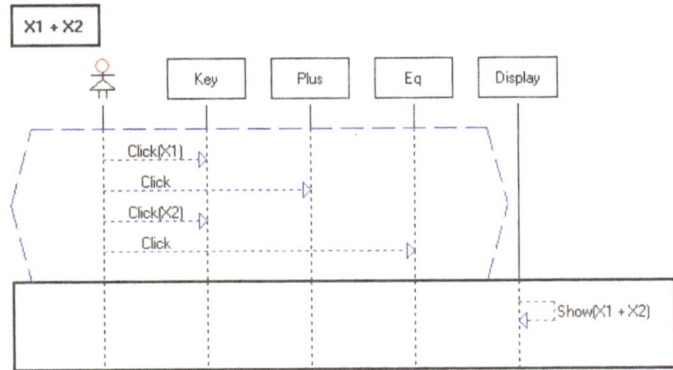

Fig. 8.5. Summing two digits

operations are written as $Arg_1\ Op\ Arg_2$ instead of the standard function representation $Op(Arg_1, Arg_2)$.

8.2 Assignments

Suppose the user wishes to specify now that when the '×' button is clicked twice, the value that is currently displayed is squared and the result is shown. For the purpose of this example, we assume that the behavior for displaying numbers as digit keys are clicked is handled by different LSCs (i.e., we are guaranteed that after clicking '1', '2' and '3', the display will show "123").

The user begins playing in, and while in the prechart he/she clicks the '×' button twice. Now, the user has to somehow refer to the currently displayed value. Note that the events that cause the display to change as digits are clicked are not in this LSC and therefore there is no predefined variable that can be referred to.

For this purpose, we introduce an **assignment** construct into the LSC language. Using an assignment, the user may save values of the properties of objects, or of functions applied to variables holding such values. The assigned-to variable stores the value for later use in the LSC. The expression on the right-hand side of the assignment contains a constant value, a reference to a property of some object (this is the typical usage) or a function applied to some predefined variables.

In our case, we would like to store the current *value* property of the display. This is done by right-clicking the GUI's display, and choosing **Store** and then **Value** from the popup menu. Since after storing a value we might like to refer to it later, and for this a meaningful name is helpful, the Play-Engine allows the user to name the assigned variable; here we use *Num* (see Fig.

8.6). Figure 8.7 shows the appropriate assignment statement generated in the LSC's prechart.

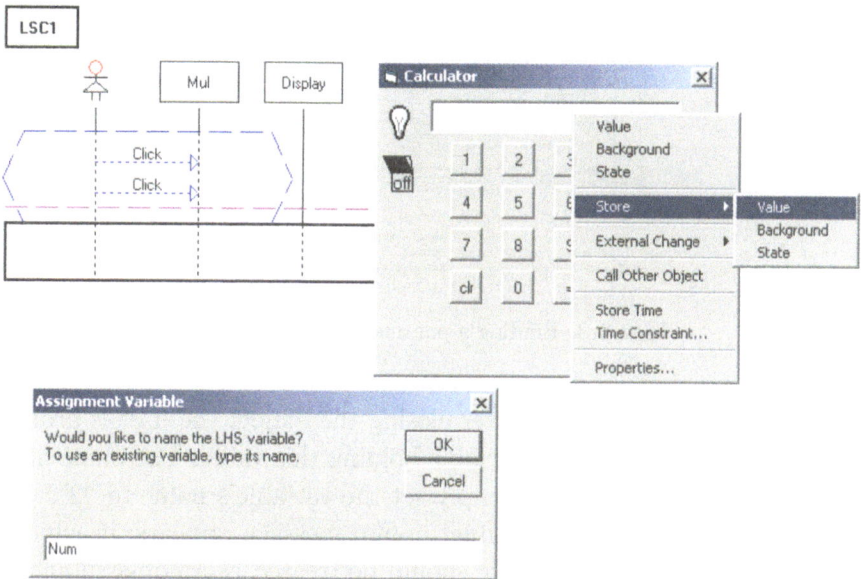

Fig. 8.6. Storing the value of an object's property

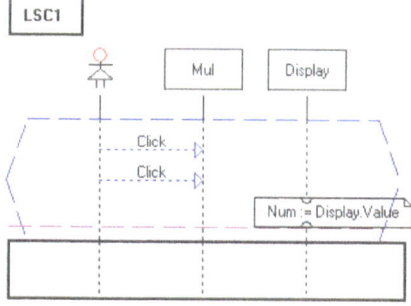

Fig. 8.7. The assignment construct

In order to specify the result of the computation, the user moves to the main chart and, as described earlier, selects the display's value property to show the *PowerOf* function. This function has two parameters, *Base* and *Exp*, and it returns $Base^{Exp}$ as a result. The user instantiates the first parameter by choosing **From LSC** and clicking on the assignment. As a result, the *Base* parameter is replaced by *Num*. For the second parameter, we wish to specify the constant '2'. To do this, the user places the mouse over **Exp** and chooses **New Value** (see Fig. 8.8). As a result, a dialog is opened where a new value

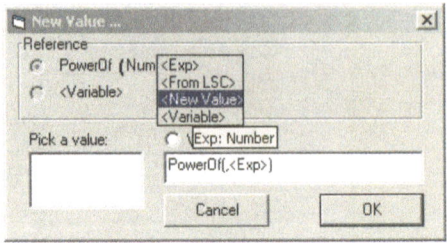

Fig. 8.8. Binding a parameter to a constant

can be entered, in this case 2. After closing the dialog, the user is prompted for a meaningful name for the variable holding this value. The name may be any string, and in this case we simply set the variable's name to "2".

After naming the variable, a final popup message appears, in which the user is asked whether this variable should be treated as a non-symbolic constant? By saying 'yes' (as should be done in this example), the user specifies that this variable should remain bound to its original value, even if the message it appears in is symbolic. The final LSC for raising a number to the power of 2 is shown in Fig. 8.9.

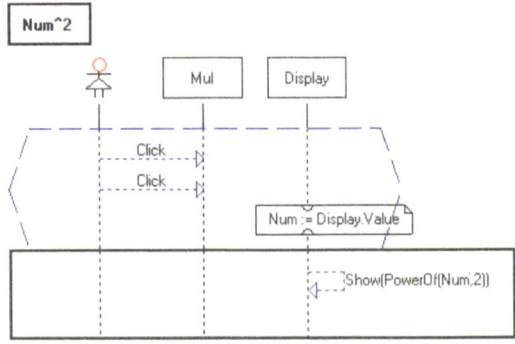

Fig. 8.9. An LSC for Num^2

It is important to note that the assignment's variable is local to the containing chart and can be used in the specification of that chart only, as opposed to the system's state variables (i.e., object properties), which may be used to communicate values between charts.

Assignments can also be used to store constant values or values returned by implemented functions. To insert such assignments, the user clicks the appropriate button on the toolbar, chooses a name for the assigned-to variable and fills the assignment details in the dialog that is opened (see Fig. 8.10). Using this dialog, the user may specify a function, as described earlier, or

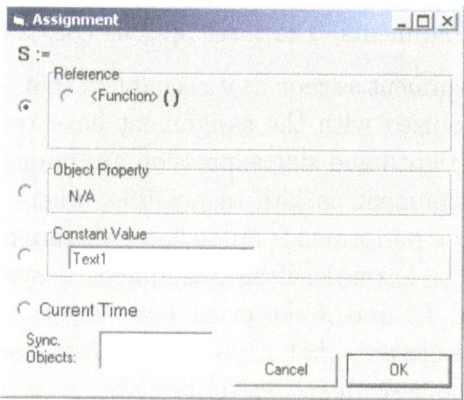

Fig. 8.10. Storing fixed values or function results

just enter a fixed value. Since the creation procedure of assignments of this kind is not started by clicking a GUI object, the assignment is not associated automatically with an object instance. In order to associate the assignment with an object, the user right-clicks the object that should be synchronized with this assignment and chooses **Synchronized** from the popup menu.

Each assignment may have several participating objects that synchronize at the location of the assignment. Synchronizing at an assignment means that none of the synchronized instances may progress beyond the assignment until all of them reach it and it is actually performed.

8.3 Playing Out

When playing out behavior, assignments are performed according to the partial order induced by the LSC. In assignments, like in messages, we distinguish between affecting a variable and using a variable. An assignment affects its assigned-to variable and uses all the variables in its right-hand side expression. The location of an assignment in the partial order is determined by the vertical order of the instance locations attached to it and by the variables used by it (e.g., $S := X + 1$ comes after the first message that affects X or after the first assignment that assigns a value to X, so that when it is evaluated X is already bound). Since assignments are now another legal form of binding a variable to a value, an assignment that affects a variable X is also considered when looking for the first location that affects this variable.

Assignments are hidden events, since they do not correspond directly to events carried out by the system. Therefore, when building a tool that monitors system runs and/or executes the LSC specification, one has to decide when to perform assignments. The three options considered were:

1. Perform the assignment as soon as it is enabled; that is, when all instances that are synchronized with the assignment have reached it and all the variables in the right-hand side expression are bound.
2. Perform the assignment as late as possible, where the latest point an assignment can be performed is immediately before one of its subsequent events occurs. For example, if an assignment is synchronized with two instances I_1 and I_2, and if the event following the assignment in I_1 is receiving a message and that message is indeed received, then only at that time will the assignment be performed.
3. Choose at random a point in the interval starting when the assignment is enabled and ending when one of its subsequent events occurs, and perform the assignment at that time.

We decided on the first of these. In many examples of systems we have modeled, performing the assignment as soon as possible seemed to be the most intuitive interpretation of the LSC. This is because when specifying reactivity, most of the time a value is stored immediately after some event occurs (e.g., clicking a button), and therefore performing the assignment as soon as possible guarantees that the value is not changed before it is stored. Another argument that supports this choice is that the first option is the most deterministic one, and is therefore easier to understand and follow.

We should comment, however, that by choosing the first option (or for that matter, any other option) as the one driving the operational semantics for the Play-Engine, we rule out possible behaviors that would have been allowed by making other semantic choices, both when executing a model and when monitoring an implementation with respect to a given model. Hence there is often more than one way to go. This is true for other such dilemmas later in the book too. Nevertheless, such decisions are necessary when building tools for model execution.

Now consider the LSC in Fig. 8.11. We would like this chart to mean the following:

> When the light changes its state, the display should show the previous state of the light.

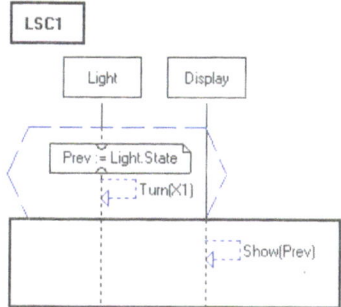

Fig. 8.11. Assignments as minimal events

In the prechart of this LSC, there is one minimal event — the assignment. Again, the question of when to perform the assignment and activate the LSC arises. Since an assignment is a hidden event, we do not consider it an event that can activate a prechart. This is because there is no strong intuition as to when to take such a step, and a policy that tries to cover all possible assignment values is impractical. We have therefore decided to perform the assignment 'just before' the next visible event occurs. Recall that a chart is activated when one of the minimal events in it occurs.

We now refine the definition of a minimal event to include all events that have no *visible* events before them according to the partial order. When such an event is detected, the hidden events that precede it are performed and only then is the visible event itself considered. To sum up, LSCs are activated only by visible events. A visible event may activate a prechart if it is minimal with respect to other visible events, but as soon as such an event is detected all the hidden events that can be performed are carried out before the visible event is.

Performing an assignment during play-out has the effect of binding the assigned-to variable with the value of the right-hand side expression at the point of evaluation. If the assignment stores a value of an object's property, the application is queried for that value. If the assignment stores the value returned by an implemented function, the function information (containing its name and the values of the actual parameters) is packed and sent to the GUI application, which in turn computes the function and returns the value to the Play-Engine. The same mechanism for function evaluation applies also when functions are used directly in messages.

Messages that use implemented functions should normally be symbolic. However, if the message is exact, the value returned by the function during play-in is kept with the message and is used in play-out, without reevaluating the function. The label of such an exact message will contain the value itself and not the string describing the function and its parameters. Assignments are by definition symbolic, and therefore a function on the right-hand side of an assignment will always be reevaluated during play-out.

During play-out, symbolic messages are matched using the unification algorithms described in Chap. 7. Messages containing implemented functions are unified according to the value returned by the function and not according to the structure of the function. Therefore, as an example, the following messages are all unifiable: $M(4), M(X1 + X2), M(Y), M(PowerOf(Y, X1))$, where $X1 = 1, X2 = 3$ and $Y = 4$.

8.4 And a Bit More Formally ...

We now show the extensions and modifications to the semantics needed to support implemented functions and assignments.

System Model and Events

An implemented function is defined as:

$$Func = Name : D_1 \times D_2 \times \ldots \times D_n \rightarrow D_F$$

where Name is the function name, $D_i \in \mathcal{D}$ is the type of its ith formal parameter and $D_F \in \mathcal{D}$ is the type of its returned value.

An object system $\mathcal{S}ys$ is modified to also contain a set of implemented functions $\mathcal{F}$:

$$\mathcal{S}ys = \langle \mathcal{D}, \mathcal{C}, \mathcal{O}, \mathcal{F} \rangle$$

We redefine a system message M_s to also contain function information if a function is used:

$$M_s = \langle Src, Dst, P, V, f, \lambda_f^F, Symbolic \rangle$$

where $f \in \mathcal{F} \cup \{\bot\}$ is a function describing a new value for P, and λ_f^F is a *function information structure*, defined for f as follows:

$$\lambda_f^F = \begin{cases} (V_1 \in f.D_1, \ldots, V_n \in f.D_n) & \text{if } f \in \mathcal{F} \\ \bot & \text{if } f = \bot \end{cases}$$

If the message uses a function $f \in \mathcal{F}$, the structure λ_f^F will contain variables as actual parameters replacing the function's formal parameters. If M_s does not use an implemented function, $\lambda_f^F = \bot$.

At this point, a message can represent a change in a property's value using a variable or a function to describe the new value. This variable or function is called the message content.

Definition 8.4.1 (message content). *The* message content Λ *of a message* M_s *is defined as:*

$$M_s.\Lambda = \begin{cases} M_s.\lambda_f^F & \text{if } \lambda_f^F \neq \bot \\ M_s.V & \text{otherwise} \end{cases}$$

LSC Specification

An LSC L is extended to contain assignments:

$$L = \langle I_L, V_L, M_L, [Pch_L], A_L, evnt, temp \rangle$$

An assignment is defined as

$$A = \langle V, I_A, C, P, f, \lambda_f^F \rangle$$

where V is the assigned-to variable, $I_A \subseteq I_L$ is the set of instances that are synchronized with the assignment, $C \in (\bigcup_{D \in \mathcal{D}} D) \cup \{\bot\}$ is a constant of some type in case the assignment stores a constant, and C is $\bot$ if not, $P \in (\bigcup_{I \in I_A} I.AppObj.\mathcal{P}) \cup \{\bot\}$ is the property stored in case the assignment stores a property value, and P is $\bot$ if not, $f \in \mathcal{F} \cup \{\bot\}$ is a function in case the assignment stores some function, and f is $\bot$ if not, and λ_f^F is a function information structure in case $f \neq \bot$. We require that one and only one of the following expressions holds for each assignment:

$$(C \neq \bot), \ (P \neq \bot) \text{ and } (f \neq \bot)$$

We say that the *assignment type* (or simply type) of A is *constant* if $C \neq \bot$, *property* if $P \neq \bot$, and *function* if $f \neq \bot$.

We extend E_L, the set of LSC events in L, to contain also hidden events of performing assignments:

$$\begin{aligned} E_L = &(\{m \in M_L \mid m.M_s \in \Sigma_{FromUser} \cup \Sigma_{ToUser} \cup \Sigma_{FromEnv} \cup \Sigma_{ToEnv}\} \\ &\times \{Send, Recv\}) \\ &\cup (\{m \in M_L \mid m.M_s \in \Sigma_{Self}\} \times \{Send\}) \\ &\cup (Pch_L \times \{Start, End\}) \cup \{Completed\} \cup \{perform(A) \mid A \in A_L\} \end{aligned}$$

We extend the notion of affecting a variable, and distinguish between *affecting* a variable and *using* a variable.

Definition 8.4.2 (affecting a variable). *An LSC message* $M \in M_L$ *affects a variable* X, *if* $M.M_s.V = X$. *An assignment* $A \in A_L$ *affects a variable* X *if* $A.V = X$.

Definition 8.4.3 (using a variable). *An LSC message $M \in M_L$ uses a variable X if $X \in M.M_s.\lambda_f^F$, and an assignment $A \in A_L$ uses a variable X if $X \in A.\lambda_f^F$.*

The notions of affecting and using a variable are extended to LSC events and locations in the natural way. By extending the above definitions to locations, the definition of the *first* location that affects a variable X now refers to assignments without any change.

The partial order $<_L$ is extended with the following two rules:

Variables - The first location that affects a variable precedes all other locations that affect or use the variable:

$$\forall l, l' \in \ell(L) : first(l, X) \wedge (\textit{affects}(l', X) \vee \textit{uses}(l', X)) \Rightarrow l <_L l'$$

Synchronize at assignments - All the instances that participate in an assignment are synchronized there:

$$\forall A \in A_L, \ \forall l_x^i, l_y^j \in loc(A) : \ l_x^i =_L l_y^j$$

Operational Semantics

The first change we apply to our operational semantics is the redefinition of minimal events, to consider only visible events, but to also allow hidden events to precede them.

Definition 8.4.4 (minimal event in a chart). *An event e is minimal in a chart L if there is no visible event e' in L such that $e' <_L e$.*

We now extend the notion of unification to apply also to functions.

Definition 8.4.5 (function unification). *Two function information structures λ_f^F and λ_g^F are unifiable (both positively and negatively) if $f(\lambda_f^F) = g(\lambda_g^F)$ (where $f(\lambda_f^F)$ is the value of f applied to the actual parameters in λ_f^F).*

Definition 8.4.6 (variable-function unification). *A variable X and a function information structure λ_f^F are positively-unifiable if $X.\omega = f(\lambda_f^F)$ or free(X). They are negatively-unifiable if $X.\omega = f(\lambda_f^F)$.*

Definition 8.4.7 (message unification). *Two system messages $M_s = \langle Src, Dst, P, V, f, \lambda_f^F, Symbolic \rangle$ and $M'_s = \langle Src', Dst', P', V', f', \lambda_{f'}^F, Symbolic' \rangle$ are Q-Unifiable (where Q is 'positively' or 'negatively') if $Src = Src', Dst = Dst', P = P'$ and their contents $M_s.\Lambda$ and $M'_s.\Lambda$ are Q-Unifiable.*

Since message variables may bind to values returned by functions during execution, we add another unification procedure to handle these cases:

Unify(X, λ_f^F, Context)

1. If $X.\omega = f(\lambda_f^F)$ then return.
2. $X.\omega \leftarrow f(\lambda_f^F)$.
3. $Bind(X, X.\omega, Context)$.

For two unifiable messages M and M', we use $Unify(M, M', Context)$ as an abbreviation of $Unify(M.\Lambda, M'.\Lambda, Context)$, and $Unify(e, e', Context)$ remains an abbreviation of $Unify(e.M, e'.M', Context)$.

Having these definitions at hand, the transition relation Δ supports implemented functions with no modifications required. However, for Δ to support assignments, two modification are needed: (1) When a minimal visible event is detected, all the assignments that come before it are carried out before the event may be considered. (2) After an assignment is performed, its assigned-to variable is bound to an appropriate value according to the assignment type.

- If $e = \langle M, t \rangle (where\ t \in \{Send, Recv\})$ then:
1. set $Context \leftarrow \emptyset$.
2. If $\exists C^L \in \mathcal{RL}$ and $\exists e' \in C^L.LSC$ such that e and e' are negatively $level_1$-unifiable and e' violates C^L, then set $\mathcal{RL} \leftarrow \mathcal{RL} \setminus \{C^L\}$. If $temp(C^L.Cut) = hot$, set $Violating \leftarrow True$.
3. For every universal LSC $L \in \mathcal{S}_\mathcal{U}$ which has an event e', positively $level_1$-unifiable with e, as a minimal event in its prechart, create a copy of L, C^L, and set $\mathcal{RL} \leftarrow \mathcal{RL} \cup \{C^L\}$. Set $C^L.Mode = PreActive$ and set its cut by $C^L.Cut \leftarrow AdvanceCut(InitialCut(L), \langle Pch_L, Start \rangle)$. Unify the variables of e and e', by $Unify(e, e', Context)$.
   For each hidden event $e'' <_L e'$, apply $\Delta(e'')$.
4. For every copy $C^L \in \mathcal{RL}$ which has an enabled event e', positively $level_1$-unifiable with e, set its cut by $C^L.Cut \leftarrow AdvanceCut(C^L.Cut, e')$. Then, if $e' = \langle M, Send \rangle$, M is synchronous and $e'' = \langle M, Recv \rangle$, set the cut by $C^L.Cut \leftarrow AdvanceCut(C^L.Cut, e'')$. Unify the variables of e and e', by $Unify(e, e', Context)$.
- If $e = Completed(C^L)$ for some $C^L \in \mathcal{RL}$, then set $\mathcal{RL} \leftarrow \mathcal{RL} \setminus \{C^L\}$.
- If $e = \langle Pch_L, End \rangle$ for some $C^L \in \mathcal{RL}$, then set
$C^L.Cut \leftarrow BeginMainCut(C^L.LSC)$ and $C^L.Mode \leftarrow Active$.
- If $e = perform(A)$ for some $A \in A_L$ s.t. $C^L \in \mathcal{RL}$, then set $C^L.Cut \leftarrow AdvanceCut(C^L.Cut, e)$ and set

$$A.V \leftarrow \begin{cases} A.C & \text{if } A.Type = constant \\ Value(A.P) & \text{if } A.Type = property \\ A.f(A.\lambda_f^F) & \text{if } A.Type = function \end{cases}$$

After having thus modified Δ, the procedures for *step* should be slightly modified so that if the new value for a property is given as a function, that function is computed and the new value is reflected in the system. The procedure for *super-step* remains unchanged.

---

step(e)

1. Apply $\Delta(e)$.
2. Change the property value according to the value in the message:
   a)

   $$O \leftarrow \begin{cases} e.M.Src \text{ if } M \in \Sigma_{ToUser} \cup \Sigma_{ToEnv} \\ e.M.Dst \text{ otherwise} \end{cases}$$

   b) $P \leftarrow e.M.P$
   c)

   $$Value(O.P) \leftarrow \begin{cases} e.M.f(e.M.\lambda_f^F) \text{ if } e.M.f \neq \bot \\ e.M.V.\omega \qquad \text{otherwise} \end{cases}$$

---

9. Conditions

In this chapter we discuss guarding conditions in LSCs, and the way their being true or false impacts execution.

9.1 Cold Conditions

Returning to the bakery panel application, suppose our user wishes to specify the following requirement:

> *When the temperature indicated by thermometer ♯1 changes, it should be shown on the console. If it increases beyond 70 degrees, the console background color should turn red.*

The LSC describing this requirement is shown in Fig. 9.1.

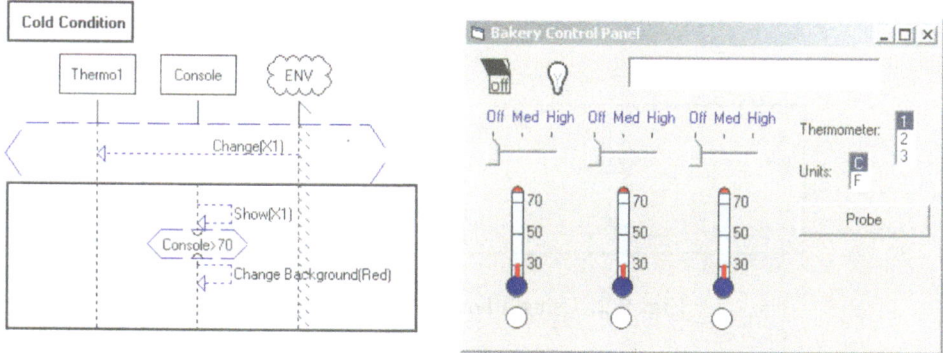

Fig. 9.1. Using a cold condition

The temperature is changed by the environment in the prechart, and as a result the console shows the new temperature in the chart body. The hexagon that follows is a **condition**. This one is a **cold** condition, denoted by a blue dashed line, and it requires the number displayed on the console to be greater than 70. If a cold condition is *true*, the chart progresses to the location that immediately follows the condition, whereas if it is *false*, the surrounding chart (or subchart; see later) is exited. In this example, if the temperature is indeed greater than 70 degrees, execution of the chart will progress and the console will change to red. If the temperature is less than or equal to 70 degrees, the chart will be exited and the console will take no action.

A condition hexagon can be stretched along several instances in the LSC in order to reach those that it refers to. To distinguish these from the instances that do not participate in the condition's definition or are not to be synchronized with it, we draw small semicircular connectors at the intersection points of a participating instance line with the condition.

9.2 Hot Conditions

Consider now a second requirement, stating the following:

> *When the main switch is turned on, the first 3-state switch is automatically set to Med, thus activating the first oven. As a result, the temperature must rise above 50 degrees, and only then should the first warning light change to green.*

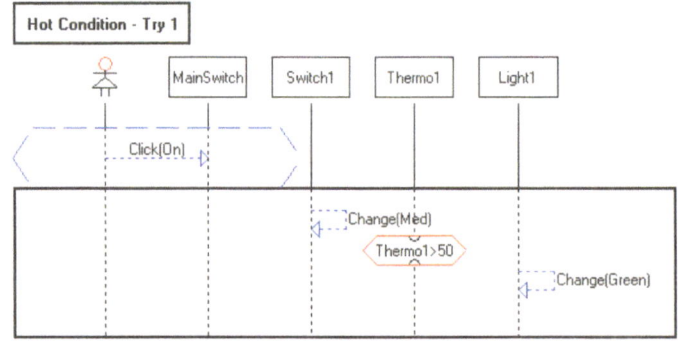

Fig. 9.2. Using a hot condition: first try

As a first try, consider the LSC in Fig. 9.2. In the prechart, the user clicks the main switch to on, and as a response, in the main chart, the first switch is set to *Med*. A condition then follows, constraining the temperature of the first thermometer to be greater than 50 degrees. This condition is **hot**, denoted by a red solid line. A hot condition *must* be true, otherwise the requirements are violated. Following this condition, the first warning light changes its color to green.

Note, however, that there is no partial order between the events and the condition in the chart body. Therefore, a scenario in which the main switch is clicked to on and as a result the light turns green, the switch is set to *Med* and only then does the temperature rise above 50 degrees, is a permissable one. This, of course, is not what we had in mind. We would like to impose a strict order, in which the light turns green only after the switch is set to *Med* and the temperature rises. We do this by synchronizing. Like assignments, conditions can also synchronize several instances. Synchronizing at a condition means that none of the synchronized instances may progress beyond the condition until all of them reach it and it is actually evaluated. In this case we synchronize the 3-state switch and the light with the condition (see Fig. 9.3). Now, there is a strict order that forces the condition to be evaluated

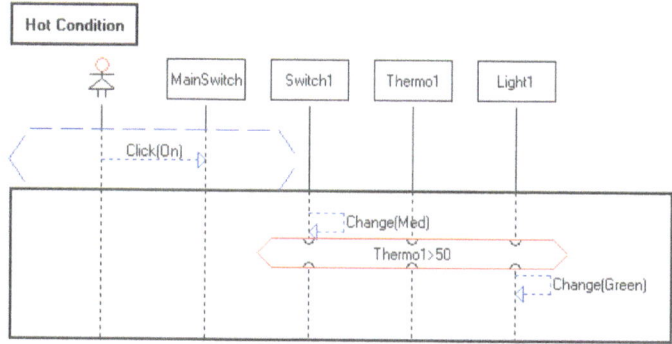

Fig. 9.3. Using a hot condition with synchronization

only after the switch is set to *Med*, and forces the light to turn green only after the condition evaluates to true.

9.3 Playing In

In order to play in a condition, the user clicks on the appropriate `Condition` button on the toolbar. In response, a condition dialog opens (see Fig. 9.4). In our current implementation, we support **conjunctive-query** conditions, namely ones that are conjunctions of basic expressions. Accordingly, each expression that is played in is attached as a new conjunct to the condition being constructed.

There are several kinds of basic expressions and different ways of playing them in, but the play-in methods are similar to the way properties are played in outside conditions. For example, to specify that the switch should be on,

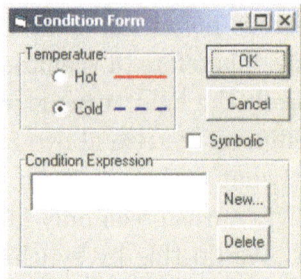

Fig. 9.4. A condition dialog

the user simply clicks it to on (if it is already on, the user can turn it off and on again). When operating objects that way, the resulting expression is always generated as an equality. To specify other kinds of relations, or to constrain objects that cannot be operated by the user (e.g., light, thermometer, etc.) the user right-clicks the object and selects the property to be constrained. In response, a basic expression dialog opens, in which the user may specify the value and the Boolean operator. Figure 9.5 shows the condition dialog after the switch was clicked to on, and the basic expression dialog, in which the color of the first warning light is constrained to be anything but green.

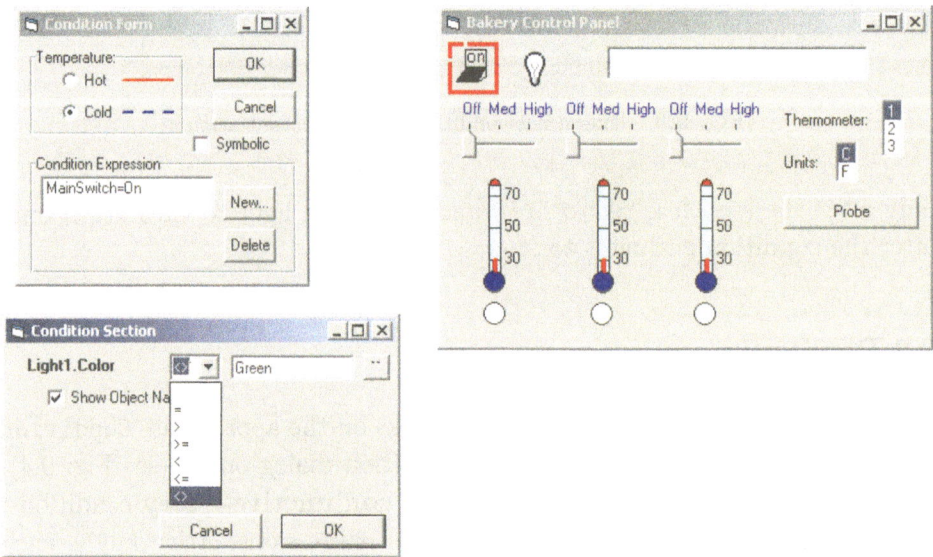

Fig. 9.5. Specifying a basic expression

As described earlier, an object can participate in a condition without having any of its property values actually constrained. This is usually done when we want the object's progress to be synchronized with the condition's evaluation, but to have no effect on its value. Synchronizing an object with a condition (i.e., making the object a non-influential part of the condition) is done by right-clicking the object and choosing **Synchronized** from the popup menu (see Fig. 9.6). Figure 9.7 shows the resulting condition in the LSC.

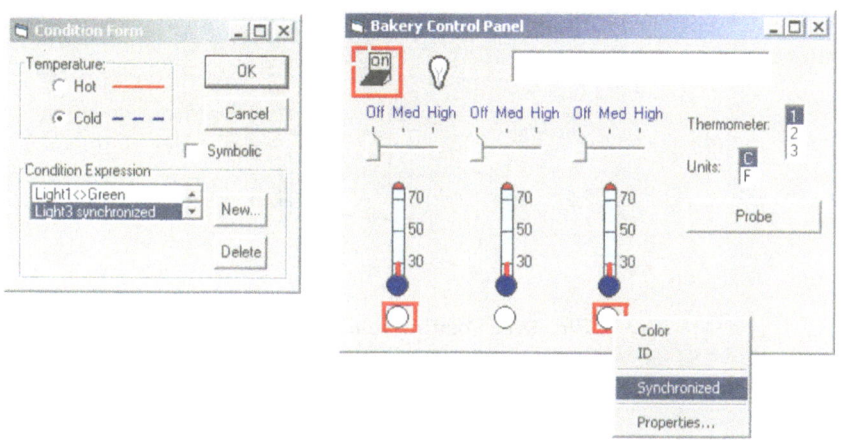

Fig. 9.6. Synchronizing an object with a condition

Since we attach importance to the intuitive manner of the play-in process, we have tried to have the user interact directly with the GUI application as much as possible. One example of this is in the way conditions are shown. When the user points to a condition in an LSC, several things show up; see Fig. 9.7. Within the LSC itself the condition is highlighted, as are all the participating instances, and the current true/false value of the condition is shown. At the same time, the GUI application (the bakery panel in our case) highlights the objects that participate in the condition, and each of them displays a tool tip that contains a description of the object's part in the condition. Since the rectangular tool tips may overlap, we have used a layout algorithm to arrange them nicely on the screen. This is done by defining an attractive force between each object and its tip and a repulsive force between every two tips, and then letting the physics of equilibrium do the rest.

Conditions may also contain basic expressions that do not refer directly to object properties. To specify such an expression, the user clicks on the **New** button in the condition dialog and as a result a condition expression dialog opens (see Fig. 9.8). Using this dialog, the user may constrain the value

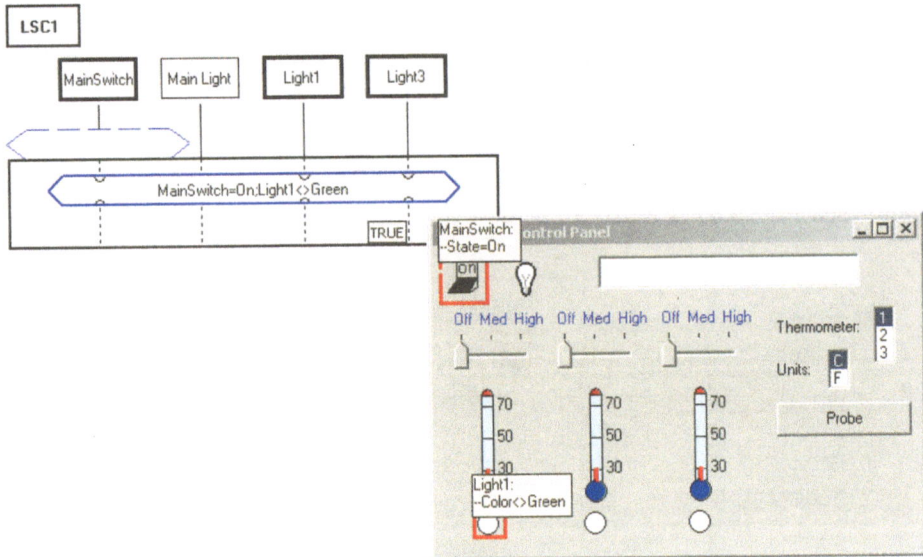

Fig. 9.7. Pointing to a condition

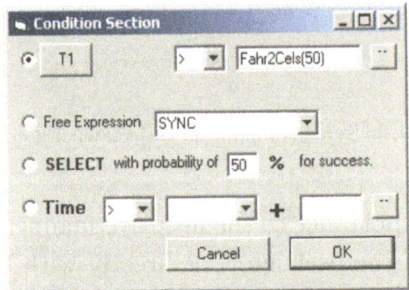

Fig. 9.8. Possible expressions in a condition

of some variable in the LSC. A variable (like an object property) can be constrained with respect to a constant value, another variable or a function applied to some variables. In this example, $T1$ is required to be greater than the value of 50 degrees Celsius converted to Fahrenheit.

In addition, there are some reserved words that can be used in conditions. A condition consisting only of the reserved word TRUE, synchronized with several instances, can be used to create a synchronization point for these instances with no other effect, because it is guaranteed to evaluate to true. Since this method for synchronizing objects is quite useful, we allow the use of the word SYNC, which is semantically equivalent to TRUE but better reflects the purpose of the condition.

A condition consisting of the reserved word **FALSE** is guaranteed to fail, and as such is useful in specifying **anti-scenarios**, i.e., scenarios that are not allowed to happen. This is achieved by placing the forbidden scenario in the prechart and the hot condition **FALSE** as the sole element in the chart body. If the forbidden scenario is successfully completed, the chart is activated and the hot condition is encountered. Since this hot condition can never be met, it causes a violation. The overall effect is to forbid the scenario in the prechart.

In addition to reserved words, one can write any string expression as a conjunct within a condition. Since such expressions have no semantical meaning, when such a condition is encountered during play-out, the user is asked whether the condition holds or not, and the run progresses accordingly. (The **Time** option shown in the dialog of Fig. 9.8 is discussed in Chap. 16.)

A condition may contain a *SELECT* basic expression, which is associated with a probability. During play-out it evaluates to true with that probability and to false with the complement probability. Although the main use of the *select* statement is within if-then-else constructs, as discussed in Chap. 10, it can be useful also in stand-alone guards. The LSC in Fig. 9.9 shows such an example. In this LSC, after the switch is clicked to on, the light

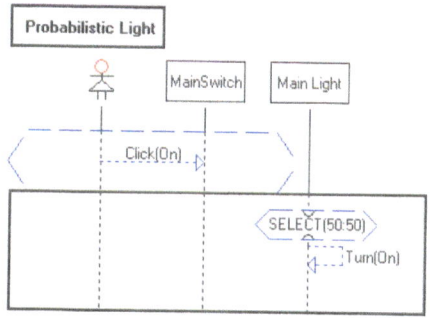

Fig. 9.9. Specifying nondeterministic behavior

turns on with a probability of 50%. Combining a *select* expression with a standard expression as a conjunctive condition results in a *guarded select*, in which progress is allowed with a given probability only if the guard (i.e., the standard expression) holds.

Expressions that do not refer to object properties are not automatically associated with object instances, and therefore a condition consisting solely of such expressions must be explicitly synchronized with some object.

9.4 Playing Out

When playing out behavior, conditions are very much like assignments. They are performed according to the partial order induced by the LSC, and are also considered hidden events.

In contrast with assignments and messages, conditions cannot affect variables but can only use them. A condition uses all the variables that appear in its basic expressions. The location of a condition in the partial order is determined therefore by the vertical order of the instance locations attached to it and by the variables it uses. For example, $X > f(Y)$ can be evaluated only after the messages that affect X and Y are sent or after the assignments that assign values to them are performed, so that when the expression is evaluated, X and Y are already bound.

Conditions are hidden, since they do not correspond directly to events carried out by the system. Therefore, the same decisions we had to make for the execution of assignments must be made for conditions. With conditions, the number of options is even greater since the temperature of the condition and its value may affect the decision about whether to advance it or not.

The case of hot conditions is easy. Since a hot condition must be true, when it is reached it is constantly evaluated and is advanced if and when it becomes true. The execution will remain stuck at that point if the specification is incorrect and the condition indeed never becomes true. Recalling that anti-scenarios are expressed using a hot false condition in the main chart, there is no point in the engine waiting for a hot condition consisting of the word FALSE to become true; the chart is therefore viewed as causing an immediate violation, and in the Play-Engine implementation it is crossed out and a violation message pops up (see Fig. 9.10).

Obviously, we could have used theorem-proving techniques to find other, less trivial, everywhere-false conditions and treat them as immediate violations too, but this is beyond the scope of our research. We have implemented only the most basic and practical feature needed to support the expression and detection of anti-scenarios.

Turning now to cold conditions, one can think of several possible policies for executing them, such as waiting for them to be true if they are currently false or waiting for them to be false if currently true, and deciding at random whether to evaluate them or evaluating them immediately. We have chosen the policy where cold conditions are evaluated immediately, mainly because this seems more intuitive for users to follow. In Chap. 16 we shall see that there are ways to explicitly require a condition to be evaluated only after a certain delay.

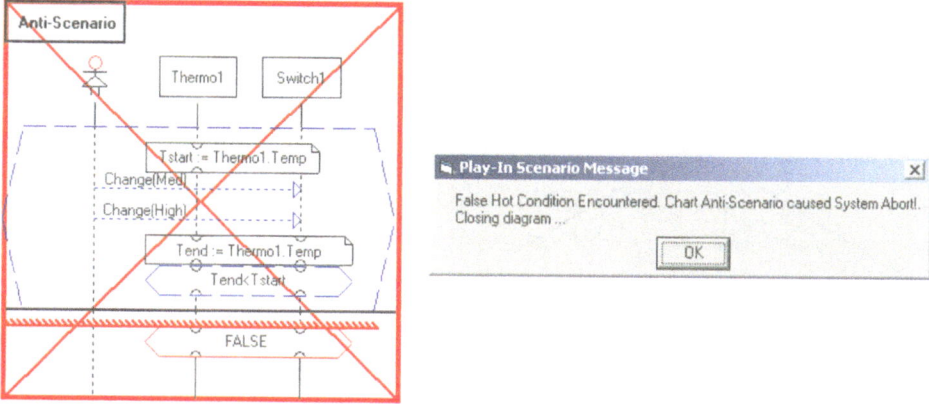

Fig. 9.10. Detecting anti-scenarios

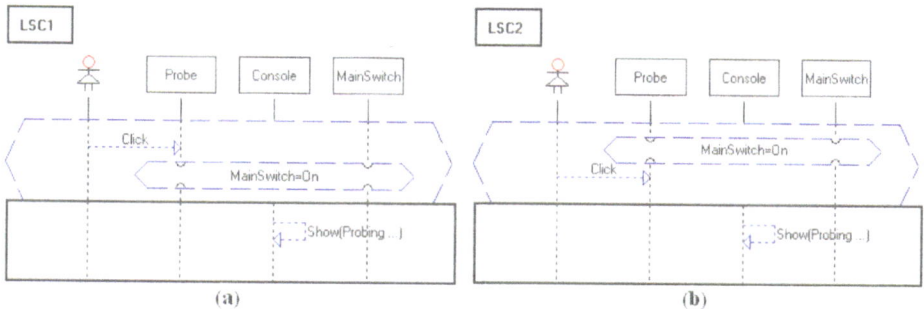

Fig. 9.11. Conditions in precharts

Let us consider now the two LSCs of Fig. 9.11. Both of these LSCs state that if the *Probe* button is clicked while the switch is on, the console should show "Probing ...".

There is however a difference between the charts. In '*LSC1*' the minimal event is the message (this is a synchronous message and therefore we refer to it as an event consisting of both the sending and the receiving), while in '*LSC2*' the minimal event is that of evaluating the condition. If we use '*LSC1*', the chart will be activated as soon as the button is clicked, and if the switch is *Off* the prechart is violated, which means that the chart stops existing since its triggering scenario is not fulfilled (see Fig. 9.12).

Conditions appearing as minimal events are treated again like assignments, because of the same considerations of intuition and practicality. When a visible event is detected, the conditions that precede it are evaluated and only then is the event considered. There is however a difference between assignments and conditions. A minimal assignment can always be performed,

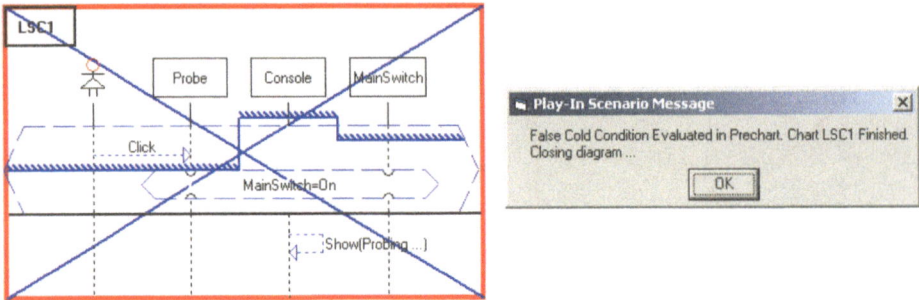

Fig. 9.12. Prechart violation

thus allowing the visible event to be considered, while in order for a condition to be advanced its value must be true. Returning to '*LSC2*' in Fig. 9.11, if the button is clicked while the switch is *Off*, the visible event of clicking the button in the chart cannot be reached because the instances cannot progress beyond the condition, and therefore the chart will not be activated at all. Actually, in order to evaluate the condition, assignments that may precede it should be performed. It is thus semantically inaccurate to say that the chart is not activated at all; it is better to say that the actions are taken 'behind the scenes' without the user being aware of them.

A prechart with the event coming before the condition, as in '*LSC1*', can be used to indicate that after some visible event occurs progress depends on some condition, while a prechart like '*LSC2*' is used to indicate that a pre-condition must hold in order for the event to even be considered.

9.5 And a Bit More Formally ...

Following the semantics skeleton, we show the extensions and modifications needed to support conditions.

System Model and Events

Conditions are entirely specification oriented, and therefore do not affect the system model.

LSC Specification

An LSC L is extended to contain conditions:

$$L = \langle I_L, V_L, M_L, [Pch_L], A_L, C_L, evnt, temp \rangle$$

A condition C in an LSC L is defined as

$$C = \langle I_C, \Psi \rangle$$

where $I_C \subseteq I_L$ is the set of instances that are synchronized with the condition and Ψ is the set of basic expressions. A basic expression $\psi \in \Psi$ is defined over the following alphabet:

$$\psi \in \{LHS \times Oper \times RHS\} \cup \{\texttt{TRUE, FALSE, SELECT(P)}, \bot\}$$

where

$$LHS \in \{O.P | O \in \mathcal{O}, P \in O.\mathcal{P}\} \cup V_L$$
$$Oper \in \{=, <, \leq, >, \geq, \neq\}$$
$$RHS \in (\bigcup_{D \in \mathcal{D}} D) \cup V_L \cup \{(f, \lambda_f^F) | f \in \mathcal{F}\}$$

The first kind of expression is used to constrain a property or a variable, by comparing it via some comparison operator with a constant value, another variable or a function. The second kind of expression consists of the reserved words (SYNC is really just an abbreviation for TRUE), the SELECT statement with probability P, and free expressions (all free expressions are reduced to $\bot$). We denote by $value(\psi)$ the result of evaluating ψ in the natural way. If ψ is of the form SELECT(P), a Boolean value is chosen at random with probability P for true, and if ψ is $\bot$ the user is prompted for a value. The value of a condition C is defined as:

$$value(C) = \bigwedge_{\psi \in \Psi} value(\psi)$$

Since conditions may also be cold or hot, the domain of the function $temp$ should be modified:

$$temp : \ell(L) \cup M_L \cup C_L \rightarrow \{hot, cold\}$$

We extend E_L, the set of *LSC events* in L, to contain also hidden events of evaluating conditions:

$$E_L = (\{m \in M_L \mid m.M_s \in \Sigma_{FromUser} \cup \Sigma_{ToUser} \cup \Sigma_{FromEnv} \cup \Sigma_{ToEnv}\}$$
$$\times \{Send, Recv\})$$
$$\cup (\{m \in M_L \mid m.M_s \in \Sigma_{Self}\} \times \{Send\})$$
$$\cup (Pch_L \times \{Start, End\}) \cup \{Completed\} \cup \{perform(A) \mid A \in A_L\}$$
$$\cup \{eval(C) \mid C \in C_L\}$$

The definition of *using variables* is modified to reflect the way conditions use them.

Definition 9.5.1 (using a variable). *An LSC message $M \in M_L$ uses a variable X if $X \in M.M_s.\lambda_f^F$, and an assignment $A \in A_L$ uses a variable X if $X \in A.\lambda_f^F$.*

A condition basic expression ψ uses a variable X if at least one of the following holds:

1. *$\psi.LHS \in V_L$ and $\psi.LHS = X$.*
2. *$\psi.RHS \in V_L$ and $\psi.RHS = X$.*
3. *$\psi.RHS = (f, \lambda_f^F)$ and $X \in \lambda_f^F$.*

A condition C uses a variable X if one of its basic expressions uses it.

The partial order $<_L$ is now extended with the following rule:

Synchronize at conditions - All the instances that participate in a condition are synchronized there:

$$\forall C \in C_L, \ \forall l_x^i, l_y^j \in loc(C) : \ l_x^i =_L l_y^j$$

Operational Semantics

Since conditions are pretty much like assignments in the sense that they are hidden events that are not considered as minimal events, most of the definitions remain unchanged.

There is however one change in the definition of enabled events, which makes sure that false hot conditions are not evaluated unless they explicitly contain the basic expression *FALSE*.

Definition 9.5.2 (enabled event). *An event e is enabled with respect to a cut C if $\uparrow(\downarrow C \cup loc(e))$ is a legal cut. That is, if the location in C of every instance participating in the event e is the one exactly prior to e, and there is no $e' <_L e$ that is not already in the down-closure of C.*

- *If $e = \langle m, Send \rangle$, m is synchronous and $e' = \langle m, Recv \rangle$, we require also that $\downarrow C \cup loc(e) \cup loc(e')$ is down-closed, thus making sure that a synchronous message will not be sent unless it can be received.*
- *If $e = eval(C), temp(C) = hot$ and $FALSE \notin C.\Psi$, we require also that $value(C) = true$.*

Next, Δ is extended with transitions for handling the evaluation of conditions:

- *If $e = \langle M, t \rangle$ (where $t \in \{Send, Recv\}$) then:*
  1. Set $Context \leftarrow \emptyset$.

2. If $\exists C^L \in \mathcal{RL}$ and $\exists e' \in C^L.LSC$ such that e and e' are negatively level$_1$-unifiable and e' violates C^L, then set $\mathcal{RL} \leftarrow \mathcal{RL} \setminus \{C^L\}$. If $temp(C^L.Cut) = hot$, set $Violating \leftarrow True$.

3. For every universal LSC $L \in \mathcal{S}_\mathcal{U}$ which has an event e', positively level$_1$-unifiable with e, as a minimal event in its prechart, create a copy of L, C^L, and set $\mathcal{RL} \leftarrow \mathcal{RL} \cup \{C^L\}$. Set $C^L.Mode = PreActive$ and set its cut by $C^L.Cut \leftarrow AdvanceCut(InitialCut(L), \langle Pch_L, Start \rangle)$. Unify the variables of e and e', by $Unify(e, e'.Context)$. For each hidden event $e'' <_L e'$, apply $\Delta(e'')$.

4. For every copy $C^L \in \mathcal{RL}$ which has an enabled event e', positively level$_1$-unifiable with e, set its cut by $C^L.Cut \leftarrow AdvanceCut(C^L.Cut, e')$. Then, if $e' = \langle M.Send \rangle$, M is synchronous and $e'' = \langle M.Recv \rangle$, set the cut by $C^L.Cut \leftarrow AdvanceCut(C^L.Cut, e'')$. Unify the variables of e and e', by $Unify(e, e'.Context)$.

- If $e = Completed(C^L)$ for some $C^L \in \mathcal{RL}$, then set $\mathcal{RL} \leftarrow \mathcal{RL} \setminus \{C^L\}$.
- If $e = \langle Pch_L, End \rangle$ for some $C^L \in \mathcal{RL}$, then set
  $C^L.Cut \leftarrow BeginMainCut(C^L.LSC)$ and $C^L.Mode \leftarrow Active$.
- If $e = perform(A)$ for some $A \in A_L$ s.t. $C^L \in \mathcal{RL}$, then set $C^L.Cut \leftarrow AdvanceCut(C^L.Cut, e)$ and set

$$A.V \leftarrow \begin{cases} A.C & \text{if } A.Type = constant \\ Value(A.P) & \text{if } A.Type = property \\ A.f(A.\lambda_f^F) & \text{if } A.Type = function \end{cases}$$

- If $e = eval(C)$ for some $C \in C^L$ s.t. $C^L \in \mathcal{RL}$, then
  1. If $value(C) = true$ then set $C^L.Cut \leftarrow AdvanceCut(C^L.Cut, e)$;
  2. If $value(C) = false$ then set $\mathcal{RL} \leftarrow \mathcal{RL} \setminus \{C^L\}$. If $temp(C) = hot$, set $Violating \leftarrow True$.

Since false hot conditions that do not explicitly contain the expression *FALSE* are not enabled, and all other conditions should be evaluated as soon as they are enabled, the procedure *super-step* remains unchanged, with the emphasized part taking care also of conditions:

---

super-step

1. Compute the set of enabled events:

$$Enabled \leftarrow \bigcup_{C^L \in \mathcal{RL}} \{e \in E_L | enabled(e)\}$$

$$Enabled \leftarrow Enabled \setminus External$$

2. If there is a *hidden* enabled event $e \in Enabled$, then
   a) Apply $\Delta(e)$.
   b) Go back to 1.
3. If there is a *visible* enabled event $e \in Enabled$, such that e does not violate any copy which is in *active* mode, then
   a) $step(e)$.
   b) Go back to 1.
4. Terminate super-step.

9.6 Bibliographic Notes

Conjunctive queries were first defined in [20]. An algorithm for synthesizing UML statecharts from UML sequence diagrams is presented in [119]. It makes use of constraints written in OCL [115] (the UML object constraints language), which are of the form $Var = Value$. These constraints are used to resolve conflicts arising from different scenarios and to join system states that identify over these variables; they can be viewed as a sort of combination of our assignments and conditions.

The layout algorithm we have used for the tool tips is a variant of the non-uniform vertex graph layout algorithm of [45], adapted to arrange a set of arbitrary rectangles in the plane.

10. Branching and Subcharts

In this chapter we discuss ways of using conditions to help control the execution flow of a chart, and how this works with the main LSC structuring mechanism — the subchart.

10.1 The If-Then-Else Construct

Consider the bakery panel with the following requirement:

> *When the main switch is clicked to on, the main light should turn on and the console's background should change to green. When the switch is clicked to off, the light should turn off and the console's background should change to white.*

In Chap. 7 we saw how variables and symbolic messages can be utilized to capture several scenarios in a single LSC. Figure 10.1 shows how a part of the above requirement is captured in a symbolic LSC. Using symbolic messages

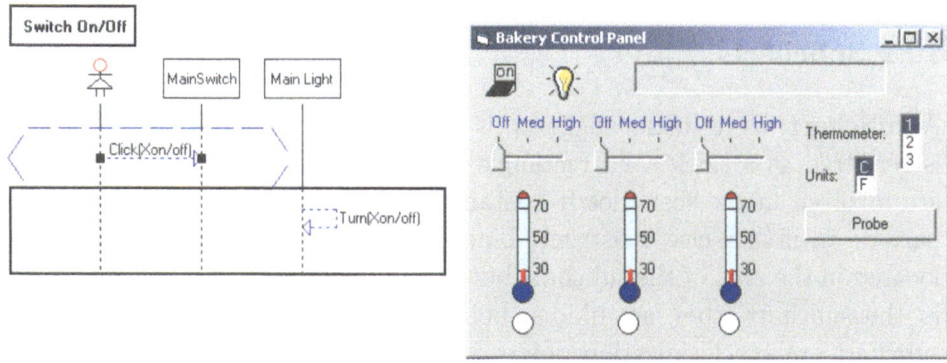

Fig. 10.1. Using symbolic messages to generalize scenarios

here is fine, since the light takes on the same state as the switch. There is, however, a problem with the background color of the console because there is no direct link between the state of the switch and the color of the console.[1] What we need here is a construct for conditional choice, which will make it possible to perform different scenario fragments, depending on some condition. Figure 10.2 shows how the problem is solved using an **if-then-else** construct.

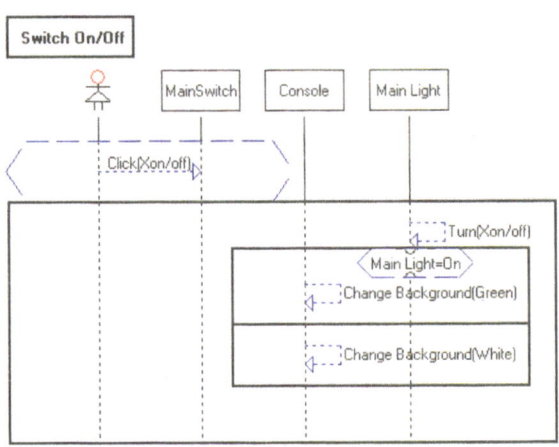

Fig. 10.2. Conditional choice using if-then-else

An if-then-else construct consists of two adjacent subcharts — the 'then' part and the 'else' part — and a controlling condition that is located at the top of the first subchart. The operational semantics is the standard conditional branching. The 'else' part is not mandatory and may be omitted.

10.2 Subcharts

A **subchart**, as its name suggests, is a well-formed fragment of a chart. It is rendered as a thick solid rectangle stretching over all the instances that are involved in the scenarios it contains, and is not restricted to appear as part of an if-then-else construct. Lines of instances that are geometrically located in the area of the subchart but do not participate in it are not shown in the subchart (they are hidden behind it). The beginning and end of a subchart are synchronization points for all participating instances. Thus, a subchart is entered only after all the instances that participate in it arrive at the locations associated with the subchart start.

---

[1] In this case such a link could be represented by an implemented function that takes an On/Off value as a parameter and returns a green/white color as a result, yet this is cumbersome and there are many cases where such links cannot be established.

This fact can be reason enough to use the subchart construct in the first place. For example, Fig. 10.3 shows an LSC containing two subcharts. By surrounding the pairs of events with subcharts, we guarantee that the two events in the first pair will both occur before those in the second pair. A

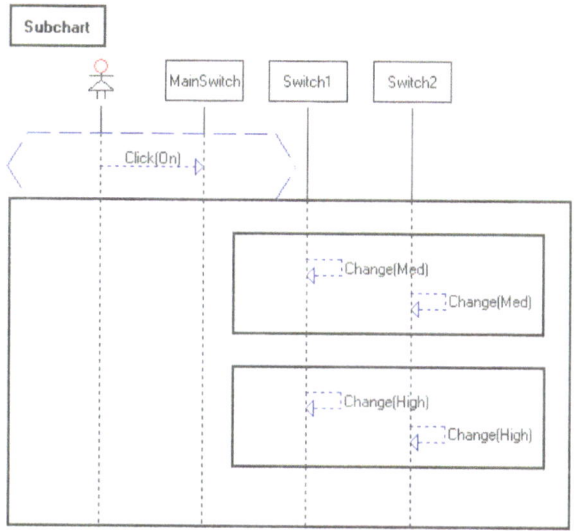

Fig. 10.3. Subcharts in LSCs

subchart is exited only after all the instances have completed their activities in it, with one exception, which we discuss next.

In the previous chapter, we said that when a cold condition evaluates to false the chart is exited. We now extend this definition. If a cold condition residing within a subchart evaluates to false, the closest surrounding subchart is exited. If there is no surrounding subchart, the chart itself is exited (as in the original definition).

Entering a subchart and exiting it are considered hidden events that are performed as soon as possible. Carrying out these events has no effect on the system model or on the values of LSC variables. Their only effect is to move the cut beyond the subchart start/end line for all participating instances.

10.3 Nondeterministic Choice

In Chap. 9 we introduced the *select* statement, used as a basic expression in conditions. In this section we show how a select statement within an if-then-else construct can be used to specify nondeterministic choice.

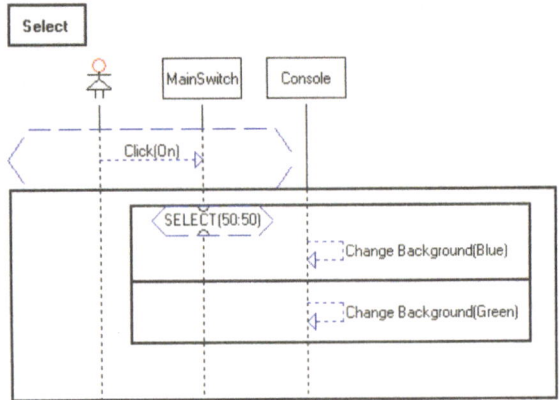

Fig. 10.4. Specifying a nondeterministic choice

The LSC in Fig. 10.4 specifies that when the user clicks the switch to on, the background color of the console turns green with probability 50% and blue with probability 50%. When executing this LSC, the Play-Engine randomly picks a value from {*true*, *false*} with the specified probabilities, executing the 'then' part or the 'else' part accordingly.

10.4 Playing In

To play in a subchart construct, the user clicks the **Subchart** button on the toolbar. In response, the Play-Engine opens a subchart wizard and places the cursor automatically in the subchart rectangle (see Fig. 10.5). The user

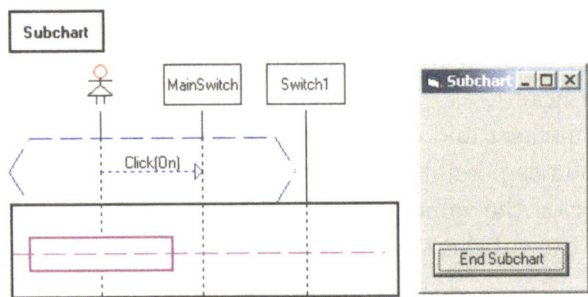

Fig. 10.5. A wizard for specifying subcharts

then simply continues playing in the scenario fragment that should be located in the subchart. Clicking the **End Subchart** button closes the subchart construct and the cursor is placed immediately after it.

In order to play in an if-then-else construct, the user clicks the `If-Then-Else` button on the toolbar. In response, the Play-Engine opens an if-then-else wizard and a condition dialog (see Fig. 10.6). The first thing the user does is

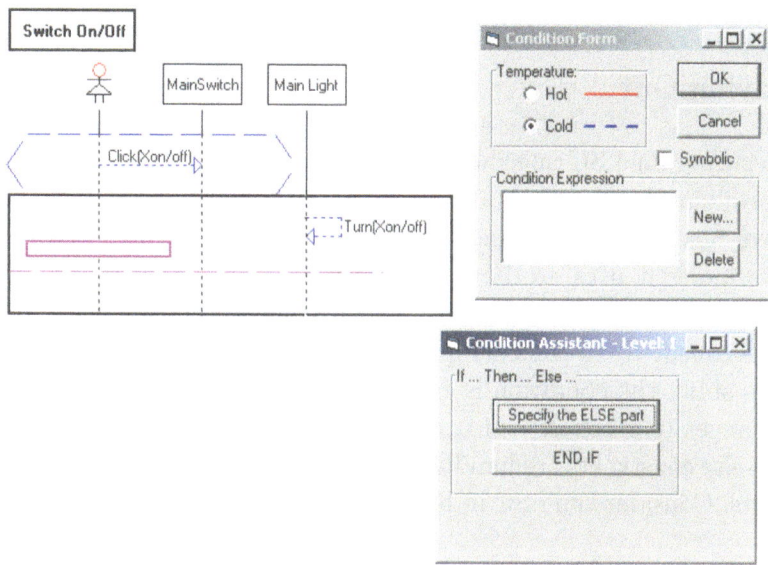

Fig. 10.6. A wizard for specifying if-then-else constructs

to specify the condition using the methods and techniques described in the previous chapter. The Play-Engine then places the cursor automatically in the 'then' part and the user simply continues playing in the subchart that should be satisfied when the condition holds (see Fig. 10.7(a)). To specify the

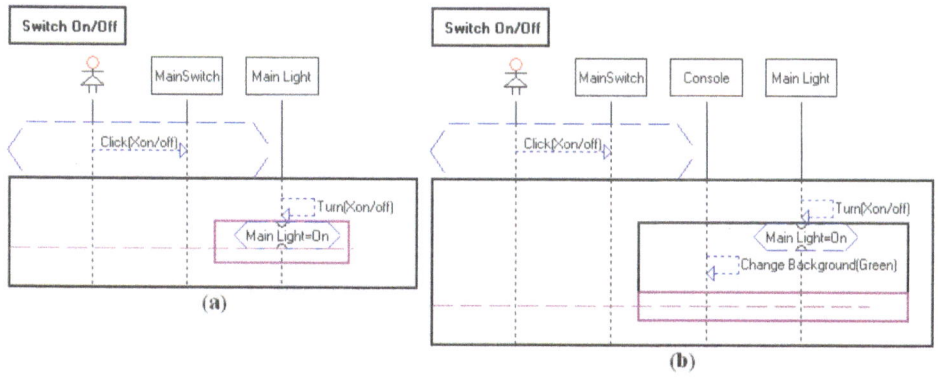

Fig. 10.7. Playing in an if-then-else

'else' part, the user clicks on `Specify the ELSE part` in the wizard and the engine creates the 'else' subchart and moves the cursor there in preparation for playing in the rest of the construct (see Fig. 10.7(b)). Clicking the `END IF` button closes the if-then-else construct and the cursor is placed immediately after it.

10.5 Playing Out

When executing an LSC specification, the condition of an if-then-else construct is evaluated as soon as all the instances that participate in the construct have reached it, assuming that the condition itself can be evaluated (all the variables it uses are bound). If the condition evaluates to true the Play-Engine executes the 'then' subchart, and if it evaluates to false the 'else' subchart is executed. In the example given in Fig. 10.2, as soon as the light changes its state, the condition is evaluated and the background color of the console changes to green or white, depending on the state of the light.

If-then-else constructs are handled somewhat differently when they appear in precharts. Consider the LSC in Fig. 10.8. The scenario in the prechart can

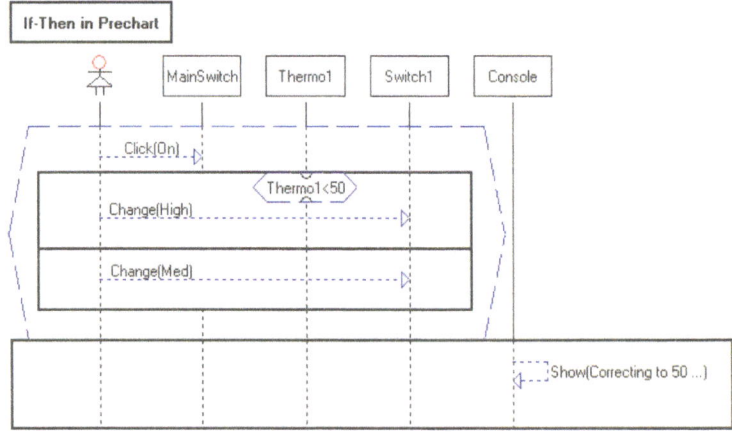

Fig. 10.8. An if-then-else in a prechart

be read in two different ways. According to the execution semantics described above, it reads:

> *Wait for the user to click the main switch to on. Immediately after that, check the temperature indicated by thermometer ♯1. If it is below 50 degrees, (enter the 'then' part and) wait for the user to set the*

*state of the first 3-state switch to High. If the temperature is at least
50 degrees, (enter the 'else' part and) wait for the user to set the state
of the first 3-state switch to Med.*

Thus, the condition of the if-then-else is evaluated an a priori unknown period
of time before any of the events in the 'then' or 'else' parts occur.

We have chosen a different semantics for an if-then-else appearing in the
prechart. According to our proposed semantics, the scenario of Fig. 10.8
reads:

*Wait for the user to click the main switch to on. Then, wait for the
user to (i) set the state of the first 3-state switch to High while the
temperature indicated by thermometer ♯1 is below 50 degrees, or (ii)
set the state of the first 3-state switch to Med while the temperature
is at least 50 degrees.*

Here, we evaluate the condition as the event occurs, thus linking the event
to a context in which the condition holds. The approach is similar to and
consistent with the one we adopted for evaluating minimal cold conditions
in precharts. We believe that this interpretation of if-then-else constructs
appearing in precharts is more intuitive and fits better with the way people
think when specifying conditional choices in a triggering scenario.

If-then-else constructs are the first constructs we have seen so far that
behave differently when monitored in a prechart and when executed in the
chart body. This subtle difference in the semantics, and hence in the execution
mechanism, evolves from the poignant difference between monitoring and
execution.

When executing an LSC specification, the play-out mechanism is responsible for generating visible events, and in the case of the Play-Engine also
for reflecting the effects of these events in the GUI representation of the system model. Hence, when an if-then-else construct is encountered in a chart
body, the execution mechanism should evaluate the condition and continue
generating any events that depend on the condition's value.

In contrast, events in precharts are *monitored* in order to see if the prechart
can be successfully completed. Since the order of events and their timing
is a priori unknown, the prechart monitoring mechanism should enable the
prechart to be completed if possible. The evaluation of a condition is a hidden
event and its timing is not dictated by the system itself, therefore choosing
to evaluate it as soon as possible will eliminate one of the courses that can
be taken by the system (e.g., evaluating a condition when it is true, and the
system later producing an event matching the case of the condition being
false). When monitoring a system, the visible events are produced by the
system itself. Therefore, the monitoring mechanism should wait for the next

event from the system and let that event dictate the choice between the 'then' and the 'else' parts, since it is that event that reflects the choice made by the system.

One could argue that there are more options for the scheduling of condition evaluation, which our semantics does not cover. For example, there could be a case where the condition holds at time T_1, later at time T_2 it becomes false, and at T_3 becomes true again. Finally, at time T_4, the system generates an event that belongs to the 'else' part. In this case, neither of the policies of evaluating the condition as soon as possible or as late as possible will monitor the if-then-else construct to completion. To overcome this, we could set things up so that the monitoring mechanism continuously monitors the condition and probably maintains two copies for the two options. However, since a prechart can have more than one if-then-else construct enabled simultaneously (referring to different objects), the number of copies needed to be maintained can easily blow up. Apart from the fact that monitoring mechanisms that try to cover all options are not practical, they lack the intuition, according to which the event is linked with the system context (condition value) in which it occurs.

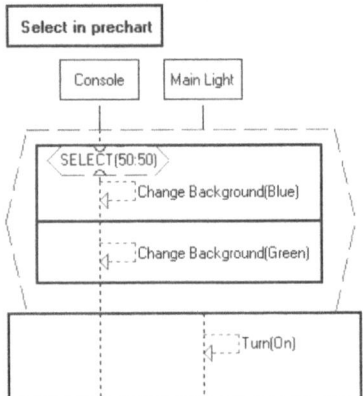

Fig. 10.9. Nondeterministic choice in a prechart

Figure 10.9 shows a nondeterministic choice in the prechart. As discussed above, a condition in an if-then-else construct that appears in a prechart is evaluated only when one of the minimal events in the 'then' part or the 'else' part occurs. The same holds for nondeterministic choice in precharts too, but with one exception. When the Play-Engine *monitors* a prechart with a nondeterministic choice, it does not randomly choose the part to be monitored, but, rather, 'agrees' with any choice made by the system.

Therefore, in this example, the Play-Engine waits for the console to change its background to green or blue, and according to the event taken by the system the Play-Engine enters the correct part of the choice. Note that when it comes to monitoring charts, the actual value of the probability that is attached to a select statement has no meaning; it just states that the two options are possible.[2]

The differences between monitoring an LSC specification and executing it are discussed in more detail in Chap. 12.

10.6 And a Bit More Formally ...

Following the semantics skeleton, we show the extensions and modifications needed to support branching and subcharts.

System Model and Events

Subcharts and if-then-else constructs are entirely specification oriented and therefore do not affect the system model.

LSC Specification

An LSC L is now extended to contain subcharts and if-then-else constructs:

$$L = \langle I_L, V_L, M_L, [Pch_L], A_L, C_L, SUB_L, ITE_L, evnt, subchart, temp \rangle$$

where SUB_L is the set of subcharts in L, ITE_L is the set of if-then-else constructs in L and $subchart$ is a mapping function.

Every LSC construct can be contained in at most one immediately surrounding subchart. The function $subchart$ returns for each construct the innermost subchart to which it belongs (if there is no such subchart it returns $\perp$). The domain of $subchart$ includes SUB_L, thus enabling nested subcharts:

$$subchart : M_L \cup A_L \cup C_L \cup SUB_L \rightarrow SUB_L \cup \{\perp\}$$

The function $subchart$ is extended to events and to instance locations in the natural way. We will also use the notation $e \in Sub$ as an abbreviation of $subchart(e) = Sub$.

The set of instances I_{Sub} participating in a subchart Sub is defined as the set of all instances that are involved in some activity in Sub:

---

[2] If, however, a probability of 0% or 100% is specified, then only the events in the corresponding subchart are allowed to occur.

$$I_{Sub} = \{I \in I_L | \ \exists M \in M_L \text{ s.t. } (subchart(M) = Sub$$
$$\wedge \ (I = M.I_{Src} \vee I = M.I_{Dst}))$$
$$\vee \ \exists A \in A_L \text{ s.t. } (subchart(A) = Sub \wedge I \in I_A)$$
$$\vee \ \exists C \in C_L \text{ s.t. } (subchart(C) = Sub \wedge I \in I_C)$$
$$\vee \ \exists Sub' \in SUB_L \text{ s.t. } subchart(Sub') = Sub \wedge I \in I_{Sub'}\}$$

An if-then-else construct ITE in L is defined as:

$$ITE = \langle I_{ITE}, C, Sub_T, Sub_E \rangle$$

where $I_{ITE} = I_C \cup I_{Sub_T} \cup I_{Sub_E}$ is the set of instances participating in the if-then-else construct, C is the main condition of the if-then-else construct, $Sub_T \in SUB_L$ is the subchart containing the 'then' part and $Sub_E \in SUB_L \cup \{\bot\}$ is the subchart containing the 'else' part (and if there is no such part, $Sub_E = \bot$).

We extend E_L, the set of *LSC events* in L, to contain also hidden events of entering subcharts and exiting them and a special event for branching in an if-then-else construct:

$$E_L = (\{m \in M_L \mid m.M_s \in \Sigma_{FromUser} \cup \Sigma_{ToUser} \cup \Sigma_{FromEnv} \cup \Sigma_{ToEnv}\}$$
$$\times \{Send, Recv\})$$
$$\cup (\{m \in M_L \mid m.M_s \in \Sigma_{Self}\} \times \{Send\})$$
$$\cup (Pch_L \times \{Start, End\}) \cup \{Completed\}$$
$$\cup \{perform(A) \mid A \in A_L\} \cup \{eval(C) \mid C \in C_L\}$$
$$\cup (SUB_L \times \{Start, End\}) \cup \{branch(ITE) \mid ITE \in ITE_L\}$$

We have to cater for the need to exit an if-then-else construct from somewhere within one of its subcharts. For this we use the virtual event (ITE, End), defined as:

$$(ITE, End) \triangleq \begin{cases} (ITE.Sub_E, End) & \text{if } ITE.Sub_E \neq \bot \\ (ITE.Sub_T, End) & \text{if } ITE.Sub_E = \bot \end{cases}$$

The partial order $<_L$ is extended with the following rules:

Synchronize at subcharts - All the instances that participate in a subchart are synchronized at its start and end.

$$\forall Sub \in SUB_L, \ \forall l_x^i, l_y^j \in loc((Sub, Start)) : l_x^i =_L l_y^j$$
$$\forall l_x^i, l_y^j \in loc((Sub, End)) : l_x^i =_L l_y^j$$

If-then-else branch - All the events in an if-then-else construct may be carried out only after the main condition has been evaluated and one of the 'then' or 'else' branches has been selected.

$$\forall ITE \in ITE_L, \ \forall e \in ITE.Sub_T \cup ITE.Sub_E : branch(ITE) <_L e$$

We must also remove from the relation $<_L$ all the pairs of locations that belong to different parts of an if-then-else construct, so that events that are in the 'else' part are not considered as coming *after* events in the 'then' part:

Disconnect If and Else - Events in 'then' subcharts should not be considered as preceding events in 'else' subcharts.

$$\forall ITE \in ITE_L, \forall l_x^i, l_y^i \text{ s.t. } l_x^i \in ITE.Sub_T \wedge l_y^i \in ITE.Sub_E : l_x^i \not<_L l_y^i$$

Operational Semantics

If-then-else constructs are the first constructs we have seen so far that behave differently when monitored in a prechart and when executed in the chart body. To correctly monitor if-then-else constructs within precharts, we should allow the execution mechanism to 'wait' outside the construct until a minimal event in the 'then' part or the 'else' part occurs. In order to allow waiting outside the if-then-else construct but to enable events inside its subcharts to occur, we extend the range of occurrences of events allowed, to include more than the set of directly enabled ones.

Definition 10.6.1 (reachable event). *A visible event e is* reachable from a cut C *if:*

1. *The event e is enabled with respect to C, or*
2. *There exists a hidden event e' such that e is reachable from the cut $C' = AdvanceCut(C, e')$.*

The reachable events are therefore all the events that are enabled, or can become enabled by propagating some hidden events.

The transition relation Δ is therefore extended with transitions for handling if-then-else constructs and with transitions allowing reachable events to occur, even if they are not directly enabled:

- If $e = \langle M, t \rangle$ *(where $t \in \{Send, Recv\}$)* then:
  1. Set $Context \leftarrow \emptyset$.
  2. If $\exists C^L \in \mathcal{RL}$ and $\exists e' \in C^L.LSC$ such that e and e' are negatively level$_1$-unifiable and e' violates C^L, then set $\mathcal{RL} \leftarrow \mathcal{RL} \setminus \{C^L\}$. If $temp(C^L.Cut) = hot$, set $Violating \leftarrow True$.
  3. For every universal LSC $L \in \mathcal{S}_{\mathcal{U}}$ which has an event e', positively level$_1$-unifiable with e, as a minimal event in its prechart, create a copy of L, C^L, and set $\mathcal{RL} \leftarrow \mathcal{RL} \cup \{C^L\}$. Set $C^L.Mode = PreActive$ and set its cut by $C^L.Cut \leftarrow AdvanceCut(InitialCut(L), \langle Pch_L, Start \rangle)$. Unify the variables of e and e', by $Unify(e, e', Context)$. For each hidden event $e'' <_L e'$, apply $\Delta(e'')$.

4. For every copy $C^L \in \mathcal{RL}$ which has a reachable event e', positively level$_1$-unifiable with e, set its cut by $C^L.Cut \leftarrow AdvanceCut(C^L.Cut, e')$. Then, if $e' = \langle M, Send \rangle$, M is synchronous and $e'' = \langle M, Recv \rangle$, set the cut by $C^L.Cut \leftarrow AdvanceCut(C^L.Cut, e'')$. Unify the variables of e and e', by $Unify(e, e', Context)$. For each hidden event $e'' <_L e'$, apply $\Delta(e'')$.

- If $e = Completed(C^L)$ for some $C^L \in \mathcal{RL}$, then set $\mathcal{RL} \leftarrow \mathcal{RL} \setminus \{C^L\}$.
- If $e = \langle Pch_L, End \rangle$ for some $C^L \in \mathcal{RL}$, then set $C^L.Cut \leftarrow BeginMainCut(C^L.LSC)$ and $C^L.Mode \leftarrow Active$.
- If $e = perform(A)$ for some $A \in A_L$ s.t. $C^L \in \mathcal{RL}$, then set $C^L.Cut \leftarrow AdvanceCut(C^L.Cut, e)$ and set

$$A.V \leftarrow \begin{cases} A.C & \text{if } A.Type = constant \\ Value(A.P) & \text{if } A.Type = property \\ A.f(A.\lambda_f^F) & \text{if } A.Type = function \end{cases}$$

- If $e = eval(C)$ for some $C \in C^L$ s.t. $C^L \in \mathcal{RL}$, then
  1. If $value(C) = true$ then set $C^L.Cut \leftarrow AdvanceCut(C^L.Cut, e)$;
  2. If $value(C) = false$ then
     a) If $subchart(C) \in \{ITE.Sub_T, ITE.Sub_E\}$ for some ITE then

     $$\text{set } C^L.Cut \leftarrow AdvanceCut(C^L.Cut, (ITE, End))$$

     b) If $subchart(C) = Sub \in SUB_L$ then

     $$\text{set } C^L.Cut \leftarrow AdvanceCut(C^L.Cut, (Sub, End))$$

     c) If $subchart(C) = \bot$ then set $\mathcal{RL} \leftarrow \mathcal{RL} \setminus \{C^L\}$;
     d) If $temp(C) = hot$, set $Violating \leftarrow True$.
- If $e = branch(ITE)$ for some $ITE \in C^L$ s.t. $C^L \in \mathcal{RL}$ then
  1. If $value(ITE.C) = true$ then set
     $C^L.Cut \leftarrow AdvanceCut(C^L.Cut, (ITE.Sub_T, Start))$;
  2. If $value(ITE.C) = false$ then

$$\text{set } C^L.Cut \leftarrow \begin{cases} AdvanceCut(C^L.Cut, (ITE.Sub_E, Start)) & \text{if } ITE.Sub_E \neq \bot \\ AdvanceCut(C^L.Cut, (ITE.Sub_T, End)) & \text{if } ITE.Sub_E = \bot \end{cases}$$

- If $e = (ITE.Sub_T, End)$ for some $ITE \in C^L$ s.t. $C^L \in \mathcal{RL}$ then

  $$\text{set } C^L.Cut \leftarrow AdvanceCut(C^L.Cut, (ITE, End))$$

- If $e = (ITE.Sub_E, End)$ for some $ITE \in C^L$ s.t. $C^L \in \mathcal{RL}$ then

  $$\text{set } C^L.Cut \leftarrow AdvanceCut(C^L.Cut, (ITE.Sub_E, End))$$

- If $e = (Sub, End)$ for some $Sub \in C^L$ s.t. $C^L \in \mathcal{RL}$ then

$$set\ C^L.Cut \leftarrow AdvanceCut(C^L.Cut, (Sub, End))$$

Finally, we modify *super-step* so it does not attempt to evaluate conditions of if-then-else constructs that are located in precharts (i.e., within copies that are *preactive*).

---

super-step

1. Compute the set of enabled events:

$$Enabled \leftarrow \bigcup_{C^L \in \mathcal{RL}} \{e \in E_L \mid enabled(e)\}$$

$$Waiting \leftarrow \bigcup_{\substack{C^L \in \mathcal{RL}, \\ C^L.Mode = PreActive}} \{e \mid e = branch(ITE)\}$$

$$Enabled \leftarrow Enabled \setminus (External \cup Waiting)$$

2. If there is a *hidden* enabled event $e \in Enabled$, then
   a) Apply $\Delta(e)$.
   b) Go back to 1.
3. If there is a *visible* enabled event $e \in Enabled$, such that e does not violate any copy which is in *active* mode, then
   a) $step(e)$.
   b) Go back to 1.
4. Terminate super-step.

10.7 Bibliographic Notes

The MSC standard also describes a higher-level way of connecting MSCs, termed hierarchical MSCs (HMSCs). An HMSC is a directed graph with one initial node and one final node. Each node in the graph is associated with a basic MSC (bMSC). Using HMSCs, one can specify the order in which different scenario fragments are to be considered, similar to the way it is done with subcharts in LSCs. HMSCs also allow one to define conditions as nodes of the underlying graph, thus allowing for conditional branching, where each branch is given as a bMSC or an HMSC. A major difference between a subchart in an LSC and a bMSC in an HMSC lies in the synchronization requirement. In LSCs, all the instances that participate in a subchart synchronize at its beginning and end, while in HMSCs there is no such requirement. The fact that an instance is allowed to proceed to the next bMSC without having to synchronize with other instances has some significant effects on behavior, as discussed in Chap. 13.

Part IV

Advanced Behavior: Multiple Charts

11. Executing Multiple Charts

In previous chapters we presented various LSC constructs. Besides discussing the play-in process for each construct, we also discussed its semantics when monitoring a system against an LSC specification, and then showed how it can be played out directly within its host LSC. However, the focus so far was on the semantics of the construct within a *single* LSC. An LSC specification will typically consist of a number (often a large number) of charts, and play-out's most subtle issues arise from their combination and interaction. In this chapter we focus on executing **multiple LSCs**, as well as on **overlapping incarnations** of a single LSC.

11.1 Simultaneous Activation of Multiple Charts

Consider the two LSCs of Fig. 11.1. They describe different actions required to be taken by the system when the main switch is clicked to on. '*LSC1*' states that the main light should turn on, and '*LSC2*' states that the first switch should be set to *Med* and the first warning light should turn green.

As the user plays out a scenario in which the main switch is clicked to on, both charts are activated. Suppose that these charts are not to be executed, but rather are viewed as a test of a system, meaning that they are to be monitored against a sequence of events generated by the system. In this case, all the Play-Engine has to do is to wait for the next event, advance the charts accordingly and check that the partial order induced by the charts is not violated. In contrast, suppose that the charts are to be *executed* by the Play-Engine, and there is no other system against which we are testing. In this case, the engine has to *choose* the next event and must then proceed to carry it out. In the above example, the three events can be chosen in any order, since they are not constrained by the LSC partial order.

Suppose now that, in addition to the two LSCs of Fig. 11.1, the specification also contains the LSC shown in Fig. 11.2, stating that when the user

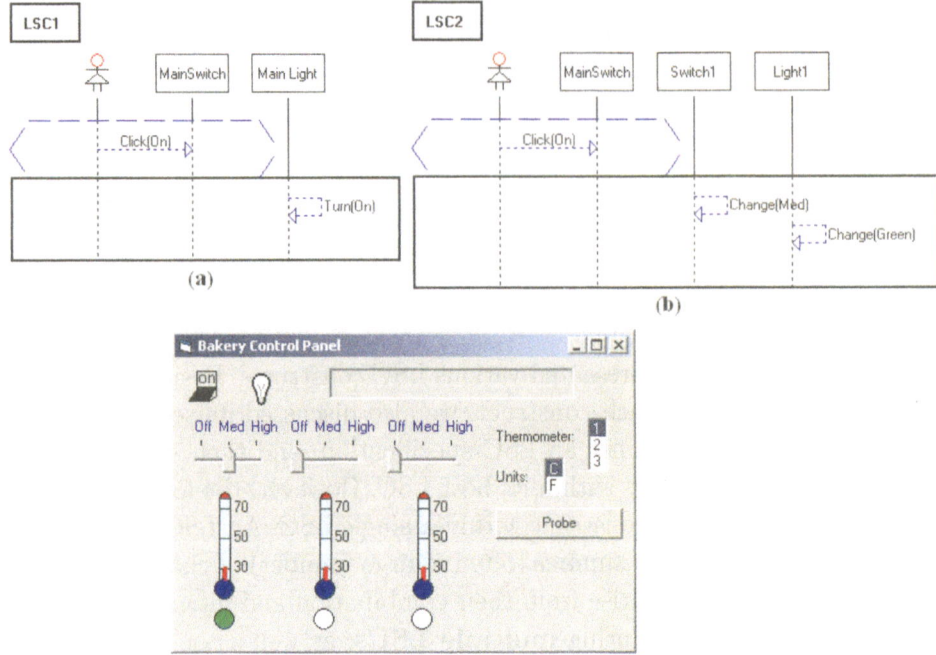

Fig. 11.1. Activating two LSCs as a result of a single event

clicks the main switch to on, the main light turns on, and only after that can the first switch and the warning light take their actions.[1]

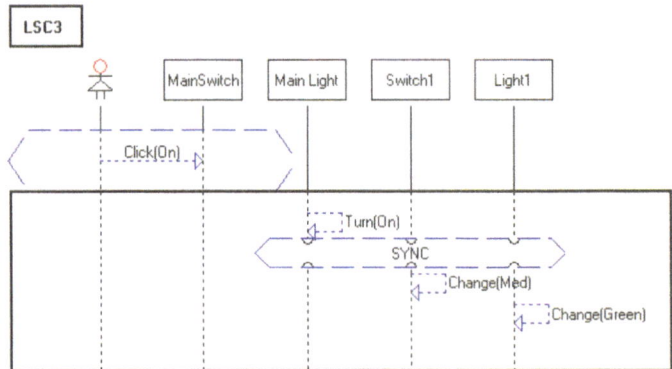

Fig. 11.2. Constraining events in other charts

---

[1] This kind of phenomenon, where different scenarios refer to the same set of actions and reactions in a somewhat different way, is quite common when preparing system requirements, where it is often the case that they are written by more than one person or in several phases.

Now, when the user clicks the switch to on, the three charts are activated. In this case, the only event that can be carried out without getting into trouble is that of turning on the light, since selecting any one of the other two events will cause a violation of '*LSC3*'. Accordingly, the algorithm underlying the play-out mechanism has been designed to allow the choice of the next event to be carried out only from among the set of events that are both enabled and do not violate any other chart.

We have seen several examples of LSCs that were activated by (i.e., their precharts contained) user actions. LSCs can also be activated by system events, thus enabling the specification of **scenario fragments** that may be shared by more than one scenario. The LSC '*Med-Green1*' in Fig. 11.3(a) states that when the first 3-state switch is set to *Med*, the first warning light changes to green. Another LSC, '*Green1-Console*', shown in Fig. 11.3(b), states that every time the first warning light changes to green, a corresponding message appears on the console.

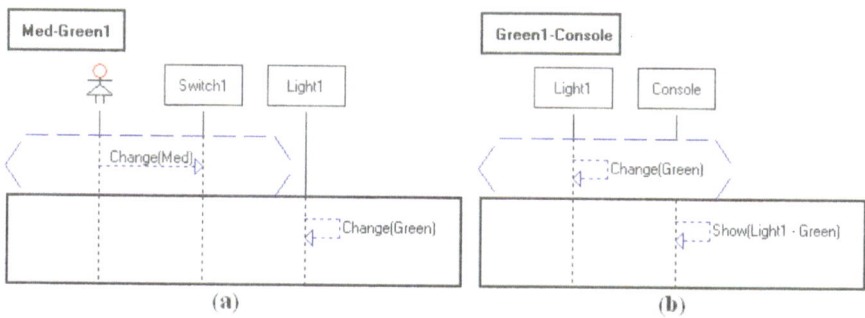

Fig. 11.3. Activation of one LSC by another

When the user sets the state of the first 3-state switch to *Med* during play-out, '*Med-Green1*' is activated. Since its prechart contains only one message, it is successfully completed and the Play-Engine executes the event in the chart body. As this event is fired, it is identified as a minimal event in the prechart of '*Green1-Console*' and this chart is activated too (see Fig. 11.4). The LSC event selected by the Play-Engine is marked by a thick red circle and all the events that are advanced simultaneously with it (in this case there is only one) are marked by thin red circles.

Sometimes, in order to progress with the execution dictated by the body of certain LSCs, we must violate the precharts of others. Consider for example a specification that contains an LSC for each pair of switch and warning light, saying that when the former is set to *Med*, the latter turns green. Suppose we have another chart saying that if the warning lights turn green in ascending

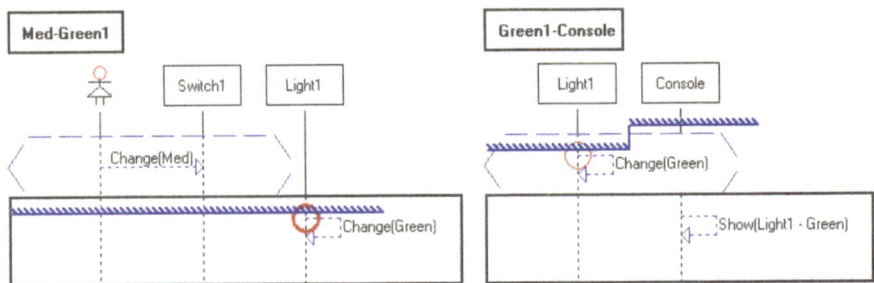

Fig. 11.4. Chain of activations in play-out

order, from 1 to 3, the console should display some message. Now, assume that the user clicks switch number 1 and then switch number 3. Figure 11.5 shows the result. After setting the first switch to *Med*, the first light turns

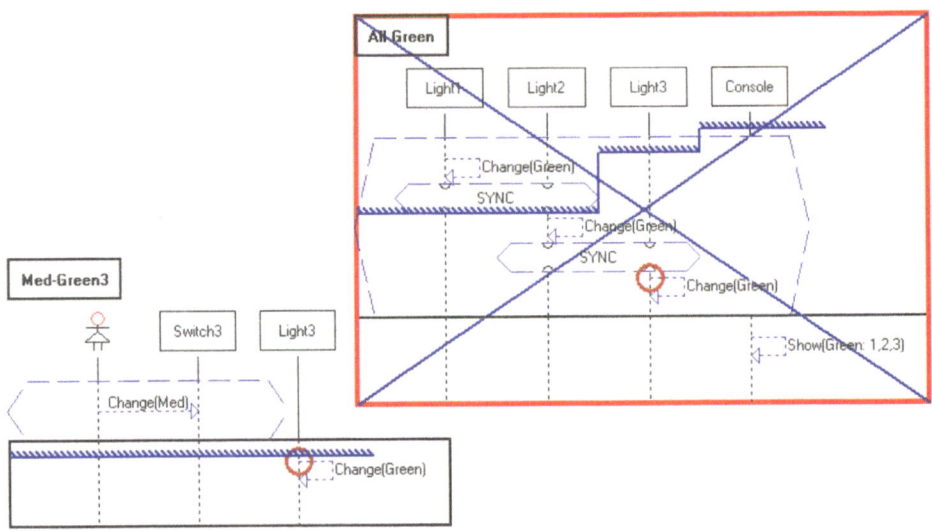

Fig. 11.5. Violating a prechart

green and activates the LSC '*All Green*' (on the right). When the user then sets the state of the third switch to *Med*, the Play-Engine has to select an event to carry out. In this case, the only enabled event is that of changing the third light to green, but clearly this event is not enabled in the LSC '*All Green*'. Precharts can obviously stay active without being completed, and unless and until a prechart is completed, the system is not constrained by the corresponding LSC at all. Thus, the Play-Engine is allowed to change the color of the third light to green and terminate the prechart before it is completed.

A careful examination of the issue of violating an LSC before its prechart completes raises the following question: why not try to violate all precharts as soon as possible, thus minimizing the set of constraints imposed on the execution. Indeed, this is a legitimate question, and a policy that selects events based on this criteria would have been a legitimate one. This kind of policy is **minimal**, in the sense that it minimizes the set of events that should be carried out, by trying to 'cut off' LSCs that do not yet obligate the execution.

We have chosen a **maximal** policy; i.e., our algorithm tries to avoid violating precharts as long as it can. Only if there is no choice left and the only events that can be carried out are ones that violate some prechart, is such an event taken and the prechart terminated. This rule applies not only to precharts. The play-out algorithm may also violate LSC copies that are in active mode and are located in a cold cut. Again, we allow this, since violating an LSC in a cold cut is not considered a violation, due to the fact that none of the instances is obligated to progress. Therefore, when an event violating such a chart is taken, it can be viewed as though the instances decided to stay in their locations and the chart could have been terminated earlier. Similarly, our reluctance to violate precharts also carries over to cold cuts of the main chart. This is also due to the maximal approach we take.

The principle behind the maximal approach is the following: We believe that users specify behavior for a reason, and they want the behavior to be executed if possible. Cold cuts are means to allow scenarios to end before they are expected, due to possible interactions with other scenarios.

To summarize, the play-out execution mechanism searches for enabled events to be carried out according to the following order:

1. If there is an enabled event that does not violate any prechart or any LSC in a cold cut, select it.
2. If there is an event that violates some prechart but does not violate any LSC in a cold cut, select it.
3. If there is an enabled event that violates an LSC in a cold cut but does not violate any LSC in a hot cut, select it.
4. Otherwise, no event can be carried out.

In the Play-Engine, the user is given full control over whether or not to allow violation of precharts and whether to allow violation of cold cuts when looking for the next event (i.e., whether to allow the Play-Engine to use steps 2 and 3 when it looks for the next event to be carried out).

11.2 Overlapping Charts

We have just seen how several LSCs can be activated simultaneously. In
this section we show how the same LSC can be activated more than once
simultaneously, resulting in several overlapping copies of the same original
chart.

Suppose the user would like to click digits and have the display continuously show the sum of the last two digits clicked. This behavior is captured
by the single LSC in Fig. 11.6.

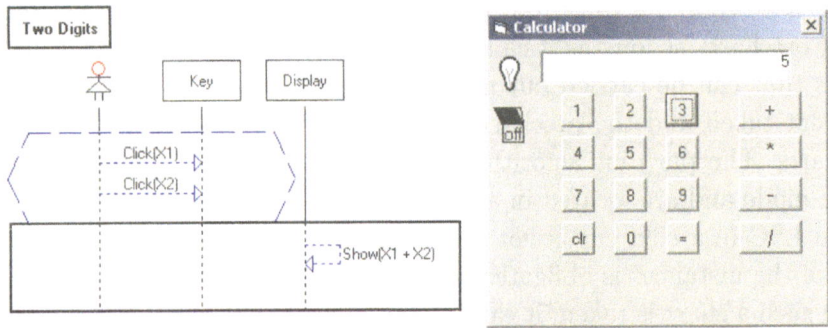

Fig. 11.6. Continuous two-digit summation

Consider the scenario in which the user clicks '2' and then '3'. Figure 11.7
shows the LSC copies that are active at the end of this scenario. The one on

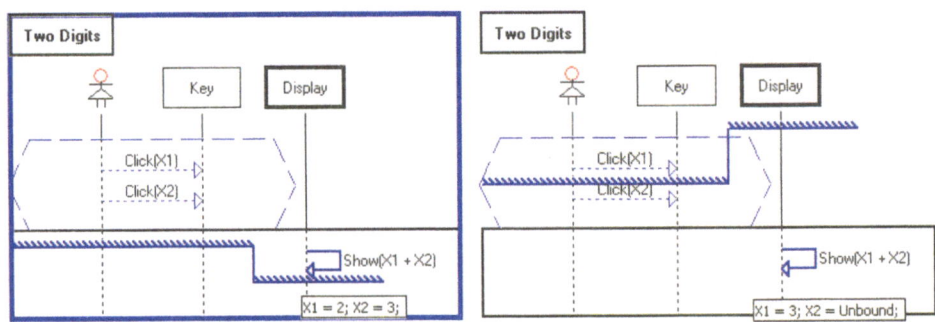

Fig. 11.7. Overlapping charts during play-out

the left is activated by the click on '2'. Then, when the user clicks '3', the
prechart completes and the display is instructed to show "5". Note that the
yellow label at the bottom (displayed when the mouse is placed over the last

message) shows that $X1$ and $X2$ are bound to 2 and 3, respectively. Another thing that occurs as a result of the user clicking '3' is the activation of a new copy of the same LSC, the reason being that clicking '3' is unifiable with a minimal event in the chart. The new copy is shown on the right in Fig. 11.7, and, as can be seen, it is waiting for the next digit to be clicked before its prechart can be completed. The tool tip in this LSC copy shows that $X1$ is bound to 3 and $X2$ is still unbound.

The fact that an LSC can be active simultaneously in several copies, each in a different cut, can be used for several purposes. One interesting use involves recursive calls. Consider the LSCs in Fig. 11.8, which constitute a scheme of a recursive computation consisting of a start, a recursive call guarded by a termination condition, and some way of specifying the returned value. Figure 11.8(a) shows that when a digit is clicked, the display's background changes to white and it then shows the digit itself. Figure 11.8(b)

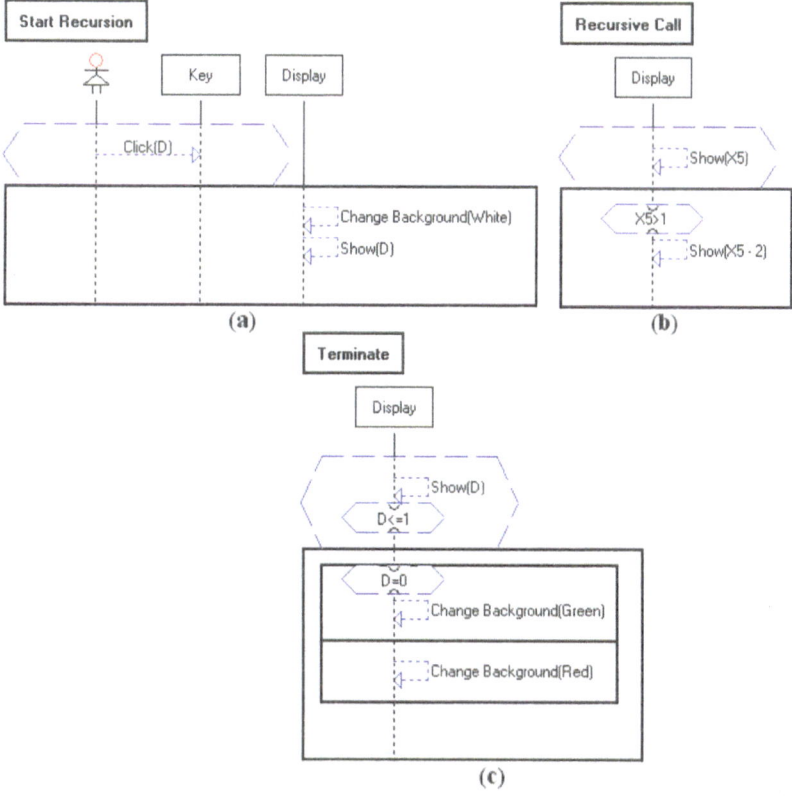

Fig. 11.8. Recursion in LSCs

consists of the recursive call. It says that every time the display shows some
value, if this value is greater than 1 a new value equal to the previous value
minus two is shown. The recursion stems from the fact that the event of
decreasing the digit in the body of the chart of Fig. 11.8(b) triggers a rein-
carnation of that very chart, as long as the digit shown is larger than 1.
Finally, the LSC of Fig. 11.8(c) says that when the display shows the value
0 or 1 its background changes to green or red, respectively. Besides looping
down and decreasing the display digit, this combination of LSCs checks par-
ity without the use of *odd* or *even* predicates: when an even digit is clicked
the display turns green, and when the digit clicked is odd the display turns
red.

Figure 11.9 shows a snapshot of the active LSCs towards the end of a run.
Figure 11.9(a) shows the '*Recursive Call*' LSC that was activated when the

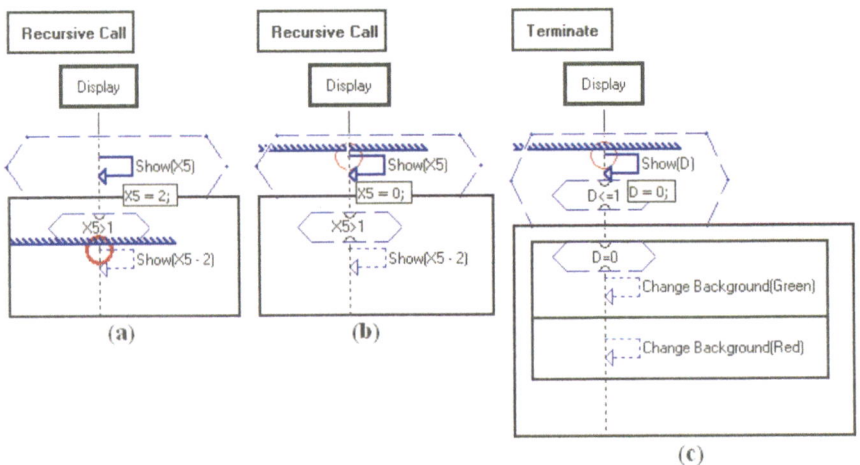

Fig. 11.9. Recursive LSCs during play-out

display showed "2". Since the variable $X5$ in this copy is bound to 2, the
cold condition holds and the display is instructed to show "0" (marked by a
thick red circle). As a result of this event, two more charts are activated. A
new copy of '*Recursive Call*' is created, this time with $X5$ bound to 0 (Fig.
11.9(b)). In this LSC the cold condition does not hold and therefore the chain
of recursive calls terminates. In addition, the LSC '*Terminate*' is activated
with $D = 0$. The cold condition in the prechart of this LSC is true and
the main chart is entered. The main condition of the if-then-else evaluates
to true, causing the background of the display to change to green and the
scenario to end.

Figure 11.10 shows how the two LSCs of Fig. 11.8(b) and 11.8(c) can be combined using nested if-then-else constructs. It is clear that this LSC can

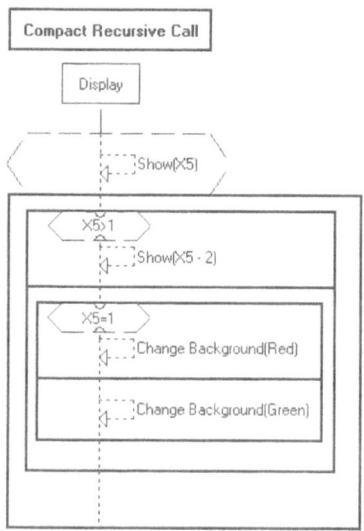

Fig. 11.10. More compact recursion

replace the two original charts, but what is particularly interesting is the fact that all three can be executed together, synchronizing on all the visible events they share.

In the above examples we saw that a single LSC can be active in more than one copy simultaneously. We should emphasize that different copies of the same LSC do not differ only in their cuts but also in the values assigned to their variables. Thus, an LSC live copy consists of a fully cloned chart, including an independent copy of its variables. We would also like to note that although the example of recursion seems a bit coarse, it is because we have used messages that denote property changes. In Chap. 14 we refine the system model with messages that better capture the notion of calling an object or sending it a control signal.

11.3 And a Bit More Formally ...

The issue of executing multiple charts is not related to the system model or to the LSC language, and is therefore relevant only to the operational semantics.

Operational Semantics

The notions of enabled events and violating events were defined in previous chapters and remain unchanged. The procedure for performing a *super-step* referred to these definitions too and avoided carrying out events that violated other LSCs. We now refine *super-step* so that it tries to avoid selecting events that violate other precharts or LSCs in cold cuts. The operational semantics assumes that both kinds of violation are permissable and does not refer to the option of the user controlling these parameters. The extension is quite straightforward.

---

super-step

1. Compute the set of enabled events:

$$Enabled \leftarrow \bigcup_{C^L \in \mathcal{RL}} \{e \in E_L | enabled(e)\}$$

$$Waiting \leftarrow \bigcup_{\substack{C^L \in \mathcal{RL}, \\ C^L.Mode = PreActive}} \{e \mid e = branch(ITE)\}$$

$$Enabled \leftarrow Enabled \setminus (External \cup Waiting)$$

2. If there is a *hidden* enabled event $e \in Enabled$, then
   a) Apply $\Delta(e)$.
   b) Go back to 1.

3. If there is a *visible* enabled event $e \in Enabled$, such that e does not violate any copy that is in *active* or *preactive* mode, then
   a) $step(e)$.
   b) Go back to 1.

4. If there is a *visible* enabled event $e \in Enabled$, such that e does not violate any copy that is in *active* mode, then
   a) $step(e)$.
   b) Go back to 1.

5. If there is a *visible* enabled event $e \in Enabled$, such that e does not violate any copy that is in *active* mode with a hot cut, then
   a) $step(e)$.
   b) Go back to 1.

6. Terminate super-step.

---

12. Testing with Existential Charts

Universal charts, which must be satisfied by any run that satisfies their prechart, 'drive' the model by their action/reaction nature. In contrast, existential charts, which can get by with only a single satisfying run, can be used as system tests or as examples of object interactions. In this chapter, we deal with the uses of existential charts and the way they are monitored by the Play-Engine.

12.1 Specifying Test Scenarios

Consider Fig. 12.1, which describes the following scenario-based test:

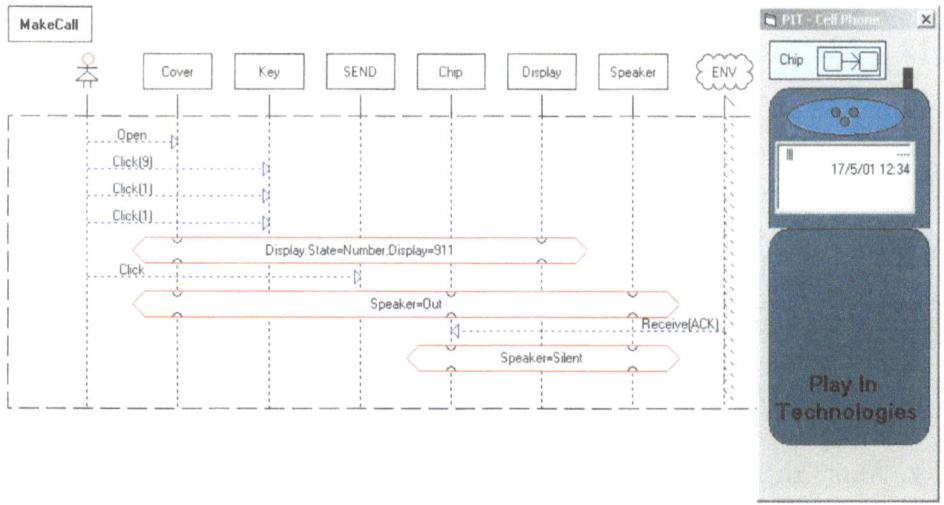

Fig. 12.1. Specifying tests with existential charts

The user first opens the cover and dials 911 (by clicking the digit keys in that order). At this point, the display is expected to change its

*mode from Date to Number and should display the number " 911".
Next, the user clicks the **Send** button. At this point the speaker should
emit an outgoing dial tone. Then, when a signal indicating that the
call was answered (denoted by the word ACK) is received from the
environment, the speaker becomes silent.*

In contrast to universal charts, this LSC does not specify how and when
the system actions are carried out (e.g., displaying a number, making a sound,
etc.), but rather constrains the behavior of the system to satisfy a set of
conditions that are expected to hold at different points in the run. We are
using it to define a **test scenario**. The required test results are specified using
hot conditions, thus enabling the chart to complete only if the conditions all
evaluate to true.

Although system tests can be described using existential charts, it is important to remember that a system can satisfy an existential LSC by producing but a single run in which the LSC is successfully traced to completion.
Therefore, in the case of nondeterministic systems, satisfying an existential
LSC cannot be considered as proving that the system always behaves in some
way, but only that it *may* behave in some way. To show that a system *always* behaves in a specified manner, one should monitor the system against
a universal LSC.

12.2 Monitoring LSCs

Rather than serving to drive the play-out, existential charts are **monitored**
and checked for their successful completion. To integrate the monitoring capabilities into our execution mechanism, recall from Sect. 5.3 that an execution
engine had to satisfy the first four requirements. We now add a fifth, yielding
the following list:

1. Identify an external stimulus and find all the requirements that should
   be considered when resolving the system's response to it (e.g., identify
   the event of flipping a switch and find all the requirements that specify
   the system's responses to the switch being flipped).
2. Apply the relevant requirements to create the sequence of system reactions. This is done iteratively, and thus includes identifying additional
   requirements that become relevant as the system is responding and applying them too (e.g., after the switch is flipped, send a signal to the
   controller, which in turn may result in sending a signal to the light and
   turning it on).

3. Identify scenarios that are forbidden according to the requirements, and avoid generating them (e.g., make sure that if the requirements say that a certain signal cannot be sent to the light while it is on, it will indeed not be sent when the light is on).
4. If a forbidden scenario actually occurs (e.g., because some other mandatory scenario forces it to), indicate a violation.
5. Indicate when an existential (provisional) scenario successfully completes.

When monitoring a chart, the Play-Engine simply tracks the events in the chart as they occur, and is not required to initiate any visible events while doing so. Existential charts are monitored in a way similar to that for monitoring precharts of universal charts. Conditions and assignments are performed and evaluated as soon as they are enabled, while the choices between 'then' and 'else' subcharts of if-then-else constructs are delayed until an event in one of the two subcharts occurs.

When (and if) a traced chart reaches its end, it is highlighted, and the user is informed that it was successfully traced to completion. The user may select the charts to be monitored in advance, thus saving the Play-Engine the need to track charts that might currently be of no interest. Figure 12.2 shows the chart from Fig. 12.1 after it was successfully traced to completion.

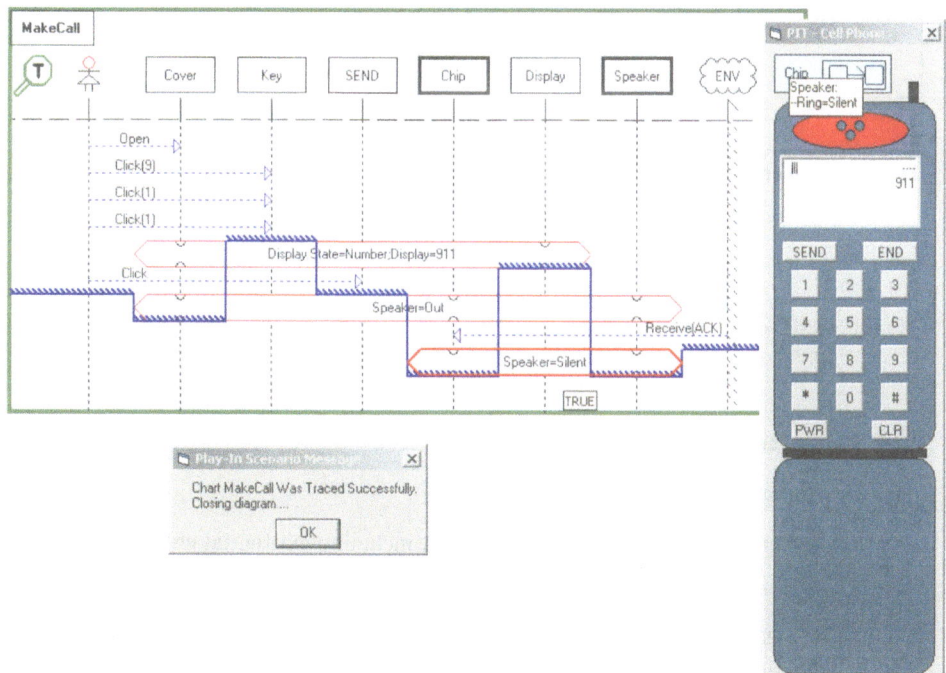

Fig. 12.2. Monitoring existential charts

As with universal charts, there could be cases where a single existential chart is activated in several overlapping copies, and at a given time during execution each one is in a different tracking status (i.e., in a different cut). This is fine, since one does not know a priori when a satisfying scenario begins, and it could be the case that such a scenario begins after some prefix of it has already been monitored. Had we allowed only a single copy for each LSC active at a time, we would definitely have missed some of the satisfying scenarios, and erroneously concluded that some existential scenario is not satisfiable.

Universal LSCs go through a *PreActive* → *Active* → *Terminate* life cycle. Existential LSCs go through a similar, though simpler, life cycle. When one of the minimal visible events in the chart occurs, the copy is created and enters the *Check* state. If the chart is violated, it is simply exited and deleted. If it completes successfully, it moves through a temporary *Completed* state where various registration and management actions are taken, and it is then exited and deleted. Figure 12.3 shows the full life cycle of LSC copies.

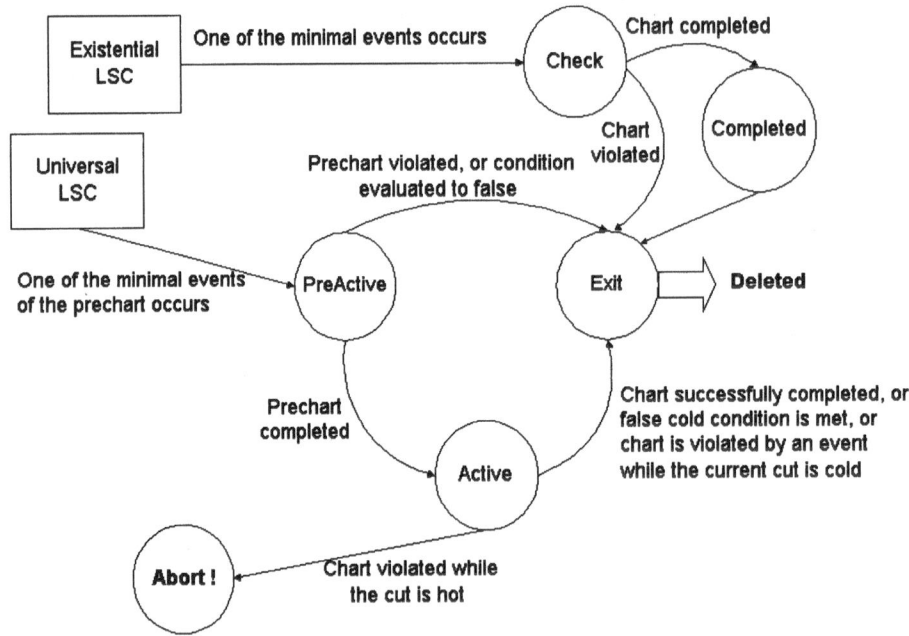

Fig. 12.3. Life cycle of LSC copies, including existential charts

Having existential LSCs at hand makes it possible to consider the notion of consistency between a system and a specification. Earlier, we defined a consistent run as one that does not violate any universal LSC in the specification. A system is **consistent with a specification** if all its runs are consistent with the specification and, in addition, each existential LSC is satisfied by some run. Note that without existential LSCs, and with a passive user, a system could be easily consistent by simply doing nothing, since an empty run trivially satisfies all the universal charts. Of course, since universal charts can have user events in their precharts, the system can be forced to react even if no existential charts are present. However, in principle, if we somehow prevented the user from taking any action (e.g., by initiating the system with locked switches, buttons, etc.), then, in the absence of existential charts, the system could do nothing and still be consistent with the specification.

12.3 Recording and Replaying

When playing out the GUI application, a run trace is produced, which includes all the user actions and the system reactions. These runs can be recorded, to provide testimonies for fulfilling existential LSCs. Figure 12.4 shows a fragment of a recorded run.

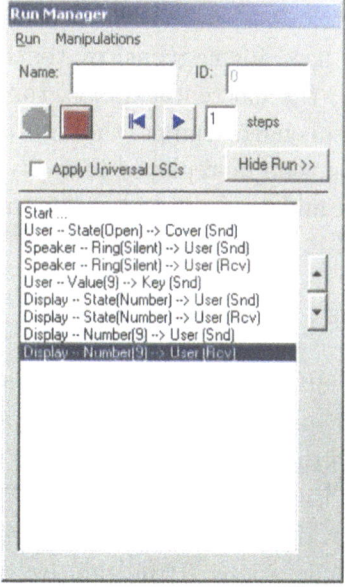

Fig. 12.4. A recorded run

Recorded runs can be saved (in XML format) and then reloaded and replayed. In replaying a run, the user may select both existential and universal charts to be traced. Existential LSCs can thus be shown to be fulfilled, and with universal charts the run shows when the charts were activated and how they participated in creating the system's reactions. And, of course, the engine notifies us if a universal chart is violated.

More importantly, runs can be imported from different sources and replayed in the same manner. These external sources can be different implementations of the specification, either given as executable programs or as more detailed design models (e.g., statecharts, labeled transition systems, etc.). Importing a run from an implementation and replaying it, while tracing all charts, can be used to show that the implementation is consistent with the requirements, in the sense that existential charts are successfully traced and universal charts are not violated.

Recorded runs can be manipulated by the user, by changing the order of events and checking whether the resulting run is also a legal one. One of the interesting possibilities that we have built into the Play-Engine is that of deleting all system reactions and leaving only user and environment actions. After applying this modification, the resulting run can be replayed. The user can then specify that universal charts should also be activated (and not only monitored). In this case, events from the recorded run are injected as before, but now the selected universal charts activate the system and trigger events as specified in their bodies.

This feature may be used for **regression testing**, in the following way. While fulfilling (part of) the existential LSCs, the runs are recorded. Later on, if some of the universal charts change, the runs can be modified to contain only user actions and can then be replayed to verify that existential LSCs are still successfully fulfilled and no universal charts are violated in the process.

12.4 On-line Testing

As discussed in the previous section, in order to test an intra-object model or an actual system implementation with respect to a given LSC specification, the system should record the generated events, and the recorded run can then be loaded into the Play-Engine and replayed.

The Play-Engine provides another, more convenient, way for testing system models and implementations. Using an *External Event Manager*, the Play-Engine can be connected through a TCP/IP connection to other programs. To test a system, we would connect it to the Play-Engine and have it send the generated events along the communication line. These events, in the format of recorded events, would be received by the Play-Engine and injected into the execution and monitoring mechanisms, in a way similar to how recorded events are injected.

The Play-Engine enables the user to inject the events upon their arrival or to have them accumulate in a queue and then inject them manually. By asking the engine to monitor all the LSCs in the specification, the user can test the system and verify that all the existential charts can be satisfied and no universal charts are violated in the process. By having it activate universal LSCs, the Play-Engine can operate in a mode where the external events are actually received from an external source and are used to trigger the system's reactions, which are generated by the engine itself.

The Play-Engine can also be instructed to send the generated events back to the communication line, and thus affect the connected program in any desired way. This feature also makes it possible to connect two Play-Engines, each executing its own specification and serving as the external environment of the other; see Sect. 21.5.

12.5 Executing and Monitoring LSCs in the Play-Engine

Prior to LSCs, scenario-based languages were used mainly to express requirements, which are later verified against system runs. The semantics of these languages is therefore oriented towards testing, and it specifies whether a set of runs generated by the system satisfies the specification. Obviously, since the language of LSCs can serve for testing as well, we would like to support this kind of semantics too. However, the fact that our main interest in this book is in *executing* some LSCs, the ones that drive the execution, while only monitoring others, affects the language's operational semantics.

Figure 12.5 illustrates how an LSC specification can be used both for driving a model and for monitoring it. When executing an LSC specification, the user may choose the LSCs that drive the model and those that will be monitored. The driving LSCs must all be universal, while the set of monitored LSCs may include both existential and universal charts. To keep the semantics clean, we require that the two sets be disjoint. In practice, the Play-Engine allows a universal LSC to both drive the model and be monitored at the same time, and we refer to such cases as if there are two identical but distinct LSCs, one in each set.

According to the conventional semantics of scenario-based languages, the set of driving LSCs is empty and all the LSCs are monitored. In this setting, events generated by the system are monitored one after the other (using *monitor event*), by applying *track event* to these events and to hidden events between them. The *track event* procedure is the basis of the LSC semantics and it computes all the actions that should be taken as a result of firing an

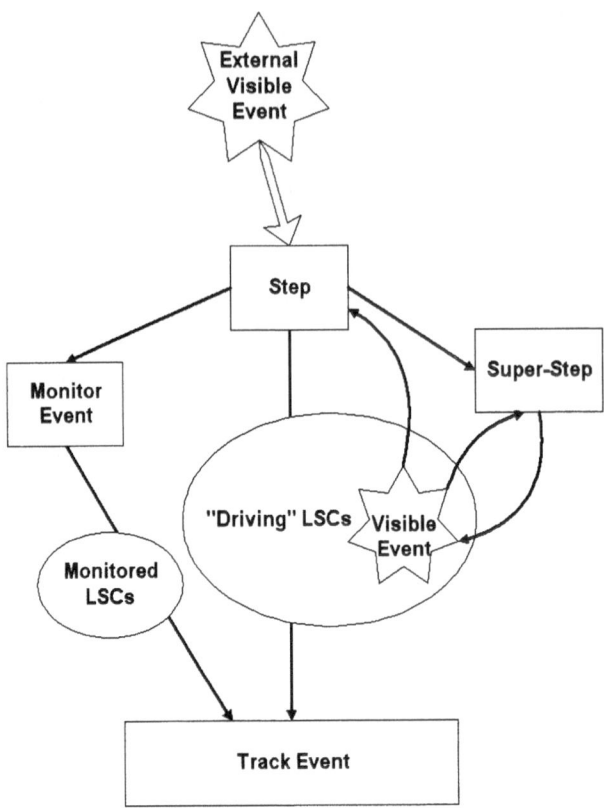

Fig. 12.5. Executing and monitoring LSCs

LSC event (e.g., advancing cuts, creating new copies, closing copies, unifying events, etc.).

As we saw in earlier chapters, the Play-Engine's execution mechanism consists of the two procedures *step* and *super-step*. These are defined at a higher level than *track event* and use the basic semantics to execute the specification. After some external event occurs, the procedure *step* monitors it as described above, except that the event is now monitored with respect to the set of driving LSCs. The event is also sent to *monitor event*, so that it affects monitored LSCs as well. Then, *super-step* searches through the driving LSCs for events that can be executed. As long as such events exist they are sent to *step*, thus monitoring them in both the driving LSCs and the monitored LSCs.

12.6 And a Bit More Formally ...

In previous chapters we defined a system model and an LSC specification. The system model is not affected by existential LSCs, and the LSC specification was already defined with existential LSCs in mind. Therefore, the only modifications that are required here are in the operational semantics.

Operational Semantics

An LSC copy of an existential LSC is in *Check* mode as long as it exists.

Definition 12.6.1 (LSC live copy). *Given an LSC L, a live copy of L, denoted by C^L, is defined as*

$$C^L = \langle LSC, Mode, Cut \rangle,$$

where LSC is a copy of the original chart, $Mode \in \{PreActive, Active, Check\}$ is the execution mode of this copy, and Cut is some legal cut of L representing the current location of the instances of L in this particular copy.

When executing an LSC specification, the user may choose the LSCs that drive the model and those that should be monitored. These two sets are required to be disjoint. The operational semantics is therefore given as:

$$Sem(\mathcal{S}) = \langle \mathcal{V}, V_0, \mathcal{S}_D, \mathcal{S}_M, \Delta[\mathcal{S}_O, \mathcal{S}_C] \rangle$$

A state $V \in \mathcal{V}$ is modified to contain not only live copies of driving LSCs ($\mathcal{RL}$) but also a set of live copies of monitored LSCs ($\mathcal{ML}$):

$$V = \langle \mathcal{RL}, \mathcal{ML}, Violating \rangle$$

The initial configuration contains no copies of driving LSCs and no copies of monitored LSCs, and is defined as:

$$V_0 = \langle \emptyset, \emptyset, False \rangle$$

$\mathcal{S}_D \subseteq \mathcal{S}_U$ is the set of driving LSCs, $\mathcal{S}_M \subseteq \mathcal{S}_U \cup \mathcal{S}_E$ is the set of LSCs the user wishes to monitor, and the two sets satisfy $\mathcal{S}_D \cap \mathcal{S}_M = \emptyset$.

The transition relation Δ is no longer applied automatically to all the LSCs in the specification and to the sets of running copies $\mathcal{RL}$, but is parameterized with two sets. The first set, $\mathcal{S}_O$, contains original LSCs that are subject to Δ. The second set, $\mathcal{S}_C$, contains the live copies that currently exist. This set contains only copies of LSCs from $\mathcal{S}_O$. The two sets are instantiated with either $(\mathcal{S}_D, \mathcal{RL})$ or $(\mathcal{S}_M, \mathcal{ML})$.

Note that if one cares only about the 'standard' part of the semantics, i.e., the part that enables a system to be tested and verified against an LSC specification, and not in executing the specification directly, this can be achieved by setting $\mathcal{S}_M = \mathcal{S}$ and $\mathcal{S}_D = \emptyset$.

The transition relation $\Delta[\mathcal{S}_O, \mathcal{S}_C]$ is modified so that it refers to its parameters and is extended to consider existential charts.

- If $e = \langle M, t \rangle$ (where $t \in \{Send, Recv\}$) then:
  1. Set $Context \leftarrow \emptyset$.
  2. If $\exists C^L \in \mathcal{S}_C$ and $\exists e' \in C^L.LSC$, such that e and e' are negatively $level_1$-unifiable and e' violates C^L, then set $\mathcal{S}_C \leftarrow \mathcal{S}_C \setminus \{C^L\}$. If $temp(C^L.Cut) = hot$, set $Violating \leftarrow True$.
  3. For every universal LSC $L \in \mathcal{S}_O$ which has an event e', positively $level_1$-unifiable with e, as a minimal event in its prechart, create a copy of L, C^L, and set $\mathcal{S}_C \leftarrow \mathcal{S}_C \cup \{C^L\}$. Set $C^L.Mode = PreActive$ and set its cut by $C^L.Cut \leftarrow AdvanceCut(InitialCut(L), \langle Pch_L, Start \rangle)$. Unify the variables of e and e', by $Unify(e, e', Context)$. For each hidden event $e'' <_L e'$, apply $\Delta(e'')$.
  4. For every existential LSC $L \in \mathcal{S}_O$ which has an event e', positively $level_1$-unifiable with e, as a minimal event in the chart body, create a copy of L, C^L, and set $\mathcal{S}_C \leftarrow \mathcal{S}_C \cup \{C^L\}$. Set $C^L.Mode = Check$, and set its cut to the beginning of the chart by $C^L.Cut \leftarrow BeginMainCut(C^L.LSC)$. Unify the variables of e and e', by $Unify(e, e', Context)$. For each hidden event $e'' <_L e'$, apply $\Delta(e'')$.
  5. For every copy $C^L \in \mathcal{S}_C$ which has a reachable event e', positively $level_1$-unifiable with e, set its cut by $C^L.Cut \leftarrow AdvanceCut(C^L.Cut, e')$. Then, if $e' = \langle M, Send \rangle$, M is synchronous and $e'' = \langle M, Recv \rangle$, set the cut by $C^L.Cut \leftarrow AdvanceCut(C^L.Cut, e'')$. Unify the variables of e and e', by $Unify(e, e', Context)$. For each hidden event $e'' <_L e'$, apply $\Delta(e'')$.
- If $e = Completed(C^L)$ for some $C^L \in \mathcal{S}_C$, then set $\mathcal{S}_C \leftarrow \mathcal{S}_C \setminus \{C^L\}$.
- If $e = \langle Pch_L, End \rangle$ for some $C^L \in \mathcal{S}_C$, then set $C^L.Cut \leftarrow BeginMainCut(C^L.LSC)$ and $C^L.Mode \leftarrow Active$.
- If $e = perform(A)$ for some $A \in A_L$ s.t. $C^L \in \mathcal{S}_C$, then set $C^L.Cut \leftarrow AdvanceCut(C^L.Cut, e)$ and set

$$A.V \leftarrow \begin{cases} A.C & \text{if } A.Type = constant \\ Value(A.P) & \text{if } A.Type = property \\ A.f(A.\lambda_f^F) & \text{if } A.Type = function \end{cases}$$

- If $e = eval(C)$ for some $C \in C^L$ s.t. $C^L \in \mathcal{S}_C$ then
  1. If $value(C) = true$ then set $C^L.Cut \leftarrow AdvanceCut(C^L.Cut, e)$.
  2. If $value(C) = false$ then
     a) If $subchart(C) \in \{ITE.Sub_T, ITE.Sub_E\}$ for some ITE then

        set $C^L.Cut \leftarrow AdvanceCut(C^L.Cut, (ITE, End))$

     b) If $subchart(C) = Sub \in SUB_L$ then

        set $C^L.Cut \leftarrow AdvanceCut(C^L.Cut, (Sub, End))$

c) If $subchart(C) = \perp$ then set $\mathcal{S}_C \leftarrow \mathcal{S}_C \setminus \{C^L\}$.

d) If $temp(C) = hot$ then set $Violating \leftarrow True$.

- If $e = branch(ITE)$ for some $ITE \in C^L$ s.t. $C^L \in \mathcal{S}_C$ then

  1. If $value(ITE.C) = true$ then set

     $C^L.Cut \leftarrow AdvanceCut(C^L.Cut, (ITE.Sub_T, Start))$

  2. If $value(ITE.C) = false$ then

$$set \ C^L.Cut \leftarrow \begin{cases} AdvanceCut(C^L.Cut, (ITE.Sub_E, Start)) \ \text{if} \ ITE.Sub_E \neq \perp \\ AdvanceCut(C^L.Cut, (ITE.Sub_T, End)) \ \ \text{if} \ ITE.Sub_E = \perp \end{cases}$$

- If $e = (ITE.Sub_T, End)$ for some $ITE \in C^L$ s.t. $C^L \in \mathcal{S}_C$ then

  $set \ C^L.Cut \leftarrow AdvanceCut(C^L.Cut, (ITE, End))$

- If $e = (ITE.Sub_E, End)$ for some $ITE \in C^L$ s.t. $C^L \in \mathcal{S}_C$ then

  $set \ C^L.Cut \leftarrow AdvanceCut(C^L.Cut, (ITE.Sub_E, End))$

- If $e = (Sub, End)$ for some $Sub \in C^L$ s.t. $C^L \in \mathcal{S}_C$ then

  $set \ C^L.Cut \leftarrow AdvanceCut(C^L.Cut, (Sub, End))$

In Chap. 5 we defined a consistent run as one that does not cause any violations.

Definition 12.6.2 (consistent run). *A run R is consistent with an LSC specification $\mathcal{S}$ if, starting from V_0, the rules of Δ can be applied to the events in R and to the hidden events generated between them, without reaching a violating transition.*

We can now define a *consistent system* with respect to an LSC specification.

Definition 12.6.3 (consistent system). *A system Sys is consistent with an LSC specification $\mathcal{S}$ if all the runs of Sys are consistent with the specification, and if for every existential LSC $L \in \mathcal{S}_E$ there exists a run that satisfies L.*

The difference between executing a specification and monitoring it is reflected in the three high-level procedures. The *step* and *super-step* procedures are used for executing the driving LSCs and the new *monitor-event* procedure is used to monitor the monitored LSCs. The procedure *step* is modified so that Δ is applied to the event to be executed, just as before, thus affecting the driving LSCs, but then the event is sent to *monitor-event*, so that it affects the monitored LSCs too. Thus, a model that is driven by some charts can simultaneously monitor other charts.

---

step(e)

1. Apply $\Delta[\mathcal{S}_D, \mathcal{RL}](e)$.
2. Change the property value according to the value in the message:
   a)
   $$O \leftarrow \begin{cases} e.M.Src \text{ if } M \in \Sigma_{ToUser} \cup \Sigma_{ToEnv} \\ e.M.Dst \text{ otherwise} \end{cases}$$

   b) $P \leftarrow e.M.P$
   c)
   $$Value(O.P) \leftarrow \begin{cases} e.M.f(e.M.\lambda_f^F) \text{ if } e.M.f \neq \bot \\ e.M.V.\omega \qquad \text{otherwise} \end{cases}$$

3. monitor-event(e).

Since the procedure *super-step* triggers the execution of events by sending them to *step*, and *step* already sends them to *monitor-event*, *super-step* remains unchanged from its latest definition in Chap. 11.

In case a sequence of visible events is to be monitored against an LSC specification, as in replaying a run, for example, the events are sent one by one to *monitor-event*. This procedure is a simple combination of a single *step* and a *super-step* which is allowed to propagate only hidden events. The input to *monitor-event* is a single event and it advances all the hidden events until none is enabled:

---

monitor-event(ev)

1. Apply $\Delta[\mathcal{S}_M, \mathcal{ML}](ev)$.
2. Compute the set of enabled events:
   $$Enabled \leftarrow \bigcup_{C^L \in \mathcal{ML}} \{e \in E_L | enabled(e)\}$$
   $$Waiting \leftarrow \bigcup_{C^L \in \mathcal{ML}} \{e \mid e = branch(ITE)\}$$
   $$Enabled \leftarrow Enabled \setminus Waiting$$

3. If there is a *hidden* enabled event $e \in Enabled$, then
   a) Apply $\Delta[\mathcal{S}_M, \mathcal{ML}](e)$.
   b) Go back to 2.
4. Terminate monitor-event.

12.7 Bibliographic Notes

The notion of a consistent system with respect to an LSC specification was given in [27]. In [46] a consistent LSC specification is defined as a specification for which there exists a set of runs such that every existential chart is satisfied by at least one run and every universal chart is satisfied by all runs. It is proved in [46] that an LSC specification is consistent if and only if it is possible to synthesize a statechart model for it, such that the model is consistent with the specification. We should remark that the results in [46] were defined for a subset of the LSC language described here that does not contain assignments and conditions, for example.

In [76] a methodology is described, supported by a tool called TestConductor, which is integrated into Rhapsody [60]. The tool is used for monitoring and testing a model using a subset of LSCs. The charts can be monitored in a way that is similar to the way we trace existential charts. Sequence diagrams created using the TestConductor allow the use of variables. However, when such a chart is to be used, the user has to manually bind the variables in the chart with concrete values. Therefore, runtime unification is not performed, and if a general scenario needs to be verified for a priori unknown objects and values, the diagram must be manually instantiated for all possible combinations.

In [29] a verification environment is described, in which LSCs are used to express requirements that can be verified against a Statemate model. The tool is commercially available with the Statemate tool. The verification is based on translating an LSC into a timed Büchi automaton, as described in [65], and it also handles timing issues. In both [29] and [76], the underlying assumption is that a system model whose reactive parts are described by statecharts has already been constructed, and the aim is to test or verify that model using sequence charts.

Part V

Advanced Behavior: Richer Constructs

13. Loops

In this chapter, we discuss how to specify iteration in LSCs, in the form of the various kinds of looping constructs the language supports.

13.1 Using Loops

Continuing with our bakery panel example, consider the following requirement:

> *If the temperature of thermometer ♯1 rises above 50 degrees, its associated warning light should flicker five times.*

This requirement can be described using an LSC with the rising of the temperature in the prechart and five pairs of messages, each denoting the change of the light to green and back to white. Clearly, to cater for larger or varying numbers of iterations, this method becomes impractical, and a **loop construct** becomes essential. Figure 13.1 shows an LSC with a simple fixed loop, in which the light changes color to green and back to white five times.

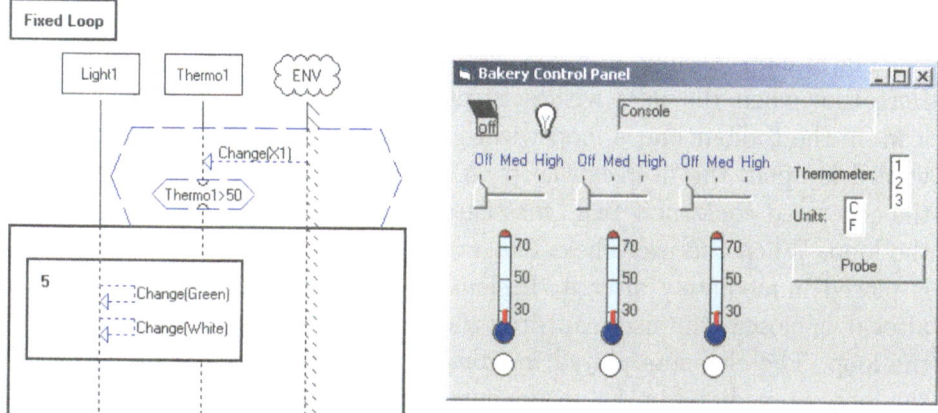

Fig. 13.1. A loop with a constant number of iterations

Now, suppose we want the light to flicker as long as the temperature remains above 50 degrees, rather than a fixed number of times. Here, the number of iterations is a priori unknown and depends on the dynamic behavior of the system. Figure 13.2 shows an LSC for this, in which the loop is unbounded (denoted by a '*'). An unbounded loop iterates forever, and can

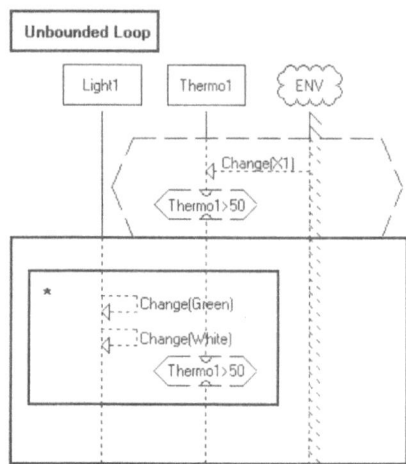

Fig. 13.2. An unbounded loop

be exited, like any other subchart, if a cold condition inside it evaluates to false. In this case, the loop will iterate and the light will keep flickering, as long as the condition is true, i.e., until the temperature decreases to below 50 degrees.

13.2 Playing In

Playing in loops is done in a way similar to that for if-then-else constructs. Here too, when the user wishes to play in a loop he/she clicks the loop icon on the toolbar and a loop wizard opens (see Fig. 13.3). As long as the wizard is open, the user can keep on playing in behavior as usual and all the generated constructs (e.g., messages, assignments, etc.) are placed inside the loop. When the user clicks **End Loop**, the loop is closed and the cursor is placed immediately after it. If elements are to be added inside the loop after it is closed, the user can drag the cursor and drop it anywhere inside the loop. The elements played in from that point on will be located inside the loop, immediately prior to the cursor.

Figure 13.4 shows an example in which the loop is fixed but the number of iterations is not given as a constant but is represented by a variable T. In

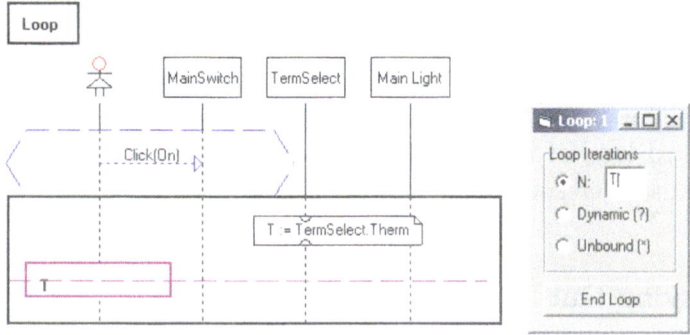

Fig. 13.3. Playing in loops

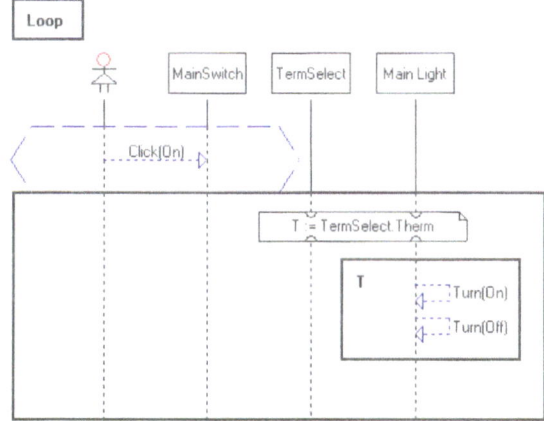

Fig. 13.4. Using a variable as the number of iterations

play-out, the loop will iterate T times, where T is the number of the currently selected thermometer in the thermometer selector. Had T changed its value within the loop body, this could not have changed the number of iterations, which is fixed in advance based on the value of T when the loop is started.

Three kinds of loops are defined in our extended language of LSCs. As we have seen, a **fixed loop** is performed a fixed number of times, which can be given as either a constant or as the value of a variable in the chart.

The second kind of loop is the **unbounded loop** we have seen, which is performed an a priori unknown number of times and is exited only when a cold condition in it evaluates to false. Note that placing a cold condition C at the beginning or end of an unbounded loop creates a *while C do* or *repeat until ¬C* construct, respectively. One can also place a cold condition with a SELECT statement in the loop, thus specifying that it should be iterated a nondeterministic number of times, governed by the probability given therein.

Having unbounded loops as part of the language is not only a matter of convenience, it increases the computational power of the language so that in the presence of integer variables it can express the full range of recursive functions; bounded loops can express only primitive recursive ones.

The third kind of loop is the **dynamic loop**, annotated with a '?', for which the user determines the number of iterations at run time.

13.3 Playing Out

During play-out, a loop can be entered, like any other subchart, only if all the instances that participate in it have reached their locations at the loop start. Before entering the loop, its maximal number of iterations is stored. If the loop is fixed, this number is known; if the loop is unbounded, the maximal number of iterations is set to infinity. If the loop is dynamic, the user is prompted on the fly for the desired number of iterations (see Fig. 13.5). The user specifies the desired number, and can also indicate whether

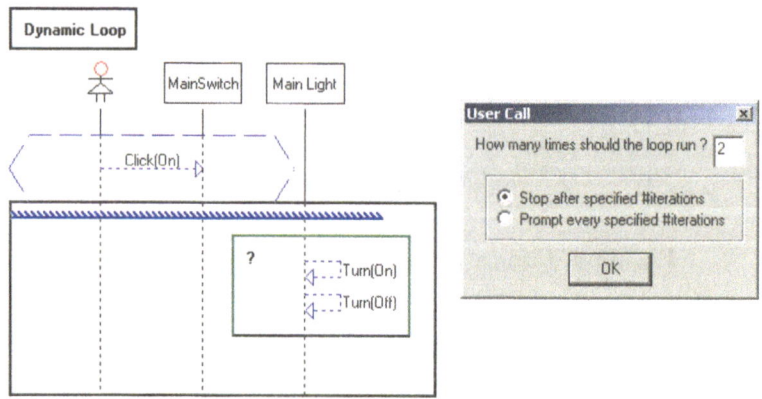

Fig. 13.5. Setting up a dynamic loop

he/she would like to be prompted again after that number of iterations is over. Dynamic loops are quite powerful when it comes to testing different behaviors of the system.

As the execution progresses and the loop is iterated, the Play-Engine provides runtime information to help the user monitor the course of execution. Figure 13.6 shows an example of such runtime information. In the top-left corner of the loop subchart, the Play-Engine indicates that the loop is currently in its second iteration out of three (denoted by 2/3), and in the top-right corner it shows the number of already completed iterations. The

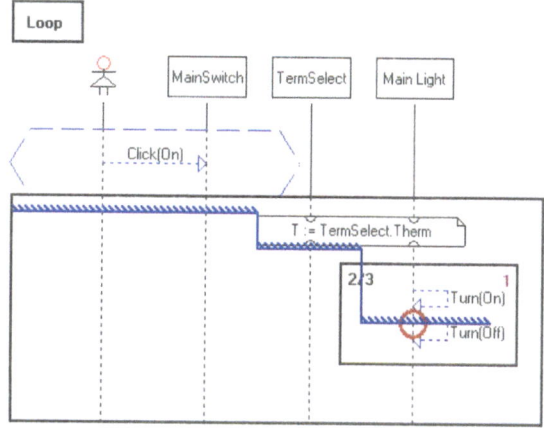

Fig. 13.6. Runtime information during loop execution

second number is important mainly because it is shown also after the loop has completed. Thus, one can know how many times each of the loops was actually performed, regardless of its expected, prescribed or maximal number of iterations. Recall that even fixed loops can be exited prior to completion due to cold conditions, so this information is never really redundant.

13.4 Using Variables Within Loops

Let us consider the LSC in Fig. 13.7. It states that after the user changes the state of the first switch three times, the console should display an appropriate message. Since we do not really care to what state the switch is set we have used a symbolic message with a variable S. But using a naive semantics here

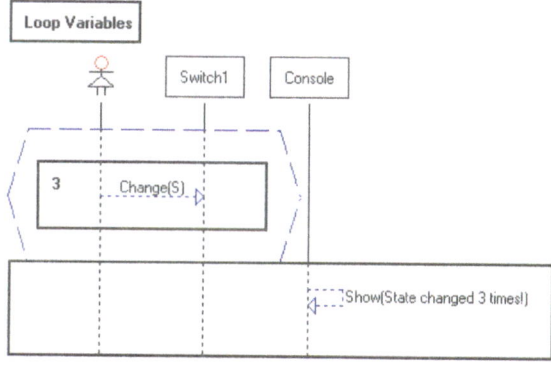

Fig. 13.7. Binding variables in loops

is problematic: Recall that as the execution progresses, variables in symbolic messages are bound to concrete values as a result of the various events being carried out. Suppose the user sets the first switch to *High*. As a result, a copy of this LSC is created, in which S is bound to *High*. If the user then changes the state of the switch to *Med*, this event will not be unified with the message in the LSC, since S is already bound to a different value. This is clearly not what we had in mind when playing in the LSC. And, indeed, we have chosen a semantics different from the one just described for variables within loops. According to the proposed semantics, every time the loop body is re-entered, all the variables that occur for the first time inside the loop (in the sense of Sect. 7.2) are freed from their bindings, thus enabling rebinding with new values. This way, the LSC of Fig. 13.7 behaves exactly as desired.

We free only variables that occur for the first time inside the loop, since if the variable used in the loop is the same as one used prior to the loop, the intention is to restrict its value in the loop to the one it was bound to before the loop was started. Figure 13.8 shows a similar LSC, except that now S is

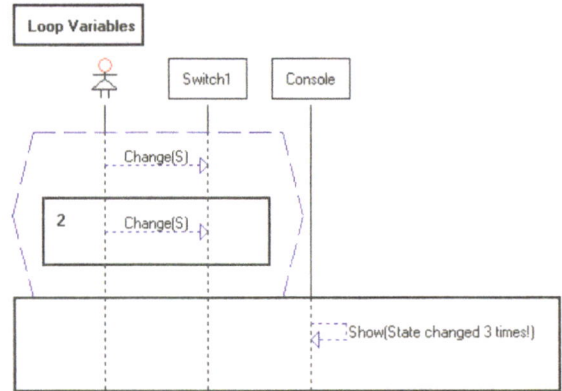

Fig. 13.8. Using an already bounded variable in a loop

bound outside the loop with the first state to which the switch is changed. In this case the two remaining occurrences can be unified only with events that change the switch to the same state, which is quite different from the meaning the semantics assigns to the LSC of Fig. 13.7.

13.5 Executing and Monitoring Dynamic Loops

In this section we discuss some of the delicate aspects concerning the differences between executing a loop in an LSC and monitoring it with respect to a given system run.

When it comes to fixed and unbounded loops, the mechanisms for executing and monitoring the loops are quite similar. In both cases, the loop is entered, and is iterated a fixed number of times, or until a false cold condition is encountered. The main difference is that when it is executing an LSC specification, the Play-Engine selects the events to be carried out, whereas when it is monitoring, the sequence of events is provided externally.

The major differences between executing and monitoring loops arise for dynamic loops. As explained, when a dynamic loop is encountered in a universal chart, the user is prompted for the desired number of iterations. This is true not only for loops within the main chart but also in the prechart. This may be somewhat counterintuitive, since in the prechart the Play-Engine *monitors* events and does not initiate them. So why can't the Play-Engine monitor a dynamic loop and determine on its own when the loop is over? Well, consider Fig. 13.9, in which, after the user flips the switch between on and off a number of times that is to be determined at runtime, the light should turn on. Suppose now that the user flips the switch to on and a copy

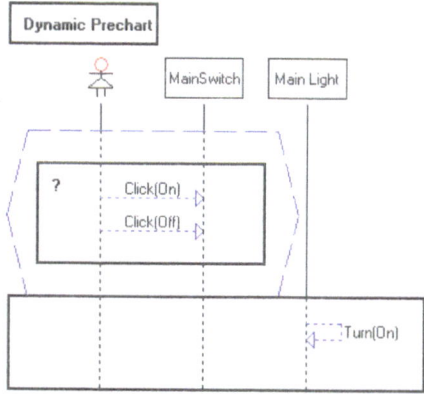

Fig. 13.9. A dynamic loop in the prechart

of this LSC is created. If the user now flips the switch to off, the Play-Engine faces the following dilemma: Should it wait for the user to continue flipping the switch or should it proceed to the main chart and initiate the event of turning the light on? Since the Play-Engine cannot resolve this dilemma on its own, the user is prompted for the number of iterations as soon as the loop is reached, even though we are in the prechart.

When a user is prompted for the number of iterations he/she may specify '0' to indicate that in the current run the loop should not be executed at all. In this case the loop is skipped and the Play-Engine continues executing the events that follow it. There could be cases, like the one in Fig. 13.9, where the loop is reached only after one of its minimal events has already occurred (since it is a minimal visible event in the prechart). In such cases the Play-Engine enters the loop and then prompts the user post factum for the desired number of iterations. If the user chooses '0', the chart is closed since the prechart was violated.

In contrast to executing universal charts, when it monitors an LSC the Play-Engine does not have to initiate execution of events at any point. Hence, dynamic loops can be used to further extend the expressive power of LSCs and to indicate sequences of events that repeat an a priori unknown number of times (including 0) but for which the number of iterations is not determined by any constant, variable or condition. Figure 13.10 shows an example of an existential LSC with two dynamic loops. This LSC can be activated either

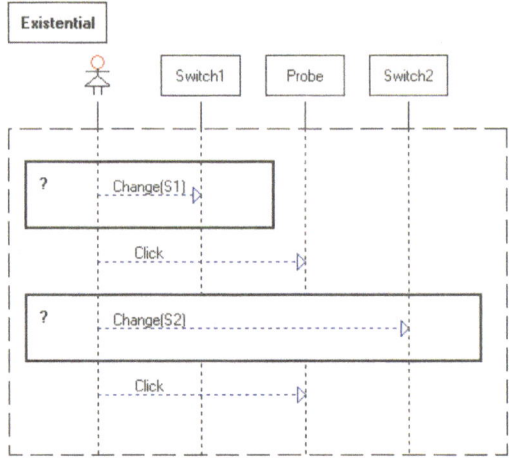

Fig. 13.10. A dynamic loop in a monitored LSC

by the user changing the state of the first switch, in which case the first loop is entered, or by the user clicking the *Probe* button, in which case the first loop is skipped, i.e., it is carried out 0 times. If the chart was started by the user changing the state of the switch, the Play-Engine will keep monitoring the incoming events and will exit the loop upon receiving the event of the probe button being clicked. In the same spirit, two probe-clicks alone also satisfy the chart, since both of the loops are carried out 0 times and the LSC completes.

Besides these differences between monitoring and executing dynamic loops, the Play-Engine is required to handle loop endings differently when they are executed and when they are monitored. During execution, when a loop reaches its end, the Play-Engine can immediately determine whether to exit the loop or return to its beginning. When monitoring dynamic loops, the Play-Engine waits before the loop end until the next event arrives. If the event matches a minimal event in the body of the loop, the execution continues from the loop's start. If it matches an event that immediately follows the loop, the loop is exited and execution continues from there.[1]

13.6 And a Bit More Formally ...

Following the semantics skeleton, we show the extensions and modifications needed to support the various kinds of loop constructs.

System Model and Events

Loop constructs are entirely specification oriented and therefore do not affect the system model.

LSC Specification

An LSC L is extended to contain loop constructs as follows:

$$L = \langle I_L, V_L, M_L, [Pch_L], A_L, C_L, SUB_L, ITE_L, LOOP_L, evnt, subchart, temp \rangle$$

where $LOOP_L$ is the set of loops in L.

A loop construct $Loop$ in $LOOP_L$ is defined as:

$$Loop = \langle Kind, \mu, Sub \rangle$$

where $Kind \in \{Fixed, Unbounded, Dynamic\}$ is the loop's kind, $\mu \in N \cup \{\infty\}$ is the loop's number of iterations, and $Sub \in SUB_L$ is the subchart containing the loop events to be iterated. We denote by $I_{Loop} = I_{Sub}$ the set of instances participating in the loop.

For the rest of this chapter, we use the term *dynamic loops* only for dynamic loops that appear in monitored LSCs. Dynamic loops in executable

---

[1] If the event matches both a minimal event in the loop's body and an event that follows the loop, our implementation chooses to go back to the loop start.

universal LSCs are considered to be fixed loops and we omit the technical details of the user being prompted (and reprompted) for their number of iterations.

We now extend E_L, the set of LSC events, with the hidden events of entering, exiting and iterating loops, and with the hidden event of skipping a dynamic loop:

$$\begin{aligned}
E_L = &(\{m \in M_L \mid m.M_s \in \Sigma_{FromUser} \cup \Sigma_{ToUser} \cup \Sigma_{FromEnv} \cup \Sigma_{ToEnv}\} \\
&\times \{Send, Recv\}) \\
&\cup (\{m \in M_L \mid m.M_s \in \Sigma_{Self}\} \times \{Send\}) \\
&\cup (Pch_L \times \{Start, End\}) \cup \{Completed\} \\
&\cup \{perform(A) \mid A \in A_L\} \cup \{eval(C) \mid C \in C_L\} \\
&\cup (SUB_L \times \{Start, End\}) \cup \{branch(ITE) \mid ITE \in ITE_L\} \\
&\cup (LOOP_L \times \{Start, End\}) \\
&\cup \{skip(Loop) \mid Loop \in LOOP_L \wedge Loop.Kind = Dynamic\}
\end{aligned}$$

Operational Semantics

As explained in the text, dynamic loops can be skipped (i.e., iterated 0 times), even if they contain visible events. When tracking a prechart of an executed universal chart or when monitoring any other chart, we have to be able to skip such loops at the occurrence of an event that follows. For this, we must refine the definition of a reachable event.

Definition 13.6.1 (reachable event). *A visible event e is reachable from a cut C if:*

1. *The event e is enabled with respect to C, or*
2. *There exists an enabled hidden event e' such that e is reachable from the cut $C' = AdvanceCut(C, e')$, or*
3. *There exists an enabled dynamic loop, Loop, such that e is reachable from the cut $C' = AdvanceCut(C, (Loop, End))$, or*
4. *There exists an enabled dynamic loop, Loop, such that $(Loop, End)$ is currently enabled from C and e is reachable from the cut $C' = AdvanceCut(C, (Loop, Start))$.*

The reachable events are therefore the events that: (1) are currently enabled; or (2) can become enabled by propagating some hidden events; or (3) can become enabled by skipping a dynamic loop; or (4) are minimal events in a dynamic loop, which is waiting just before its end location.

The transition relation $\Delta[\mathcal{S}_O, \mathcal{S}_C]$ is now extended with transitions for handling loop iterations and skipping (monitored) dynamic loops:

- If $e = \langle M, t \rangle$ (where $t \in \{Send, Recv\}$) then:

1. Set $Context \leftarrow \emptyset$.

2. If $\exists C^L \in \mathcal{S}_C$ and $\exists e' \in C^L.LSC$, such that e and e' are negatively level$_1$-unifiable and e' violates C^L, then set $\mathcal{S}_C \leftarrow \mathcal{S}_C \setminus \{C^L\}$. If $temp(C^L.Cut) = hot$, set $Violating \leftarrow True$.

3. For every universal LSC $L \in \mathcal{S}_O$ which has an event e', positively level$_1$-unifiable with e, as a minimal event in its prechart, create a copy of L, C^L, and set $\mathcal{S}_C \leftarrow \mathcal{S}_C \cup \{C^L\}$. Set $C^L.Mode = PreActive$ and set its cut by $C^L.Cut \leftarrow AdvanceCut(InitialCut(L), \langle Pch_L, Start \rangle)$. Unify the variables of e and e', by $Unify(e, e', Context)$. For each hidden event $e'' <_L e'$, apply $\Delta(e'')$.

4. For every existential LSC $L \in \mathcal{S}_O$ which has an event e', positively level$_1$-unifiable with e, as a minimal event in the chart body, create a copy of L, C^L, and set $\mathcal{S}_C \leftarrow \mathcal{S}_C \cup \{C^L\}$. Set $C^L.Mode = Check$, and set its cut to the beginning of the chart by $C^L.Cut \leftarrow BeginMainCut(C^L.LSC)$. Unify the variables of e and e', by $Unify(e, e', Context)$. For each hidden event $e'' <_L e'$, apply $\Delta(e'')$.

5. For every copy $C^L \in \mathcal{S}_C$ which has a reachable event e', positively level$_1$-unifiable with e, set its cut by $C^L.Cut \leftarrow AdvanceCut(C^L.Cut, e')$. Then, if $e' = \langle M, Send \rangle$, M is synchronous and $e'' = \langle M, Recv \rangle$, set the cut by $C^L.Cut \leftarrow AdvanceCut(C^L.Cut, e'')$. Unify the variables of e and e', by $Unify(e, e', Context)$. For each hidden event $e'' <_L e'$, apply $\Delta(e'')$.

- If $e = Completed(C^L)$ for some $C^L \in \mathcal{S}_C$, then set $\mathcal{S}_C \leftarrow \mathcal{S}_C \setminus \{C^L\}$.

- If $e = \langle Pch_L, End \rangle$ for some $C^L \in \mathcal{S}_C$, then set
$C^L.Cut \leftarrow BeginMainCut(C^L.LSC)$ and $C^L.Mode \leftarrow Active$.

- If $e = perform(A)$ for some $A \in A_L$ s.t. $C^L \in \mathcal{S}_C$, then set $C^L.Cut \leftarrow AdvanceCut(C^L.Cut, e)$ and set

$$A.V \leftarrow \begin{cases} A.C & \text{if } A.Type = constant \\ Value(A.P) & \text{if } A.Type = property \\ A.f(A.\lambda_f^F) & \text{if } A.Type = function \end{cases}$$

- If $e = eval(C)$ for some $C \in C^L$ s.t. $C^L \in \mathcal{S}_C$ then

1. If $value(C) = true$ then set $C^L.Cut \leftarrow AdvanceCut(C^L.Cut, e)$.

2. If $value(C) = false$ then

   a) If $subchart(C) \in \{ITE.Sub_T, ITE.Sub_E\}$ for some ITE then

   set $C^L.Cut \leftarrow AdvanceCut(C^L.Cut, (ITE, End))$

   b) If $subchart(C) = Sub \in SUB_L$ then

   set $C^L.Cut \leftarrow AdvanceCut(C^L.Cut, (Sub, End))$

c) If $subchart(C) = \bot$ then set $\mathcal{S}_C \leftarrow \mathcal{S}_C \setminus \{C^L\}$.

d) If $temp(C) = hot$ then set $Violating \leftarrow True$.

- If $e = branch(ITE)$ for some $ITE \in C^L$ s.t. $C^L \in \mathcal{S}_C$ then
  1. If $value(ITE.C) = true$ then set
     $C^L.Cut \leftarrow AdvanceCut(C^L.Cut, (ITE.Sub_T, Start))$.
  2. If $value(ITE.C) = false$ then

$$set\ C^L.Cut \leftarrow \begin{cases} AdvanceCut(C^L.Cut, (ITE.Sub_E, Start)) & \text{if } ITE.Sub_E \neq \bot \\ AdvanceCut(C^L.Cut, (ITE.Sub_T, End)) & \text{if } ITE.Sub_E = \bot \end{cases}$$

- If $e = (ITE.Sub_T, End)$ for some $ITE \in C^L$ s.t. $C^L \in \mathcal{S}_C$ then

$$set\ C^L.Cut \leftarrow AdvanceCut(C^L.Cut, (ITE, End))$$

- If $e = (ITE.Sub_E, End)$ for some $ITE \in C^L$ s.t. $C^L \in \mathcal{S}_C$ then

$$set\ C^L.Cut \leftarrow AdvanceCut(C^L.Cut, (ITE.Sub_E, End))$$

- If $e = (Sub, End)$ for some $Sub \in C^L$ s.t. $C^L \in \mathcal{S}_C$ then

$$set\ C^L.Cut \leftarrow AdvanceCut(C^L.Cut, (Sub, End))$$

- If $e = skip(Loop)$ for some $Loop \in C^L$ s.t. $C^L \in \mathcal{S}_C$ then

$$set\ C^L.Cut \leftarrow AdvanceCut(C^L.Cut, (Loop, End))$$

- If $e = (Loop, Start)$ for some $Loop \in C^L$ s.t. $C^L \in \mathcal{S}_C$ then

$$set\ C^L.Cut \leftarrow AdvanceCut(C^L.Cut, (Loop, Start))$$

  For every variable $V \in V_L$ that is used in $Loop$ for the first time, set $V.\omega \leftarrow \bot$.

- If $e = (Loop, End)$ for some $Loop \in C^L$ s.t. $C^L \in \mathcal{S}_C$ and $Loop.Kind \neq Dynamic$ then
  1. Set $\mu \leftarrow \mu - 1$.
  2. If $\mu > 0$ then

$$set\ C^L.Cut \leftarrow AdvanceCut(C^L.Cut, (Loop, Start))$$

  For every variable $V \in V_L$ that is used in $Loop$ for the first time, set $V.\omega \leftarrow \bot$.
  3. If $\mu = 0$ then

$$set\ C^L.Cut \leftarrow AdvanceCut(C^L.Cut, (Loop, End))$$

Since the events of entering, exiting and iterating loops are additional forms of hidden events, the procedures *step* and *super-step* handle them with no modifications. The procedure *monitor-event* has to be modified so that it does not propagate the hidden event of ending a dynamic loop, but rather leaves the cut positioned just prior to the loop end in order to be able to accept events that appear after the loop start as well as ones that appear after the loop end.

---

monitor-event(ev)

1. Apply $\Delta[\mathcal{S}_M, \mathcal{ML}](ev)$.
2. Compute the set of enabled events:

$$Enabled \leftarrow \bigcup_{C^L \in \mathcal{ML}} \{e \in E_L \mid enabled(e)\}$$

$$Waiting \leftarrow \bigcup_{C^L \in \mathcal{ML}} \{e \mid e = branch(ITE)\}$$

$$\cup \bigcup_{C^L \in \mathcal{ML}} \{e \mid e = (Loop.End) \wedge Loop.Kind = Dynamic\}$$

$$Enabled \leftarrow Enabled \setminus Waiting$$

3. If there is a *hidden* enabled event $e \in Enabled$, then
   a) Apply $\Delta[\mathcal{S}_M, \mathcal{ML}](e)$.
   b) Go back to 2.
4. Terminate monitor-event.

13.7 Bibliographic Notes

The original definition of the MSC standard [123] allows the specification of repeated interactions by means of a *loop* expression. The number of possible repetitions can be constrained by upper and lower bounds. Setting both bounds to be the same causes the loop to iterate an exact number of times, and setting the upper bound to infinity yields an unbounded loop. The number of iterations of fixed loops in MSCs can be specified with a constant only and not with a variable. Since conditions are not given a precise semantics with regard to the scope they are defined in, they cannot be used in MSCs to construct 'while-do' and 'repeat-until' constructs.

If an MSC contains a loop with proper upper and lower bounds, meaning that the former is larger than the latter, a system would satisfy this MSC only if the loop is iterated for a number of times that is in the specified range. However, the MSC standard does not say anything about the number of iterations that such a loop should be performed had we wished to take an executable approach like the one we have for LSCs. This is fine for MSCs, since they are oriented towards testing, but it is not enough for LSCs, which have to be executable.

As discussed in the bibliographic notes for Chap. 10, the MSC standard also describes a higher-level way of connecting MSCs, hierarchical MSCs (HMSCs). The underlying graph of an HMSC may contain cycles, thus allowing for the specification of loops, which are repeated sequences of bMSCs (basic MSCs). As is the case with subcharts, a major difference between a loop in an LSC and in an HMSC lies in the synchronization requirement. In LSCs, all the instances that participate in a loop synchronize at the beginning and end of the loop, while in HMSCs there is no such requirement. It has been observed in several papers, e.g., [10], that allowing processes to progress along the HMSC with each object being in a different node may introduce irregular behavior, and is the cause of undecidability of certain properties. Undecidability results and ways to restrict HMSCs in order to avoid such problems can be found in [9, 40, 57, 56].

14. Transition to Design

So far, we have seen how the play-in/play-out approach and its implementation in the Play-Engine help in the process of capturing and validating scenario-based behavioral requirements. As we have seen, the graphical user interface of the system is used extensively in both play-in and play-out. In the former the GUI objects are used to specify user actions and system reactions, and in the latter they are used to reflect the system reactions as the specification is executed, and to allow the user to input external events. We have also seen how existential LSCs can be used to specify system tests and how they can be monitored in the Play-Engine for successful completion. If we indeed want to think of our methodology and tool as being useful not only for requirements but also for specifying the system's actual implementable behavior, we have to talk about making a smooth transition from the requirements phase into the design phase. This chapter is devoted to discussing some of the issues raised by this possibility.

14.1 The Design Phase

In many development methodologies, the design phase begins with a requirements specification, usually given as a text document, following which scenarios are constructed (say, in some variant of sequence diagrams) to show the interaction between the objects comprising the system. The scenarios are considered to be an initial step towards formalizing the requirements. Using play-in and play-out, the designer is given a head start: He/she can begin the design phase with the requirements specification already given as a set of executed and debugged LSCs, describing the allowed, necessary and forbidden interactions between the system and its users and environment. This specification is thus highly suitable as a basis for the design phase.

Beginning with this LSC specification, we can imagine the design phase as consisting of the following activities, which would typically be carried out as part of an incremental and iterative (possibly spiral-like) process:

- Identifying 'internal' objects (i.e., objects that are not represented in the GUI of the system) and their properties. This activity is usually affected not only by the original behavioral requirements but also by other considerations, such as non-functional constraints, robustness of the design, design patterns, etc.
- Adding properties (e.g., state variables) to existing objects, both graphical and internal.
- Describing the interactions between the objects comprising the system in increasing levels of detail. To do this, the designer identifies the methods of each object, through which it can be called, and the parameters to be passed when invoking each of them. Then, existing LSCs and newly created ones are refined with method calls, interleaved with the original property changes of the objects. These method calls are used to show the control flow that triggers the changes in the various values of the properties.
- Refining objects into sets of sub-objects and composing (clustering) sets of objects into compound objects. During these processes, we allow the use of appropriate levels of detail in the inter-object scenarios, and preserve the meanings of these scenarios under the refinement and composition of objects.
- Constantly making sure that the design is consistent with the original requirements. This is usually done by maintaining some kind of traceability between the requirements and the design.

The following sections show how the play-in/play-out approach and the Play-Engine are extended to support most of these aspects in the transition from requirements to design. We do note, however, that although the issue of object refinement and composition is extremely important, we have not yet worked it into our methodology and implementation. This is one of the main topics for our future work; see Chap. 21.

14.2 Incorporating Internal Objects

Figure 14.1 shows a simple LSC stating that each time the user changes the state of the switch, the light should change its state accordingly. In the requirements analysis phase, one does not have (and usually does not wish) to be more specific than this. However, it is clear that the way the LSC is currently specified, we do not know how the light is notified about the user action and how it decides to turn on or off.

Let us assume that as a first step towards the design the user decides that the communication between the switch and the light will be carried via a new internal object — a *controller*. The Play-Engine allows the addition of

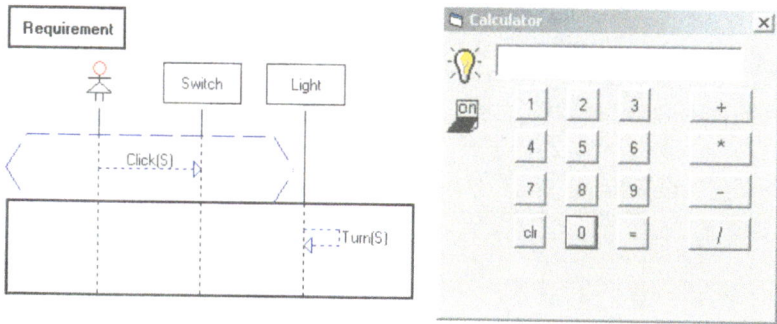

Fig. 14.1. High-level requirements

internal (i.e., GUI-less) objects on the fly. After creating an internal object, the user may specify properties for this object using an appropriate dialog. See Fig. 14.2. The user may specify a name for the newly created object (in

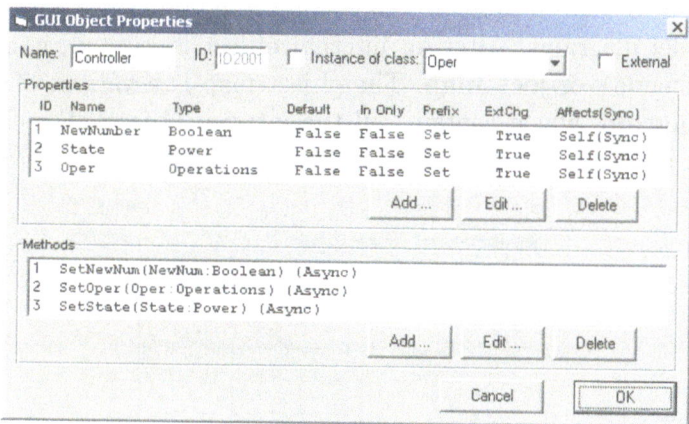

Fig. 14.2. Dialog for defining application objects

this case 'Controller') and define new properties for it. The bottom section of the dialog, termed 'Methods', is discussed in the next section.

After filling in all the details and closing the dialog, the object is added to the set of application objects and can be used in the LSCs and during play-in and play-out. Figure 14.3 states that after the switch is flipped, the information is first transferred to the controller, which sets its *state* property to be the same as the switch, and only then does it reach the light. Note that even the LSC of Fig. 14.3 does not specify *how* the information is passed between the objects, but only that it reaches an intermediate object that is responsible for forwarding it to the light.

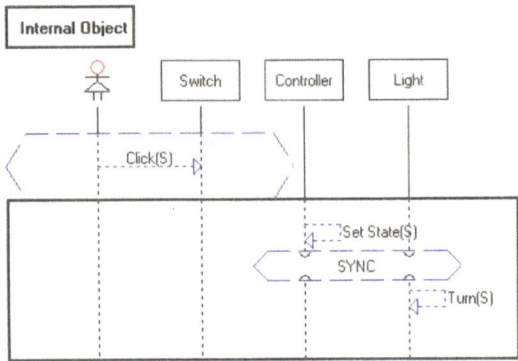

Fig. 14.3. Using an internal object in an LSC

One point needs to be addressed here: if an internal object is not represented in the GUI, how can it be used in playing in and playing out? We have decided to visually represent internal objects in a way similar to how they are represented in most object-oriented methodologies and tools — by object model diagrams. After an internal object is created, it is added to the Play-Engine's **object map**. The object map is a variant of an **object model diagram**, which contains all the internal objects. For each object, the object map displays its sets of properties (see Fig. 14.4). Properties of

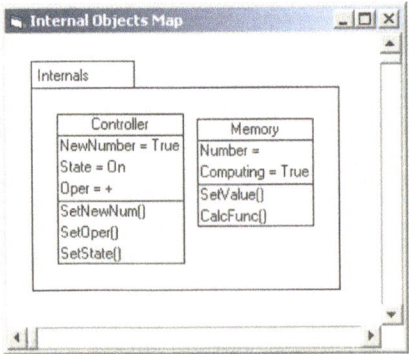

Fig. 14.4. Visualizing internal objects in an object map

internal objects are like properties of GUI objects, and are used to reflect various attributes of the objects. Since property values of internal objects cannot be visually reflected, as they can for graphical properties of GUI objects, the value of each property is written next to the property name in the object map, thus enabling the user to view the system state at a glance.

Since the process of transition into design may entail adding new properties to existing GUI objects, as well as to internal objects, the Play-Engine allows the addition of properties to GUI objects too. But since new properties of GUI objects are not known to the GUI application, they cannot be visually rendered in the GUI itself. To examine the current values of such properties, the user right-clicks an object and selects **Properties** from the popup menu. In response, the Play-Engine displays a list of all the object's properties together with their current values.

14.3 Calling Object Methods

Continuing with our example, suppose that the user now wishes to specify how the information is transferred from the switch that was clicked by the user, via the newly added controller, to the light, so it can change its state. We do this by adding methods to every object that needs to be called, and then calling these methods to transfer the desired information.

Methods are means for transferring data or control signals between objects. Each object can have an arbitrary number of methods, which other objects can call in order to transfer the required information. Every method has a name and a set of parameters defined over the application types. A method can be either synchronous or asynchronous, thus specifying whether the calling and the called objects synchronize when the method is called. The list of methods is shown both in the object dialog (as seen in the bottom section of the dialog in Fig. 14.2) and in the bottom part of the object rectangle in the object map (as seen in Fig. 14.4).

In our example, we add two identical methods $SetState(S)$, with S ranging over $\{On,\ Off\}$, one to the controller and one to the light. We then move into play-in mode and play in a call from the switch to the controller. Figure 14.5 shows the basic steps in playing in such interactions. The user first right-clicks the switch and selects **Call Other Object** (see Fig. 14.5(a)). As a result, the switch is highlighted and a tooltip appears above it showing "**From**" (see (b)). Next, the user right-clicks the target object. The Play-Engine knows that the user is currently in the process of specifying a method call, and therefore the opened popup menu contains a list of all the methods of the target object (see (b)). After one of the methods is selected, a dialog opens up, in which the user instantiates the parameters of the method with concrete values or with variables from the LSC (see (c)). When this process is over, a message going from the caller object to the called object is added to the LSC (see (d)).

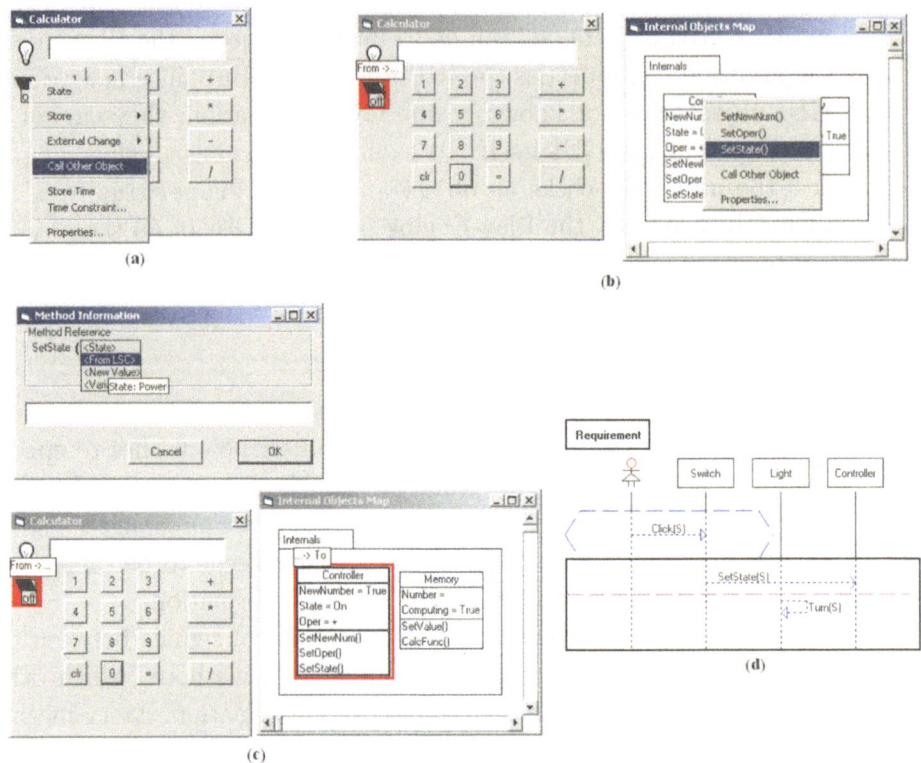

Fig. 14.5. Playing in interactions with internal objects

Repeating this process, but with the controller as the source and the light as the target, completes the desired interaction, resulting in the LSC of Fig. 14.6.

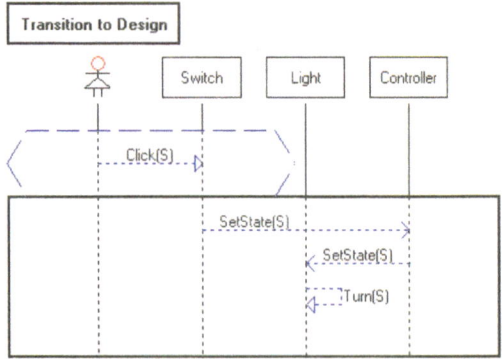

Fig. 14.6. From the Switch to the Light via the Controller

Adding this control flow information to a chart that initially contains only requirements-level interaction between the system and its environment helps fill the gap between *what* the system should do and *how* it does it. In our example, the 'what' part is given in the initial LSC, stating that the light should reflect the state of the switch, and the 'how' part is given in the final LSC by the interactions between the objects, which are interleaved with those appearing in the original scenario. These interactions show how seemingly unrelated events become related, by explicitly showing the sequence (or sequences) of events that can lead from one to the other.

As discussed at the beginning of the chapter, by starting with LSCs created by, or on behalf of, the user, developers can achieve direct traceability between the behavioral requirements and the design. Although the determination of internal objects, their properties and their methods can be affected by various considerations other than the behavioral requirements, these objects and properties should be integrated into the system in a way that satisfies the requirements that caused their addition but does not violate any other requirements. After internal objects are added and the interaction between objects is played in, the user may play out various scenarios and verify that the system still behaves as expected.

In addition to all of this, continuous consistency between the requirements and the design, as it evolves, can be checked using existential LSCs. Suppose that after the initial LSC of Fig. 14.1 is developed, a corresponding test is formulated, as shown in the existential LSC of Fig. 14.7. This LSC can

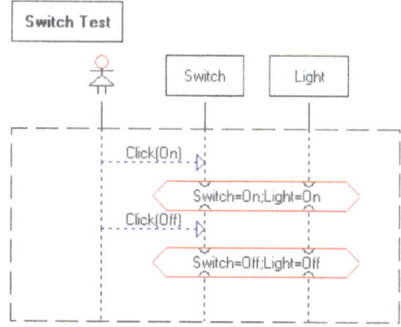

Fig. 14.7. Regression testing with existential LSCs

then be checked for satisfiability by clicking the switch to on and then to off, and verifying that the two hot conditions evaluate to true when they are reached. By leaving the existential chart unmodified, the designer may prove the correctness of the modified universal LSC (i.e., the one in Fig. 14.6) by repeating the same sequence of actions and showing that this sequence satisfies the test described by the existential LSC.

As shown in Chap. 12, a comprehensive set of system tests can be formulated as a set of existential LSCs. In the requirements phase, this set can be checked for satisfiability, and for each test a satisfying run should be recorded. At any point during the design phase this set can then be used for regression testing of the requirements, as follows. Each recorded run is modified to contain only external events (i.e., events that were generated by the user or the environment). These runs are then replayed, but with the new universal charts now driving the execution, and the original existential charts being monitored. Since the existential tests do not (and for this purpose, indeed should not) specify how the results are achieved but only that they are indeed eventually achieved, the new sequences of events generated by the modified universal LSCs should still satisfy the tests.

Another way of performing regression testing to check for consistency between the original LSCs — those on the requirements level — and the modified, design-level LSCs would be to keep copies of the original LSCs and then to simply execute the system, with both the old and the new LSCs driving the execution. Figure 14.8 shows the initial and the final LSCs of our example being executed simultaneously.

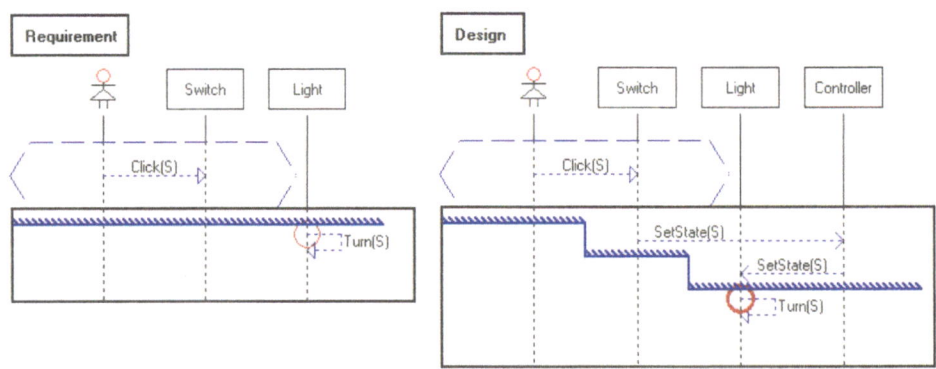

Fig. 14.8. Consistency between requirements and design

14.4 Playing Out

Messages representing method calls can be symbolic (just like the usual kind of message). To support their execution, our unification algorithm is extended, so that messages that are sent between the same two objects, and which represent the same method, can be unified if all their variables can be pairwise unified.

When LSCs containing method calls are played out, the Play-Engine highlights the involved objects and animates the interaction by drawing arrows between them. Thus, the play-out mechanism does not only let end-users validate requirements but can also be used beneficially for demonstrating, reviewing and debugging a design. Figure 14.9 shows how the interaction between objects is animated during play-out. Note that the arrows are not limited to being within the GUI application or the object map, but can run from one to the other. Send events are animated by arrows that start out with

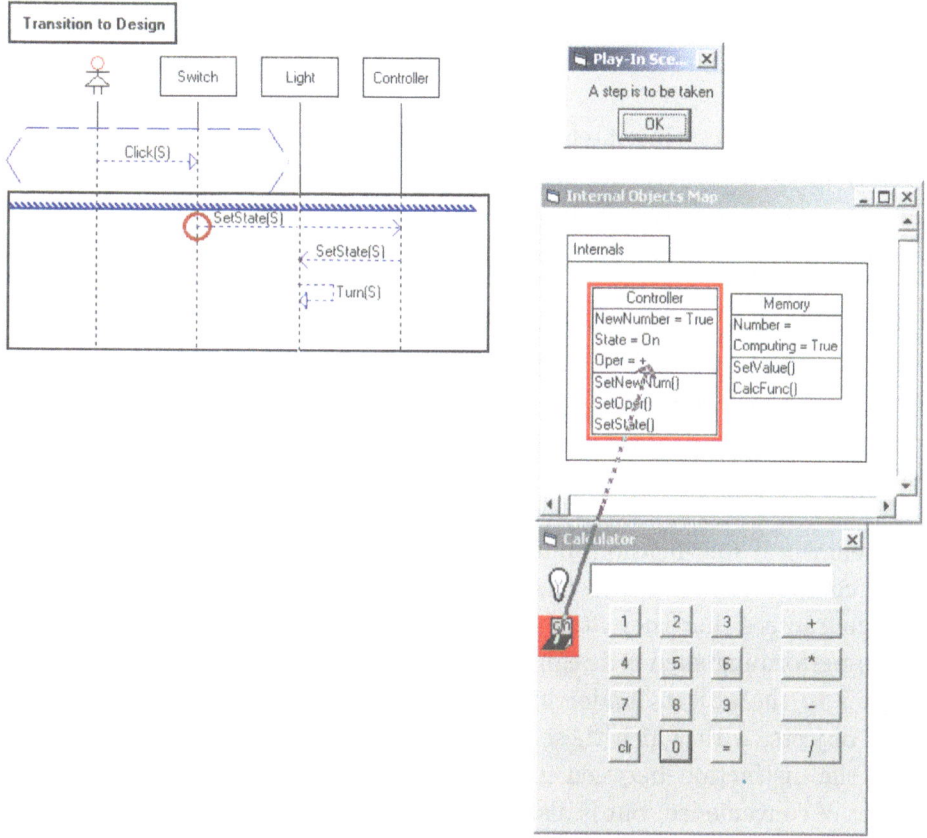

Fig. 14.9. Animating interactions between objects

a solid line (the sender) and end up with a dashed line (the receiver), while receive events will be drawn the other way around. Synchronous messages are shown as full solid arrows.

14.5 External Objects

Often, a reactive system works in the presence of other elements, besides the user who interacts with it. These might include other systems, components, machines, computers, sensors, and even other humans or elements from nature. The collection of all these elements is referred to as the system's *environment*. When playing in the required behavior of a reactive system, it is necessary to be able to express its interaction with this environment. As we have already seen, the Play-Engine allows the user to specify how the environment interacts with the system in a way similar to the interaction with the end-user. However, such interactions with the environment are limited to changes in object properties, and are thus suited to interactions with nature (e.g., the external temperature rising, devices breaking down, etc.), but less so to true communication with interfacing systems (e.g., receiving data or control signals).

The need to describe interactions with interfacing systems usually arises already in the requirements analysis phase, although there are cases where these aspects of the system may be ignored. For example, when specifying the behavioral requirements of a communication-guided missile, chances are that we cannot ignore the control signals received from the guiding control unit. In contrast, when specifying the requirements of an automatic teller machine (ATM), we could probably describe the ATM as an integral system, and describe the communication with the remote bank server at a later phase.

When it comes to design, it is often the case that the design of a system is carried out by more than one person, each responsible for a set of components. In such cases, every designer in the team is aware of the entire behavioral specification, but is allowed to refine the specification of only those components for which he/she is responsible, and must do so in a way that guarantees that they fit in correctly within the overall system behavior. While performing such a design task it is convenient for each team member to refer to the objects under his/her responsibility as internal, and to the other objects, with which these are to interact, as external. As we shall see next, the distinction between internal and external objects is not merely a matter of convenience, but is also reflected in the executable semantics of the language.

To support the aforementioned design tasks within the language of LSCs and the play-in/play-out approach, we first extend the LSC language with the ability to refer to external objects. Technically, within the Play-Engine, external objects are implemented as internal objects, i.e., non-GUI ones, and are distinguished from the usual internal objects by their **external** flag being set to true.

Having external objects within the specification entails more than just partitioning the external environment into its components and giving them names. In contrast to the external environment discussed in Chap. 5, external objects are not limited to changing property values of internal objects. External objects can have properties of their own, indicating their being in different states (e.g., active, ready for communication, etc.). They can also *call* system objects and be called by them, thus modeling the interaction with external systems.

Figure 14.10 shows an LSC, in which the switch instance represents an external object, and is therefore annotated with a small cloud.

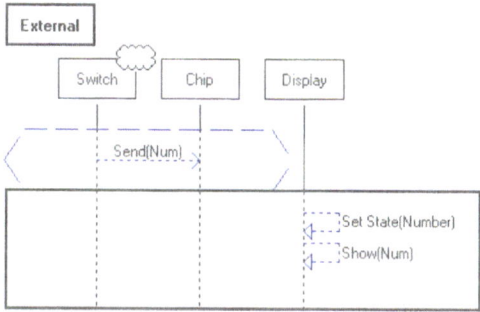

Fig. 14.10. External objects in LSCs

When playing out scenarios and testing the system's behavior, we would like to be able to control the behavior of external objects, much like we control the actions of the user and the external environment. As an example, consider the LSC in Fig. 14.11, which describes a simple interaction between two interfaces. Suppose that we are given the task of creating a detailed design for *Interface_2*. For simplicity, assume that this entails adding a single implementation object, *Impl_2*, and a simple interaction with it. The detailed design is given in the LSC of Fig. 14.12. Note that the interfacing object *Interface_1* is now considered external.

To check our design, we would now like to use the play-out techniques in the standard way. Recall, however, that property changes of internal objects and method calls between objects are not carried out by the user; rather, they are performed by the Play-Engine as part of its super-steps. In our example, we would like to activate the prechart of '*Detailed Design*' by initiating the call from *Interface_1* to *Interface_2*. If the actions of *Interface_1* were dependent upon the values of its properties, we would have also liked to be able to change these values, and thus control the behavior of this object.

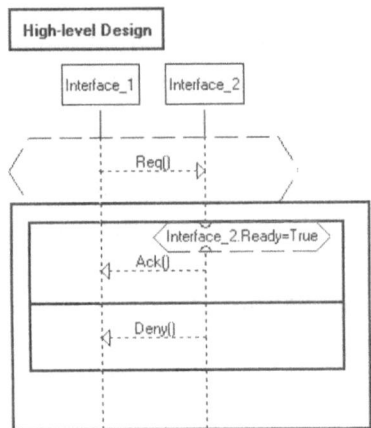

Fig. 14.11. High-level interaction between interfaces

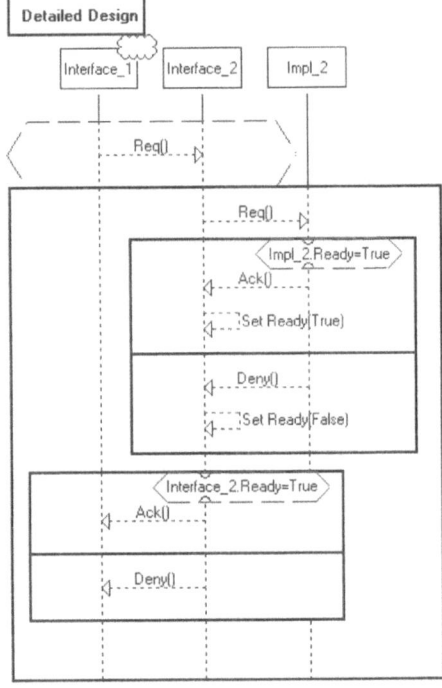

Fig. 14.12. Detailed design of Interface_2

To support this, the execution mechanism of the Play-Engine is modified so that it does not initiate events that originate from external objects, much as it does not initiate events from the user or the external environment. While playing out, the user can change property values of external objects and can initiate calls from external objects to objects that are internal to the system. Thus, it is the user who controls the behavior of external components and systems while the system under development is being executed and analyzed. This extension to the play-out mechanism provides a way for validating component-based requirements and designs, by allowing the independent execution of each part and then combining the LSCs in the various parts into a fully integrated requirements or design specification. Section 21.5 in our Future Work chapter describes our work on linking several Play-Engines together, and is particularly relevant to the above discussion.

14.6 And a Bit More Formally ...

Following the semantics skeleton, we show the extensions and modifications needed to support method calls, and internal and external objects.

System Model and Events

The system model is extended to include method calls and to distinguish between internal and external objects.

A method with n formal parameters is defined as:

$$Method = Name(D_1, D_2, \ldots, D_n)$$

where $Name$ is the method name and $D_i \in \mathcal{D}$ is the type of its ith parameter.

A class is modified to have a set of methods, through which its object instances can be called:

$$C = \langle Name, \mathcal{P}, \mathcal{M} \rangle$$

Next, an object can be declared as external:

$$O = \langle Name, C, \mathcal{PV}, External \rangle$$

where $External$ is a Boolean flag, set to true in external objects and to false in all other objects.

We now redefine a system message M_s to also contain method information if it represents a method call:

$$M_s = \langle Src, Dst, P, V, f, \lambda_f^F, m, \lambda_m^M, Symbolic \rangle$$

where $m \in \mathcal{M} \cup \{\bot\}$ is the method represented by the message and λ_m^M is a *method information structure* for m, defined as follows:

$$\lambda_m^M = \begin{cases} (V_1 \in m.D_1, \dots, V_n \in m.D_n) & \text{if } m \in \mathcal{M} \\ \bot & \text{if } m = \bot \end{cases}$$

If the message represents a method call $m \in \mathcal{M}$, then λ_m^M contains variables as actual parameters that replace the method's formal parameters. If M_s does not represent a method call, then $\lambda_m^M = \bot$. We require that each message represent either a property change or a method call:

$$\forall M_s : \ (M_s.P \neq \bot) \oplus (M_s.m \neq \bot)$$

Since method calls can also be synchronous and asynchronous, the definition of synchronous messages is modified to reflect this.

Definition 14.6.1 (synchronous system messages). *A message M_s is synchronous if $M_s.P \neq \bot \wedge M_s.P.Sync = true$ or $M_s.m \neq \bot \wedge M_s.m.Sync = true$. A self message is also synchronous.*

The alphabet of possible messages of $\mathcal{S}ys$ is extended to include messages going between objects within the system and not only between objects and the environment:

$$\begin{aligned} \Sigma \quad &= \Sigma_{FromUser} \cup \Sigma_{ToUser} \cup \Sigma_{FromEnv} \cup \Sigma_{ToEnv} \cup \Sigma_{Self} \cup \Sigma_{Calls} \\ \Sigma_{FromUser} &= \{M_s \mid Src = User \ \wedge \ P \in class(Dst).\mathcal{P}\} \\ \Sigma_{ToUser} &= \{M_s \mid Dst = User \ \wedge \ P \in class(Src).\mathcal{P} \ \wedge \ P.Affects = User \ \wedge \\ & \quad P.InOnly = False\} \\ \Sigma_{FromEnv} &= \{M_s \mid Src = Env \ \wedge \ P \in class(Dst).\mathcal{P} \ \wedge \ P.ExtChg = True \ \wedge \\ & \quad P.InOnly = False\} \\ \Sigma_{ToEnv} &= \{M_s \mid Dst = Env \ \wedge \ P \in class(Src).\mathcal{P} \ \wedge \ P.Affects = Env \ \wedge \\ & \quad P.InOnly = False\} \\ \Sigma_{Self} &= \{M_s \mid Dst = Src \ \wedge \ P \in class(Src).\mathcal{P} \ \wedge \ P.Affects = Self \ \wedge \\ & \quad P.InOnly = False\} \end{aligned}$$

The set of *system events*, $\mathcal{E}$, is extended accordingly:

$$\begin{aligned} \mathcal{E} = &((\Sigma_{FromUser} \cup \Sigma_{ToUser} \cup \Sigma_{FromEnv} \cup \Sigma_{ToEnv} \cup \Sigma_{Calls}) \times \{Send, Recv\}) \\ & \cup (\Sigma_{Self} \times \{Send\}) \end{aligned}$$

LSC Specification

The set of LSC events is extended to contain messages that represent interactions between system objects:

$E_L =$
$\quad (\{m \in M_L \mid m.M_s \in \Sigma_{FromUser} \cup \Sigma_{ToUser} \cup \Sigma_{FromEnv} \cup \Sigma_{ToEnv} \cup \Sigma_{Calls}\}$
$\qquad \times \{Send, Recv\})$
$\quad \cup (\{m \in M_L \mid m.M_s \in \Sigma_{Self}\} \times \{Send\})$
$\quad \cup (Pch_L \times \{Start, End\}) \cup \{Completed\}$
$\quad \cup \{perform(A) \mid A \in A_L\} \cup \{eval(C) \mid C \in C_L\}$
$\quad \cup (SUB_L \times \{Start, End\}) \cup \{branch(ITE) \mid ITE \in ITE_L\}$
$\quad \cup (LOOP_L \times \{Start, End\})$
$\quad \cup \{skip(Loop) \mid Loop \in LOOP_L \wedge Loop.Kind = Dynamic\}$

The notion of a message *affecting* a variable is extended. Now, an LSC message $M \in M_L$ *affects* a variable X also if the variable is used as a parameter in a method call.

Definition 14.6.2 (affecting a variable). *An LSC message $M \in M_L$ affects a variable X, if $M.M_s.V = X$ or $X \in M.M_s.\lambda_m^M$. An assignment $A \in A_L$ affects a variable X if $A.V = X$.*

Operational Semantics

The operational semantics is changed in two ways. First, the notion of message unification is extended to support method calls. Then, the set of external events is extended to include send events that originate from external objects, so that these events will not be candidates for execution in the procedure *super-step*.

We now extend the notion of unification to apply also to method calls, so that two method information structures are unifiable if they represent the same method and their variables are pairwise unifiable.

Definition 14.6.3 (method unification). *Two method information structures $\lambda_{m_1}^M$ and $\lambda_{m_2}^M$ are Q-unifiable (where Q is 'positively' or 'negatively') if:*

$m_1 = m_2$
$\quad \wedge \ \forall i : \ \lambda_{m_1}^M.V_i \text{ and } \lambda_{m_2}^M.V_i \text{ are Q-unifiable.}$

The message content Λ of a message M_s is modified to refer to methods when relevant.

Definition 14.6.4 (message content).

$$M_s.\Lambda = \begin{cases} M_s.\lambda_f^F & \text{if } \lambda_f^F \neq \bot \\ M_s.\lambda_m^M & \text{if } \lambda_m^M \neq \bot \\ M_s.V & \text{otherwise} \end{cases}$$

Definition 14.6.5 (message unification). *Two system messages*
$M_s = \langle Src, Dst, P, V, f, \lambda_f^F, m, \lambda_m^M, Symbolic \rangle$ *and*
$M'_s = \langle Src', Dst', P', V', f', \lambda_{f'}^F, m', \lambda_{m'}^M, Symbolic' \rangle$ *are Q-unifiable (where Q is 'positively' or 'negatively') if* $Src = Src', Dst = Dst', P = P', m = m'$ *and their contents are Q-unifiable.*

Since message variables may bind to values as a result of unifying different method information structures during execution, we add another unification procedure to handle such cases:

Unify(λ_m^M, $\lambda_m^{M'}$, Context)

1. For $i = 1, \ldots, n$:
   a) Unify($\lambda_m^M.V_i$, $\lambda_m^{M'}.V_i$, Context)

Having these definitions, the transition relation Δ supports method calls with no modifications. In Chap. 5, we defined the set of external events as send events that are initiated by the user or the environment:

$$External = \{ \bigcup_{L \in S} \langle m, Send \rangle \mid m.M_s.Src \in \{User, Env\}\}$$

We now modify this definition to include send events from all external objects. For brevity, we will refer to *User* and *Env* as external objects and will not treat them separately:

$$External = \{ \bigcup_{L \in S} \langle m, Send \rangle \mid m.M_s.Src.External = true\}$$

Having modified the set of external events, the procedure *super-step* remains unchanged.

14.7 Bibliographic Notes

Constructing a program from a requirements specification is the long-known general and fundamental **synthesis problem**. This chapter was devoted to discussing briefly a methodology, supported by the Play-Engine tool, for refining a set of requirements given as LSCs into a design also given as an LSC specification. Since we use the same language and the same pattern of thought for both phases, the synthesis problem becomes a lot easier. In the development scheme outlined in [43], an important facet is the ability to synthesize an intra-object implementation from the inter-object requirements. This is a whole lot harder than our LSC-to-LSC process, or the problem of generating lower-level code from an already intra-object system model (which is really but a high-level kind of compilation). The duality between the inter-object scenario style for requirements and the intra-object statechart style for design renders useful synthesis a truly difficult task.

There has been a lot of work on the limited case of state-machine synthesis from variants of classical message sequence charts. This problem is a lot easier than synthesis from LSCs, since MSCs do not enable expressing forbidden or mandatory behavior, so there is very little in the way of real constraints on behavior. Also, some of the synthesis papers do not even allow the system to be simultaneously in different charts, and so really relate to a single chart only. Work on synthesis from MSCs includes the SCED method [66, 67, 68], based on the algorithm of [15], and synthesis in the framework of ROOM charts [77]. Other relevant work appears in [108, 10, 18, 72]. New efforts on synthesis appear in [5, 119].

A lot of work has also been carried out on synthesizing state-based systems from requirements given in **temporal logic**. Due to the expressive power of temporal logic, this problem is closely related to synthesizing from LSCs. The early work on such synthesis considered **closed systems** that do not interact with the environment [83, 34]. In this case, a program can be extracted from a constructive proof that the formula is satisfiable. This approach is not suitable for synthesizing **open systems** that interact with the environment, since satisfiability implies the existence of an environment in which the program satisfies the formula but the synthesized program cannot restrict the environment. Later work in [98, 96, 1, 121] dealt with the synthesis of open systems from linear temporal logic specifications. The realizability problem is reduced to checking the non-emptiness of tree automata, and a finite state program can be synthesized from an infinite tree accepted by the automaton. The problems of realizability checking and synthesis from linear temporal logic have been shown to be 2EXPTIME-complete. Work on synthesis from branching temporal logics, based on alternating tree automata

[73], show that the synthesis problems for CTL and CTL* are EXPTIME and 2EXPTIME complete, respectively. In [97] synthesis of a distributed reactive system is considered. Given an architecture — a set of processors and their interconnection scheme — a solution to the synthesis problem yields finite state programs, one for each processor, whose joint behavior satisfies the specification. It is shown in [97] that the realizability of a given specification over a given architecture is undecidable. Previous work assumed the easy architecture of a single processor, and then realizability was decidable.

Turning to LSCs, there is the work described in [65], which synthesizes a timed Büchi automaton from a single LSC (and code can then be derived from the automaton). A more general approach appears in [46], where the synthesis problem for a multiple-chart LSC specification is tackled by first defining consistency, then showing that an LSC specification is consistent iff it is satisfiable by a state-based object system, and finally synthesizing a satisfying system as a collection of finite state machines or statecharts. A global automaton for the entire system is constructed, which is then distributed between the objects in the system. Construction of the global automaton in [46] causes a state explosion problem, which must be tackled somehow in order for the algorithm to become practical. Also, the LSCs in [46] are restricted: for example, conditions are excluded and specific restrictions on the interaction of the environment with the system are assumed.

Another approach that tries to bridge the gap between requirements and design by using a common representation for both is called **genetic software engineering** (GSE) [33], in which a requirement written in natural language is formalized by a 'behavior tree'. All such trees are then integrated into a single tree. This comprehensive system behavior tree is transformed by a variety of manipulations and projections into a components architecture diagram, and then into many component trees, each describing the internal behavior of a single component. GSE is also similar to our approach in that it uses a richer specification language than conventional sequence charts (e.g., it can specify anti-scenarios).

The software cost reduction (SCR) method described in [55] also allows the specification and simulation of requirements for reactive systems. The SCR method provides a tabular notation for specifying the required relation between system and environment variables and also uses a GUI in the final phase of simulation. According to this method, requirements are first described using nondeterministic and possibly incomplete relations between variables, and then the specification is modified, with the aid of an automated tool, to be deterministic and can then be simulated. The process of refining the requirements and making them deterministic can also be viewed as a kind of design. SCR is different from our work in the languages used (i.e., tables of variables vs. visual notations) and in the requirement that the final model should be deterministic.

A methodology supported by a tool called LTSA for specifying and analyzing labeled transition systems (LTSs) is presented in [81, 114]. This tool works with an animation framework called SceneBeans [99], yielding a nicely animated executable model. The model has to be an LTS, which is more akin to the intra-object statecharts than to inter-object sequence based behavior, and it will usually be larger and more detailed than sequence charts. The behavior can be either written in FSP [80] and compiled into LTSs, or described as MSCs and transformed using a synthesis algorithm into LTSs [114]. An interesting idea would be to use SceneBeans as an animation engine to describe the behavior of internal (non-GUI) objects in our Play-Engine.

15. Classes and Symbolic Instances

In Chap. 7 we showed how scenarios can be generalized using symbolic messages. Symbolic messages are but one aspect of defining generic scenarios — the simpler one. This chapter addresses symbolic object instances, which is the more complicated and more powerful aspect of genericity.

Many systems feature multiple objects that are instances of the same **class**, which is one of the central maxims of the object-oriented paradigm. For example, a communication system contains many phones, and a railroad control system has many trains and terminals and possibly also many distributed controllers. We would like to be able to specify inter-object scenario-based behavior in a general way, on the level of classes and their parameterized instances, not necessarily restricting them to concrete objects. Not surprisingly, the issue of executing such behavior is quite subtle, since figuring out exactly what is going on, and in which objects, must be continuously done on the fly. In this chapter, we extend the LSC language with symbolic instances and discuss playing in and playing out the resulting specifications, including the delicate semantic issues that arise.

15.1 Symbolic Instances

Consider a telephone network consisting of four phones, one central switchboard and four channels, each connecting one phone to the switch. Figure 15.1 shows a graphical user interface for this system. Now, suppose we would like to say that for every phone, when the 'C' button is clicked, the display should be cleared. Figure 15.2 shows an LSC describing this requirement for *Phone1*. To specify the same requirement for the other telephones, the LSC should be replicated for each phone. This may become very inconvenient and inefficient when the number of phones is large, and may also become impossible in systems where the number of phones is unknown (dynamic creation and destruction of objects) or in parameterized systems where the number of phones is fixed, but is given as a parameter.

To solve these problems and to enable the creation of more compact LSC specifications, we introduce **symbolic instances**. Recall that every object

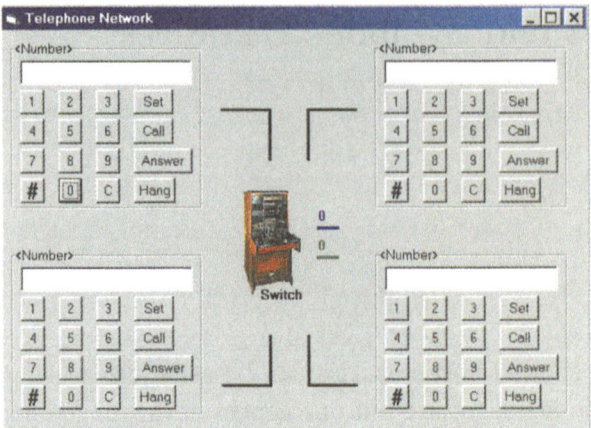

Fig. 15.1. NetPhone: the GUI for a telephone network

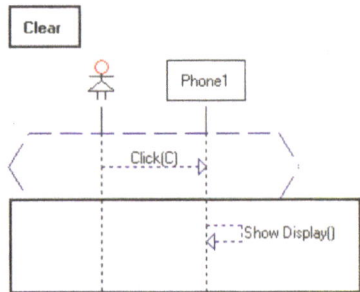

Fig. 15.2. A concrete scenario for clearing a display

in our system model is an instance of some specific class. A symbolic instance represents an entire class rather than one concrete object, and can bind to concrete objects at runtime. Figure 15.3 shows an LSC where one of the instances is symbolic and represents the class *Phone* (denoted by 'Phone::'). The chart states that its scenario should hold for every actual phone of class *Phone* in the system, regardless of the number of actual phones and whether these phones are static or were created dynamically during the system run.

15.2 Classes and Objects

Before we get into the more complex features of symbolic instances, let us spend some time on how classes and objects show up in the play-in/play-out methodology. Classes in object-orientation are used to describe sets of objects that share a common behavior. The objects themselves are commonly referred to as the class instances. Classes are usually introduced in the design

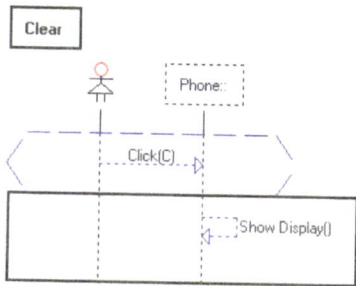

Fig. 15.3. A generalized scenario for clearing the display of any phone

phase, where the behavior of each class is given in an intra-object style, say, using a statechart or code, thus describing how each of the objects in the class behaves under different circumstances.

In the play-in/play-out approach, we are not interested in how each of the objects behaves as an independent entity, but, rather, in how a set of objects interacts in an inter-object style to satisfy certain desired (or undesired) scenarios. Therefore, classes in our approach serve more as interfaces, i.e., as place holders for sets of objects that are interchangeable in the specified scenarios. Put another way, classes are not used to describe the overall common behavior of sets of concrete objects, but, more operationally, to specify that in certain scenarios any concrete object from the set of class instances can be used, and that the scenario should still hold (or that a forbidden scenario is not allowed to hold for any instance of the class).

The Play-Engine provides several ways to create classes and objects and to associate them with others. A class can be created from scratch, or can be based on an already existing object. In the former case, the user names the class and specifies the class properties and methods. In the latter case, the class properties and methods are derived from those of the object on which the class is based. Creating classes based on existing objects is very useful in cases where the GUI application comes with sets of similar objects, and one would like to handle them in identical ways. Note that a class is not restricted to have either GUI objects as instances or internal objects, but may contain instances of both kinds. For example, in our telephone system, we could create a 'backup' switch as an internal object and then let both the GUI switch and the internal switch be instances of a *Switch* class.

An alternative way to associate objects with classes is to start with a class and then create objects based on that class. After creating some classes, the concrete objects may be associated with them via class property dialogs. The Play-Engine supports the creation of (multiple) internal objects using a single mouse click. Currently, it supports one level of classes and one level of objects, but this could be easily extended to support class inheritance, by defining a class hierarchy and associating each object with the class from which it is derived. A symbolic instance representing a class C can then bind to a concrete object O if O is either an instance of C or is an instance of a class C' that (indirectly) inherits from C.

15.3 Playing with Simple Symbolic Instances

Specifying that a certain instance represents a class rather than a concrete object is done at the end of playing in the scenario. Thus, the scenario is first played in just as in the non-symbolic case. When this is completed, the user selects the desired instance and turns it into a symbolic one by choosing Symbolic from the instance popup menu (see Fig. 15.4).[1]

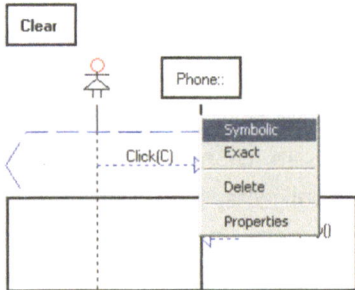

Fig. 15.4. Declaring LSC instances to be symbolic

As for playing out, we have shown in previous chapters that when a system event occurs, it is unified with the relevant LSC events. With symbolic instances, the extended unification principle we will be using is obtained by relaxing the requirement for identical senders and receivers: From now on, we do not require that the senders of the two events should be the exact same object, but we allow one of them to be a class to which the other belongs. The same holds for the message's receivers.

The execution mechanism is now modified as follows. When an event e occurs, the precharts of universal charts are scanned for minimal events that can be unified with e according to the new definition. Note that since e has occurred, its sender and receiver are already bound. If a unifiable event is found, a copy of the relevant universal chart is created and the symbolic

---

[1] At the time of writing (February 2003) we are in the process of modifying the Play-Engine so that playing in will be possible even when some of the instances in the chart are symbolic.

sender and receiver instances (if they exist) are bound to the actual sender and receiver, respectively. The same holds for events located in precharts of already created copies. Thus, events associated with symbolic instances cannot be carried out as such; events actually carried out must be in fact connected to actual objects. After a symbolic instance binds to a concrete object it remains bound to it until the LSC completes.

15.4 Symbolic Instances in the Main Chart

Suppose that we would like our phone to have the property that any digit the user clicks will be transmitted over the channel appropriately associated with the phone. Simply adding a symbolic instance representing a *Channel::* is not good enough, since there is a major difference between the way the phone and channel symbolic instances are identified in this scenario. The *Phone::* instance is bound to an actual phone as the result of a user action. The channel, however, should be bound by the Play-Engine's execution mechanism (not by the user), so that the message from the actual phone is sent via the correct actual channel without the need for a user-triggered action during execution. What we need here is the information as to which channel should bind to the *Channel::* symbolic instance.

One option for obtaining this information is to use static binding, derived from an object model that can have each phone associated with a channel by a special relationship denoted by *itsChannel*. This information can then be used in the LSC. We suggest a somewhat more general approach, using **binding expressions**, which can involve any available properties of the instance. If the first event involving a symbolic instance is in the prechart, the instance will be bound to an actual object as the result of unification with some other event, but if the event is in the chart body the execution mechanism should be able to trigger it, and the object to be bound with the instance should be identified using a binding expression, as follows.

Figure 15.5 shows how the *Channel::* instance is specified as binding with the actual channel associated with the phone (the example assumes that this association is defined by the use of a common ID). After the *Phone::* instance is bound, the assignment can be performed and the value of the *ID* variable is determined, following which the binding expression of the *Channel::* instance (shown as .ID = ID in the small oval above the instance name[2]) can be evaluated and the appropriate channel is bound. A binding expression is evaluated as soon as all the variables it uses are bound.

---

[2] The '.' preceding the ID property indicates a self reference.

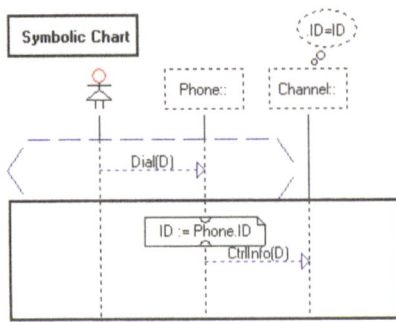

Fig. 15.5. Binding expressions for symbolic instances

Recall that in order to turn an instance into a symbolic one, the user right-clicks it and selects the **Symbolic** option from a popup menu. To support symbolic instances that are to be bound by the execution mechanism, upon making this selection the Play-Engine checks whether the first event of the instance is located in the prechart or in the chart body. If the event is in the chart body, a wizard opens up, with which the user may specify the binding expression for the symbolic instance (see Fig. 15.6). A binding expression —

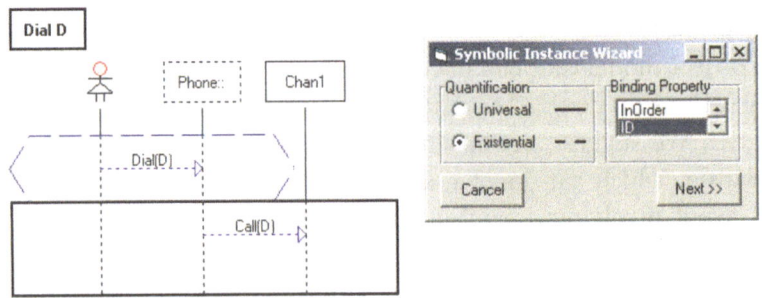

Fig. 15.6. A wizard for specifying binding expressions

like a basic expression in a condition construct — is of the form P $Oper$ RHS, where P is a property of the class represented by the symbolic instance, $Oper$ is a comparison operator, and RHS may be a constant value, a variable or a function applied to some specified parameters.

The binding-expression approach can be used to associate objects using any navigation expressions derivable from an object model diagram. We have not implemented this feature yet, since our Play-Engine has not yet been set up to fully support object model diagrams with general object associations, but we definitely plan to do so in the near future. For each such navigation association, a property can be automatically extracted (e.g., *itsChannel* would be derived in the case of a one-to-one association between a phone and its channel, *itsChannel$_i$* for the ith channel in the case of a one-to-many association, etc.).

15.5 Quantified Binding

Nothing we have said so far forbids the situation where a binding expression is satisfied by more than one object. This raises the options of the engine choosing one object at random on the fly, or treating such cases as errors, or somehow binding to all satisfying objects. Since there are cases where we would like only one instance to bind and others for which we would like them all to bind (see example below), we have decided to allow both possibilities, in the hot/cold spirit of the original definition of LSCs: The association of a symbolic instance with a binding expression can be made existential or universal. In the existential case (denoted by a dashed instance header and expression oval), one of the objects satisfying the binding expression is chosen at random and the instance is bound to it, and in the universal case (denoted by solid lines) a new copy is created for each satisfying object.

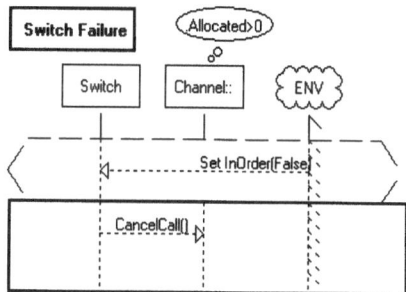

Fig. 15.7. Using universally quantified symbolic instances

The LSC in Fig. 15.7 shows the power of this approach. Whenever the central switch becomes out of order (in our example, this can happen as a result of some external environment stimulus), we want it to send a *CancelCall* message to all the channels that are currently allocated to a conversation. This is done using a universally quantified *Channel::* instance associated with a binding expression that is true for all allocated channels (no matter how many channels the system has and no matter how many of them are allocated). Figure 15.8 shows one copy of this LSC immediately before the symbolic channel instance binds to a concrete channel. When the binding expression

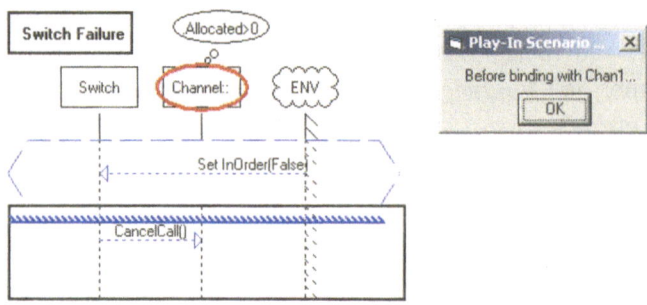

Fig. 15.8. Binding an instance during play-out

is evaluated, a different copy is created for each satisfying object. These LSC copies are then added to the set of active copies and continue executing as if they were not created from the same original chart.

15.6 Reusing a Scenario Prefix

Figure 15.9(a) raises an interesting issue concerning multiple bindings of a symbolic instance. The LSC in the figure states that if some phone sends the message *Call(1)* to the switch and then some other[3] phone sends the same message to the switch, the switch sends an error message to the second phone. By way of illustration, suppose *Phone1* is the first to send the message to the switch. As a consequence, the left-hand instance in the chart is bound to *Phone1*. Now, *Phone2* sends the message to the switch, the right-hand instance binds to *Phone2*, and the chart completes its execution by sending the error message from the switch to *Phone2*; see Fig. 15.9(b). This is fine.

Now suppose that a third phone, *Phone3*, sends the same message to the switch. The pair of events of *Phone1* and then *Phone3* sending the same message satisfies the prechart of the LSC in Fig. 15.9(a), and the chart body should therefore be executed. But this is a problem since after binding the right-hand instance to *Phone2*, the LSC copy completes execution and stops existing, and the first event of *Phone1* sending the message is 'lost', making it impossible for a second event to cause another satisfaction of the same chart.

We solve this problem as follows. When an instance in an already activated LSC copy is bound to an object as the result of an event, the binding and consequent propagation of the execution are carried out in a new separate copy (in this case Fig. 15.9(b)). In addition, the original copy is left open, with the cut positioned as it was in the first active copy before the binding,

---

[3] The second calling phone must be different from the first one, recalling that an object cannot be represented by more than one instance in an LSC.

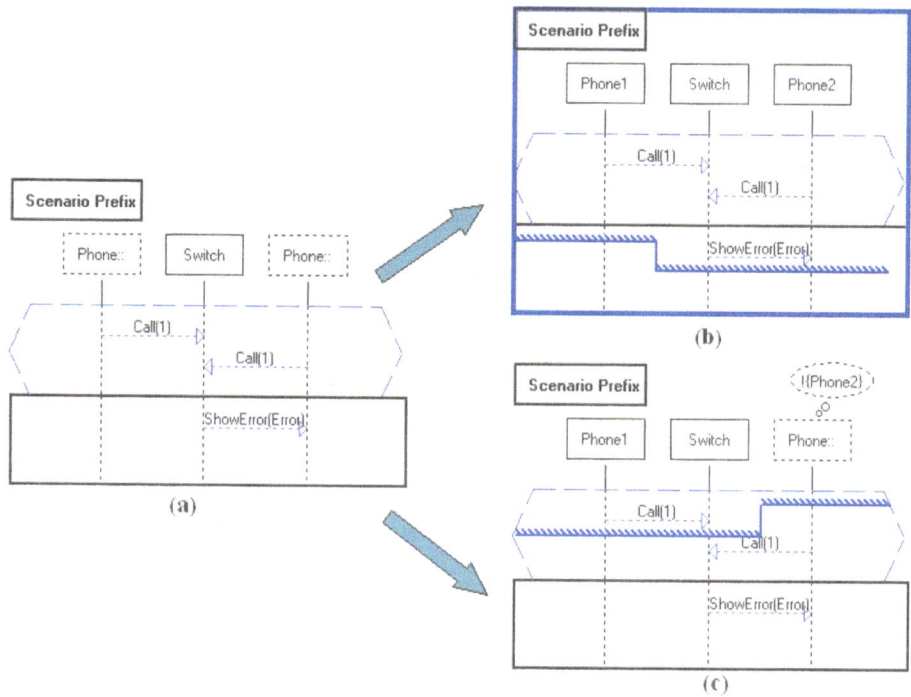

Fig. 15.9. Retaining scenario prefixes for reuse

but with the symbolic instance in this remaining copy being restricted in a binding expression to not bind to the same object again. The original copy of Fig. 15.9(a), with its new binding expression, is shown in Fig. 15.9(c). In this way, prefixes of scenarios are kept open for reuse. Proceeding with our example, when *Phone3* sends the message to the switch, a new copy is created, based on the original copy of Fig. 15.9(c), in which *Phone3* is bound to the right-hand instance. Then, in the original copy of Fig. 15.9(c), *Phone3* is added to the set of objects to which the right-hand instance cannot bind, thus making it possible for yet another phone to bind to this instance. By the way, during this described scenario, additional LSC copies are created. For example, each sending of *Call(1)* by *Phone2* and *Phone3* is also a minimal event and therefore causes the creation of new copies of this LSC; also, sending *Call(1)* by *Phone3* after *Phone2* completes the copy created when *Phone2* sent the message, etc. For clarity, we have focused here only on some of the copies.

If the engine determines that the set of forbidden objects of a symbolic instance (together with the objects of the same class that are already present in the chart and therefore cannot bind to the symbolic instance) becomes equal to the set of all objects in the system that are instances of the same class, the LSC copy is closed, since it has a symbolic instance that cannot bind to any more objects.

The same mechanism is adopted also for events that cause violation of a prechart. If an event e associated with object O occurs, and is unifiable with an event e' associated with a symbolic instance I (among other things, this means, of course, that O is an instance of the class represented by I), and e' is not enabled, this should be a violation. However, for the reasons discussed earlier, we want the scenario prefix to be kept open for other objects to bind to later. Therefore, a new copy is created, in which I is bound to O, and this copy is violated and closed.[4] The original copy adds O to the set of restricted objects of I, thus forbidding O to bind to I later on in the execution.

15.7 Symbolic Instances in Existential Charts

In Chap. 12 we saw how existential charts can be used to specify system tests and how they are monitored for successful completion. When an LSC is monitored, its events are propagated when matching events are generated by the tested system. Since the events that are generated by the system are actual events, in which the sending and receiving objects are concrete and known, there is no need for binding expressions in existential LSCs, and the symbolic instances bind with concrete objects only as a result of system events.

Now, a universal LSC can also be monitored, but since when it is created we do not specify whether it is going to be used for execution or monitoring or both, binding expressions are used anyway. Therefore, even in the case of monitoring a universal chart, instances can bind to concrete objects in between system events, as a result of evaluating binding expressions.

15.8 An Advanced Example: NetPhone

Using the NetPhone GUI and the play-in methodology, one can specify a variety of behaviors for the telephone network. In this section we show a simple, but non-trivial example of describing a requirement for this system, which strongly utilizes symbolic instances. The requirement, which involves a phone setting its own number, is as follows:

---

[4] Creating a copy, violating it and closing it is done so that the user can be visually notified of the effects of this most recent event.

> When the user dials a number and then clicks the Set button, then:
> 1. If the number is already occupied by another phone an error message is shown.
> 2. Otherwise, the number is associated with the current phone as its telephone number, and is stored in the database as such. The number is also displayed in the top-left corner of the phone's GUI.

Since our GUI does not contain a database object, we first add it as an internal object, called *PhoneDB*, and we can then play in the requirement. We now discuss this behavior in some detail, since it entails a chain of messages going from the phone to the switch, from there to the database, and then back to the phone. Note that in our model each phone is associated with a unique ID. This ID serves only to distinguish between the phone objects, and is different from the phone's number, which is used to call the phone from other phones. The channels are also associated with unique IDs that serve to distinguish between them, and it will be convenient to associate each phone with the channel that has the same ID. Other 1–1 relations between phones and channels could have been established in various different ways.

The LSC '*Click Set*' (Fig. 15.10(a)) shows that when the user clicks the *Set* button the phone's ID number, *Phone.ID*, is stored in the variable *ID* and the currently displayed number is stored in *N*. The phone then calls the switch's *SetNumber* method with *ID* and *N*. The LSC '*Verify Number*' (Fig. 15.10(b)) shows that when *some* phone (the instance is symbolic but dashed) calls the switch's *SetNumber* method with parameters *ID* and *N*, the *PhoneDB* is searched for a phone ID associated with the number *N* (denoted by the implemented function *RetrieveKey*). If the result returned in the *PhoneDB* state variable *QResult* is the empty string(denoted by no value in the condition), then no phone is associated with this number, and the switch therefore asks the *PhoneDB* to associate the phone's *ID* with the number *N* and to store this information in the database. Otherwise, if the retrieved ID is not the same as the initiating phone ID, the number *N* is already associated with a different phone, and an error message should be shown on the initiating phone's display. LSC '*Set in DB*' (Fig. 15.10(c)) shows that when the switch asks the *PhoneDB* to associate the phone that has an ID equal to the number stored in the variable *ID* with the number stored in the variable *N*, the *PhoneDB* actually stores the information in the DB (using an implemented function). If the operation was successful, the switch sends *AckNumber* to the phone, which has an ID equal to *ID*. Otherwise, an error message is sent to this phone, indicating that the operation of linking the ID with the new number has failed. The final LSC, '*AckNumber*' (Fig. 15.10(d)), simply states that when a phone receives the *AckNumber* message with the acknowledged

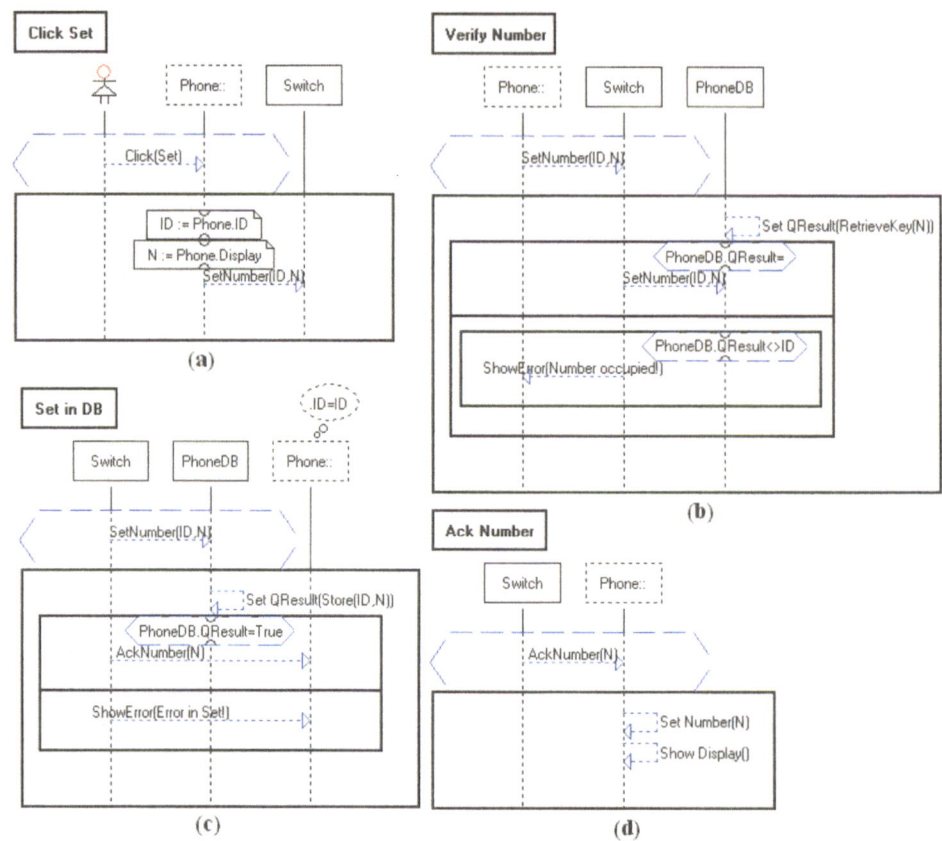

Fig. 15.10. A phone setting its own number

number N as a parameter, the phone's number is set to N (which, in turn, is reflected in the GUI by showing this number on the top-left corner of the phone) and the phone's display is cleared by showing an empty string.

We have extended the NetPhone to include LSCs for establishing calls, answering calls, conference calls, hanging up, and many other scenarios. Our method of using binding expressions to characterize symbolic instances allows each phone to set its phone number at runtime, but to use the *number* property in binding expressions in order to refer to the required phone when describing interactions between telephones. This could not have been done using static instances and relationships only.

15.9 And a Bit More Formally ...

Here are the extensions and modifications needed to support symbolic instances and their binding during execution.

System Model and Events

The system model we have defined so far already contains classes and defines the relationships between classes and objects. Hence, no modifications are needed here.

LSC Specification

Until now, all we needed to know about an LSC instance was the object it represented, and this was given by the *AppObj* function. Since instances can now be symbolic, and thus represent classes rather than objects, we modify the definition of an instance as follows:

$$I = \langle \ell, O, C, \psi, Mode, \Phi \rangle$$

where $O \in \mathcal{O} \cup \{\bot\}$ is the concrete object represented by I (with $O = \bot$ if I is symbolic), $C \in \mathcal{C} \cup \{\bot\}$ is the class represented by I (with $C = \bot$ if I is not symbolic), $\psi \in \{P \times Oper \times RHS\}$ is the binding expression of I, which is a basic condition expression restricting the property $P \in C.\mathcal{P}$ to certain values, as discussed in Chap. 9, $Mode \in \{Existential, Universal\}$ is the instance quantification, and $\Phi \subseteq \mathcal{O}$ is a set of *forbidden objects* that the instance is not allowed to bind to. We also modify the range of *AppObj* to reflect these changes:

$$AppObj : \bigcup_{L \in \mathcal{S}} I_L \to \mathcal{O} \cup \mathcal{C}$$

We will use the predicate *symbolic(I)* as an abbreviation of $I.C \neq \bot$. We now define the relation $X \preccurlyeq Y$, where $X \in \mathcal{O}$ and $Y \in \mathcal{O} \cup \mathcal{C}$, to denote that either X and Y are the same object or Y is the class to which X belongs:[5]

$$X \preccurlyeq Y \triangleq (X \in \mathcal{O} \wedge (X = Y \vee class(X) = Y))$$

We extend the relation $\preccurlyeq$ so it can also have instances as arguments in the natural way (i.e., the relation refers to the objects or classes represented by the instances).

---

[5] Recall from Chap. 4 that every object belongs to exactly one class.

The instances to which an LSC message $M \in M_L$ refers can now be symbolic. Therefore, we relax the requirement that the instances represent the same concrete objects as in the associated system message, and allow them to also represent the classes to which the concrete objects belong:

$$M = \langle I_{Src}, I_{Dst}, M_S \rangle$$

where $M_S.Src \preccurlyeq AppObj(I_{Src})$ and $M_S.Dst \preccurlyeq AppObj(I_{Dst})$.

We now extend E_L, the set of LSC events, with the hidden event of binding a symbolic instance with a concrete object:

$E_L =$

$\quad (\{m \in M_L \mid m.M_s \in \Sigma_{FromUser} \cup \Sigma_{ToUser} \cup \Sigma_{FromEnv} \cup \Sigma_{ToEnv} \cup \Sigma_{Calls}\}$
$\quad\quad \times \{Send, Recv\})$
$\quad \cup (\{m \in M_L \mid m.M_s \in \Sigma_{Self}\} \times \{Send\})$
$\quad \cup (Pch_L \times \{Start, End\}) \cup \{Completed\}$
$\quad \cup \{perform(A) \mid A \in A_L\} \cup \{eval(C) \mid C \in C_L\}$
$\quad \cup (SUB_L \times \{Start, End\}) \cup \{branch(ITE) \mid ITE \in ITE_L\}$
$\quad \cup (LOOP_L \times \{Start, End\})$
$\quad \cup \{skip(Loop) \mid Loop \in LOOP_L \wedge Loop.Kind = Dynamic\}$
$\quad \cup \{bind(I) \mid I \in I_L \wedge symbolic(I)\}$

The events of binding symbolic instances with concrete objects do not refer to bindings that occur as a result of unifying events, but only to the act of binding a symbolic instance when its binding expression is enabled. As opposed to all the other events we have seen so far, a $bind(I)$ event is *enabled* when all the variables it *uses* are bound, regardless of the instances' locations as depicted by the current cut.

Operational Semantics

Prior to the addition of symbolic instances, one could tell whether two LSC messages were unifiable by looking only at their associated system messages. Hence, the definition for message unification was:

Definition 15.9.1 (message unification). *Two system messages*
$M_s = \langle Src, Dst, P, V, f, \lambda_f^F, m, \lambda_m^M, Symbolic \rangle$ *and*
$M'_s = \langle Src', Dst', P', V', f', \lambda_{f'}^F, m', \lambda_{m'}^M, Symbolic' \rangle$ *are Q-unifiable (where Q is 'positively' or 'negatively') if $Src = Src', Dst = Dst', P = P', m = m'$ and their contents are Q-unifiable.*

This definition then served in the definition of unifiable events as follows:

Definition 15.9.2 (level$_1$-unification).

1. *A system event $e_s = \langle m_s, t \rangle$ and an LSC event $e_l = \langle m_l, t' \rangle$, with $t, t' \in \{Send, Recv\}$ are Q-level$_1$-unifiable (where Q is 'positively' or 'negatively') if $t = t'$, $m_l.M_s$ and m_s are Q-unifiable, $AppObj(m_l.I_{Src}) = m_s.Src$, and $AppObj(m_l.I_{Dst}) = m_s.Dst$.*
2. *Two LSC events $e = \langle m, t \rangle$ and $e' = \langle m', t' \rangle$, with $t, t' \in \{Send, Recv\}$, are Q-level$_1$-unifiable if $t = t'$, $m.M_s$ and $m'.M_s$ are Q-unifiable, $AppObj(m.I_{Src}) = AppObj(m'.I_{Src})$ and $AppObj(m.I_{Dst}) = AppObj(m'.I_{Dst})$.*

Since we are never really interested in unifying two system events but rather in unifying a system event with an LSC event or unifying two LSC events, and since the unification now depends also on the LSC instances, we must modify these two definitions. First, we do not check the actual objects of the system messages but rather leave this check to the event unification. Second, we no longer require the objects to be identical, and it suffices that one is an instance of the other.

Definition 15.9.3 (message unification). *Two system messages*
$M_s = \langle Src, Dst, P, V, f, \lambda_f^F, m, \lambda_m^M, Symbolic \rangle$ *and*
$M'_s = \langle Src', Dst', P', V', f', \lambda_{f'}^F, m', \lambda_{m'}^M, Symbolic' \rangle$ *are Q-unifiable (where Q is 'positively' or 'negatively') if they represent the same property or method (i.e., $P = P'$ and $m = m'$), and their contents are Q-unifiable.*

Definition 15.9.4 (level$_2$-unification).

1. *A system event $e_s = \langle m_s, t \rangle$ and an LSC event $e_l = \langle m_l, t' \rangle$, with $t, t' \in \{Send, Recv\}$, are Q-level$_2$-unifiable (where Q is 'positively' or 'negatively') if $t = t'$, $m_l.M_s$ and m_s are Q-unifiable, $m_s.Src \preccurlyeq m_l.I_{Src}$, $m_s.Src \notin m_l.I_{Src}.\Phi$, $m_s.Dst \preccurlyeq m_l.I_{Dst}$, and $m_s.Dst \notin m_l.I_{Dst}.\Phi$.*
2. *Two LSC events $e = \langle m, t \rangle$ and $e' = \langle m', t' \rangle$, with $t, t' \in \{Send, Recv\}$, are Q-level$_2$-unifiable if $t = t'$, $m.M_s$ and $m'.M_s$ are Q-unifiable and*

$$((m.I_{Src} \preccurlyeq m'.I_{Src} \;\wedge\; AppObj(m.I_{Src}) \notin m'.I_{Src}.\Phi)$$
$$\vee (m'.I_{Src} \preccurlyeq m.I_{Src} \;\wedge\; AppObj(m'.I_{Src}) \notin m.I_{Src}.\Phi))$$

and

$$((m.I_{Dst} \preccurlyeq m'.I_{Dst} \;\wedge\; AppObj(m.I_{Dst}) \notin m'.I_{Dst}.\Phi)$$
$$\vee (m'.I_{Dst} \preccurlyeq m.I_{Dst} \;\wedge\; AppObj(m'.I_{Dst}) \notin m.I_{Dst}.\Phi))$$

So far, the effect of unifying events was a possible binding of variables with new values. However, now, unifying events may result also in binding symbolic instances with concrete objects. We therefore define the act of unifying two $level_2$-*unifiable* LSC events $e = \langle m, t \rangle$ and $e' = \langle m', t \rangle$ as follows:

Unify(e, e', Context)

1. Unify($e.m, e'.m'$, Context).
2. If $symbolic(e.m.I_{Src})$ and $e'.m'.I_{Src} \preccurlyeq e.m.I_{Src}$ then bind the symbolic instance with the concrete object:
   a) $e.m.I_{Src}.O \leftarrow e'.m'.I_{Src}.O$.
   b) $e.m.I_{Src}.C \leftarrow \perp$.
3. If $symbolic(e'.m'.I_{Src})$ and $e.m.I_{Src} \preccurlyeq e'.m'.I_{Src}$ then bind the symbolic instance with the concrete object:
   a) $e'.m'.I_{Src}.O \leftarrow e.m.I_{Src}.O$.
   b) $e'.m'.I_{Src}.C \leftarrow \perp$.
4. If $symbolic(e.m.I_{Dst})$ and $e'.m'.I_{Dst} \preccurlyeq e.m.I_{Dst}$ then bind the symbolic instance with the concrete object:
   a) $e.m.I_{Dst}.O \leftarrow e'.m'.I_{Dst}.O$.
   b) $e.m.I_{Dst}.C \leftarrow \perp$.
5. If $symbolic(e'.m'.I_{Dst})$ and $e.m.I_{Dst} \preccurlyeq e'.m'.I_{Dst}$ then bind the symbolic instance with the concrete object:
   a) $e'.m'.I_{Dst}.O \leftarrow e.m.I_{Dst}.O$.
   b) $e'.m'.I_{Dst}.C \leftarrow \perp$.

A system event $e_s = \langle m_s, t \rangle$ and an LSC event $e_l = \langle m_l, t \rangle$ are also unified along the same lines, except that the system event is guaranteed to have concrete objects as the sender and receiver of the message:

Unify(e_s, e_l, Context)

1. Unify($e_s.m_s, e_l.m_l$, Context).
2. If $symbolic(e_l.m_l.I_{Src})$ and $e_s.m_s.Src \preccurlyeq e_l.m_l.I_{Src}$ then bind the symbolic instance with the concrete object:
   a) $e_l.m_l.I_{Src}.O \leftarrow e_s.m_s.Src$.
   b) $e_l.m_l.I_{Src}.C \leftarrow \perp$.
3. If $symbolic(e_l.m_l.I_{Dst})$ and $e_s.m_s.Dst \preccurlyeq e_l.m_l.I_{Dst}$ then bind the symbolic instance with the concrete object:
   a) $e_l.m_l.I_{Dst}.O \leftarrow e_s.m_s.Dst$.
   b) $e_l.m_l.I_{Dst}.C \leftarrow \perp$.

The transition relation $\Delta[\mathcal{S}_O, \mathcal{S}_C]$ should now be modified to contain also the effects of binding symbolic instances caused by event unification, and extended with transitions for handling the hidden events of binding symbolic instances as their binding expressions become enabled:

- If $e = \langle M, t \rangle$ (where $t \in \{Send, Recv\}$) then:
  1. Set $Context \leftarrow \emptyset$.
  2. If $\exists C^L \in \mathcal{S}_C$ and $\exists e' \in C^L.LSC$, such that e and e' are negatively level$_2$-unifiable and e' violates C^L, then:
     a) Set $\mathcal{S}_C \leftarrow \mathcal{S}_C \setminus \{C^L\}$.
     b) If $temp(C^L.Cut) = hot$, set $Violating \leftarrow True$.
     c) If $symbolic(e'.M.I_{Src})$ or $symbolic(e'.M.I_{Dst})$ then create an identical copy C'^L of C^L, set $\mathcal{S}_C \leftarrow \mathcal{S}_C \cup \{C'^L\}$, and in the copy set
     $$e'.M.I_{Src}.\Phi \leftarrow e'.M.I_{Src}.\Phi \cup \{e.M.Src\} \quad \text{if } symbolic(e'.M.I_{Src})$$
     $$e'.M.I_{Dst}.\Phi \leftarrow e'.M.I_{Dst}.\Phi \cup \{e.M.Dst\} \quad \text{if } symbolic(e'.M.I_{Dst})$$
  3. For every universal LSC $L \in \mathcal{S}_O$ which has an event e', positively level$_2$-unifiable with e, as a minimal event in its prechart, create a copy of L, C^L, and set $\mathcal{S}_C \leftarrow \mathcal{S}_C \cup \{C^L\}$. Set $C^L.Mode = PreActive$ and set its cut by $C^L.Cut \leftarrow AdvanceCut(InitialCut(L), \langle Pch_L, Start \rangle)$. Unify the variables of e and e', by $Unify(e, e', Context)$. For each hidden event $e'' <_L e'$, apply $\Delta(e'')$.
  4. For every existential LSC $L \in \mathcal{S}_O$ which has an event e', positively level$_2$-unifiable with e, as a minimal event in the chart body, create a copy of L, C^L, and set $\mathcal{S}_C \leftarrow \mathcal{S}_C \cup \{C^L\}$. Set $C^L.Mode = Check$, and set its cut to the beginning of the chart by $C^L.Cut \leftarrow BeginMainCut(C^L.LSC)$. Unify the variables of e and e', by $Unify(e, e', Context)$. For each hidden event $e'' <_L e'$, apply $\Delta(e'')$.

  5. For every copy $C^L \in \mathcal{S}_C$ that has a reachable event e' positively level$_2$-unifiable with e:
     a) If $symbolic(e'.M.I_{Src})$ or $symbolic(e'.M.I_{Dst})$ then create an identical copy of C^L, C'^L, set $\mathcal{S}_C \leftarrow \mathcal{S}_C \cup \{C'^L\}$, and in the copy set
     $$e'.M.I_{Src}.\Phi \leftarrow e'.M.I_{Src}.\Phi \cup \{e.m.Src\} \quad \text{if } symbolic(e'.M.I_{Src})$$
     $$e'.M.I_{Dst}.\Phi \leftarrow e'.M.I_{Dst}.\Phi \cup \{e.m.Dst\} \quad \text{if } symbolic(e'.M.I_{Dst})$$
     b) Set $C^L.Cut \leftarrow AdvanceCut(C^L.Cut, e')$.
     c) If $e' = \langle M, Send \rangle$, M is synchronous and $e'' = \langle M, Recv \rangle$, set $C^L.Cut \leftarrow AdvanceCut(C^L.Cut, e'')$.
     d) Unify the events e and e', $Unify(e, e', Context)$.
     e) For each hidden event $e'' <_L e'$, apply $\Delta(e'')$.
- If $e = Completed(C^L)$ for some $C^L \in \mathcal{S}_C$, then set $\mathcal{S}_C \leftarrow \mathcal{S}_C \setminus \{C^L\}$.
- If $e = \langle Pch_L, End \rangle$ for some $C^L \in \mathcal{S}_C$, then set $C^L.Cut \leftarrow BeginMainCut(C^L.LSC)$ and $C^L.Mode \leftarrow Active$.
- If $e = perform(A)$ for some $A \in A_L$ s.t. $C^L \in \mathcal{S}_C$, then set $C^L.Cut \leftarrow AdvanceCut(C^L.Cut, e)$ and set

$$A.V \leftarrow \begin{cases} A.C & \text{if } A.Type = constant \\ Value(A.P) & \text{if } A.Type = property \\ A.f(A.\lambda_f^F) & \text{if } A.Type = function \end{cases}$$

- If $e = eval(C)$ for some $C \in C^L$ s.t. $C^L \in \mathcal{S}_C$ then
  1. If $value(C) = true$ then set $C^L.Cut \leftarrow AdvanceCut(C^L.Cut, e)$.
  2. If $value(C) = false$ then
     a) If $subchart(C) \in \{ITE.Sub_T, ITE.Sub_E\}$ for some ITE then

        set $C^L.Cut \leftarrow AdvanceCut(C^L.Cut, (ITE, End))$

     b) If $subchart(C) = Sub \in SUB_L$ then

        set $C^L.Cut \leftarrow AdvanceCut(C^L.Cut, (Sub, End))$

     c) If $subchart(C) = \bot$ then set $\mathcal{S}_C \leftarrow \mathcal{S}_C \setminus \{C^L\}$.
     d) If $temp(C) = hot$ then set $Violating \leftarrow True$.
- If $e = branch(ITE)$ for some $ITE \in C^L$ s.t. $C^L \in \mathcal{S}_C$ then
  1. If $value(ITE.C) = true$ then set
     $C^L.Cut \leftarrow AdvanceCut(C^L.Cut, (ITE.Sub_T, Start))$.
  2. If $value(ITE.C) = false$ then

$$set\ C^L.Cut \leftarrow \begin{cases} AdvanceCut(C^L.Cut, (ITE.Sub_E, Start)) & \text{if } ITE.Sub_E \neq \bot \\ AdvanceCut(C^L.Cut, (ITE.Sub_T, End)) & \text{if } ITE.Sub_E = \bot \end{cases}$$

- If $e = (ITE.Sub_T, End)$ for some $ITE \in C^L$ s.t. $C^L \in \mathcal{S}_C$ then

  set $C^L.Cut \leftarrow AdvanceCut(C^L.Cut, (ITE, End))$

- If $e = (ITE.Sub_E, End)$ for some $ITE \in C^L$ s.t. $C^L \in \mathcal{S}_C$ then

  set $C^L.Cut \leftarrow AdvanceCut(C^L.Cut, (ITE.Sub_E, End))$

- If $e = (Sub, End)$ for some $Sub \in C^L$ s.t. $C^L \in \mathcal{S}_C$ then

  set $C^L.Cut \leftarrow AdvanceCut(C^L.Cut, (Sub, End))$

- If $e = skip(Loop)$ for some $Loop \in C^L$ s.t. $C^L \in \mathcal{S}_C$ then

  set $C^L.Cut \leftarrow AdvanceCut(C^L.Cut, (Loop, End))$

- If $e = (Loop, Start)$ for some $Loop \in C^L$ s.t. $C^L \in \mathcal{S}_C$ then

  set $C^L.Cut \leftarrow AdvanceCut(C^L.Cut, (Loop, Start))$

For every variable $V \in V_L$ that is used in $Loop$ for the first time, set $V.\omega \leftarrow \bot$.

- If $e = (Loop, End)$ for some $Loop \in C^L$ s.t. $C^L \in \mathcal{S}_C$ and $Loop.Kind \neq Dynamic$ then
  1. Set $\mu \leftarrow \mu - 1$.
  2. If $\mu > 0$ then

     set $C^L.Cut \leftarrow AdvanceCut(C^L.Cut, (Loop, Start))$

     For every variable $V \in V_L$ that is used in $Loop$ for the first time, set $V.\omega \leftarrow \bot$.
  3. If $\mu = 0$ then

     set $C^L.Cut \leftarrow AdvanceCut(C^L.Cut, (Loop, End))$

- If $e = bind(I)$ for some symbolic instance $I \in C^L$ s.t. $C^L \in \mathcal{S}_C$, then:
  1. $S \leftarrow \{O \in \mathcal{O} \mid O \preccurlyeq I,\ O \text{ satisfies } I.\psi \text{ and } \not\exists I' \in C^L \text{ s.t. } I'.O = O\}$.
  2. If $S = \emptyset$ then $\mathcal{S}_C \leftarrow \mathcal{S}_C \setminus \{C^L\}$.
  3. If $I.Mode = Existential$ then
     a) Set $I.O = O$, for some $O \in S$.
     b) Set $I.C = \bot$.
  4. If $I.Mode = Universal$ then perform the following for every $O \in S$:
     a) Create an identical copy C'^L of C^L.
     b) Set $\mathcal{S}_C \leftarrow \mathcal{S}_C \cup \{C'^L\}$.
     c) Set $I.O = O$.
     d) Set $I.C = \bot$.
     Finally, set $\mathcal{S}_C \leftarrow \mathcal{S}_C \setminus \{C^L\}$.

Since the events of binding symbolic instances with objects that satisfy their binding expressions are simply additional forms of hidden events, the procedures *step*, *super-step* and *monitor-event* handle them with no modifications needed.

15.10 Bibliographic Notes

Deriving object relations from the object model diagram and utilizing these relations during execution was discussed in [44] and is implemented in the Rhapsody tool [60].

Extending LSCs with symbolic instances was first described in [84]. In that paper we also discuss the rather technical problem of redundant activation of symmetric precharts, and a proposed solution. However, since the issue is not treated in the current implementation of the Play-Engine, we have decided to omit it from the book.

In [64] there is a description of work (carried out independently of ours) that deals with relating instance lines in LSCs to objects and classes, as part of an ongoing effort to establish a verification environment for UML models. The resulting decisions made in [64] are different from ours, since the goals were quite different; we have executability of LSCs as one of our main goals, while the main purpose of LSCs in [64] is to serve as a basis for testing an intra-object model or implementation.

16. Time and Real-Time Systems

In this chapter, we extend the language of LSCs and the Play-Engine with means for dealing with time. We use a single discrete clock that is linked to the host computer's internal clock. We also assume the synchrony hypothesis. Hence, in terms of playing out the behavior on an actual simulating computer, we essentially have a real-time mechanism. The resulting extension is extremely expressive.

16.1 An Example

Let us return to the cellular phone example, and consider the requirement discussed in Chap. 7:

> *Every time the user opens or closes the cover, the antenna should automatically open or close as well.*

The LSC in Fig. 16.1 captures this requirement. Now, suppose we change the requirement as follows:

> *Every time the user opens or closes the cover, the antenna should automatically open or close between two and four seconds later.*

This requirement refers to the time passage between events, and in order to express it we have to extend the language of LSCs with timing constructs. The LSC in Fig. 16.2 shows how this requirement is expressed in the extended language. After the cover is opened (closed), the current time is stored in the variable T. Before the antenna is allowed to open (close) we make sure, using a hot condition, that the current time is greater than or equal to $T + 2$. Since a hot condition must be met, the execution must wait until the condition becomes true, thus forcing the required delay. Finally, after the antenna opens (closes), we check, again using a hot condition, that the current time is no more than $T + 4$, thus making sure that the interval's upper bound was not violated.

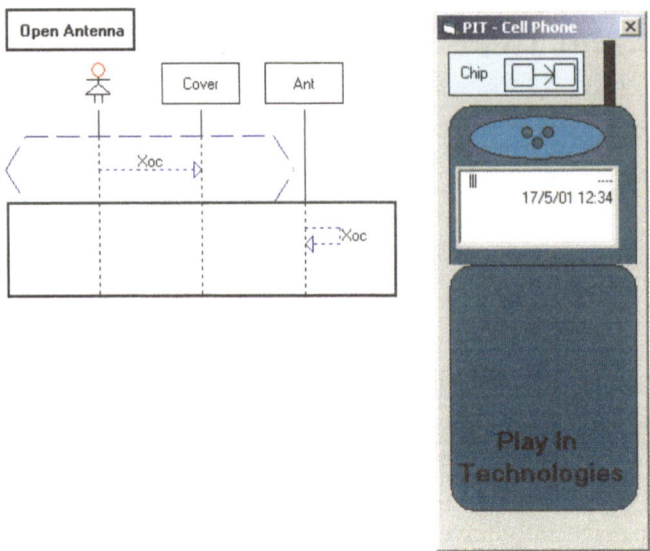

Fig. 16.1. Opening and closing the antenna automatically

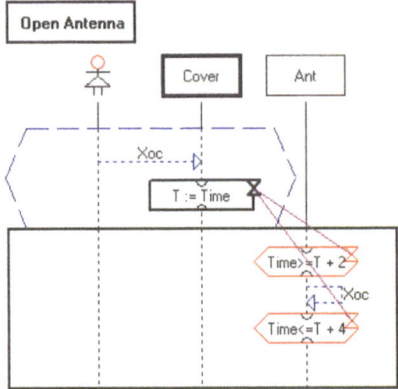

Fig. 16.2. Opening and closing the antenna within a specified time interval

16.2 Adding Time to LSCs

Many kinds of reactive systems must explicitly refer to time and react to its passage. For this purpose, a variety of programming language constructs have been proposed, including delays, timeouts, watchdogs and clock variables. Temporal logic, for example, has been extended by a variety of constructs to enable quantification of time, including bounded temporal operators, freeze quantifiers and the use of explicit clock variables. Visual scenario-based languages, such as MSCs, have also been extended with timers, delay intervals, drawing rules and timing marks. Many of these approaches are referred to in the bibliographic notes at the end of this chapter.

To extend the language of LSCs to deal with time, we adopt the basic philosophy of Alur and Henzinger, according to which a real-time system can be viewed as a discrete system with clock variables. We apply this approach in our setting by adding a special single **clock** object with one property, Time, and one method, Tick. The new object and its method can be referred to in the charts by a special instance (with a clock icon) and a special constant Tick event. The main technical observation underlying this chapter is that by using these new elements with constructs already existing in our language, such as assignments and conditions, and, significantly, by exploiting the hot and cold dichotomy that pervades our entire approach, we are able to capture a rich set of **timing constraints** and time-based behavior.

An important point here is that we have chosen to assume the **synchrony hypothesis**, although we did not have to do so in order to make semantic sense of our extension. This is a well-known abstraction of real-time systems, according to which the system events themselves consume no actual time, and time may pass only between events. As we shall see later, the synchrony hypothesis makes our life a bit simpler when it comes to executing a time-enriched LSC specification.

16.3 Hot Timing Constraints

A timing constraint in the extended LSC language can be defined by a combination of assignments and conditions. Figure 16.3 shows how to express three of the most common timing constraints in scenario-based visual languages. A **vertical delay** interval indicates the minimal and maximal delays allowed between two consecutive events along an instance line. Such an interval is expressed in our language using the following steps (see Fig. 16.3(a), and note the small sand-clock icons added to the assignment and condition boxes):

Store time: The time is stored immediately after the first event. According to our semantics, assignments are performed as soon as they are reached. Hence, the value of the variable will be the time instant at which the event occurs.

Specify minimal delay: The minimal delay is specified by placing a hot condition of the form *Time > Time-Variable + Min-Delay* just before the second event. According to the described semantics, hot conditions are evaluated continuously until they become true. Therefore, this condition will be advanced only after the required period has passed. Such a condi-

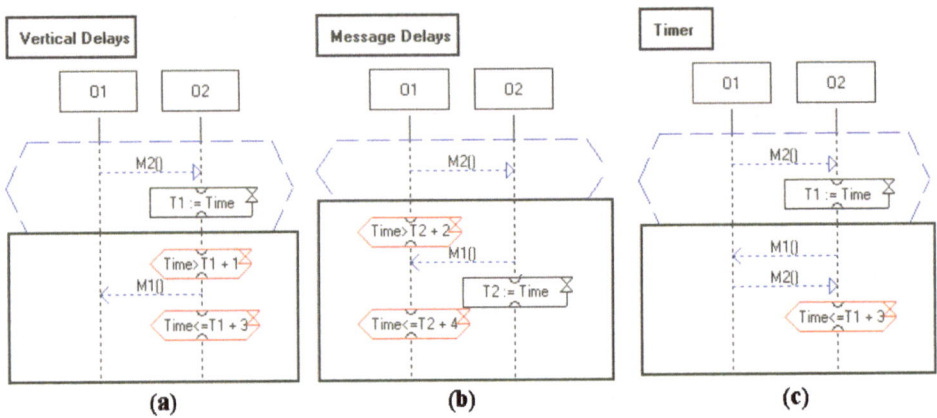

Fig. 16.3. Expressing common timing constraints in LSCs

tion may be reached after the required lower bound on time has passed, in which case it will be advanced immediately.

Specify maximal delay: The maximal delay is specified by placing a hot condition of the form *Time < Time-Variable + Max-Delay* just after the second event. If the condition is reached before the maximal delay has elapsed, it will evaluate to true and will be advanced immediately, causing no delay or violation. If the condition is reached after the maximal delay has elapsed, it evaluates to false, and since time cannot decrease the condition will never hold and it is therefore treated as a constant *False* condition, causing a violation of the requirements.

A **message delay** interval indicates the minimal and maximal delays allowed from the moment a message is sent until it is received. This kind of delay interval is specified like a vertical delay, except that here the time is stored on one instance line and is checked on another (Fig. 16.3(b)). Note that the assignment and the first condition in the figure are not related by the LSC partial order, so that the condition may be reached before the assignment. However, recall that a condition that *uses* (refers to) an unbound variable cannot be evaluated. Thus, in this case, the condition will not be evaluated until the assignment is performed.

The ITU-TS Recommendation Z.120 document provides **timers** for expressing timing constraints within a single MSC, and along a single instance. Such a timer can be set to a value, reset to 0, and observed for timeout, and can be used to express a minimal delay between two consecutive events or a maximal delay between two or more consecutive events. However, timers cannot be shared among different instances in an MSC and can therefore be used to constrain events occurring only within a single object. Our LSC equivalent for a timer is also specified as a vertical constraint, except that the maximal delay condition can be placed arbitrarily far from the place where the time is stored (Fig. 16.3(c)), and we are not limited to a single instance, as we shall soon see.

Here now are some more complex examples of timing constraints that can be expressed in the extended LSCs.

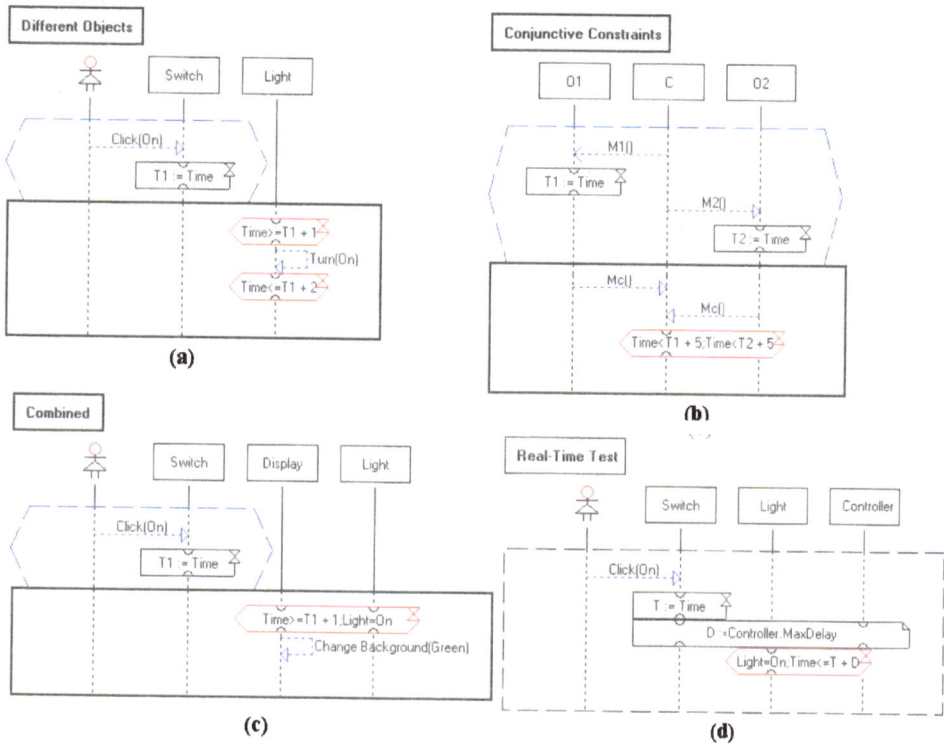

Fig. 16.4. Expressing more complex timing constraints

Figure 16.4(a) shows how events occurring in different objects can be related by a timing constraint. The LSC in this figure says that whenever the switch is turned on, the light should turn on after no less than one time unit and no more than two time units. (As we shall see later, the actual duration of time units can be determined by the user, so we sometimes use specific time units and sometimes use the more general term.) This very natural requirement cannot be expressed by the previous three standard time constructs, unless the communication between the switch and the light is given explicitly in the chart. However, this kind of constraint is often desired, especially in the requirements analysis phase, without having to get into the details of implementation.

Figure 16.4(b) shows the use of conjunctive timing constraints. The LSC shows a scenario where object C sends messages to $O1$ and $O2$ and expects messages in reply from both objects. C is willing to accept the replies no later than five time units after the first object received its message. Conjunctive timing constraints are very useful when it is impossible to know the exact execution order between multiple events that can affect some other event.

Figure 16.4(c) shows how conditions can be used to combine timing constraints with conventional constraints. In this LSC, when the switch is turned on, the display should change its background color to green, but only if the light is on, and no earlier than 1 time unit after the switch event. When the condition is reached, execution will be advanced only if and when both of these are true.

The combination of real-time constraints and regular ones can be taken one step further, as seen in Fig. 16.4(d). This is an existential LSC, which describes a simple test stating our expectation that the light should be on no more than D time units after the switch was turned on. Or, in other words, that if the light is still off later than D units after the switch was turned on, we are in trouble. The value of D is taken from the *MaxDelay* state variable of the controller, which may change dynamically during the system run. Note that since this LSC represents a test, it does not have to specify how the result of the light being on is achieved but only that it indeed is.

16.4 Cold Timing Constraints

In the previous section we used hot conditions to force an event to occur only after a certain amount of time has elapsed (by a minimal delay) and to cause a violation if the constraint is not satisfied (by a maximum delay). The availability of cold conditions further enriches the expressive power of time-enriched LSCs. A cold timing constraint with a minimal delay states that if a certain event occurs after a specified period of time, the scenario continues, otherwise the chart is exited. A cold constraint with a maximal delay states that if the event occurred within the specified period of time, the chart (or subchart) continues, otherwise the rest of it is simply ignored.

Figure 16.5 shows an example. The Queen of Hearts instructs the rabbit to come to her palace in five seconds, and proceeds to look at her watch, noting the time. The rabbit meets Alice and tells her he is late (the message is cold, so he doesn't *have* to do this, but *can*). Alice hurries the rabbit up, and upon arriving at the Queen's palace he reports to her. The Queen then checks

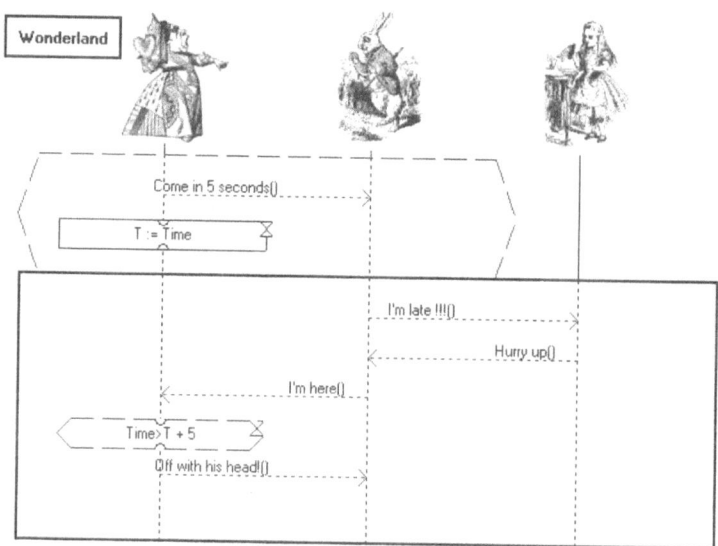

Fig. 16.5. Having a cold time in Wonderland

whether more than five seconds have passed since the last time she looked at her watch. If this is the case, she issues an order to remove the rabbit's head; otherwise, the scenario ends with the rabbit's anatomy intact...

16.5 Time Events

Reactive real-time systems are often required to react to the passage of time, and not only to refer to it when constraining the timing of other events of interest. An example of such a requirement could be:

> *The controller should probe the thermometer for a temperature value*
> *every* 100 *milliseconds, and if the result is more than* 60 *degrees, it*
> *should deactivate the heater and send a warning to the console.*

To express such requirements, generally termed **time events**, a special object instance representing the clock is available, and can it be added to the LSCs. Within this instance one can refer to the Tick event, which represents an actual clock tick, i.e., the passage of a single time unit. This event can be placed in a prechart to trigger desired actions, or in the main chart, thus explicitly forcing delays.

Figure 16.6 shows an LSC that describes the above requirement.

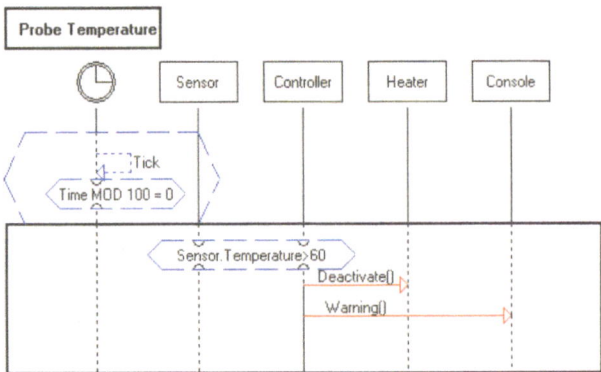

Fig. 16.6. Time events in LSCs

16.6 Playing In

In order for the user to be able to refer to time while remaining within the intuitive convenience of GUI-oriented play-in, we have added a global clock object (accessible directly from the upper toolbar of the engine's layout: see Fig. 16.7). To specify a Tick event, the user simply clicks the clock's `Tick` button on the toolbar.

Fig. 16.7. The clock object in the Play-Engine's toolbar

In order to specify timing constraints, the user needs to store time in time variables and to restrict time with respect to these variables. Although we use the existing constructs of assignments and conditions for these activities, the Play-Engine provides more direct ways to define the timed versions of these constructs.

To store the time at any point during play-in, the user right-clicks the relevant object and chooses `Store Time` from the popup menu (see Fig. 16.8(a)). In response, the Play-Engine displays a popup dialog in which the user is requested to name the time variable.

To specify a timing constraint, the user right-clicks the constrained object and chooses `Time Constraint...` from the popup menu (Fig. 16.8(b)). In response, a timing constraint dialog opens up, in which the user specifies the time variable, the delay and the constraint operator (Fig. 16.8(c)).

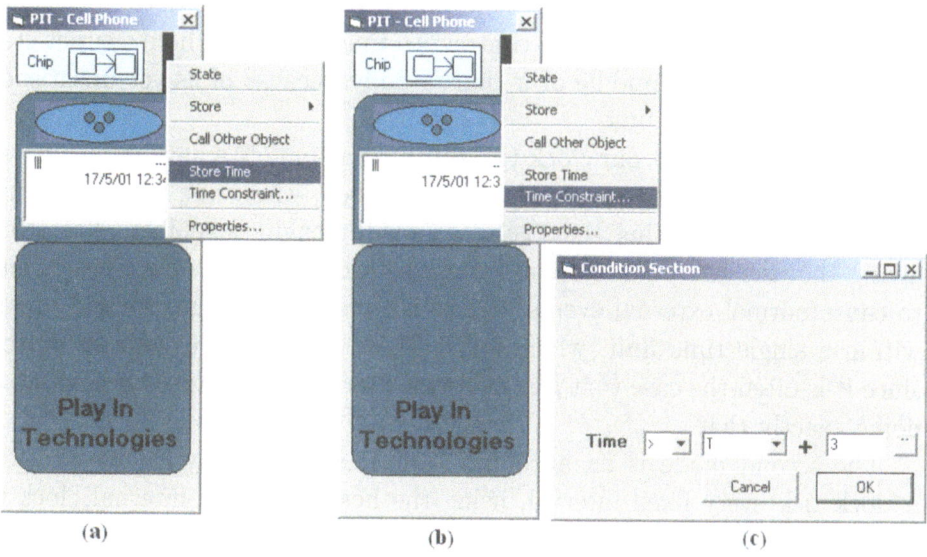

Fig. 16.8. Playing in a timing constraint

We have also added the following feature to the Play-Engine's interface: placing the mouse over a timed assignment causes the engine to draw thin indication lines from it to all the timing constraints it may affect (see Fig. 16.2), and placing it over a timing constraint shows such lines drawn to all the timed assignments that may affect it. We should add that the algorithm for doing this is non-trivial, as it has to take into account the partial order in the chart, the bindings of variables, and a number of additional things.[1]

16.7 Playing Out

As emphasized throughout the book, our target is not merely to construct an off-line modeling medium, but to produce an executable formalism — for which the execution mechanism essentially constitutes the operational semantics — and to build the tool that executes the specifications. These goals raise a host of new issues when time is included as part of the language, and this section discusses the way we deal with them.

We have already seen that during execution the Play-Engine generates only system events; it does not cause events that should be triggered by the user or by the external environment. In this sense, the clock is considered part

---

[1] We have actually implemented this algorithm for assignments and conditions in general, and not only for those that deal with time.

of the system's external environment, and the Play-Engine does not trigger clock ticks on its own. Hence, in contrast to time-less LSCs, here a super-step can terminate in the middle of a chart's body because of as-yet unsatisfied minimal-delay constraints.

So how indeed does our clock tick during play-out? We have implemented two means for this. The first is a manual mode, where the user can cause a tick by simply clicking the `Tick` icon on the engine's toolbar. Note that giving the user the power to control clock ticks, over and above the ability to cause normal external events, makes it possible to trigger several events within a single time unit, which can be used to set up realistic scenarios, since it is often the case that a real-world external environment is capable of doing exactly that.

The second mode is an automatic one. Here, the Play-Engine triggers a clock tick every fixed interval, using the host machine's internal clock to obtain the actual time information. The interval length, relative to the real clock, is determined by the engine's user, and a natural thing to do would be to set the interval to be the time unit used in the requirements themselves, or the smallest such unit (e.g., if the time units are seconds, then the time interval could be set to 1000 ms). Allowing for true control over the execution/simulation speed, at least insofar as the host machine's clock allows, this gets us as close as can be hoped to having a 'really' real-time system model (that is, on a general-purpose computer, as opposed to working on a special-purpose real-time operating system).[2]

The Play-Engine performs a lot of additional work during execution that is not related to actually executing the specified events and actions (e.g., finding the next event to be taken, monitoring the activated LSCs and displaying their progress graphically, etc.). Therefore, we have to somehow confront the problem of model vs. implementation, which is particularly acute in the real-time arena. The synchrony hypothesis makes this easier. When our Play-Engine executes the model, the clock keeps ticking and the system waits for external stimuli. When such a stimulus arrives, our execution mechanism freezes the clock and performs the sequence of events that constitutes the system's response to that stimulus (this is the super-step). When the sequence is completed, the clock's operation is resumed, thus causing the effect of zero-time actions. We could just as easily not adopt the synchrony assumption that freezes the clock when this kind of additional engine-specific 'meta-work' is carried out, but rather let the clock continue to tick when events and functions from the model itself are applied. However, doing so would mean that since the Play-Engine executes on a single-processor PC

---

[2] If the interval between ticks is made sufficiently large, the user can trigger several end-user and environment events within a single time unit in this mode too.

the requirements are captured correctly only if the target system also runs on a single-processor platform.

16.8 Unification of Clock Ticks

The clock Tick event is denoted in LSCs as a self message, going from the clock instance to itself. Although this message appears to be like any other one, its unification with the Tick event must be handled in a special way. To illustrate the problematic nature of this special message, consider the LSC in Fig. 16.9.

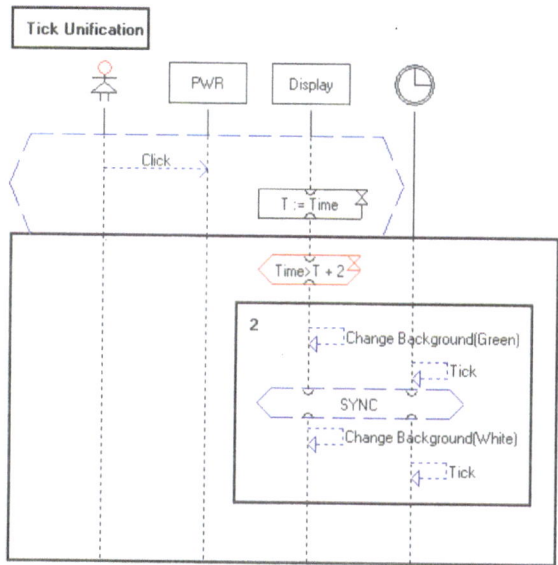

Fig. 16.9. Unification of Tick messages with the Tick event

This LSC says that every time the user clicks the PWR button, the display waits for three time units and then changes its color to green and then to white, twice. Between every two changes of color there is a delay of at least one time unit. The clock Tick event is being used here to explicitly indicate the passage of time, as an alternative to the timing constraints described earlier.

There is however a problem with this chart. In order to advance beyond the first timing constraint, three time units must elapse. The passage of each time unit is caused by a Tick event, but as the first such event occurs it will be unified with the Tick messages in the chart and will cause the chart's violation (because of the semantics of events, which causes violation if an event occurs out of sequence). This problem complicates the task of specifying timed specifications, especially in the case where a Tick message must appear in the prechart, since having such a message forbids the occurrence of other ticks until the chart completes (unless these ticks are specified explicitly in the chart body).

To overcome this problem we handle the unification of Tick events differently: Recall that we use positive unification when looking for events that can be propagated simultaneously, whereas we use negative unification to find events that violate currently active LSCs. In the case of clock ticks, we do not want the occurrence of a Tick event to be considered a violation because of Tick messages that appear elsewhere in the LSC. Therefore, Tick events can be positively unified (so that minimal events are found and Tick messages are advanced when required), but they are not negatively unifiable. Thus, a Tick event in a chart does not prevent other Tick events from happening.

Chapter 17 discusses an alternative way of specifying that a Tick event is not allowed to happen as long as a specific LSC is active.

16.9 The Time-Enriched NetPhone Example

In Chap. 15 we introduced the telephone network example, and used it to illustrate the power of symbolic instances. We now extend this NetPhone system with a number of time-related features. For example, Fig. 16.10(b) shows the LSC for an auto-dial feature:

> *If a phone that is not in automatic mode tries to call some number, following which the "Receiver Busy..." message appears on the display, then if the user clicks the* call *button within five seconds from the time the message appeared, the phone enters automatic mode.*

The LSC in Fig. 16.10(c) shows the behavior of a phone in automatic mode. As soon as it enters this mode the phone stores the current time in Ts. It then displays "Automatic Mode", and enters an (unbounded) loop, which iterates for as long as the display shows "Automatic Mode", but no longer than 30 seconds from when the mode was entered. The loop's control is captured by the cold condition therein, whose semantics prescribes exiting the current subchart — i.e., the loop — upon becoming false. The first thing the phone does inside the loop is to store the current time in $T1$ and to try calling the desired number. It then waits one second for the communication protocol to be over and checks the message on the display. If it says "Receiver Busy ...", the display is set to show "Automatic Mode" again. Then there

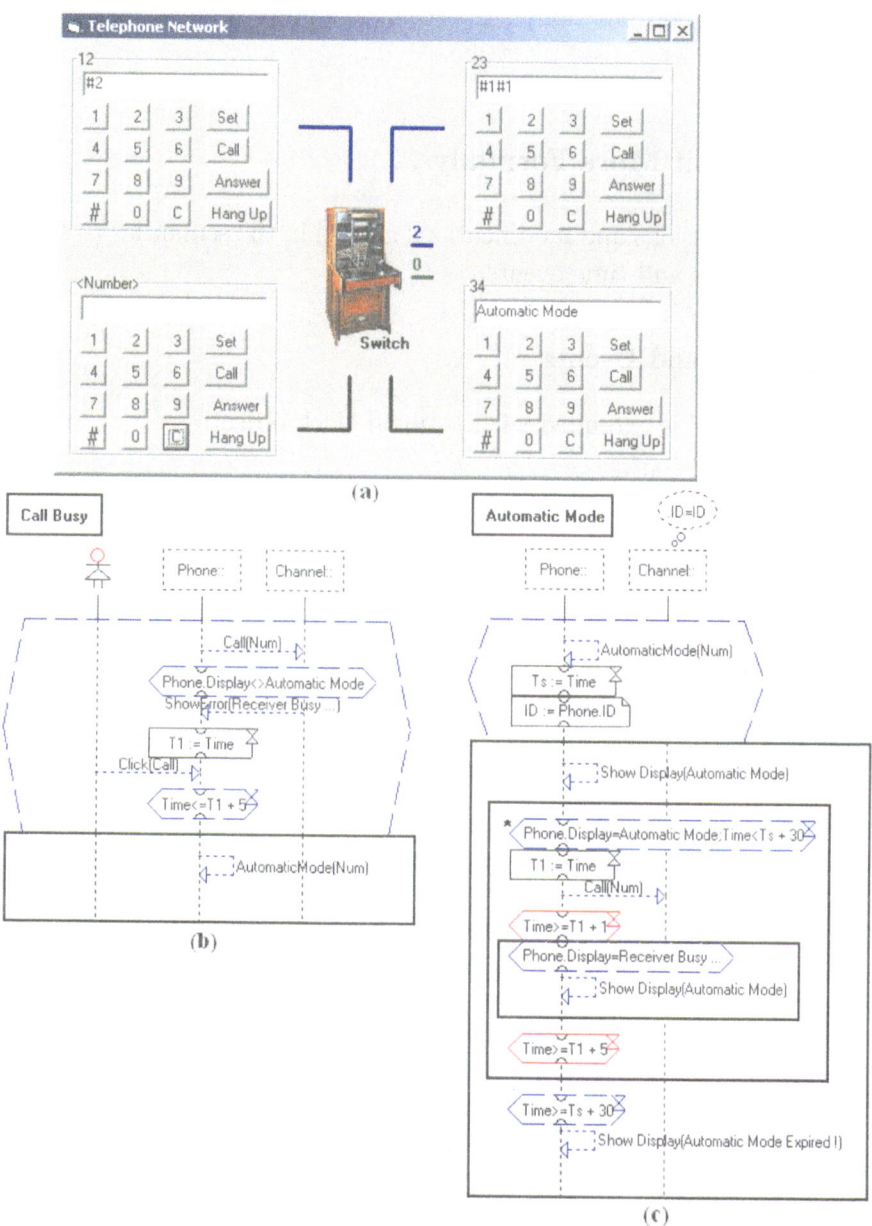

Fig. 16.10. Some time-related behavior of the NetPhone system

is a hot constraint that forces a five second wait before there is an attempt
to reconnect. After the loop, there is a cold time constraint: If the loop was
exited after 30 seconds or more (i.e., it was exited not because a conversation
was established), the display shows that the automatic mode has expired.

Since the condition is cold, if the loop exits before 30 seconds have elapsed (by establishing a conversation[3]), the scenario simply ends without showing this last message.

16.10 And a Bit More Formally ...

Here are the extensions and modifications needed in the semantics to support timing constraints and time events.

System Model and Events

The system model is extended with a global clock object:

$$\mathcal{S}ys = \langle \mathcal{D}, \mathcal{C}, \mathcal{O}, \mathcal{F}, Clock \rangle$$

The clock is an external object with one *Time* property and one *Tick* method:

$$Clock.\mathcal{P} = \{Time\}$$
$$Clock.\mathcal{M} = \{Tick\}$$
$$Clock.External = True$$

The alphabet of possible messages of $\mathcal{S}ys$ is extended to include clock ticks:

$$
\begin{aligned}
\Sigma \quad &= \Sigma_{FromUser} \cup \Sigma_{ToUser} \cup \Sigma_{FromEnv} \cup \Sigma_{ToEnv} \cup \Sigma_{Self} \cup \Sigma_{Calls} \\
&\quad \cup \Sigma_{Clock} \\
\Sigma_{FromUser} &= \{M_s \mid Src = User \wedge P \in class(Dst).\mathcal{P}\} \\
\Sigma_{ToUser} &= \{M_s \mid Dst = User \wedge P \in class(Src).\mathcal{P} \wedge P.Affects = User \wedge \\
&\quad P.InOnly = False\} \\
\Sigma_{FromEnv} &= \{M_s \mid Src = Env \wedge P \in class(Dst).\mathcal{P} \wedge P.ExtChg = True \wedge \\
&\quad P.InOnly = False\} \\
\Sigma_{ToEnv} &= \{M_s \mid Dst = Env \wedge P \in class(Src).\mathcal{P} \wedge P.Affects = Env \wedge \\
&\quad P.InOnly = False\} \\
\Sigma_{Self} &= \{M_s \mid Dst = Src \wedge P \in class(Src).\mathcal{P} \wedge P.Affects = Self \wedge \\
&\quad P.InOnly = False\} \\
\Sigma_{Calls} &= \{M_s \mid Dst, Src \in \mathcal{O} \wedge m \in class(Dst).\mathcal{M}\} \\
\Sigma_{Clock} &= \{M_s \mid Dst = Src = Clock \wedge m = Tick\}
\end{aligned}
$$

---

[3] If a connection was indeed established, the receiving phone initiates a sequence of actions — not shown in this LSC — which results in the display changing to show the number of that phone, thus causing our loop to exit as it should before the full 30 seconds have elapsed, by making the controlling condition false.

The set of *system events*, $\mathcal{E}$, is extended accordingly:

$$\mathcal{E} = ((\Sigma_{FromUser} \cup \Sigma_{ToUser} \cup \Sigma_{FromEnv} \cup \Sigma_{ToEnv} \cup \Sigma_{Calls}) \times \{Send, Recv\})$$
$$\cup ((\Sigma_{Self} \cup \Sigma_{Clock}) \times \{Send\})$$

LSC Specification

We modify the definitions of assignments and conditions so that they can refer to time, as explained in the text.

An assignment is defined as:

$$A = \langle V, I_A, C, P, f, \lambda_f^F, Timed \rangle$$

where $Timed \in \{True, False\}$ is a flag indicating whether A is a timed assignment. We require that one and only one of the following expressions holds for each assignment:

$$(C \neq \bot), \ (P \neq \bot), \ (f \neq \bot), \ (Timed = true)$$

We say that the *assignment type* of A is *time* if $Timed = true$.

The set of a condition's basic expressions is extended to include also timing constraints:

$$\psi \in \{LHS \times Oper \times RHS\} \cup \{\text{TRUE, FALSE, SELECT(P)}, \bot\}$$
$$\cup \ \{Time \times Oper \times V_L \times RHS\}$$

where

$$LHS \in \{O.P | O \in \mathcal{O}, P \in O.\mathcal{P}\} \cup V_L$$
$$Oper \in \{=, <, \leq, >, \geq, \neq\}$$
$$RHS \in (\bigcup_{D \in \mathcal{D}} D) \cup V_L \cup \{(f, \lambda_f^F) | f \in \mathcal{F}\}$$

A timing constraint is therefore a basic expression, in which the constrained (left) part is the reserved word *Time*, and the constraint is the sum of the values of a (time) variable and a delay. The latter can be any constant, variable or function expression. If ψ is a time constraint, $value(\psi)$ is computed by evaluating ψ in the natural way, where *Time* is replaced by the current value of $Clock.Time$.

Finally, we extend E_L, the set of LSC events, with the visible event of the clock ticking:

$$E_L =$$
$$(\{m \in M_L \mid m.M_s \in \Sigma_{FromUser} \cup \Sigma_{ToUser} \cup \Sigma_{FromEnv} \cup \Sigma_{ToEnv} \cup \Sigma_{Calls}\}$$
$$\times \{Send, Recv\})$$
$$\cup (\{m \in M_L \mid m.M_s \in \Sigma_{Self} \cup \Sigma_{Clock}\} \times \{Send\})$$
$$\cup (Pch_L \times \{Start, End\}) \cup \{Completed\}$$
$$\cup \{perform(A) \mid A \in A_L\} \cup \{eval(C) \mid C \in C_L\}$$
$$\cup (SUB_L \times \{Start, End\}) \cup \{branch(ITE) \mid ITE \in ITE_L\}$$
$$\cup (LOOP_L \times \{Start, End\})$$
$$\cup \{skip(Loop) \mid Loop \in LOOP_L \wedge Loop.Kind = Dynamic\}$$
$$\cup \{bind(I) \mid I \in I_L \wedge symbolic(I)\}$$

Operational Semantics

First, we modify the definition of message unification so that Tick events are not negatively-unifiable.

Definition 16.10.1 (message unification). *Two system messages*
$M_s = \langle Src, Dst, P, V, f, \lambda_f^F, m, \lambda_m^M, Symbolic \rangle$ *and*
$M'_s = \langle Src', Dst', P', V', f', \lambda_{f'}^F, m', \lambda_{m'}^M, Symbolic' \rangle$ *are Q-unifiable (where Q is 'positively' or 'negatively') if they represent the same property or method $P = P' \wedge m = m'$ and their contents are Q-unifiable. If $m = m' = Tick$, M_s and M'_s are only positively-unifiable.*

The transition relation $\Delta[\mathcal{S}_O, \mathcal{S}_C]$ is now modified to handle time assignments and time constraints correctly, and is also extended with transitions for handling the *Tick* event.

- If $e = \langle M, t \rangle$ *(where $t \in \{Send, Recv\}$)* then:
1. If $e.M.m = Tick$ then set $Clock.Time \leftarrow Clock.Time + 1$.
2. Set $Context \leftarrow \emptyset$.
3. If $\exists C^L \in \mathcal{S}_C$ and $\exists e' \in C^L.LSC$, such that e and c' are negatively level$_2$-unifiable and e' violates C^L, then:
   a) Set $\mathcal{S}_C \leftarrow \mathcal{S}_C \setminus \{C^L\}$.
   b) If $temp(C^L.Cut) = hot$, set $Violating \leftarrow True$.
   c) If $symbolic(e'.M.I_{Src})$ or $symbolic(e'.M.I_{Dst})$ then create an identical copy C'^L of C^L, set $\mathcal{S}_C \leftarrow \mathcal{S}_C \cup \{C'^L\}$, and in the copy set
   $$e'.M.I_{Src}.\Phi \leftarrow e'.M.I_{Src}.\Phi \cup \{e.M.Src\} \quad \text{if } symbolic(e'.M.I_{Src})$$
   $$e'.M.I_{Dst}.\Phi \leftarrow e'.M.I_{Dst}.\Phi \cup \{e.M.Dst\} \quad \text{if } symbolic(e'.M.I_{Dst})$$
4. For every universal LSC $L \in \mathcal{S}_O$ which has an event e', positively level$_2$-unifiable with e, as a minimal event in its prechart, create a copy of L, C^L, and set $\mathcal{S}_C \leftarrow \mathcal{S}_C \cup \{C^L\}$. Set $C^L.Mode = PreActive$ and set its cut by $C^L.Cut \leftarrow AdvanceCut(InitialCut(L), \langle Pch_L, Start \rangle)$. Unify the variables of e and e', by $Unify(e, e', Context)$. For each hidden event $e'' <_L e'$, apply $\Delta(e'')$.

5. For every existential LSC $L \in \mathcal{S}_O$ which has an event e', positively level$_2$-unifiable with e, as a minimal event in the chart body, create a copy of L, C^L, and set $\mathcal{S}_C \leftarrow \mathcal{S}_C \cup \{C^L\}$. Set $C^L.Mode = Check$, and set its cut to the beginning of the chart by $C^L.Cut \leftarrow BeginMainCut(C^L.LSC)$. Unify the variables of e and e', by $Unify(e, e', Context)$. For each hidden event $e'' <_L e'$, apply $\Delta(e'')$.

6. For every copy $C^L \in \mathcal{S}_C$ that has a reachable event e' positively level$_2$-unifiable with e:

   a) If $symbolic(e'.M.I_{Src})$ or $symbolic(e'.M.I_{Dst})$ then create an identical copy of C^L, C'^L, set $\mathcal{S}_C \leftarrow \mathcal{S}_C \cup \{C'^L\}$, and in the copy set
   $$e'.M.I_{Src}.\Phi \leftarrow e'.M.I_{Src}.\Phi \cup \{e.m.Src\} \quad \text{if } symbolic(e'.M.I_{Src})$$
   $$e'.M.I_{Dst}.\Phi \leftarrow e'.M.I_{Dst}.\Phi \cup \{e.m.Dst\} \quad \text{if } symbolic(e'.M.I_{Dst})$$

   b) Set $C^L.Cut \leftarrow AdvanceCut(C^L.Cut, e')$.

   c) If $e' = \langle M, Send \rangle$, M is synchronous and $e'' = \langle M, Recv \rangle$. set $C^L.Cut \leftarrow AdvanceCut(C^L.Cut, e'')$.

   d) Unify the events e and e', $Unify(e, e', Context)$.

   e) For each hidden event $e'' <_L e'$, apply $\Delta(e'')$.

- If $e = Completed(C^L)$ for some $C^L \in \mathcal{S}_C$ then set $\mathcal{S}_C \leftarrow \mathcal{S}_C \setminus \{C^L\}$.
- If $e = \langle Pch_L, End \rangle$ for some $C^L \in \mathcal{S}_C$, then set
$C^L.Cut \leftarrow BeginMainCut(C^L.LSC)$ and $C^L.Mode \leftarrow Active$.
- If $e = perform(A)$ for some $A \in A_L$ s.t. $C^L \in \mathcal{S}_C$, then $C^L.Cut \leftarrow AdvanceCut(C^L.Cut, e)$ and

$$A.V \leftarrow \begin{cases} A.C & \text{if } A.Type = constant \\ Value(A.P) & \text{if } A.Type = property \\ A.f(A.\lambda_f^F) & \text{if } A.Type = function \\ Clock.Time & \text{if } A.Type = time \end{cases}$$

- If $e = eval(C)$ for some $C \in C^L$ s.t. $C^L \in \mathcal{S}_C$ then
1. If $value(C) = true$ then set $C^L.Cut \leftarrow AdvanceCut(C^L.Cut, e)$.
2. If $value(C) = false$ then
   a) If $subchart(C) \in \{ITE.Sub_T, ITE.Sub_E\}$ for some ITE then

   $$set\ C^L.Cut \leftarrow AdvanceCut(C^L.Cut, (ITE, End))$$

   b) If $subchart(C) = Sub \in SUB_L$ then

   $$set\ C^L.Cut \leftarrow AdvanceCut(C^L.Cut, (Sub, End))$$

   c) If $subchart(C) = \bot$ then set $\mathcal{S}_C \leftarrow \mathcal{S}_C \setminus \{C^L\}$.
   d) If $temp(C) = hot$ then set $Violating \leftarrow True$.

- If $e = branch(ITE)$ for some $ITE \in C^L$ s.t. $C^L \in \mathcal{S}_C$ then
  1. If $value(ITE.C) = true$ then set
     $C^L.Cut \leftarrow AdvanceCut(C^L.Cut, (ITE.Sub_T, Start))$
  2. If $value(ITE.C) = false$ then

$$set\ C^L.Cut \leftarrow \begin{cases} AdvanceCut(C^L.Cut, (ITE.Sub_E, Start)) \text{ if } ITE.Sub_E \neq \bot \\ AdvanceCut(C^L.Cut, (ITE.Sub_T, End))\ \ \text{ if } ITE.Sub_E = \bot \end{cases}$$

- If $e = (ITE.Sub_T, End)$ for some $ITE \in C^L$ s.t. $C^L \in \mathcal{S}_C$ then

$$set\ C^L.Cut \leftarrow AdvanceCut(C^L.Cut, (ITE, End))$$

- If $e = (ITE.Sub_E, End)$ for some $ITE \in C^L$ s.t. $C^L \in \mathcal{S}_C$ then

$$set\ C^L.Cut \leftarrow AdvanceCut(C^L.Cut, (ITE.Sub_E, End))$$

- If $e = (Sub, End)$ for some $Sub \in C^L$ s.t. $C^L \in \mathcal{S}_C$ then

$$set\ C^L.Cut \leftarrow AdvanceCut(C^L.Cut, (Sub, End))$$

- If $e = skip(Loop)$ for some $Loop \in C^L$ s.t. $C^L \in \mathcal{S}_C$ then

$$set\ C^L.Cut \leftarrow AdvanceCut(C^L.Cut, (Loop, End))$$

- If $e = (Loop, Start)$ for some $Loop \in C^L$ s.t. $C^L \in \mathcal{S}_C$ then

$$set\ C^L.Cut \leftarrow AdvanceCut(C^L.Cut, (Loop, Start))$$

  For every variable $V \in V_L$ that is used in $Loop$ for the first time, set $V.\omega \leftarrow \bot$.
- If $e = (Loop, End)$ for some $Loop \in C^L$ s.t. $C^L \in \mathcal{S}_C$ and $Loop.Kind \neq Dynamic$ then
  1. Set $\mu \leftarrow \mu - 1$.
  2. If $\mu > 0$ then

$$set\ C^L.Cut \leftarrow AdvanceCut(C^L.Cut, (Loop, Start))$$

     For every variable $V \in V_L$ that is used in $Loop$ for the first time, set $V.\omega \leftarrow \bot$.
  3. If $\mu = 0$ then

$$set\ C^L.Cut \leftarrow AdvanceCut(C^L.Cut, (Loop, End))$$

- If $e = bind(I)$ for some symbolic instance $I \in C^L$ s.t. $C^L \in \mathcal{S}_C$, then:
  1. $S \leftarrow \{O \in \mathcal{O} \mid O \preccurlyeq I, O \text{ satisfies } I.\psi \text{ and } \nexists I' \in C^L \text{ s.t. } I'.O = O\}$.

2. If $S = \emptyset$ then $\mathcal{S}_C \leftarrow \mathcal{S}_C \setminus \{C^L\}$.
3. If $I.Mode = Existential$ then
   a) Set $I.O = O$, for some $O \in S$.
   b) Set $I.C = \perp$.
4. If $I.Mode = Universal$ then perform the following for every $O \in S$:
   a) Create an identical copy C'^L of C^L.
   b) Set $\mathcal{S}_C \leftarrow \mathcal{S}_C \cup \{C'^L\}$.
   c) Set $I.O = O$.
   d) Set $I.C = \perp$.
   Finally, set $\mathcal{S}_C \leftarrow \mathcal{S}_C \setminus \{C^L\}$.

16.11 Bibliographic Notes

There are essentially four popular classes of syntactic constructs for express-ing timing constraints in (variants of) MSCs: **timers** [9, 123], **delay inter-vals** [9, 86], **drawing rules** and **timing marks** [17]. For a detailed survey and comparison of the different time notations in sequence charts the reader is referred to [13].

Recommendation Z.120 [91] provides timers for expressing timing con-straints within a single MSC, and along a single instance. Timers cannot be shared among different instances in an MSC and can therefore be used to constrain events occurring only within a single object.

Delay intervals are also used to express timing constraints in a single MSC. They may express three types of constraints: An **event associated** interval [86] indicates the global minimal and maximal delays within which the event should occur with respect to a previous event in the trace. A **message de-livery** interval indicates the minimal and maximal delays allowed from the moment a message is sent until it is received. A **processor speed** interval indicates the minimal and maximal delays allowed between two consecutive events along an instance line. The author of [86] generalizes the message de-livery and processor speed delay intervals by using the semantic notion of **consecutive events**. In addition, the syntax of MSCs is extended in [86] with **precedence edges** that connect unrelated events and thus allow the user to provide delay intervals for them. While precedence edges indeed allow the expression of additional timing constraints, they may result in a cluttered graph.

In some versions of the UML [17, 115], timing constraints in sequence diagrams can be represented by drawing rules and timing marks. Horizon-tally drawn arrows indicate synchronous messages, while downward slanted arrows indicate a required delay between the send and receive events of the message. To describe more quantitative timing constraints, timing marks can be attached to the diagram. These are Boolean expressions placed in braces, and they can constrain particular events or the entire diagram. Timing marks are not shown visually in the diagram.

In [65], an automata-based semantics for LSCs is presented. While the LSC language in [65] does not contain some of our other extensions (e.g., symbolic instances and forbidden elements), time is indeed dealt with. LSCs can be annotated by timers and by delay intervals. Thus, the timing constraints are between pairs of events that are either on the same instance line or are connected by a message. The LSC is unwound into a timed Büchi automaton with unique clocks serving each constraint.

Turning now to temporal logics, these are usually interpreted over linear traces or branching computation trees. Temporal logic formulas disregard aspects of visualization or the fact that two constrained events may occur in different objects/processes. An extensive survey of notations for timing constraints in temporal logics, comparisons of them and a discussion of their expressive power can be found in [6].

A common way of introducing real time in temporal logic is by replacing the unrestricted temporal operators by time-bounded versions [70]. For example, the **time-bounded operator** $\Diamond_{[1,3]}$ is interpreted as 'eventually within one to three time units'. This notation can relate only adjacent temporal contexts, so that there appears to be no direct way of expressing the following property for example: "every stimulus p is followed by a response q and then by another response r, such that r is within five time units of the stimulus p" [6]. This shortcoming can be remedied by extending temporal logic with explicit references to the times of temporal contexts, for example by **freeze quantifiers** [7]. The freeze quantifier '$x.$' binds the associated variable x to the time of the current temporal context. For example, the formula $\Diamond x.\phi$ binds the variable x to the time of the state at which ϕ 'eventually' becomes true.

Another way of writing real-time requirements is based on standard **first-order logic**. The syntax uses a dynamic state variable T — the clock variable — and first-order quantification of global variables over the time domain. The clock variable T assumes in each state the value of the corresponding time. Examples of using this method for expressing timing constraints can be found in several places, such as [94, 95].

Timed automata [4] serve as the semantic basis for many of the timing models in the literature, and are extensively used for model-checking properties of such models. An extensive survey of the theory of timed automata and their role in specification and verification of real-time systems appears in [3].

Time is, of course, handled in many other non-scenario-based formalisms, mainly to specify maximal delays for an operation to be carried out (e.g., *Delay* in the Ada programming language [61]) or for a state to be exited (e.g., the **squiggle** notation proposed in the initial statecharts paper [42], and **timeout** constructs for states in tools like Statemate or Rhapsody [48, 53, 60]).

The time extensions to LSCs that are discussed in this chapter were first presented in [51], which is also the source for most of the examples presented in the chapter. In our extensions to LSCs we adopt the basic philosophy of Alur and Henzinger [8], according to which a real-time system can be viewed as a discrete system with clock variables. The synchrony hypothesis, which we adopt in our operational semantics and in the Play-Engine implementation, was first proposed by Berry as part of the Esterel language [14]. For a detailed discussion regarding the problems and challenges in the transition between models of real-time systems and their implementation, see [112].

We showed earlier how timing constraints can be combined with standard conditions to form timed guards. Placing a maximal delay in conjunction with a 'regular' guard is somewhat similar to the notion of **delayed deadline**, as it appears in [107].

17. Forbidden Elements

So far, we have shown how the language of LSCs and its various proposed extensions are used to specify what a system *can* do and what it *must* do. Of course, the fact that we have hot elements at our disposal allows us to lay out a variety of constraints on the allowed behavior, outlawing parts that we do not want. The ultimate in such disallowed behavior are anti-scenarios, where we use a hot false condition to forbid an entire scenario, the one appearing in the prechart, from occurring.

In this chapter, we introduce a more direct and flexible means for disallowing behavior, **forbidden elements**. With these one can specify events that are not allowed to occur or conditions that are not allowed to hold during specific intervals within a chart's execution. We also show how forbidden elements can be used to express **invariants**, i.e., expressions that must hold during specified execution intervals. Using invariants, we can express assumptions over the system's runs and can also force the system to adhere to them. And, again, the hot/cold dichotomy causes this LSC extension to become particularly powerful. It also renders the specification of many kinds of often-needed constraints more convenient and explicit.

17.1 Example: A Cruise Control System

We shall be using a simple car panel with an automatic cruise control system as our example here. Figure 17.1 shows a graphical user interface and an object map of the target system, together with a sample LSC. The GUI consists of a steering wheel, acceleration and brake pedals, a speedometer, and a switch for turning the cruise control system on and off. The object map contains three internal objects: the cruise control unit, the car's main control unit and the engine. The LSC in this figure describes what happens when the driver hits the brake pedal. Using an unbounded loop with a cold condition and timing constructs, the speed is decreased at a rate of 5 km/h every second, until it reaches 0.

Now suppose we would like to specify that this process of deceleration terminates not only when the car stops, but also when the user presses the

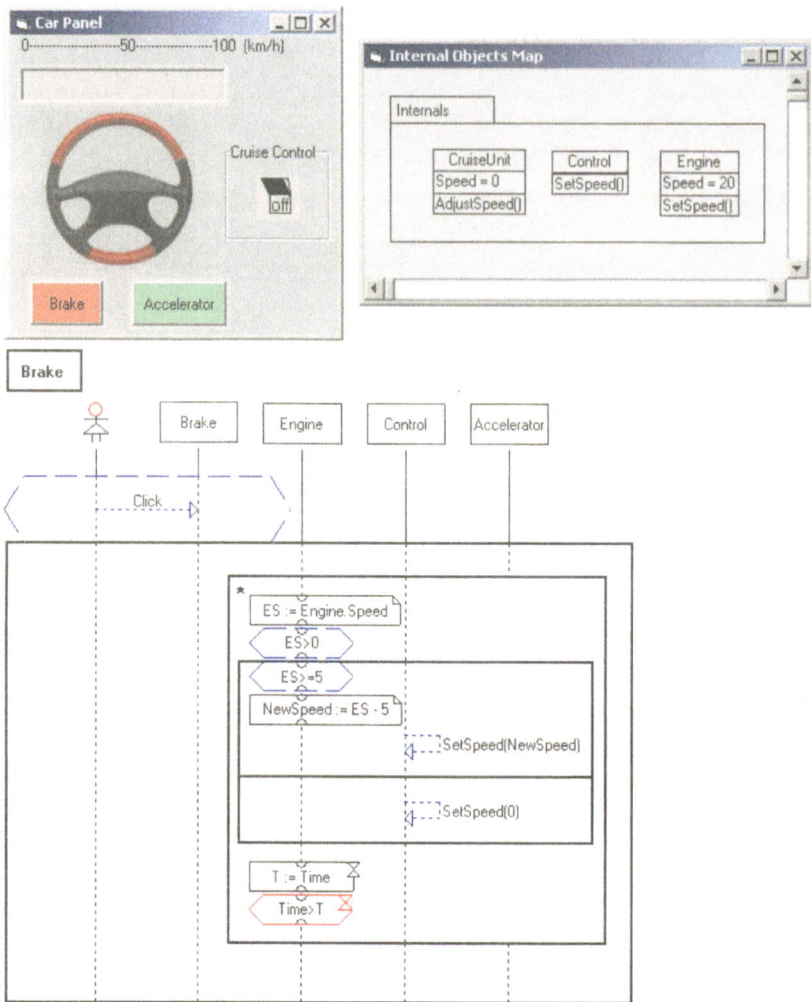

Fig. 17.1. Hitting the brakes

accelerator. Since hitting the accelerator is an event, we cannot refer to it using a cold condition in the loop. To overcome this shortcoming we introduce the new construct of a **forbidden message**, which appears in this example at the bottom of Fig. 17.2.

17.2 Forbidden Messages

Forbidden messages are messages that are not allowed to occur within a given scope. In the example of Fig. 17.2, we would like to say that the event of the

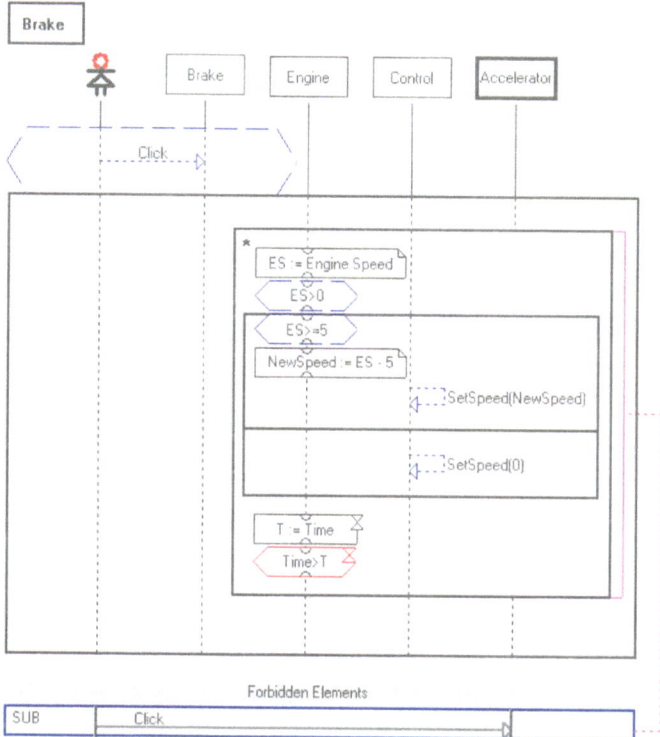

Fig. 17.2. Stop deceleration when pressing the accelerator

user pressing the accelerator is not allowed to happen inside the deceleration loop. In the general spirit of LSCs, forbidden messages can be **hot** or **cold**. If a hot forbidden message occurs while the chart is in the forbidden scope, this is considered a violation of the requirements, whereas a cold forbidden message occurring merely causes the forbidden scope to be gracefully exited, causing no error. In our example, the forbidden message is cold, thus causing the termination of the loop the instant the accelerator is pressed, regardless of the situation of the execution within the loop.

Cold forbidden messages can be used to control the flow of LSC execution by events whose exact time of occurrence is not known. In contrast, hot forbidden messages can be used to unequivocally state that certain events are simply not allowed to happen (or are strongly postulated not to happen) within a given scope. The temperature of a forbidden message has a somewhat different meaning from that of a conventional message. The temperature of a standard message represents the obligation for the message to be received if sent, while the temperature of a forbidden message represents the obligation for the message not to be sent, i.e., not to take place at all.

We thus draw forbidden messages in a neutral color — grey — while the message's surrounding rectangle is drawn in blue or red according to the temperature. Cold forbidden messages and their rectangles are still drawn using dashed lines, while the hot ones are drawn with solid lines.

All the forbidden messages are located in a special area at the bottom of the LSC, separated by the **Forbidden Elements** header. Each forbidden message is surrounded by its own (red or blue) small rectangle to emphasize that these messages are not related to each other and are not restricted by any partial order.

Figure 17.3 shows an example of using a hot forbidden message. In it, *O1*

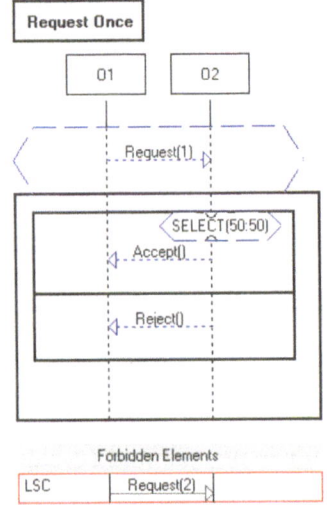

Fig. 17.3. Using hot forbidden messages

sends *Request(1)* to *O2*. In response, *O2* may reply with either "Accept" or "Reject". The forbidden message asserts that as long as the LSC is active (the forbidden scope is written to the left of the rectangle), *O1* is not allowed to send *Request(2)* to *O2*. This hot forbidden message serves two purposes. First, it can be used to capture our assumption that *O1* indeed does not send *Request(2)* to *O2* until it receives a reply. If the forbidden message does occur, the Play-Engine will issue an error message, indicating a violation of the requirements, and the chart will be crossed out in red. Second, this kind of hot forbidden message can be used to force the Play-Engine to select events in some desired order during LSC execution. If, for example, the event of *O1* sending *Request(2)* to *O2* is enabled in some other chart, the Play-Engine will not carry it out until the first chart has completed, and if these are the only two charts, the Play-Engine will first cause $O2$ to reply to $O1$ and only then will it issue the next request.

To insert a forbidden message into an LSC, the user clicks on the **Forbidden Elements** button in the toolbar. In response, the cursor moves to the forbidden elements area, and there the user plays in the message as if it were a conventional one.

17.3 Generalized Forbidden Messages

Forbidden messages come in four flavors, or, rather, four levels of generality. The user determines the level by right-clicking the message and choosing a value from the **Forbid What** submenu (see Fig. 17.4).

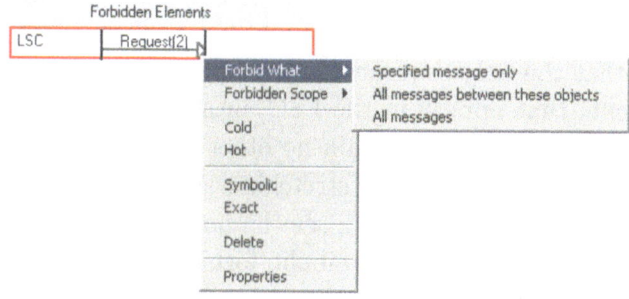

Fig. 17.4. Specifying the level of generality for a forbidden message

The first two levels of generality (i.e., the two most specific) are set by se-lecting **Specified message only**. If the message is *exact* (i.e., not symbolic) then only the exact message that was played in is forbidden. If the message is symbolic, all the messages that are unifiable with it are forbidden. Recall that when trying to unify messages for checking whether there is a violation, we used negative unification, where variables must be already bound to the same value in order to be unifiable. This was done in this way because we did not want a message of the form $m(x)$ to be considered a violation when $m(3)$ occurs, if the value of x is unknown. But now, if we specify that $m(x)$ is a forbidden message, we would certainly like any message of the form $m(c)$ with some constant value c to be considered a violation. Therefore, when checking for violations of forbidden messages we use positive unification. The top two messages in Fig. 17.5 show how these first two levels of generality show up in the forbidden elements area of the chart.

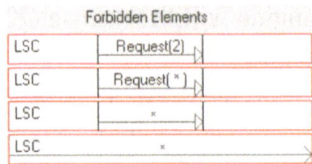

Fig. 17.5. Generality levels of forbidden messages

The next level of generality is obtained by selecting **All messages between these objects**. Setting a message to this level means that all the messages going from the sender of the message to its receiver are forbidden. These kinds of messages are denoted by an arrow going between the objects and labeled with '*'; see the third message in Fig. 17.5.

The maximal generality level is obtained by selecting **All messages**. Setting a message to this level means that *all* messages are forbidden. Setting the scope of such a message to be the entire LSC (see Sect. 17.6 for how this is done) means that the only sequences of events that are allowed are those that contain events that appear in the LSC, in an order matching the one induced by the LSC, and which contain no other events at all. These kinds of messages are denoted by an arrow stretching across the full width of the message rectangle and labeled with '*'; see the bottom message in Fig. 17.5.

Note that the parameter of the symbolic forbidden message (the second line in Fig. 17.5) is given by a '*' and not by a specific name. This is to indicate the fact that any value can be unified with the parameter. If we want to forbid only messages with a specific value that is a priori unknown but will be determined during execution, an existing variable from the LSC can be used as the parameter of the forbidden message, and the variable name will then appear as the parameter of the forbidden message. The LSC in Fig. 17.6 says that $O1$ is not allowed to make two identical requests before the first one is answered.

17.4 Symbolic Instances in Forbidden Messages

Consider the LSC shown in Fig. 17.7. It refers to the telephone network system of Chaps. 15 and 16, and states that when the user clicks the **Call** button on any of the phones in the system, the phone delays for one time unit and then sends a *Call(0)* message to the central switch. It also says, utilizing the forbidden messages mechanism, that during that time no other phone may call the switch, and if some phone does, the LSC should exit immediately.

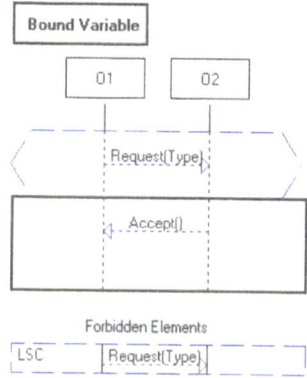

Fig. 17.6. Using an existing LSC variable in a forbidden message

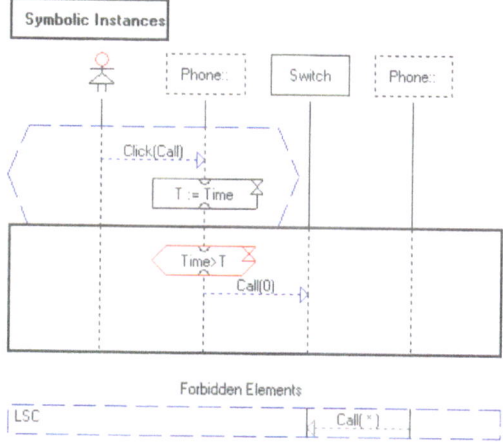

Fig. 17.7. Symbolic instances in forbidden messages

This example raises the following question: Suppose that the chart is activated by the user clicking on phone1. Clearly, if phone2 calls the switch while phone1 is waiting for the time unit to elapse, this should be considered a violation. But, what happens if phone1, not phone2, calls the switch during that period by sending the message *Call(2)* (we deliberately chose a message that does not unify with any other message in the chart body)? Should that be considered a violation?

We have decided that it is not. According to our semantics, the forbidden message, if specified with a source or target class line that is different from some instance that represents a specific object or class in the chart, should refer to the disjoint set that contains all objects other than those that are already represented by instances in the chart. Here, the forbidden message

refers to all the phones *except* phone1. This decision is consistent with the
fact that the same object cannot be represented by two instance lines in the
same LSC. The decision also allows us to restrict phone1 by adding another
forbidden message originating from the first instance, whereas choosing the
alternative option would have made it impossible to restrict all objects except
for phone1.

17.5 Forbidden Conditions

Returning to our cruise control example, consider the LSC in Fig. 17.8. It

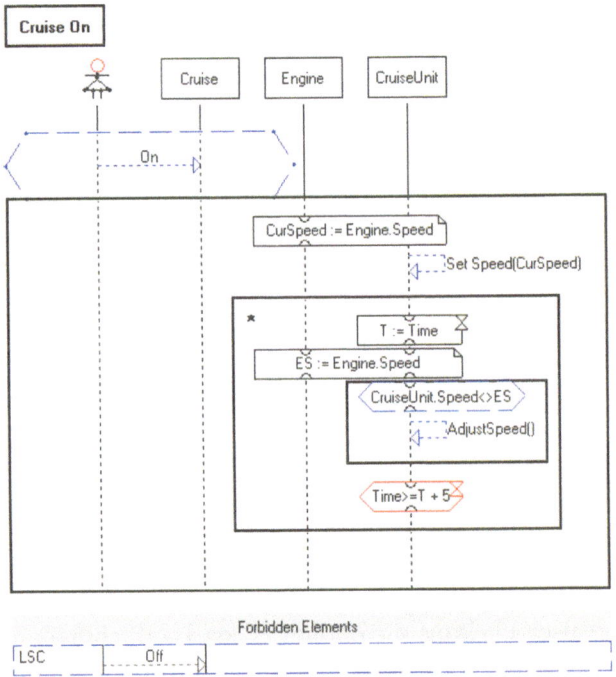

Fig. 17.8. Turning on the cruise control system

states that when the driver turns on the cruise control system, the cruise
unit stores the current speed of the car and then enters an infinite loop, in
which it adjusts the speed every 5 seconds (the call to *AdjustSpeed* activates
a different LSC that we have not shown here). Since the user may turn off the
cruise control system at any time, specifying this user action as a forbidden
message has the effect of deactivating the operation of the cruise unit as soon
as the cruise switch is turned off.

Now suppose we have specified that the cruise switch is turned off automatically as a side effect of the user hitting the brakes or the accelerator (see Fig. 17.9). Naturally, we would like to deactivate the cruise control operation

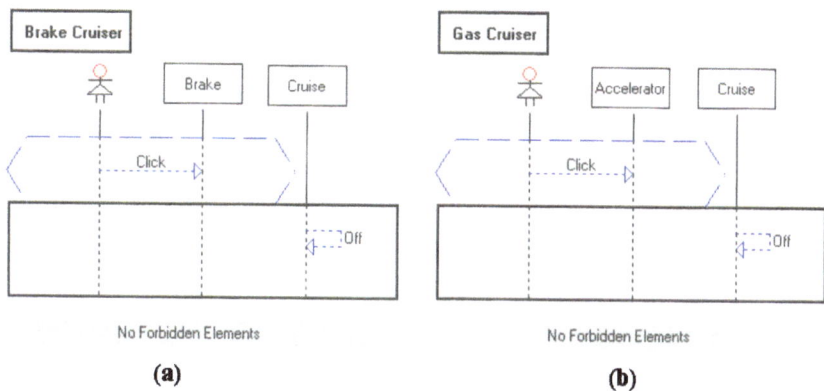

Fig. 17.9. Deactivating cruise control with the brakes or accelerator

in these cases too. We could add another forbidden (self) message in Fig. 17.8 to disallow the switch being turned off, thus having the same effect as the existing forbidden message. Instead, we offer a more elegant solution.

What we really care about is the state of the switch and not the reason for it being turned off. Thus, what we really need is a cold condition constraining the switch to be on. Where should such a condition be located? We could put it at the beginning of the loop, thus making sure that no *AdjustSpeed* event occurs while the switch is off. However, if the switch is turned off immediately after being turned on, the cruise unit will still store the new speed. Although this is not the end of the world, the point is that we want a condition that will be forced to hold not only at some discrete points during the run but throughout entire run intervals.

To make this possible, we extend the LSC language with **forbidden conditions**, which are not allowed to hold anywhere within the scope associated with them. Figure 17.10 shows an example of a cold forbidden condition that constrains the switch to be on as long as the LSC is active. As with forbidden messages, as soon as a cold forbidden condition evaluates to true, its forbidden scope is exited.

Forbidden conditions may also be hot, and can thus be used to really force properties during execution. If a hot forbidden condition becomes true, this is considered a violation of the requirements and is indicated with a red cross over the chart and an error message, as with forbidden messages. In Fig. 17.11, for example, the hot condition constrains the engine speed to be

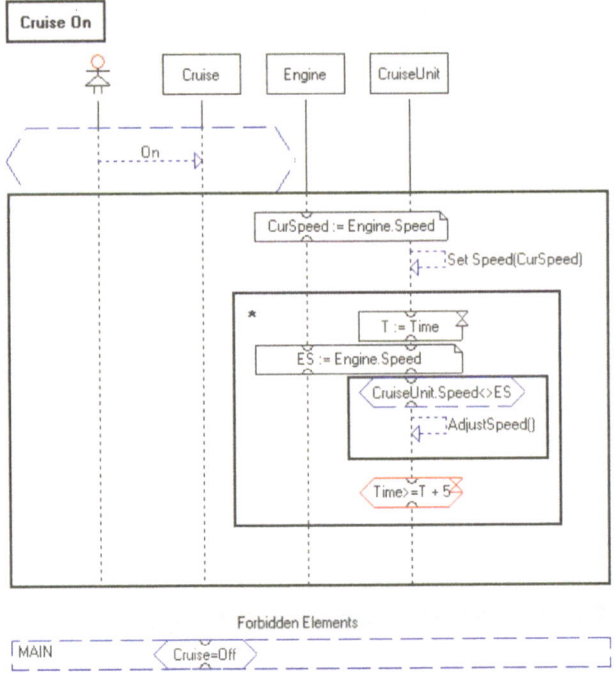

Fig. 17.10. A cold forbidden condition

no greater than 100 km/h. By associating this condition with the entire LSC, even the act of turning on the cruise control system while the car is running at a speed greater than 100 km/h will trigger a violation of the forbidden condition and the prechart will not complete.

Hot forbidden conditions can also be used to enforce some specific order between unrelated events. Consider, for example, the two LSCs in Fig. 17.12. The LSC "*Trigger*" states that when the cruise switch is turned on, $O1$ resets its *Done* flag to false, then it sends *Req1* to $O2$, and finally it sets its *Done* flag to true. The second LSC, "*Response*", shows that after a certain delay from the moment the request sent from $O1$ is received by $O2$, $O2$ replies with *Accept*. In this LSC there is a hot forbidden condition that forbids $O1$ to have its *Done* flag set to true throughout the entire LSC. Now, suppose the switch is turned on. $O1$ first resets its flag to false, then sends the message to $O2$, and this message activates a copy of "*Response*". Although $O2$ has to wait before replying to $O1$, the Play-Engine cannot advance the first chart in the meantime, because it will cause a violation of the second LSC. Therefore, the Play-Engine waits for the required delay to elapse and for $O2$ to send the reply. Only then, after the second LSC completes, is the constraint no longer

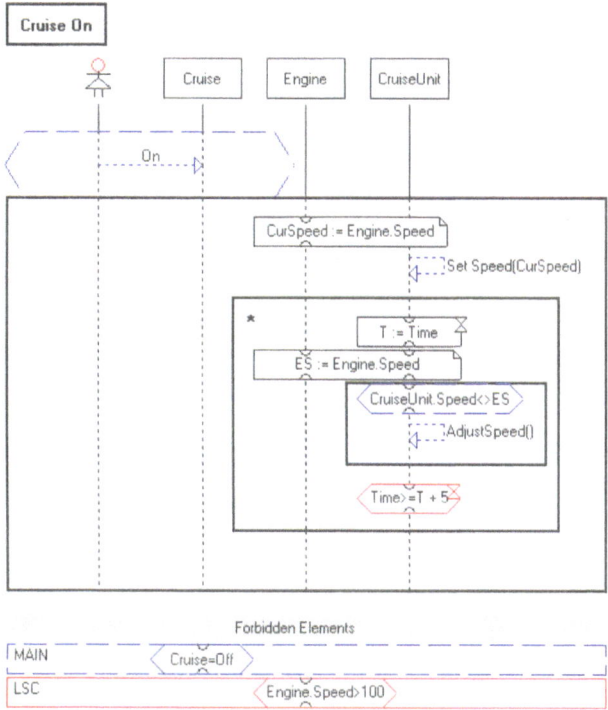

Fig. 17.11. Using a hot forbidden condition to enforce a safety invariant

obligating, and the first chart can be completed too by setting the *Done* flag to true.

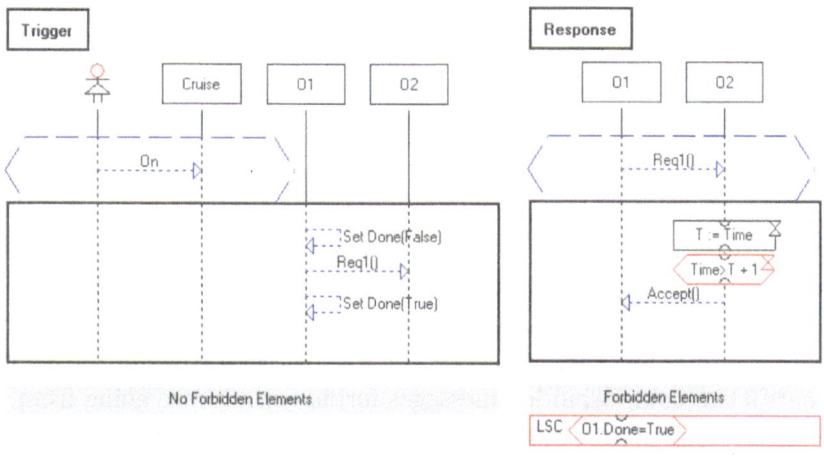

Fig. 17.12. Using a hot forbidden condition to enforce the order of execution

17.6 Scoping Forbidden Elements

Forbidden elements can be restricted to various scopes in an LSC. The forbidden scope can be the entire LSC, its prechart, its main chart, or any subchart thereof. The user determines the scope by right-clicking the message and selecting a value from the **Forbidden Scope** submenu (see Fig. 17.13).

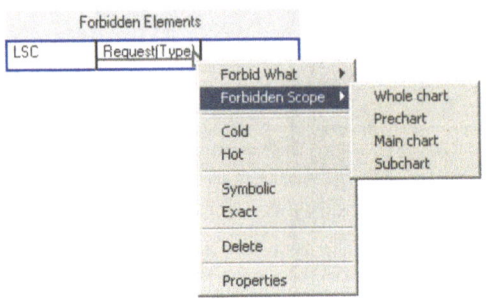

Fig. 17.13. Selecting the scope of a forbidden message

The scope is written on the left side of the forbidden message's bounding rectangle, and when the mouse is placed over the message a thin dashed line connecting it to its scope is shown. In addition, when the mouse is placed over a subchart, the Play-Engine graphically connects it to all its relevant forbidden messages (see Fig. 17.14).

Figure 17.14 actually raises a priority issue. The bottom two messages restrict the same subchart. The first is a hot restriction, and says that all messages going from $O1$ to $O2$ are strictly forbidden. The second is cold, and says that if any message occurs while execution is inside the subchart, the subchart should be exited. Suppose now that $O1$ sends a message M to $O2$. Which of the following should happen? Should the subchart exit, or should this be interpreted as a violation of the requirements?

We adopt the second approach, according to which hot forbidden messages take precedence over (or are more **dominant** than) cold ones. We feel it is more intuitive to have stricter restrictions overriding less strict ones. A similar question arises when two cold forbidden messages are violated simultaneously and one's scope contains the other. The LSC in Fig. 17.15 states that when $O1$ sends a request to $O2$, $O2$ accepts it with a 50% probability. The first of the chart's two cold forbidden messages forbids only those going from $O1$ to $O2$, but throughout the entire chart, while the second forbids *all* messages, but only within the subchart. Now suppose that $O1$ again sends a message M to $O2$. This can result in either exiting the subchart or exiting the whole

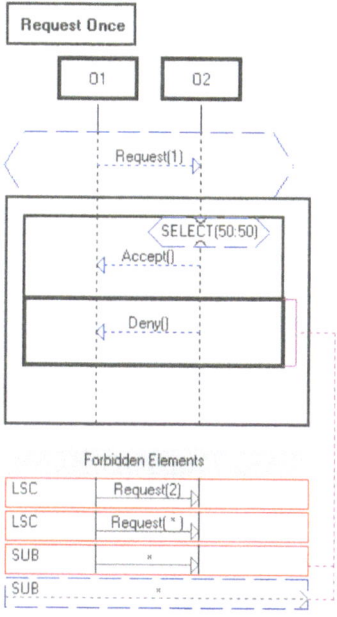

Fig. 17.14. Overlapping scopes of forbidden messages

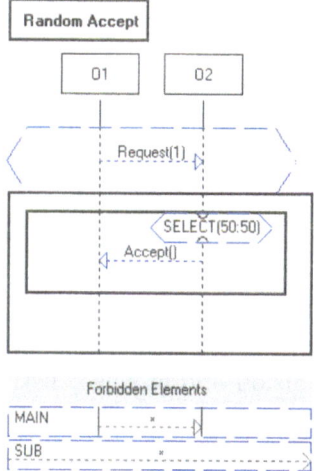

Fig. 17.15. Violating contained scopes

chart. We adopt the approach according to which the larger scope takes precedence. This choice seems the most intuitive, and it also eliminates the need to explain why a scope that is restricted by a message is not exited when the message occurs.

17.7 Playing Out

Forbidden elements are played in like conventional ones, i.e., the user moves the cursor to the forbidden area and then the elements are played in normally.

Turning to play-out, the process of executing an LSC specification calls for the Play-Engine to monitor events as they are carried out by the system or the environment, and to trigger events according to the bodies of universal charts. Events that are carried out by the environment (i.e., the user, the external environment, the clock and the external objects) are beyond the control of the Play-Engine, and it therefore cannot prevent them from occurring. If such an event does occur while being forbidden, it is the duty of the Play-Engine to indicate this misbehavior visually and to report it to the user.

As far as events that are generated by the system are concerned, the Play-Engine selects such events one at a time, in such a way as to make sure that the next event that is carried out will not violate any active LSCs (and if possible will not violate any pre-active LSCs either). Now that LSCs have been endowed with forbidden messages, the Play-Engine has additional work to do. Not only does it have to look for events that appear in the chart and are not enabled, but it also has to scan the forbidden messages looking for possible violations. Unlike finding non-enabled events, a task that involves a simple search through the chart, forbidden messages are considered to be violating only if the current cut is inside the message's forbidden scope.

When the specification contains forbidden conditions, the Play-Engine makes an additional effort, and before choosing an event to be carried out it simulates the immediate impact on the system of doing so. (Of course, this is required only for events that change object properties and not for events that merely transfer information between objects.) If a hot forbidden condition with a currently active scope would become true by this, the event is not selected to be executed. Cold forbidden conditions are not considered in the act of ruling out events, since we think of them more as means for controlling the flow of execution and less as constraints that are not allowed to happen.

Hence, the process of checking whether an event e causes a violation in an LSC L consists of the following steps:

1. Go through the forbidden conditions in L. If there is one with a currently active scope that will become true as a result of carrying out e, add it to an initially empty collection of conditions.
2. If the collection of conditions contains a hot condition, e is violating.
3. If e is currently enabled in L, it is not violating.

4. Go through the forbidden messages in L. If there is one with a currently active scope that can be positively-unified with e, add it to an initially empty collection of messages.
5. If the collection of messages contains a hot message, e is violating.
6. If the collection of messages contains only cold messages, e is not violating.
7. If there are no relevant forbidden messages and there is an event in L negatively-unifiable with e that is currently not enabled, e is violating.
8. Otherwise, e is not violating.

Actually, when the Play-Engine looks for events to be carried out, it first selects those that do not violate even cold forbidden messages, and only if no such events exist, does it allow for ones that violate cold forbidden messages.

If a forbidden message occurs, the Play-Engine crosses out the violated chart, encircles the forbidden message that caused the violation and issues a warning or an error message, depending on the message's temperature. In the

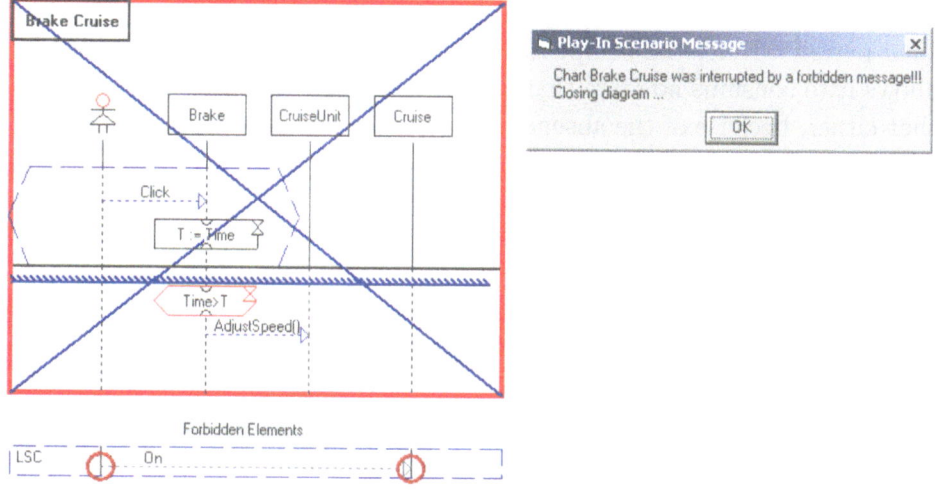

Fig. 17.16. Interrupting a chart by a cold forbidden message

example shown in Fig. 17.16, it is assumed that the driver is not supposed to turn on the cruise control for at least 1 second from the moment he/she hits the brake pedal. The figure shows the reaction of the Play-Engine when this scenario indeed occurs; in this case, the deceleration is terminated and the chart is exited, causing no violation.

17.8 Using Forbidden Elements with Time

Forbidden elements can be used to induce simple but useful (and quite common) timing constraints. For example, suppose we wish to specify that a set of events should be carried out within one time unit; or, in other words, that it should not be interrupted by clock ticks. This can be achieved, as shown in Chap. 16, by specifying a maximal delay on the set of events. A simpler and more elegant way of doing this would be to specify the 'Tick' event as a forbidden message that restricts the set of events (e.g., the entire chart or a subchart). Figure 17.18 shows an example.

A cold forbidden 'Tick' event placed so as to restrict an unbounded loop can be used to specify a restriction of the form: "the system should do as much as it can within a single time unit".

Forbidden conditions can also be used to restrict the amount of time something should take. In the LSC of Fig. 17.17, for example, $O1$ requests $O2$ to perform something. This may be an iterative computation, for which initial results can be obtained quickly and then refined for better quality as time permits. Here, the computation loop is guarded by a **watchdog** that allows it to consume no more than 3 time units (and in this case no less than that either, because of the absence of any other means of loop termination).

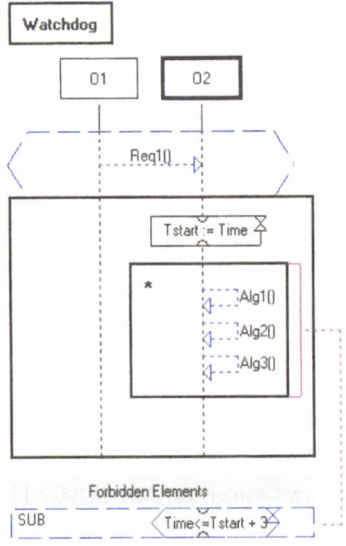

Fig. 17.17. Specifying a watchdog with forbidden conditions

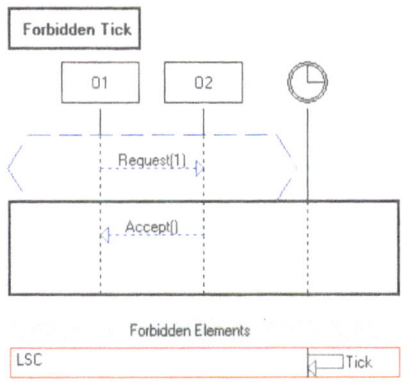

Fig. 17.18. Forcing an LSC to complete within a single time unit

17.9 A Tolerant Semantics for LSCs

The LSC semantics that we define throughout the book prescribes that an event e that occurs during execution is considered to be violating an LSC L if e appears in L but is not enabled. Other events, i.e., those that do not appear in L, are not restricted in this way, and may occur at any time. Now that LSCs are extended with forbidden messages, events that do not appear in a chart may also be restricted to not occur while the chart is executed. There is, however, a problem with this semantics: it makes it very difficult to specify the kind of behavior where some event has to appear in a certain place, but doing so without forbidding it to occur in other places during the execution.

Endowed with the expressive power of forbidden elements, a reasonable alternative semantics would be one that prescribes that events should not be restricted at all by the LSC, unless explicitly restricted using forbidden elements. And, indeed, the Play-Engine has been designed to support this 'tolerant' semantics too. We could have implemented the alternative semantics on the execution level — meaning that it would apply to all LSCs — or on the single-LSC level. We have decided to adopt the second, more expressive, approach. Thus, the user can declare each LSC as being **strict** or **tolerant**. A strict LSC is one that behaves the way we have seen all along; namely, it does not allow events that appear in it to occur when they are not enabled. A tolerant LSC allows occurrences of all events, unless they are explicitly not allowed by the forbidden elements mechanism.

Figure 17.19 shows an example of a tolerant LSC (marked with `Tolerant` to the right of its name; strict LSCs have no added annotation). In this example, if the driver switches between the accelerator and the brake pedals

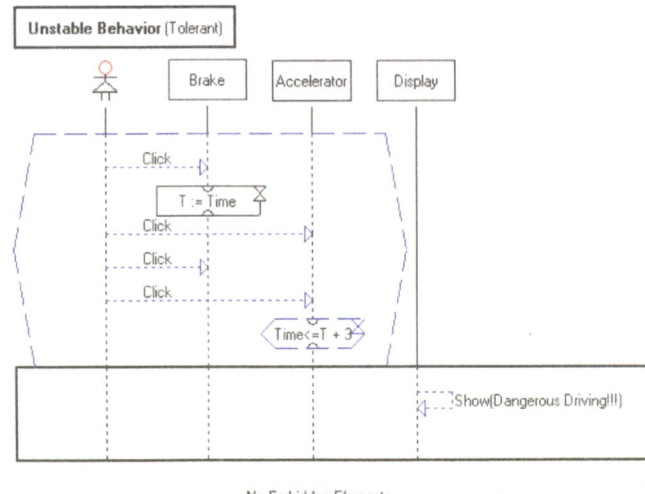

Fig. 17.19. Using a tolerant LSC to detect dangerous driving

twice within 3 seconds, this is considered dangerous driving and an appropriate message appears on the display. Since this LSC is tolerant, the user may press the brake pedal or the accelerator several times before switching to the other. In a strict LSC this would have been considered a violation, but in this tolerant LSC all that matters is that the specified events occurred in the specified order within the specified time limit.

17.10 And a Bit More Formally ...

Here are the extensions and modifications needed in the semantics to support forbidden elements and the tolerant semantics.

System Model and Events

Forbidden messages and conditions are entirely specification oriented and therefore do not affect the system model.

LSC Specification

An LSC L is extended to contain forbidden messages and forbidden conditions and may be declared as either strict or tolerant, as follows:

$$L = \langle I_L, V_L, M_L, [Pch_L], A_L, C_L, SUB_L, ITE_L, LOOP_L, \overline{M}_L, \overline{C}_L, Strict, evnt, subchart, temp\rangle$$

where $\overline{M}_L$ is the set of forbidden messages, $\overline{C}_L$ is the set of forbidden conditions, and $Strict \in \{True, False\}$ indicates whether the LSC is strict or tolerant.

A forbidden message $\bar{M} \in \overline{M}_L$ is a 3-tuple

$$\bar{M} = \langle M, Level, Scope \rangle$$

where M is an LSC message, $Level \in \{Message, Objects, All\}$ is the *generality level* of the forbidden message, and $Scope \in \{LSC, Pre, Main\} \cup SUB_L$ is the forbidden scope restricted by the message.

A forbidden condition $\bar{C} \in \overline{C}_L$ is a pair

$$\bar{C} = \langle C, Scope \rangle$$

where C is an LSC condition and $Scope$ is defined as above.

Forbidden messages and conditions are also associated with temperatures. Therefore, we extend the domain of the function *temp*:

$$temp : \ell(L) \cup M_L \cup C_L \cup \overline{M}_L \cup \overline{C}_L \rightarrow \{hot, cold\}$$

Finally, we extend E_L, the set of LSC events, to include the hidden events of evaluating forbidden conditions:

$$
\begin{aligned}
E_L = \ & (\{m \in M_L \mid m.M_s \in \Sigma_{FromUser} \cup \Sigma_{ToUser} \cup \Sigma_{FromEnv} \cup \Sigma_{ToEnv} \cup \Sigma_{Calls}\} \\
& \quad \times \{Send, Recv\}) \\
& \cup (\{m \in M_L \mid m.M_s \in \Sigma_{Self} \cup \Sigma_{Clock}\} \times \{Send\}) \\
& \cup (Pch_L \times \{Start, End\}) \cup \{Completed\} \\
& \cup \{perform(A) \mid A \in A_L\} \cup \{eval(C) \mid C \in C_L\} \\
& \cup (SUB_L \times \{Start, End\}) \cup \{branch(ITE) \mid ITE \in ITE_L\} \\
& \cup (LOOP_L \times \{Start, End\}) \\
& \cup \{skip(Loop) \mid Loop \in LOOP_L \wedge Loop.Kind = Dynamic\} \\
& \cup \{bind(I) \mid I \in I_L \wedge symbolic(I)\} \\
& \cup \{evalf(\bar{C}) \mid \bar{C} \in \overline{C}_L\}
\end{aligned}
$$

Operational Semantics

Forbidden messages and conditions are considered only when the current LSC cut contains locations that are within their associated scope. To capture precisely this notion of a cut being in a scope, we define an *active scope*.

Definition 17.10.1 (active scope). *A scope $S \in \{LSC, Pre, Main\} \cup SUB_L$ is active in an LSC live copy C^L if one of the following holds:*

1. $S = LSC$.
2. $S = Pre$ and $C^L.Mode = PreActive$.
3. $S = Main$ and $C^L.Mode \in \{Active, Check\}$.
4. $S \in SUB_L$ and $\forall I \in I_S, loc((S, Start)) <_L C^L.Cut(I) <_L loc((S, End))$.

Recall that $Cut(I)$ denotes the location of instance I in Cut. Since the start and end of a subchart are synchronization points for all its instances, it is sufficient to check any instance in the subchart to see if the subchart is active. We will use the predicate notation $active(S)$ to indicate that a scope S is active.

We explained in the text that when looking for a violation in the set of forbidden messages we use positive-unification. Moreover, since forbidden messages can be in one of several levels of generality, we should define a different algorithm for checking whether a forbidden message is unifiable with a regular one.

Definition 17.10.2 (forbidden message unification). *A system message M_s and a forbidden message $\bar{M}$ are unifiable if one of the following holds:*

1. $\bar{M}.Level = All$.
2. $\bar{M}.Level = Objects$ and $M_s.Src \preceq \bar{M}.M.I_{Src} \wedge M_s.Dst \preceq \bar{M}.M.I_{Dst}$.
3. $\bar{M}.Level = Message$ and M_s and $\bar{M}.M$ are positively-unifiable.

Checking for unification of an *LSC message* M_l with a forbidden message $\bar{M}$ is defined similarly, with $M_s.Src$ and $M_s.Dst$ replaced by $M_l.I_{Src}$ and $M_l.I_{Dst}$, respectively.

Before modifying the transition relation, we define a utility function that gets as input a set of forbidden messages and returns one of the *dominant* messages in the set. A hot message is more dominant than a cold one, and one cold message is more dominant than another if the former's scope contains that of the latter. Note that if two forbidden messages are active, their scopes must be identical or one scope must be contained in the other.

---

dominant(S)

1. If $\exists \bar{M} \in S$ s.t. $temp(\bar{M}) = hot$ then return $\bar{M}$.
2. If all messages are cold then
   a) Set $\bar{M}$ to be any message in S.
   b) $S \leftarrow S \setminus \{\bar{M}\}$.
   c) While $S \neq \emptyset$ do
       i. Choose a message $\bar{M}' \in S$.
      ii. $S \leftarrow S \setminus \{\bar{M}'\}$.
     iii. If $\bar{M}.Scope \subset \bar{M}'.Scope$ then set $\bar{M} \leftarrow \bar{M}'$.
   d) Return $\bar{M}$.

The function *dominant* is defined in the same way for sets of forbidden conditions.

The definition of a violating event is now modified, so that events that appear in an LSC and are not enabled in it are considered violating only if the LSC is strict.

Definition 17.10.3 (violating event). *An event e violates a chart L in a cut C if $L.Strict \stackrel{!}{=} True$ and $e \in M_L \times \{Send, Recv\}$, but e is not enabled with respect to C.*

The transition relation $\Delta[\mathcal{S}_O, \mathcal{S}_C]$ is now modified to handle unification with forbidden messages and to evaluate forbidden conditions. The transition relation assumes that if it is applied to a forbidden condition, the condition holds and its forbidden scope is active. These assumptions are later guaranteed by the various execution functions, i.e., step, super-step and monitor-event. $\Delta[\mathcal{S}_O, \mathcal{S}_C]$ is therefore given as:

- If $e = \langle M, t \rangle$ *(where $t \in \{Send, Recv\}$) then:*
  1. If $e.M.m = Tick$ then set $Clock.Time \leftarrow Clock.Time + 1$.
  2. Set $Context \leftarrow \emptyset$.
  3. If $\exists C^L \in \mathcal{S}_C$ and $\exists \bar{M} \in C^L.LSC.\overline{M}_L$, such that $e.M$ and $\bar{M}$ are unifiable and $active(\bar{M}.Scope)$, and there is no enabled event e' positively level$_2$-unifiable with e, then:
      a) Set $S \leftarrow \{\bar{M} \in C^L.LSC.\overline{M}_L | Unifiable(e.M, \bar{M}) \wedge active(\bar{M}.Scope)\}$.
      b) Set $\bar{M} \leftarrow dominant(S)$.
      c) If $temp(\bar{M}) = hot$ then
          i. Set $\mathcal{S}_C \leftarrow \mathcal{S}_C \setminus \{C^L\}$.
          ii. Set $Violating \leftarrow True$.
      d) If $temp(\bar{M}) = cold$ then
          i. If $\bar{M}.Scope \in \{LSC, Pre, Main\}$ then set $\mathcal{S}_C \leftarrow \mathcal{S}_C \setminus \{C^L\}$.
          ii. If $\bar{M}.Scope = Sub \in SUB_L$ then set

$$C^L.Cut \leftarrow AdvanceCut(C^L.Cut, (Sub, End))$$

  4. If $\exists C^L \in \mathcal{S}_C$ and $\exists e' \in C^L.LSC$, such that e and e' are negatively level$_2$-unifiable and e' violates C^L, then:
      a) Set $\mathcal{S}_C \leftarrow \mathcal{S}_C \setminus \{C^L\}$.
      b) If $temp(C^L.Cut) = hot$, set $Violating \leftarrow True$.
      c) If $symbolic(e'.M.I_{Src})$ or $symbolic(e'.M.I_{Dst})$ then create an identical copy C'^L of C^L, set $\mathcal{S}_C \leftarrow \mathcal{S}_C \cup \{C'^L\}$, and in the copy set

$$e'.M.I_{Src}.\Phi \leftarrow e'.M.I_{Src}.\Phi \cup \{e.M.Src\} \quad \text{if } symbolic(e'.M.I_{Src})$$
$$e'.M.I_{Dst}.\Phi \leftarrow e'.M.I_{Dst}.\Phi \cup \{e.M.Dst\} \quad \text{if } symbolic(e'.M.I_{Dst})$$

5. For every universal LSC $L \in \mathcal{S}_O$ which has an event e', positively level$_2$-unifiable with e, as a minimal event in its prechart, create a copy of L, C^L, and set $\mathcal{S}_C \leftarrow \mathcal{S}_C \cup \{C^L\}$. Set $C^L.Mode = PreActive$ and set its cut by $C^L.Cut \leftarrow AdvanceCut(InitialCut(L), \langle Pch_L, Start \rangle)$. Unify the variables of e and e', by $Unify(e, e', Context)$. For each hidden event $e'' <_L e'$, apply $\Delta(e'')$.

6. For every existential LSC $L \in \mathcal{S}_O$ which has an event e', positively level$_2$-unifiable with e, as a minimal event in the chart body, create a copy of L, C^L, and set $\mathcal{S}_C \leftarrow \mathcal{S}_C \cup \{C^L\}$. Set $C^L.Mode = Check$, and set its cut to the beginning of the chart by $C^L.Cut \leftarrow BeginMainCut(C^L.LSC)$. Unify the variables of e and e', by $Unify(e, e', Context)$. For each hidden event $e'' <_L e'$, apply $\Delta(e'')$.

7. For every copy $C^L \in \mathcal{S}_C$ that has a reachable event e' positively level$_2$-unifiable with e:

   a) If $symbolic(e'.M.I_{Src})$ or $symbolic(e'.M.I_{Dst})$ then create an identical copy of C^L, C'^L, set $\mathcal{S}_C \leftarrow \mathcal{S}_C \cup \{C'^L\}$, and in the copy set

   $$e'.M.I_{Src}.\Phi \leftarrow e'.M.I_{Src}.\Phi \cup \{e.m.Src\} \quad \text{if } symbolic(e'.M.I_{Src})$$
   $$e'.M.I_{Dst}.\Phi \leftarrow e'.M.I_{Dst}.\Phi \cup \{e.m.Dst\} \quad \text{if } symbolic(e'.M.I_{Dst})$$

   b) Set $C^L.Cut \leftarrow AdvanceCut(C^L.Cut, e')$.

   c) If $e' = \langle M, Send \rangle$, M is synchronous and $e'' = \langle M, Recv \rangle$, set $C^L.Cut \leftarrow AdvanceCut(C^L.Cut, e'')$.

   d) Unify the events e and e', $Unify(e, e', Context)$.

   e) For each hidden event $e'' <_L e'$, apply $\Delta(e'')$.

- If $e = Completed(C^L)$ for some $C^L \in \mathcal{S}_C$ then set $\mathcal{S}_C \leftarrow \mathcal{S}_C \setminus \{C^L\}$.
- If $e = \langle Pch_L, End \rangle$ for some $C^L \in \mathcal{S}_C$, then set $C^L.Cut \leftarrow BeginMainCut(C^L.LSC)$ and $C^L.Mode \leftarrow Active$.
- If $e = perform(A)$ for some $A \in A_L$ s.t. $C^L \in \mathcal{S}_C$, then set $C^L.Cut \leftarrow AdvanceCut(C^L.Cut, e)$ and set

$$A.V \leftarrow \begin{cases} A.C & \text{if } A.Type = constant \\ Value(A.P) & \text{if } A.Type = property \\ A.f(A.\lambda_f^F) & \text{if } A.Type = function \\ Clock.Time & \text{if } A.Type = time \end{cases}$$

- If $e = eval(C)$ for some $C \in C^L$ s.t. $C^L \in \mathcal{S}_C$ then
  1. If $value(C) = true$ then set $C^L.Cut \leftarrow AdvanceCut(C^L.Cut, e)$.
  2. If $value(C) = false$ then
     a) If $subchart(C) \in \{ITE.Sub_T, ITE.Sub_E\}$ for some ITE then

        set $C^L.Cut \leftarrow AdvanceCut(C^L.Cut, \langle ITE, End \rangle)$

b) If $subchart(C) = Sub \in SUB_L$ then

$$set\ C^L.Cut \leftarrow AdvanceCut(C^L.Cut, (Sub, End))$$

c) If $subchart(C) = \bot$ then set $\mathcal{S}_C \leftarrow \mathcal{S}_C \setminus \{C^L\}$.

d) If $temp(C) = hot$ then set $Violating \leftarrow True$.

- If $e = branch(ITE)$ for some $ITE \in C^L$ s.t. $C^L \in \mathcal{S}_C$ then
  1. If $value(ITE.C) = true$ then set
     $C^L.Cut \leftarrow AdvanceCut(C^L.Cut, (ITE.Sub_T, Start))$
  2. If $value(ITE.C) = false$ then

$$set\ C^L.Cut \leftarrow \begin{cases} AdvanceCut(C^L.Cut, (ITE.Sub_E, Start)) & \text{if } ITE.Sub_E \neq \bot \\ AdvanceCut(C^L.Cut, (ITE.Sub_T, End)) & \text{if } ITE.Sub_E = \bot \end{cases}$$

- If $e = (ITE.Sub_T, End)$ for some $ITE \in C^L$ s.t. $C^L \in \mathcal{S}_C$ then

$$set\ C^L.Cut \leftarrow AdvanceCut(C^L.Cut, (ITE, End))$$

- If $e = (ITE.Sub_E, End)$ for some $ITE \in C^L$ s.t. $C^L \in \mathcal{S}_C$ then

$$set\ C^L.Cut \leftarrow AdvanceCut(C^L.Cut, (ITE.Sub_E, End))$$

- If $e = (Sub, End)$ for some $Sub \in C^L$ s.t. $C^L \in \mathcal{S}_C$ then

$$set\ C^L.Cut \leftarrow AdvanceCut(C^L.Cut, (Sub, End))$$

- If $e = skip(Loop)$ for some $Loop \in C^L$ s.t. $C^L \in \mathcal{S}_C$ then

$$set\ C^L.Cut \leftarrow AdvanceCut(C^L.Cut, (Loop, End))$$

- If $e = (Loop, Start)$ for some $Loop \in C^L$ s.t. $C^L \in \mathcal{S}_C$ then

$$set\ C^L.Cut \leftarrow AdvanceCut(C^L.Cut, (Loop, Start))$$

For every variable $V \in V_L$ that is used in $Loop$ for the first time, set $V.\omega \leftarrow \bot$.

- If $e = (Loop, End)$ for some $Loop \in C^L$ s.t. $C^L \in \mathcal{S}_C$ and $Loop.Kind \neq Dynamic$ then
  1. Set $\mu \leftarrow \mu - 1$.
  2. If $\mu > 0$ then

$$set\ C^L.Cut \leftarrow AdvanceCut(C^L.Cut, (Loop, Start))$$

For every variable $V \in V_L$ that is used in $Loop$ for the first time, set $V.\omega \leftarrow \bot$.

3. If $\mu = 0$ then

$$set\ C^L.Cut \leftarrow AdvanceCut(C^L.Cut, (Loop, End))$$

- If $e = bind(I)$ for some symbolic instance $I \in C^L$ s.t. $C^L \in \mathcal{S}_C$, then:
  1. $S \leftarrow \{O \in \mathcal{O} \mid O \preccurlyeq I, O \text{ satisfies } I.\psi \text{ and } \nexists I' \in C^L \text{ s.t. } I'.O = O\}$.
  2. If $S = \emptyset$ then $\mathcal{S}_C \leftarrow \mathcal{S}_C \setminus \{C^L\}$.
  3. If $I.Mode = Existential$ then
     a) Set $I.O = O$, for some $O \in S$.
     b) Set $I.C = \bot$.
  4. If $I.Mode = Universal$ then perform the following for every $O \in S$:
     a) Create an identical copy C'^L of C^L.
     b) Set $\mathcal{S}_C \leftarrow \mathcal{S}_C \cup \{C'^L\}$.
     c) Set $I.O = O$.
     d) Set $I.C = \bot$.
     Finally, set $\mathcal{S}_C \leftarrow \mathcal{S}_C \setminus \{C^L\}$.

- If $e = eval f(\bar{C})$ for some $\bar{C} \in C^L$ s.t. $C^L \in \mathcal{S}_C$, then (it is guaranteed that $value(\bar{C}) = true$)
  1. If $temp(\bar{C}) = hot$ then
     a) Set $\mathcal{S}_C \leftarrow \mathcal{S}_C \setminus \{C^L\}$.
     b) Set $Violating \leftarrow True$.
  2. If $temp(\bar{C}) = cold$ then
     a) If $\bar{C}.Scope \in \{LSC, Pre, Main\}$ then set $\mathcal{S}_C \leftarrow \mathcal{S}_C \setminus \{C^L\}$.
     b) If $\bar{C}.Scope = Sub \in SUB_L$ then set

$$C^L.Cut \leftarrow AdvanceCut(C^L.Cut, (Sub, End))$$

To complete the modifications in the formal semantics caused by forbidden messages and conditions, we need to modify the procedures *super-step* and *monitor-event*. As opposed to conventional conditions, which are evaluated according to the partial order induced by the LSC, forbidden conditions should affect the course of execution immediately upon becoming true. Therefore, they should be given precedence over other hidden events, both in *super-step* and in *monitor-event*. We begin with the changes in *monitor-event*:

---

monitor-event(ev)

1. Apply $\Delta[\mathcal{S}_M.\mathcal{ML}](ev)$.
2. Compute the set of forbidden conditions:

$$Forbidden \leftarrow \bigcup_{C^L \in \mathcal{ML}} \{\bar{C} \in \overline{C}_L | \; active(\bar{C}.Scope) \wedge value(\bar{C}.C) = true\}$$

3. If $Forbidden \neq \emptyset$ then
   a) $\bar{C} \leftarrow dominant(Forbidden)$.
   b) Apply $\Delta[\mathcal{S}_M.\mathcal{ML}](eval f(\bar{C}))$.
   c) Go back to 2.
4. Compute the set of enabled events:

$$Enabled \leftarrow \bigcup_{C^L \in \mathcal{ML}} \{e \in E_L | enabled(e)\}$$

$$Waiting \leftarrow \bigcup_{C^L \in \mathcal{ML}} \{e \mid e = branch(ITE)\}$$

$$\cup \bigcup_{C^L \in \mathcal{ML}} \{e | e = (Loop, End) \wedge Loop.Kind = Dynamic\}$$

$$Enabled \leftarrow Enabled \setminus Waiting$$

5. If there is a *hidden* enabled event $e \in Enabled$, then
   a) Apply $\Delta[\mathcal{S}_M.\mathcal{ML}](e)$.
   b) Go back to 2.
6. Terminate monitor-event.

As the Play-Engine selects events to be carried out, it avoids choosing ones that are unifiable with active hot forbidden messages, and tries to defer events that are unifiable with cold forbidden messages. Moreover, it avoids choosing events that will cause active hot forbidden conditions to become true. To capture this behavior formally, we define *hot-forbidden* events and *cold-forbidden* events.

Definition 17.10.4 (hot-forbidden event). *An event e is* hot-forbidden *in a chart L being in a cut C if e is not enabled with respect to C, and if, in addition, one of the following holds:*

- $\exists \bar{M} \in \overline{M}_L$ *s.t.* $active(\bar{M}.Scope) \wedge temp(\bar{M}) = hot \wedge Unifiable(e.M, \bar{M})$
- $e.M.P \neq \perp$ *(i.e., e represents a change in the value of a property) and* $\exists \bar{C} \in \overline{C}_L$ *s.t.* $temp(\bar{C}) = hot \wedge active(\bar{C})$ *and $\bar{C}$ will become true if the current value of P is replaced with the value in $e.M$.*

Definition 17.10.5 (cold-forbidden event). *An event e is cold-forbidden in a chart L being in a cut C if e is not enabled with respect to C and $\exists \bar{M} \in \overline{M}_L$ s.t. $active(\bar{M}.Scope) \wedge temp(\bar{M}) = cold \wedge Unifiable(e.M, \bar{M})$.*

We can now continue with the modified *super-step*:

---

super-step

1. Compute the set of forbidden conditions:

$$Forbidden \leftarrow \bigcup_{C^L \in \mathcal{RL}} \{\bar{C} \in \overline{C}_L \mid active(\bar{C}.Scope) \wedge value(\bar{C}.C) = true\}$$

2. If there is a forbidden condition in *Forbidden*, then
   a) $\bar{C} \leftarrow dominant(Forbidden)$.
   b) Apply $\Delta[\mathcal{S}_C, \mathcal{RL}](evalf(\bar{C}))$.
   c) Go back to 1.

3. Compute the set of enabled events:

$$Enabled \leftarrow \bigcup_{C^L \in \mathcal{RL}} \{e \in E_L \mid enabled(e)\}$$

$$Waiting \leftarrow \bigcup_{\substack{C^L \in \mathcal{RL}, \\ C^L.Mode = PreActive}} \{e \mid e = branch(ITE)\}$$

$$Enabled \leftarrow Enabled \setminus (External \cup Waiting)$$

4. If there is a *hidden* enabled event $e \in Enabled$, then
   a) Apply $\Delta[\mathcal{S}_C, \mathcal{RL}](e)$.
   b) Go back to 1.

5. If there is a *visible* enabled event $e \in Enabled$, such that e does not violate and is neither hot-forbidden nor cold-forbidden in any copy that is either in *active* or *preactive* mode, then
   a) *step(e)*.
   b) Go back to 1.

6. If there is a *visible* enabled event $e \in Enabled$, such that e does not violate and is neither hot-forbidden nor cold-forbidden in any copy that is in *active* mode, then
   a) *step(e)*.
   b) Go back to 1.

7. If there is a *visible* enabled event $e \in Enabled$, such that e does not violate and is not hot-forbidden in any copy that is in *active* mode with a hot cut, then
   a) *step(e)*.
   b) Go back to 1.

8. Terminate super-step.

17.11 Bibliographic Notes

Forbidden conditions can be used to construct invariants, which are to be true during the behavior described in an LSC specification. The use of invariants in programming languages, mainly for capturing the semantics of loops and for specifying **pre-conditions** and **post-conditions**, is one of the most fundamental ideas in program semantics and verification. It was first proposed by Floyd in [37] and was given a significant push by Hoare's work in [58].

In the **Eiffel** programming language [87], invariants are part of the language itself. They are used to specify pre- and post-conditions for object methods, and also to capture **class-level invariants**, i.e., conditions that are asserted to hold during the entire life cycle of a class.

In **interval temporal logic** (ITL) [89, 90], a variant of temporal logic geared towards expressing properties that hold along specified intervals, one can specify that a variable has some value during an interval, or that an event, usually indicated by a change in a variable value, is not allowed to happen during an interval. These capabilities resemble our forbidden conditions and forbidden messages, respectively.

Part VI

Enhancing the Play-Engine

18. Smart Play-Out   (with H. Kugler)

In this chapter we provide a brief overview of **smart play-out**[1], a predictive strengthening of the play-out mechanism, which uses methods from program verification — mainly **model-checking**.

The chapter should not be viewed as describing another Play-Engine feature, but, rather, as a broader and more recent approach to the very idea of executing scenario-based requirements. Also, the material described here is somewhat less complete than that appearing in the rest of the book; for example, it has not yet been worked out for several features of the LSCs language. The same applies to the robustness and scope of the implementation of smart play-out, as compared with that of the rest of the Play-Engine. We expect to be able to provide a more detailed report on smart play-out in the near future, as well as a more powerful implementation.

18.1 Introduction

In recent years, formal specification and verification techniques are beginning to be applied to the development of complex reactive systems. Major obstacles that still prevent even wider usage of such methods include the facts that errors are found relatively late in the development process and that high expertise is required to correctly capture the properties to be verified. There has been a particular surge in interest in the verification of software-based reactive systems, especially given the success of verification techniques in hardware development. Due to the size and complexity of such systems, it is desirable to understand all the system requirements, and to make sure they are consistent, before moving on to the implementation phase. In classic verification, a model is first constructed and then verified against well-defined requirements, whereas one of the main points of this chapter is that verification techniques can be beneficially applied to the requirements themselves too. Alternatively, if one adopts the more ambitious potential of play-in/play-out, leading to systems specified solely in a scenario-based fashion, then smart

---

[1] Smart play-out is the central topic of the Ph.D. work of Hillel Kugler (cosupervised by Amir Pnueli), who is also the main co-author of this chapter.

play-out can be viewed as utilizing verification techniques to *run* programs rather than to verify them.

Recall that play-out is actually an iterative process, where after each step taken by the user the Play-Engine computes a super-step, i.e., a sequence of events carried out by the system as a response to the event input by the user. However, the play-out mechanism is, in general, rather naive. For example, there can be many possible sequences that are valid responses to a user event, and some of these may not constitute 'correct' super-steps. We consider a super-step to be correct if when it is executed no active universal chart is violated. By acting blindly by the 'book' of requirements, reacting to a user-generated event with the first action it encounters as a possible reaction to that event, the naive play-out process could very well follow a sequence of events that eventually causes violation, even though some other sequence might have been chosen that would have completed successfully. We will illustrate this shortly.

From a conceptual point of view, the potential of many possible sequences of reactions to a user event is due to the fact that LSCs is a declarative, inter-object language, and as such it enables the formulation of high-level requirements in pieces (e.g., scenario fragments), leaving open details that may depend on the implementation. Technically, the two sources of this non-determinism are the partial order semantics among events in each chart, and different charts containing scenarios that do not have explicit information about their interrelationship. These features are very useful in early requirements stages, but can cause undesired underspecification when one attempts to execute them. Smart play-out attempts to remove these sources of non-determinism during execution. Thus, depending on whether we view play-in/play-out as a requirements method or an implementation, smart play-out either 'helps' the system fulfil its requirements or strengthens its very execution mechanism.

The smart play-out process uses a powerful program verification technique, called model-checking, to find a 'correct' super-step if one exists, and otherwise proving that such a super-step does not exist. In our implementation, the procedure can be applied anew at the occurrence of each user event in order to examine the different potential super-steps and to find a correct sequence of system reactions if there is one. Once found, the smart play-out module feeds this sequence into the Play-Engine, which then executes it to completion as a super-step. Model-checking thus drives the execution.

We do not assume that the reader of this chapter is an expert in verification or model-checking. To get a clear idea of what this chapter describes, it suffices to know that model-checking is a method by which a desired behavioral property of a reactive system is verified over a given system (the model) through exhaustive enumeration (explicit or implicit) of all the states reachable by the system and the behaviors that traverse through them. Compared to other verification approaches, model-checking has two main advantages. First, it is fully automatic, and its application requires no user supervision or complex mathematical expertise. Second, when the design fails to satisfy the checked-for property, the model-checker is able to produce a counterexample that demonstrates some behavior that falsifies the property. In our smart play-out approach, we make use of these two advantages. Recent years have seen intensive research on developing ever-stronger and more efficient model-checking algorithms, which renders the approach successful in various industrial settings. It also serves to boost our own motivation in seeking ways to make smart play-out more powerful.

18.2 Being Smart Helps

We now use some simple examples to illustrate the role and possible usage of smart play-out. Consider the two charts of Fig. 18.1. The first, 'LSC1', states that when the phone's cover is opened the display sets its state to show a number (rather than the current time), the antenna opens and the speaker becomes silent. It is important to realize that this LSC does not enforce any particular order on these three events, since they are relevant to different objects. The play-out mechanism will choose one order for execution, in a way that is not controllable by the user.

The second chart in the figure, 'LSC2', states that whenever the antenna opens, the display should be showing the current time (and this is a hot condition), it should then set its state to show a number, and only then should the speaker become silent. (The order of these last two events is enforced by the SYNC condition.)

Assuming that these are the only two specified charts of the system, and that the user opens the cover during play-out, the play-out mechanism chooses the events in an order that results in the charts shown in Fig. 18.2, which describes the situation during the execution. The first event the engine has chosen to take is the topmost, i.e., setting the display's state to show a number. The second is opening the antenna. As this event occurs, 'LSC2' is activated but cannot progress, since the display shows a number and not the current time, so the hot condition is false. 'LSC1' is also not allowed to progress, since the event of the speaker turning silent violates 'LSC2'. Therefore, no progress is allowed at all and the super-step terminates. Note that the location of the event of the speaker becoming silent is also hot (denoted by a solid line from that location) so that the entire cut depicted in Fig. 18.2

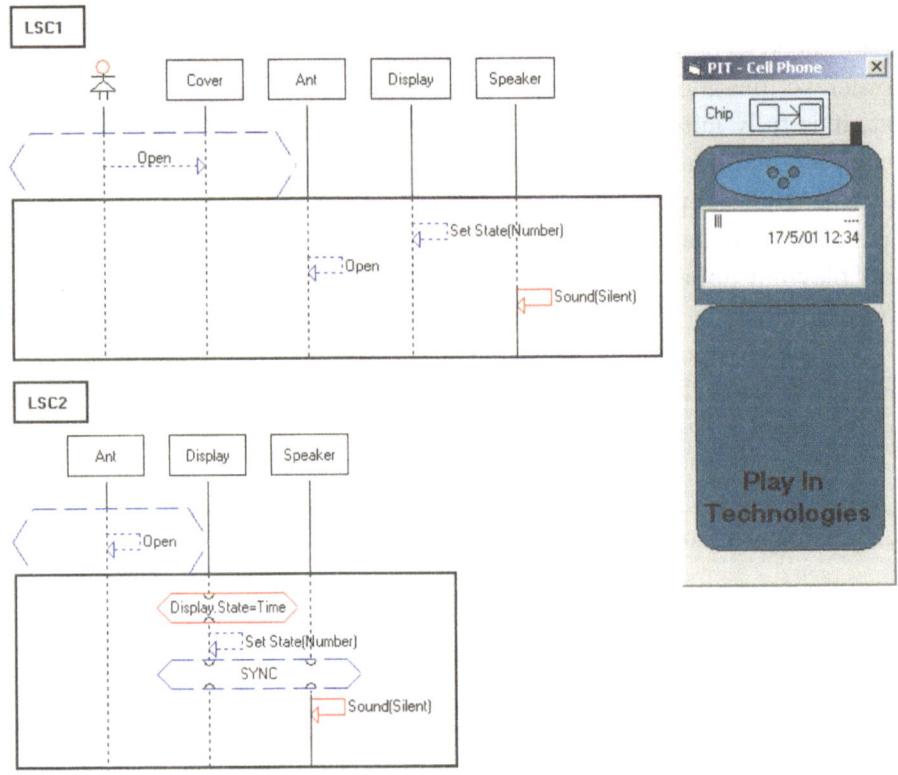

Fig. 18.1. Opening the cover of a cellular phone

is also hot. Now, it could be the case that the user decides not to do anything else, and, hence, the cut will not progress. This is clearly a violation of the requirements, since hot cuts must eventually make progress, and it was caused by what we call an 'incorrect' super-step.

If we apply the smart play-out process to this example, it computes and carries out a different order of events, as shown in Fig. 18.3. The first event taken after the cover is opened is that of opening the antenna. This event activates '*LSC2*', but this time the display still shows the current time. The hot condition is thus evaluated to true and propagated. The display now changes its state to show a number, thus making progress in both charts. Next, the synchronization condition is successfully passed, and the event of the speaker becoming silent can be performed, causing the successful completion of both charts.

There are situations in which there exists no correct super-step. Consider, for example, the two charts '*Green First*' and '*Red First*' in Fig. 18.4. When the user clicks on the *PWR* button, both charts are activated. However,

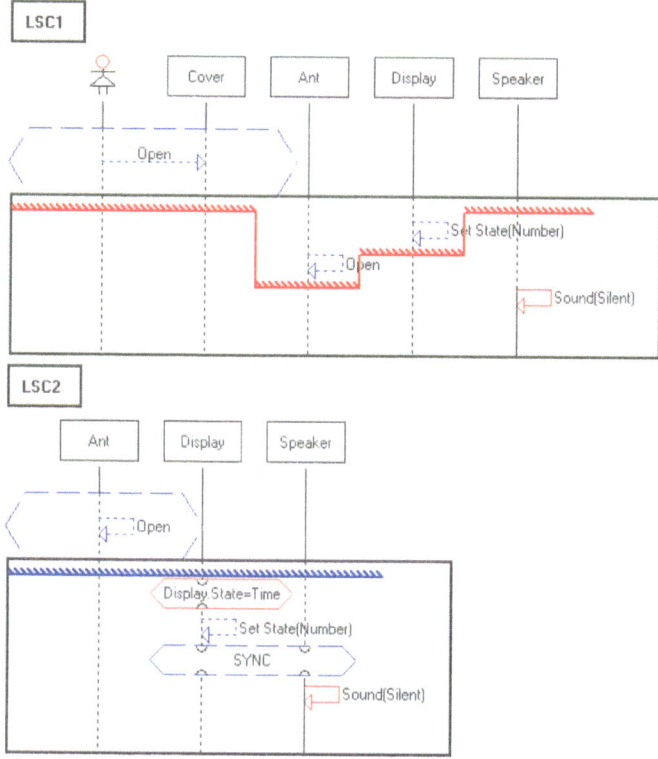

Fig. 18.2. Naive play-out

there is no way to satisfy them both since they require the events *Change background*(*Green*) and *Change background*(*Red*) to occur in contradicting order. Smart play-out proves in this case that no legal super-step exists and announces this to the user. While this is a very simple example, such contradictions can be a lot more subtle, arising as a result of the interaction between several charts. In large specifications this can be very hard to analyze manually. The smart play-out framework would prove that in such cases no correct super-step exists.

Another situation in which smart play-out is useful is in detecting the existence of an infinite loop. Consider the three LSCs of Fig. 18.5. The first, '*LSC1*', states that when the phone's antenna is opened the reception in the display is set to value 2. The second chart in the figure, '*LSC2*', states that whenever the reception in the display is set to value 2, it should later be set to value 4, while the third chart, '*LSC3*', requires that setting the reception in the display to value 4 will later cause the reception value to be set to 2. These three charts together will cause an infinite reaction if the antenna is

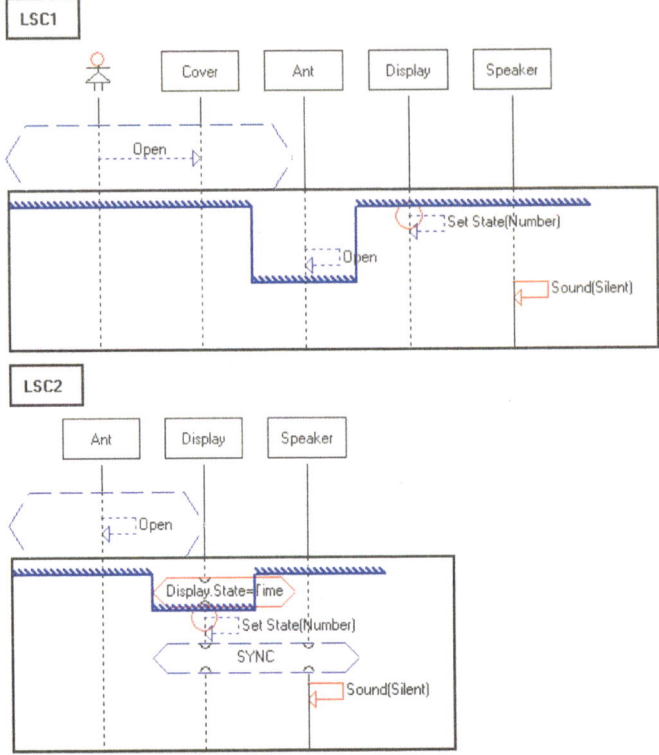

Fig. 18.3. Using smart play-out instead

opened, in which '*LSC2*' and '*LSC3*' repetitively activate each other. The play-out mechanism would indeed execute this 'infinite loop' while smart play-out will detect this situation and notify the user.

Smart play-out can be used to satisfy existential charts. As discussed earlier, existential LSCs may be used to specify system tests. Smart play-out can then be used to find a trace that satisfies the chart without violating universal charts on the way. Figure 18.6 shows a test, in which user and external environment actions are performed and expected system responses are described using conditions. In this chart, the user opens the cover and enters the number 4050. In response, the display is expected to show the dialed number. Next, the user clicks the 'SEND' button and the phone's speaker is expected to ring. Finally, when a signal from the environment indicating the acceptance of the call (denoted by the "ACK" reserved word) is received by the phone's chip, the speaker turns silent. Smart play-out finds a trace satisfying the chart and all the activated universal charts and

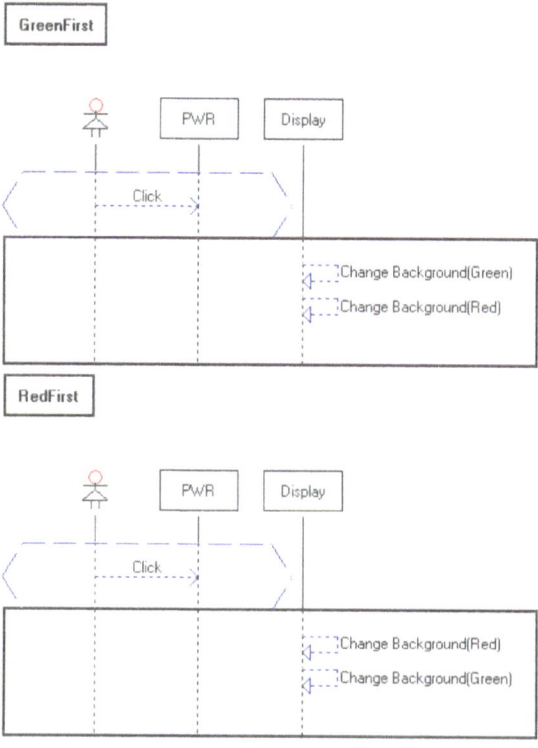

Fig. 18.4. Inconsistent LSCs

the execution is then shown by the Play-Engine. More information on using smart-play to satisfy existential charts can be found in Sect. 18.6.

18.3 The General Approach

The approach we use is to formulate the play-out task as a verification problem, and to use the counterexample provided by a model-checking algorithm as the desired super-step. The system on which we perform model-checking is constructed according to the universal charts in the LSC specification. We define a transition relation from the LSC specification, which is designed to allow progress of active universal charts but prevents any violations. The system is initialized to reflect the status of the application just after the last external event occurred, including the current values of object properties, information on the universal charts that were activated as a result of the most recent external events, and the progress in all precharts.

The model-checker is then given a property claiming that always (in the temporal sense) at least one of the universal charts is active. In order to

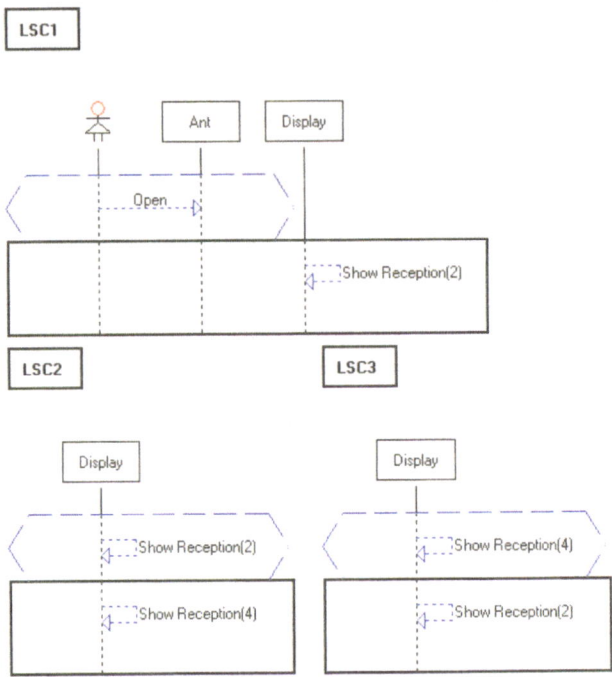

Fig. 18.5. Infinite loop

falsify the property, the model-checker searches for a run in which eventually none of the universal charts is active, i.e., all active universal charts complete successfully, and, by the definition of the transition relation, no violations occurred in the process. Such a counterexample is exactly the desired super-step. If the model-checker verifies the property then no correct super-step exists. The next section provides details on how we construct the input to the model checker.

It is important to note that smart play-out (at least as it stands when this was written — February 2003) does not backtrack over super-steps. Thus, we may get to a situation where no correct super-step exists due to moves the system made in previous super-steps, which could perhaps have been done differently. This demonstrates the difference between smart play-out, which looks one super-step ahead, and full synthesis, which performs a complete analysis. Moreover, currently smart play-out is limited to a rather restricted version of the LSCs language, as we discuss later.

It should also be emphasized that from a computational complexity point of view smart play-out, being based on model-checking, is more problematic then naive play-out. First, model-checking is in general undecidable for infinite-state systems. Second, even for finite-state systems, the time complex-

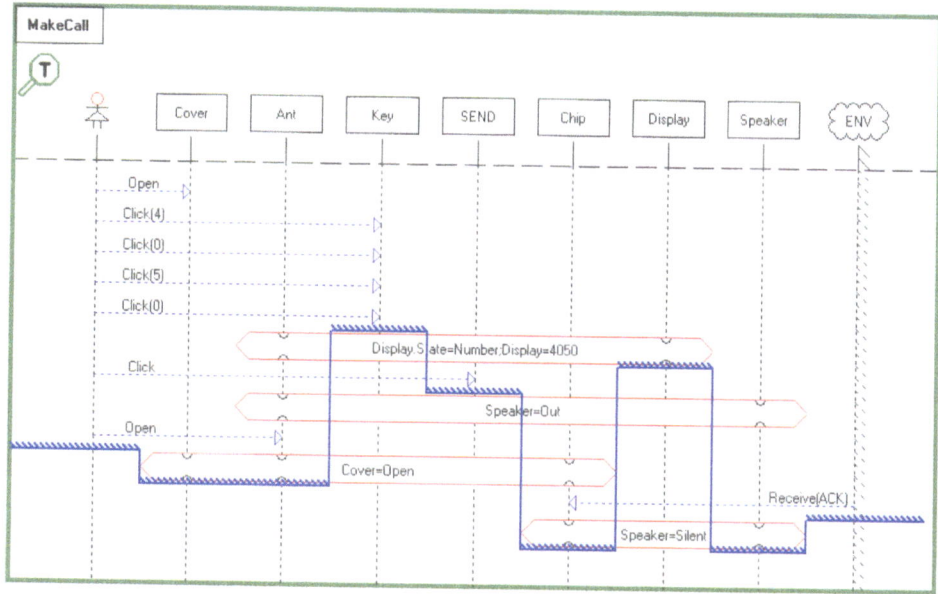

Fig. 18.6. Smart play-out satisfying an existential chart

ity of the problem turns its application to real-world systems into a major challenge.

Having said all this, our goal in future research on smart play-out is to extend the subset of LSCs that is supported and to improve the efficiency of the algorithms. We shall address several aspects of this in the remaining parts of the chapter.

18.4 The Translation

A formal definition of the operational semantics of LSCs as implemented in the Play-Engine appears in Appendix A. Central to the semantics is a symbolic transition system, where the states are the set of LSC copies (which contain cuts that specify progress), and LSC events correspond to the transitions. The transition system is then used to define the play-out execution mechanism. Roughly speaking, play-out selects an enabled event that does not cause a violation in any of the universal LSC copies and executes it, iterating this process until no such enabled events exist. If, at a certain stage in the super-step, there are several enabled events, the play-out mechanism chooses one of them in an uncontrollable way that is a function of the concrete implementation of the Play-Engine and the particular LSC specification executed. No special effort is made to prefer a certain event over another. The choice is purely 'local', and does not take into account the effects this may have down the line.

Smart play-out uses model-checking algorithms to make a 'global' decision on the super-step level. The technique takes into account the effects of choosing a particular enabled event, and makes the actual choice in a way that guarantees successful completion of the super-step, if possible.

Our main focus is to search for a correct behavior of the system when several charts act together. Accordingly, we construct a transition system with one process for each actual object. A state in this system indicates the currently active charts and the location of each object therein. The transition relation restricts the transitions of each process to moves that are allowed by *all* the currently active charts. Note that our translation does not explicitly construct the cuts for each chart (which by itself causes an exponential growth in the size of the initial representation).

We now provide more details on how to translate a play-out problem into a model-checking problem. In the rest of this section, we use terms that were defined in the more formal sections of the book.

An LSC specification $S = S_U \cup S_E$ consists of a set of charts, where each chart $m \in S$ is existential or universal. We denote by $pch(m)$ the prechart of chart m. Assume that the set of universal charts in S is $S_U = \{m_1, m_2, ..., m_t\}$, and that the objects participating in the specification are $O = \{O_1, ..., O_n\}$.

We define a transition system with the following variables:

act_{m_i} – determining if universal chart m_i is active. Its value is 1 when m_i is active and 0 otherwise.

$msg^s_{O_j \to O_k}$ – denoting the sending of message msg from object O_j to object O_k. Its value is set to 1 at the occurrence of the send and is changed to 0 at the next state.

$msg^r_{O_j \to O_k}$ – denoting the receipt by object O_k of message msg sent by object O_j. Its value is set to 1 at the occurrence of the receive and is changed to 0 at the next state.

l_{m_i, O_j} – denoting the location of object O_j in chart m_i. It ranges over $0 \cdots l^{max}$, where l^{max} is the last location of O_j in m_i.

$l_{pch(m_i), O_j}$ – denoting the location of object O_j in the prechart of m_i. It ranges over $0 \cdots l^{max}$, where l^{max} is the last location of O_j in $pch(m_i)$.

Throughout this chapter, we assume the asynchronous mode of messages, in which a send and a receive are separate events; however, smart play-out supports the synchronous mode too. We denote by $f(l) = evnt(l)$ the event associated with location l, and use the convention that primed variables denote the value of a variable in the next state, while unprimed variables relate to the current state.

The following subsections show the definition of the transition relation, organized by the various features of the LSC language.

Messages

We first define the transition relation for the location variable when the location corresponds to the sending of a message:

$$l'_{m_i,O_j} = \begin{cases} l & \text{if } l_{m_i,O_j} = l-1 \wedge msg^s_{O_j \to O_k}{}' = 1 \\ l-1 & \text{if } l_{m_i,O_j} = l-1 \wedge msg^s_{O_j \to O_k}{}' = 0 \end{cases}$$

Intuitively, if object O_j is at location $l-1$ in chart m_i, and the next location of O_j corresponds to the sending of message msg from O_j to O_k, then if in the next state the message is sent, the location is advanced; otherwise it remains where it is. It is important to notice that the event $msg^s_{O_j \to O_k}$ may not be allowed to occur at the next state due to the happenings in some other chart. This is one of the places where the interaction between the different charts becomes important.

As for the receipt of events, given that n is the location in which message msg is sent from object O_j to object O_k in m_i, we define the transition relation as:

$$l'_{m_i,O_k} = \begin{cases} l & \text{if } l_{m_i,O_k} = l-1 \wedge l_{m_i,O_j} \geq n \wedge msg^r_{O_j \to O_k}{}' = 1 \\ l-1 & \text{if } l_{m_i,O_k} = l-1 \wedge (l_{m_i,O_j} < n \vee msg^r_{O_j \to O_k}{}' = 0) \end{cases}$$

If object O_k is at location $l-1$ in chart m_i, and the next location of O_k corresponds to the receipt of the message msg sent by object O_j, and this message has already been sent, then if in the next state the message is received, the location is advanced; otherwise it remains where it is.

We now define the transition relation for the variable that determines the occurrence of a send event (the receive case is similar):

$$msg^s_{O_j \to O_k}{}' = \begin{cases} 1 & \text{if } \phi_1 \wedge \phi_2 \\ 0 & \text{otherwise} \end{cases}$$

$$\phi_1 \triangleq \bigvee_{m_i \in S_\mathcal{U} \wedge msg^s_{O_j \to O_k} \in Messages(m_i)} act_{m_i} = 1$$

$$\phi_2 \triangleq \bigwedge_{m_i \in S_\mathcal{U} \wedge msg^s_{O_j \to O_k} \in Messages(m_i)} (act_{m_i} = 0 \vee \psi(m_i))$$

$$\psi(m_i) \triangleq \bigvee_{l_t \text{ s.t. } f(l_t) = msg^s_{O_j \to O_k}} (l_{m_i,O_j} = l_t - 1 \wedge l'_{m_i,O_j} = l_t)$$

Let us explain. In order for the event of sending msg from O_j to O_k to occur, we require two conditions to hold, which are expressed by the formulas ϕ_1 and ϕ_2, respectively. The first, ϕ_1, states that at least one of the main charts in which this message appears is active. The assumption is that message communication is caused by universal charts that are active and does not occur spontaneously. The second requirement, ϕ_2, states that all active charts must 'agree' on the message. For an active chart m_i that contains $msg^s_{O_j \to O_k}$, we require that object O_j progresses to a location l_t corresponding to this message, as expressed by the formula $\psi(m_i)$. Formula ϕ_2 states that for all charts m_i containing $msg^s_{O_j \to O_k}$ (that is, $msg^s_{O_j \to O_k} \in Messages(m_i)$), either the chart is not active or the message can occur (that is, $\psi(m_i)$ holds). According to the semantics of LSCs, if a message does not appear in a chart explicitly, it (i.e., its sending and receipt) is allowed to occur between the messages that do appear, without violating the chart. This is reflected in ϕ_2 by the fact that the conjunction is only over the charts containing $msg^s_{O_j \to O_k}$.

Precharts

The prechart of a universal chart describes the scenario which, if completed successfully, forces the scenario described in the main chart to occur. The main chart becomes active if all locations of the prechart have reached maximal positions, which is what successful completion of the prechart means. A central feature of play-out is that a sequence of events in a super-step may cause the activation of some additional universal chart, which now must also be completed successfully as part of the same super-step. For this purpose precharts are monitored, and locations along instance lines are advanced when messages are sent and received.

The transition relation for a location variable in a prechart is similar to the one defined for locations in the main chart, with one major difference: precharts are allowed to be violated. If a message is sent or received while it is not enabled in the prechart, the prechart is 'reset' by moving all its instances back to their initial locations. This reset action allows the prechart to start 'looking' for another way to be satisfied. In fact, when the model-checker searches for a 'correct' super-step it often *tries* to violate a prechart in order not to get into the obligation of having to satisfy the corresponding main chart. When all locations in the prechart reach their maximal positions, they too are reset.

Formally, if the prechart location is $l_{pch(m_i), O_j} = l - 1$, and the next location corresponds to a message sending, then its transition relation is given by:

$$l'_{pch(m_i),O_j} = \begin{cases} l & \text{if } msg^s_{O_j \to O_k}{}' = 1 \\ 0 & \text{if } msg^s_{O_j \to O_k}{}' = 0 \wedge \Phi(m_i) \\ l - 1 & \text{otherwise} \end{cases}$$

$$\Phi(m_i) \triangleq \bigvee_{msg^s_{O_x \to O_y} \in Messages(m_i)} \Psi^s(msg^s_{O_x \to O_y})$$

$$\vee \bigvee_{msg^r_{O_x \to O_y} \in Messages(m_i)} \Psi^r(msg^r_{O_x \to O_y})$$

$$\vee \bigwedge_{O_j \in Obj(m_i)} (l_{pch(m_i),O_j} = l^{max}_{pch(m_i),O_j})$$

$$\Psi^s(msg^s_{O_x \to O_y}) \triangleq \begin{cases} 1 & \text{if } l_{m_i,O_x} = l_x - 1 \wedge f(l_x) \neq msg^s_{O_x \to O_y} \wedge \\ & msg^s_{O_x \to O_y}{}' = 1 \\ 0 & \text{otherwise} \end{cases}$$

$$\Psi^r(msg^r_{O_x \to O_y}) \triangleq \begin{cases} 1 & \text{if } l_{m_i,O_y} = l_y - 1 \wedge f(l_y) \neq msg^r_{O_x \to O_y} \wedge \\ & msg^r_{O_x \to O_y}{}' = 1 \\ 0 & \text{otherwise} \end{cases}$$

Ψ^s (respectively, Ψ^r) checks whether a send (respectively, receive) event occurred while not enabled by its sender (respectively, receiver) instance in the chart. $\Phi(m_i)$ checks whether all locations have reached their maximal position.

Activation of Charts

For a universal chart m_i, we define the transition relation for act_{m_i} as follows:

$$act'_{m_i} = \begin{cases} 1 & \text{if } \phi(pch(m_i)) \\ 0 & \text{if } \phi(m_i) \\ act_{m_i} & \text{otherwise} \end{cases}$$

$$\phi(m_i) \triangleq \bigwedge_{O_j \in Obj(m_i)} (l'_{m_i,O_j} = l^{max}_{m_i,O_j})$$

The main chart m_i becomes active when all locations of the prechart reach maximal positions, and it stops being active when all locations of the main chart reach maximal positions.

Object Properties and Conditions

Although the basic strength of scenario-based languages like LSCs is in showing message communication, the LSC language has the ability to reason about the properties of objects too. Object properties can be referenced in condition constructs, and these can be hot or cold. According to the semantics of LSCs, if a cold condition is true the chart progresses to the location that immediately follows the condition, whereas if it is false the surrounding (sub)chart is exited. A hot condition, on the other hand, must always be met, otherwise the requirements are violated and the system aborts. To support this kind of reasoning, we have to update the value of each property as the system runs.

More formally, let $P_{O_k}^t$ denote the tth property of object O_k, defined over a finite domain D. For many of the object properties there are simple rules — defined when the application and the GUI are constructed — that relate the value of the property to message communication. Accordingly, suppose that message msg received by O_k from O_j has the effect of changing property P^t of object O_k to the value $d \in D$. We then add to the transition relation of process O_j the clause

$$P_{O_k}^t{}' = d \ \text{ if } \ msg_{O_j \to O_k}^r{}' = 1$$

In this way, the values of the properties are updated as the objects send and receive messages.

Object properties can be referred to in conditions. In fact, we take a condition expression to be a Boolean function over the domains of the object properties, $C : D^1 \times D^2 \times \cdots \times D^r \to \{0, 1\}$, so that a condition can relate to the properties of several objects. Here, the properties appearing in the condition are $P_1, P_2, \ldots, P_r$.

A condition affects the transition relation of the location of a participating object. Here is how we deal with a hot condition: To simplify the presentation of the definition, we assume only two objects participating in the condition. In the general case, of course, there could be a single object or many objects. If object O_j is at location $l_j - 1$ and object O_k is at location $l_k - 1$ in chart m_i, and if their next locations correspond to the hot condition C, we define:

$$l'_{m_i, O_j} = \begin{cases} l_j & \text{if } C(d_j, d_k)' = 1 \wedge l_{m_i, O_j} = l_j - 1 \wedge l_{m_i, O_k} = l_k - 1 \\ l_j - 1 & \text{if } l_{m_i, O_j} = l_j - 1 \wedge ((C(d_j, d_k)' = 0 \vee l_{m_i, O_k} \neq l_k - 1) \end{cases}$$

Object O_j moves to location l_j if both objects participating in the condition are ready for the evaluation of the condition expression, being at locations $l_j - 1$ and $l_k - 1$, respectively, and the condition C holds. Here, d_j and d_k are the values of properties $P_{O_j}^s$ and $P_{O_k}^t$, respectively. The transition relation thus ensures synchronization of the objects when evaluating the condition and allows progress only if the condition expression holds, thus preventing violation of the chart. In this definition, we assume that there are two objects, O_j and O_k, constrained by the condition, whereas, as mentioned, in the general case there could be a single object or several.

For a cold condition we define:

$$l'_{m_i,O_j} = \begin{cases} l_j & \text{if } C(d_j, d_k)' = 1 \wedge l_{m_i,O_j} = l_j - 1 \wedge l_{m_i,O_k} = l_k - 1 \\ l_s & \text{if } C(d_j, d_k)' = 0 \wedge l_{m_i,O_j} = l_j - 1 \wedge l_{m_i,O_k} = l_k - 1 \\ l_j - 1 & \text{if } l_{m_i,O_j} = l_j - 1 \wedge l_{m_i,O_k} \neq l_k - 1 \end{cases}$$

The difference between this and the previous definition for a hot condition is that here, if the objects are ready for the evaluation of the condition but the condition does not hold, the smallest surrounding (sub)chart is exited, as per the semantics of LSCs. Here, l_s is the location of object O_j at the end of the surrounding (sub)chart. In such a case, all the other objects will also synchronize their exit of this (sub)chart. Note that this is a 'peaceful exit', and it does not constitute a violation of the universal chart m_i.

Assignments

Among other things, assignments enable us to refer to system properties after they are set. In the assignment $x := d$, the value d may be a constant, a property value of some object, or the value obtained by applying some function to other values. To handle assignments we add to our translation a Boolean variable $assign(x, d)$ that is set to 1 exactly when the assignment is performed. Actually, these variables are used only for notational clarity, since in the implementation they can be computed from the values of the location variables. The translation is straightforward:

$$x' = \begin{cases} d & \text{if } l_{m_i,O_k} = l - 1 \wedge l'_{m_i,O_k} = l \wedge assign(x, d) \\ x & \text{otherwise} \end{cases}$$

Intuitively, if object O_k is at location $l - 1$ in chart m_i, and the next location of O_k corresponds to the assignment $x := d$, the value of x is set to d.

We also add to the system a Boolean variable x_{bound}, which determines whether variable x is already bound to a concrete value. After an assignment is evaluated, x_{bound} is set to 1. More information about this appears in the "Symbolic Messages" subsection below.

Assignments are local to a chart. Typically, the variable x on the left-hand side of the assignment will be used later in the chart, as part of a condition or a symbolic message.

Symbolic Messages

A symbolic message is of the form $msg(x)$, where x is a parameter ranging over a finite domain D. (Actually, a message can have more than one variable, but for clarity we explain the simple case of a single variable.) It represents concrete messages of the form $msg(d)$, where $d \in D$. Using symbolic messages it is possible to describe generic scenarios, which are typically instantiated and bound to concrete values during play-out.

To handle $msg(x)$ in smart play-out, we add a variable representing the parameter x, which can be bound to a concrete value as the result of the occurrence of a concrete message or an assignment. The binding of this variable also affects other messages in the same chart that are parameterized by x, binding them to the same value. Once the variables of a symbolic message are bound to concrete values, the usual rules concerning message communication apply to it, so that the message will affect the transition relation in a way similar to that of a regular message.

Formally, for a symbolic message of the form $msg(x)$ we add a variable $x \in D$ and a Boolean variable x_{bound} that determines whether variable x is already bound to a concrete value. Initially, we set x_{bound} to 0, and we define the transition relation as follows:

$$x'_{bound} = \begin{cases} 1 & \text{if } \phi_1 \vee \phi_2 \vee x_{bound} = 1 \\ 0 & \text{otherwise} \end{cases}$$

$$\phi_1 \triangleq l_{m_i,O_j} = l - 1 \wedge l'_{m_i,O_j} = l \wedge \bigvee_{d \in D} msg(d)' = 1$$

$$\phi_2 \triangleq \bigvee_{l_t \text{ s.t. } f(l_t)=assign(x)} (l_{m_i,O_k} = l_t - 1 \wedge l'_{m_i,O_k} = l_t)$$

Thus, x_{bound} is changed to 1 if the concrete message $msg(d)$ occurs, with $d \in D$ (as defined by ϕ_1), or when x appears in the left-hand side of an assignment that is being evaluated (as defined by ϕ_2).

The transition relation for the variable x is defined as follows:

$$x' = \begin{cases} d & \text{if } l_{m_i,O_j} = l - 1 \wedge l'_{m_i,O_j} = l \wedge (msg(d)' = 1 \vee assign(x,d)' = 1) \\ x & \text{otherwise} \end{cases}$$

The first case corresponds to the binding of x to the value d, as the result of the occurrence of the concrete message $msg(d)$ or as the result of x being assigned the value d. Otherwise, x remains unchanged.

We now define the transition relation for the location variable when the location corresponds to a symbolic message:

$$l'_{m_i,O_j} = \begin{cases} l & \text{if } l_{m_i,O_j} = l - 1 \wedge \bigvee_{d \in D} \left(msg(d)' = 1 \wedge x'_{bound} = 1 \wedge x' = d \right) \\ l - 1 & \text{if } l_{m_i,O_j} = l - 1 \wedge \bigwedge_{d \in D} \left(msg(d)' = 0 \vee x'_{bound} = 0 \vee x' \neq d \right) \end{cases}$$

Intuitively, if object O_j is at location $l-1$ in chart m_i, and the next location of O_j corresponds to a symbolic message, then the location is advanced if the message $msg(d)$ occurs and x is bound to the value $d \in D$.

If-Then-Else

The transition relation of the if-then-else construct is a variation on the way conditions are handled earlier. All participating objects are synchronized when the condition is evaluated and when entering and exiting the 'then' and 'else' parts.

$$l'_{m_i,O_j} = \begin{cases} l_j & \text{if } C(d_j, d_k)' = 1 \wedge l_{m_i,O_j} = l_j - 1 \wedge l_{m_i,O_k} = l_k - 1 \\ l_j^e & \text{if } C(d_j, d_k)' = 0 \wedge l_{m_i,O_j} = l_j - 1 \wedge l_{m_i,O_k} = l_k - 1 \\ l_j - 1 & \text{if } l_{m_i,O_j} = l_j - 1 \wedge l_{m_i,O_k} \neq l_k - 1 \\ l_j^e - 1 & \text{if } l_{m_i,O_j} = l_j^e - 1 \wedge l_{m_i,O_k} \neq l_k^e - 1 \\ l_j^x & \text{if } (l_{m_i,O_j} = l_j^x - 1 \wedge l_{m_i,O_k} \neq l_k^x - 1) \\ & \quad \vee (l_{m_i,O_j} = l_j^e - 1 \wedge l_{m_i,O_k} = l_k^e - 1) \end{cases}$$

Here, l_j^e and l_k^e are the locations of objects O_j and O_k at the beginning of the else subchart, and l_j^x and l_k^x are the locations of these objects at the end of the else subchart, respectively.

Loops

A loop is a sub-chart whose behavior is iterated, and all objects are synchronized at the beginning and end of each iteration. Loops can be of two basic types, bounded or unbounded; see Chap. 13. The transition relation should synchronize the objects at the beginning and end of each iteration, and for the bounded case a counter variable is added to ensure that the given bound is not exceeded.

To simplify the presentation of the definition, we assume that there are only two objects participating in the loop, O_j and O_k, and that they end the loop at locations l_j^e and l_k^e, respectively. (In the general case, of course, there could be a single object or many objects.)

For the bounded case, where the loop is iterated N times, and where l_j^e is the first location of object O_j after the loop and l_j^b is the first location of

O_j inside the loop, we add a loop variable x, initialized to 1, and add the following conjunct to the transition relation:

$$l'_{m_i,O_j} = \begin{cases} l^e_j & \text{if } x = N \wedge l_{m_i,O_j} = l^e_j - 1 \wedge l_{m_i,O_k} = l^e_k - 1 \\ l^b_j & \text{if } x < N \wedge l_{m_i,O_j} = l^e_j - 1 \wedge l_{m_i,O_k} = l^e_k - 1 \end{cases}$$

$$x' = \begin{cases} x+1 & \text{if } x < N \wedge l_{m_i,O_j} = l^e_j - 1 \wedge l_{m_i,O_k} = l^e_k - 1 \\ 1 & \text{if } x = N \wedge l_{m_i,O_j} = l^e_j - 1 \wedge l_{m_i,O_k} = l^e_k - 1 \end{cases}$$

Intuitively, if the objects do not exit the loop by the variable x reaching the required number of iterations N, they reiterate the loop (object O_j moves to its loop start location l^b_j). The transition relation synchronizes the objects at the beginning and end of each iteration. The loop variable x is incremented in each iteration of the loop.

For an unbounded loop we do not add a loop variable, and the transition relation is defined as follows:

$$l'_{m_i,O_j} = l_b \text{ if } l_{m_i,O_j} = l_j - 1 \wedge l_{m_i,O_k} = l_k - 1$$

When they reach the end of the loop the objects always change locations to their start loop ones. The loop can be exited by a cold condition being evaluated to false inside the loop, as explained earlier.

The Model-Checking Formula

To compute a super-step in the execution of an LSC system using a model checker, the system is initialized according to the current locations of instances in precharts, while all locations in the main charts are set to 0. The main chart's activation state is also initialized to reflect the current state. After each external event, the Play-Engine decides which precharts have completed and sets their corresponding main charts to be active. We also set the properties of the objects to reflect their current value.

The model checker is then given the following property to prove, stating that it is always the case that at least one of the universal charts is active:

$$G(\bigvee_{m_i \in \mathcal{S}_\mathcal{U}} (act_{m_i} = 1))$$

As explained earlier, falsifying this property amounts to finding a run that leads to a point at which all active universal charts have completed successfully, with no violations — which is exactly the desired super-step.

18.5 Current Limitations

Features Not Covered

Smart play-out, being based on model-checking, cannot support the LSC language in full. We now briefly discuss those LSC features that are either not supported yet or are supported only in part. Some of these we believe we know how to handle, but have not yet worked out the details.

String variables: Model checkers can handle only finite-state systems. In the Play-Engine all types are indeed finite, although using a string type with a large maximal length would make model-checking infeasible in practice. In our current implementation of smart play-out, string variables are not supported. In the future we intend to use abstractions, either automatic or proposed by an advanced user, to enable smart play-out to handle strings or infinite types.

Dynamic loops: We explained earlier how smart play-out handles fixed loops and unbounded loops. A third type of loop is the dynamic loop, in which the user determines the number of times the loop is iterated. How to perform this interaction with the user while in smart play-out and how to handle some of the subtle semantic issues regarding dynamic loops require further research.

External objects: When the chart body contains interactions with entities that are external to the system — the user, environment, external objects or time — we cannot guarantee that all maximal positions are reached within a single super-step, because play-out cannot initiate moves that are not made by the system. Currently smart play-out has limitations in handling these situations and we are working on trying to overcome them.

Multiple active copies of a chart: In order to identify the activation of a universal chart it is sometimes necessary to maintain several copies of the same prechart, each one in a different stage of the prechart's scenario. A universal chart may also be reactivated before its main chart completes, causing several copies of the main chart to be active simultaneously. In the absence of unbounded loops, the maximal number of simultaneously active charts and precharts is bounded and can be easily computed. Actually, we predict that in most practical cases these bounds will be small, because in order for the bound to be large there must be a very strong correlation between the messages in the prechart and the main chart, and this is usually not the case. In any case, we have not yet dealt with multiple active copies of the same chart.

Implemented functions: As explained in Sect. 18.4, message communication can have an effect on the values of object properties. If there is a simple rule relating the value of a property to message communication, this can be fully handled in the transition relation. In cases where implemented functions are used, the situation is more complicated. We plan to investigate several directions in trying to deal with implemented functions in smart play-out. Currently we use a practical approach, creating a symbolic trace of events that is bound to actual values at a later stage, iteratively. This approach, however, is not guaranteed to produce a correct super-step; in such cases the problem will be indicated during execution of the super-step.

Probabilistic nondeterminism: Smart play-out handles probabilistic nondeterministic choices without taking into account the probabilities. The nondeterminism is directly reflected in the transition relation, and smart play-out can thus consider all possible choices when searching for a satisfying run. Future research directions may include taking into account the probabilities obtained by analyzing the probability of a satisfying run, or finding a satisfying run with the highest probability, etc. Recent work on probabilistic verification and probabilistic model-checking may be relevant here too.

Classes and symbolic instances: Extending live sequence charts to handle symbolic instances enhances the expressive power of the LSC language and thus makes smart play-out a harder challenge. For the general case in which the number of objects is not bounded the problem is undecidable. The current Play-Engine implementation does not allow dynamic creation and destruction of objects, so that their number is fixed per specification. Even so, applying the smart play-out idea to specifications with symbolic instances is a difficult challenge, which we are currently investigating.

Time: Extending LSCs with time can introduce undecidability results when attempting to apply smart play-out. Our work focuses on characterizing interesting cases in which smart play-out can be performed, and handling them efficiently. Another research direction is dealing with continuous time instead of the discrete time approach used in the Play-Engine.

Forbidden elements: The use of forbidden elements is another recent extension of LSCs, which is not yet covered in the smart play-out. We believe that it does not present new fundamental limitations, and hope to work out the details soon.

The Semantics of Smart Play-Out

Although we have made an effort to base play-out and smart play-out on the same LSC semantics, there are still some small differences, for a number of reasons. One reason is that play-out implements 'violation policies', i.e., it first tries to find an event that does not violate a prechart and only if that is impossible does it choose a violating event. In contrast, smart play-out does not implement such policies and 'cares' only about finding a correct super-step. This difference, however, is not an inherent limitation, and in the future we may consider adding information to the smart play-out process that will allow it to implement different violation policies.

A similar difference is that smart play-out sometimes allows more nonde-terminism — for example, in deciding when a certain LSC construct should be evaluated. There are some cases (e.g., assignments) in which we believe this freedom is not necessary and we plan to modify our translation scheme to capture the same semantics as in the standard play-out. There are situ-ations, however, in which the smart play-out approach has the potential to capture a more realistic and convenient semantics, such as in certain cases of evaluating conditions and in determining exactly when a prechart has been activated. We plan to further investigate these possibilities, while gaining more experience in using LSCs for more realistic examples.

18.6 Satisfying Existential Charts

An additional powerful way to utilize the techniques we have developed for calculating a super-step is in satisfying an existential LSC. Here the smart play-out approach enhances the Play-Engine's capabilities by automatically finding a satisfying run for a given existential chart. To do this using only the standard play-out we would have to designate the existential LSC as a monitored chart, and then run play-out as we see fit, trying on our own to cause the chart to be traced to completion.

In this section we briefly describe some of the ways in which smart play-out provides extended analysis capabilities for satisfying existential charts. We illustrate the ideas using a biological model of the development of parts of the egg-laying system of the nematode **Caenorhabditis elegans**, fondly called **C. elegans** by the research community.

Satisfying from Any Configuration

When formulating a play-out task as a verification problem, the system must be initialized to reflect the status of the application, in particular, the current values of all object properties. For the purpose of using smart play-out for satisfying existential charts, it is often useful to relax this constraint and allow the setting of a more general initial configuration.

Consider the C. elegans model whose GUI appears in Fig. 18.7. The GUI contains elements representing simplified versions of the worm's gonad, in-cluding its anchor cell (AC), and the six vulval precursor cells (VPCs). During

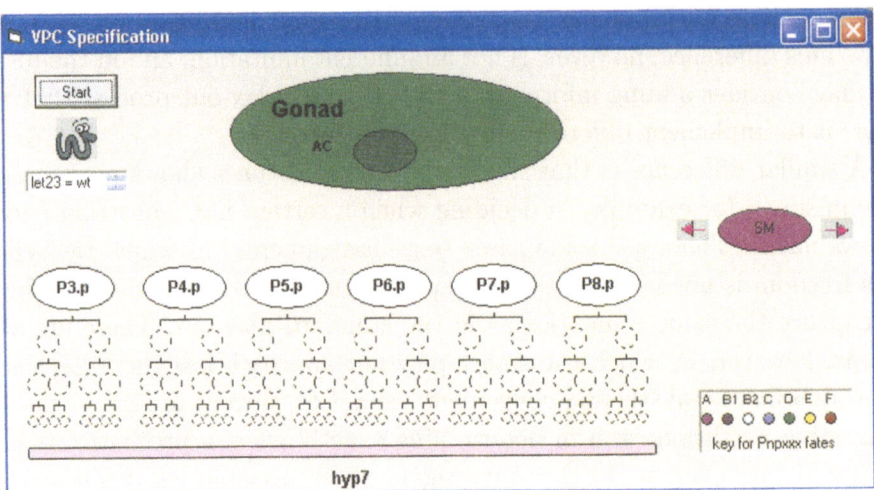

Fig. 18.7. GUI for part of the egg-laying system of C. elegans

normal development, three of the six VPCs are induced by the AC to execute vulval (primary or secondary) fates. Induced cells go through three rounds of cell division, resulting in 22 cells that form the worm's vulva. Uninduced cells adopt a tertiary (non-vulva) fate, and divide only once. The GUI in the figure represents the developmental decisions that occur during a discrete window of time, and it was constructed to directly reflect the way biologists represent the relevant part of the anatomy of C. elegans. Its form is natural and clear for anyone working on C. elegans vulval development.

The general behavioral scheme of our C. elegans model is that during the experimental setup the user can perform various genetic manipulations and cell ablations. After this setup stage, the development starts (captured during the modeling by clicking the **Start** button), and the egg-laying subsystem evolves; the different cells communicate and adopt different fates. The behavior is strongly dependent on the types of mutations that occurred at the initial stages.

This is consistent with the relevant biological data obtained from C. elegans researchers. Large parts of this data are of the 'condition-result' kind, and are usually gathered in an experiment triggered by a certain set of circumstances (conditions), following which an observation is made and the results recorded. The condition is often a set of perturbations, such as mutating genes or exposing cells to an altered environment. Another example includes observations of the effects of anatomical manipulations (e.g., cell destruction or tissue transplantation) on the behavior of the remaining structures. To model such condition-result experiments, the prechart of the LSC is played in to represent the experimental setup (i.e., the alterations that were introduced to the biological system), and the main chart captures the observed behavior (e.g., cell fates adopted during development). Thus, most of the interactions between experimentalists and the biological system they investigate, and therefore also between them and our biological model, involve modifications to the initial configuration of the system.

As an example, consider the task of satisfying the existential chart of Fig. 18.8, which states that some time after the system starts development, the *P7.p* cell adopts a tertiary fate, which shows up in the GUI by the cell being colored yellow. We instruct the smart play-out module to find a way to

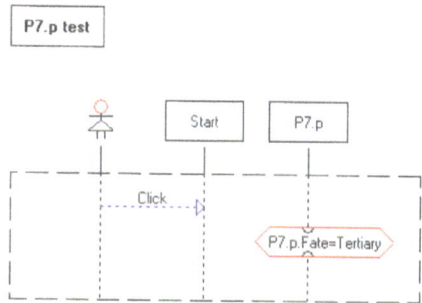

Fig. 18.8. Cell *P7.p* adopts a tertiary fate

initialize the system with some combination of mutations and cell ablations, which leads to the chart being satisfied. This corresponds to trying to find the experimental conditions that lead to the desired result. If the system succeeds, it informs the user of the initial configuration that it used to satisfy the chart, as shown in Fig. 18.9. Notice the mutation of *dig-1*, which enables

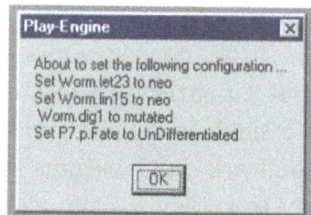

Fig. 18.9. Notifying the user of the initial configuration used

the scenario of 'displacement of the gonad' to be activated, as described in Fig. 18.10, and leads *P7.p* to adopt a tertiary fate, as desired.

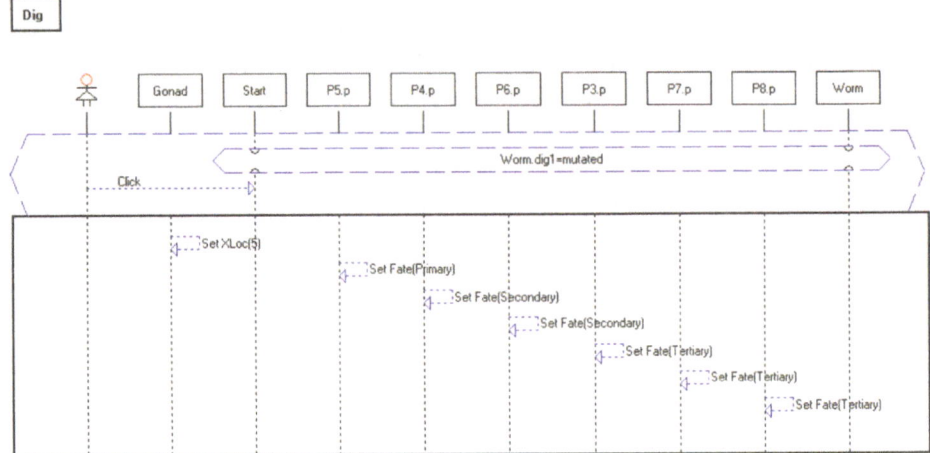

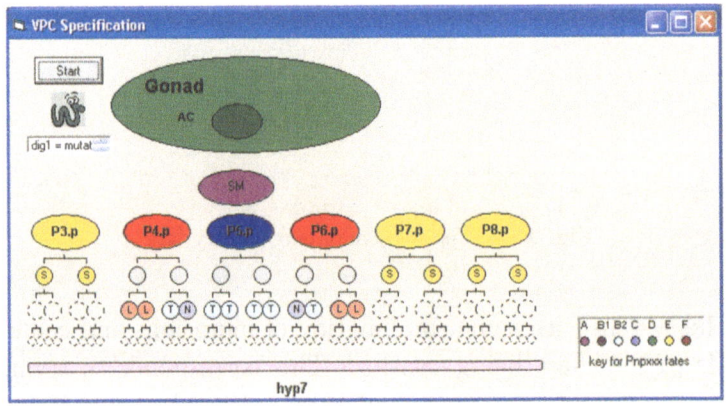

Fig. 18.10. Displacing the gonad (DIG) mutation

Finding Different Satisfying Runs

When using smart play-out to satisfy an existential LSC, it can be very helpful to obtain not only a single satisfying run but many such runs, if they exist. Our experience in the work on C. elegans showed that in certain cases the fact that there is a way to satisfy a given existential chart did not come as a surprise to the biology experts. However, they were often surprised by the different ways of satisfying it, sometimes by scenarios that they initially did not think were relevant.

To make it possible to find a number of satisfying runs within the smart play-out framework, the Play-Engine can be instructed to record a satisfying run and to transform it automatically into an anti-scenario. Figure 18.11

shows the anti-scenario obtained from the satisfying run of the '*Dig*' scenario discussed above. We can now add this anti-scenario to the LSC specification

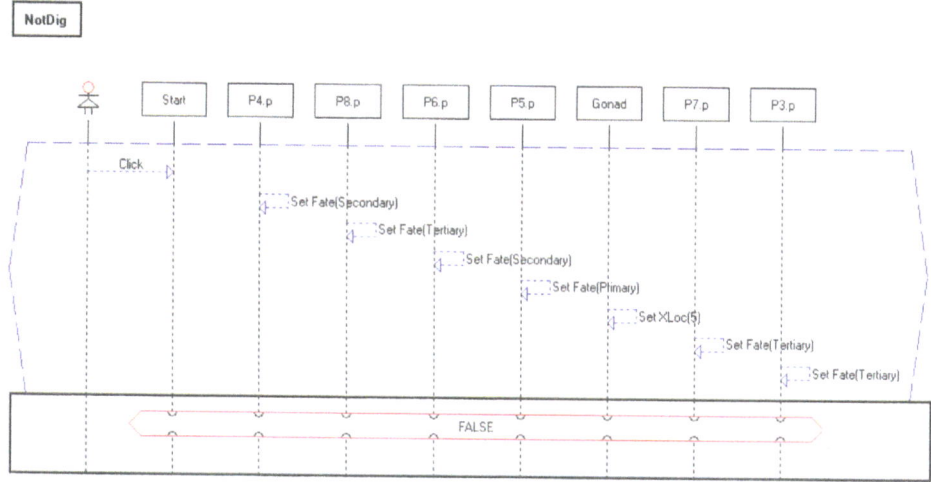

Fig. 18.11. Automatically generated anti-scenario for the DIG mutation

and go back to the smart play-out procedure, asking it again to satisfy the original existential chart. However, now it does so after enriching the specification with the new anti-scenario, so that the first solution will not be detected, since the first satisfying scenario is now forbidden. Indeed, a different satisfying run is found, which starts with the 'loss-of-function' mutation (*lof*) of the *let-23* gene, resulting in a *vulvaless* phenotype: all six VPC cells, and in particular *P7.p*, adopt a tertiary fate. See Figs. 18.12 and 18.13.

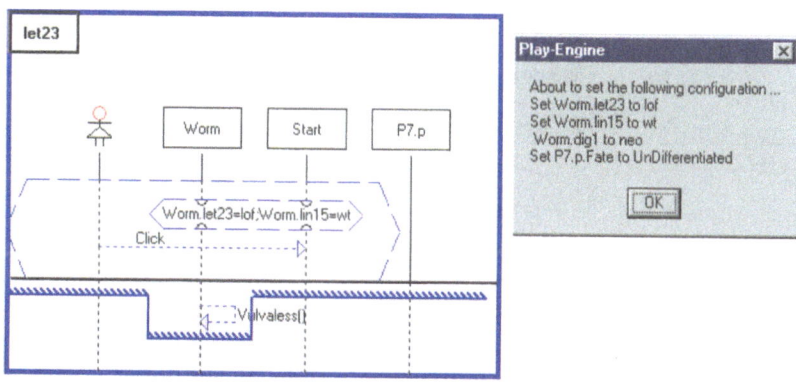

Fig. 18.12. Another way for *P7.p* to become tertiary

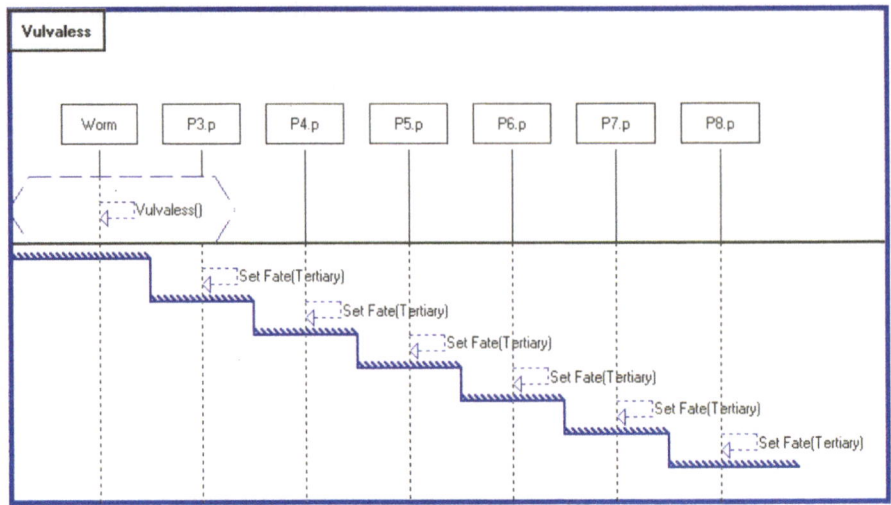

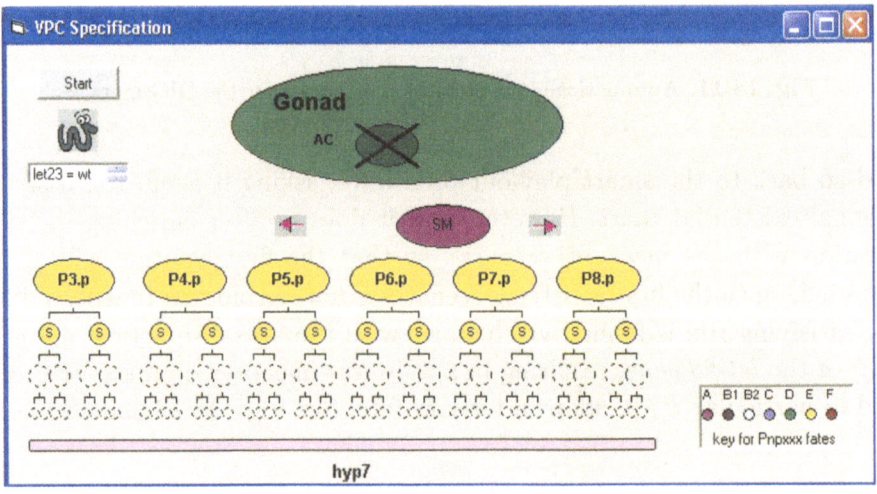

Fig. 18.13. The vulvaless scenario

18.7 Bibliographic Notes

Smart play-out was first described in [47], and is the central topic of the Ph.D. work of H. Kugler. For a survey on model checking, with a wealth of information, see [22].

Preliminary results on using LSCs for the modeling and analysis of C. elegans development appear in [63], and are the central topic of the Ph.D. work of N. Kam. This recent modeling and analysis project helped inspire some of the features described in Sect. 18.6. For further information about C. elegans vulva development, see [38, 79].

19. Inside and Outside the Play-Engine

In this chapter, we give a brief overview of the Play-Engine's architecture, and provide schematic descriptions of the way it handles its two main functions, play-in and play-out.

19.1 The Engine's Environment

Figure 19.1 shows the main components that participate in the play-in and play-out processes, and how the Play-Engine itself fits in. The top cloud represents the various graphical user interfaces that can be used for playing in and playing out. Among other things, they include mock-ups of electronic devices, dialogs and forms used in software systems, object model diagrams, etc. The *Application Interface* is implemented by any GUI application that wants to interact with the Play-Engine. It is used by the engine to instruct the GUI application to perform various commands, such as changing values of properties, highlighting objects, etc. The *Play-Engine Interface* is implemented by the Play-Engine, and is used by the GUI application to notify the Play-Engine of various events, such as right-clicking on an object or changing a property's value (e.g., flipping a switch, dragging a slider, etc.).

The Play-Engine is responsible for generating the LSC specifications during play-in and executing them during play-out. When playing in, the user specifies the behavior of the target system using a GUI representation of that system and an object model diagram for the GUI-less objects. As this is happening, the GUI application notifies the Play-Engine of events, using the *Play-Engine Interface*. In response, the Play-Engine generates an LSC for each played-in scenario. These LSCs are then added to the LSC specification.

During play-out, the user operates the GUI application and/or the object model diagram in a similar way, and events are again generated and sent to the Play-Engine using the *Play-Engine Interface*. This time, the Play-Engine monitors the LSC specification and generates events as dictated by the universal charts. The effects of these events on the GUI application are reflected in the GUI by commands sent from the Play-Engine to the GUI application, using the *Application Interface*.

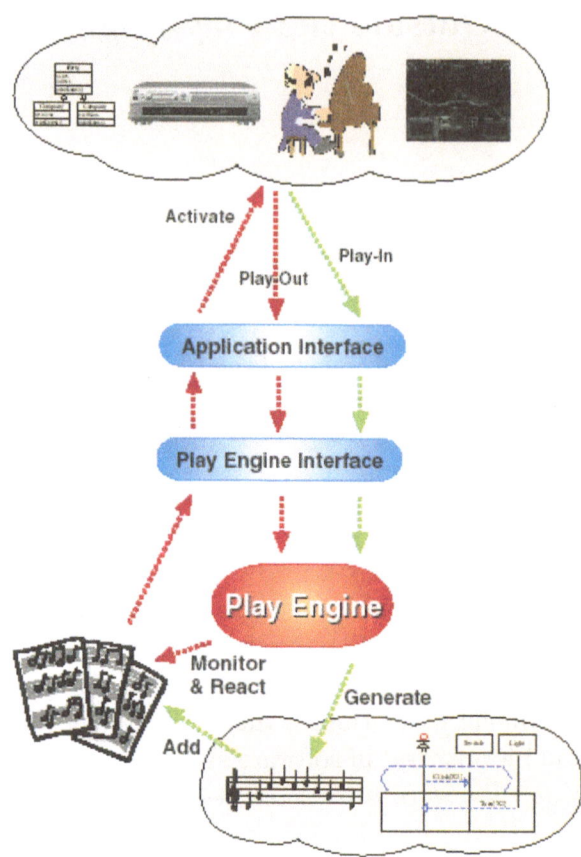

Fig. 19.1. The Play-Engine in its environment

We now zoom in, and take a somewhat closer look at the main components of the Play-Engine itself that are involved in play-in and play-out.

19.2 Playing In

Figure 19.2 shows how the play-in process is handled. The user specifies scenarios by playing in events for GUI objects using the GUI application, and events for internal and external objects using the object map. In the former case, the GUI application sends the events to the Play-Engine via the *Play-Engine Interface*, and from there the events are transferred to the *GUI Manager*, which is the Play-Engine's point of contact with the GUI application.

In the latter case, where the user plays in via the object map, the events are transmitted in a similar way to the *ObjectMap Manager*, which is the

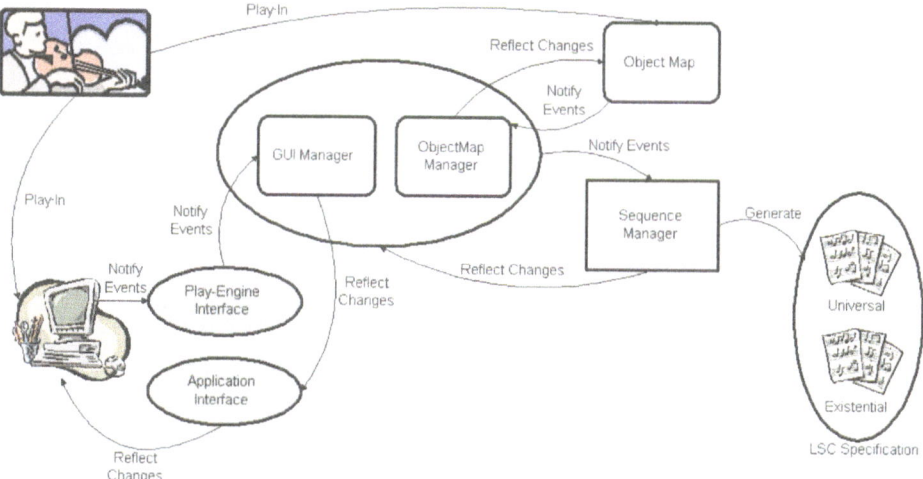

Fig. 19.2. The play-in process

Play-Engine's point of contact with the object map. (In this case, however, the communication occurs directly inside the Play-Engine.) The *GUI Manager* and the *ObjectMap Manager* provide identical interfaces (denoted by the surrounding ellipse) to the other modules in the Play-Engine, and these indeed do not distinguish between GUI objects and internal objects.

Next, the *GUI Manager* and the *ObjectMap Manager* forward the events to the *Sequence Manager*, which is the module responsible for generating the LSC specification. Recall that during play-in, the user specifies system reactions by right-clicking objects and specifying new values for their properties. The *Sequence Manager* is also responsible for conducting this interaction with the user, a process that begins with the right-click event, continues with opening the different menus and dialogs, and ends with instructing the GUI application or the object map to visually reflect the change of value in the object's graphical representation. The instruction that causes these changes to show goes through the chain of interfaces described above, and if it is designated for the GUI application, it is sent to it by calling the *Application Interface* implemented by the GUI application.

19.3 Playing Out

Figure 19.3 shows how the complementary play-out process is handled. Just like with play-in, the user operates the GUI application and the object map, and the generated events are sent through the chain of interfaces until they

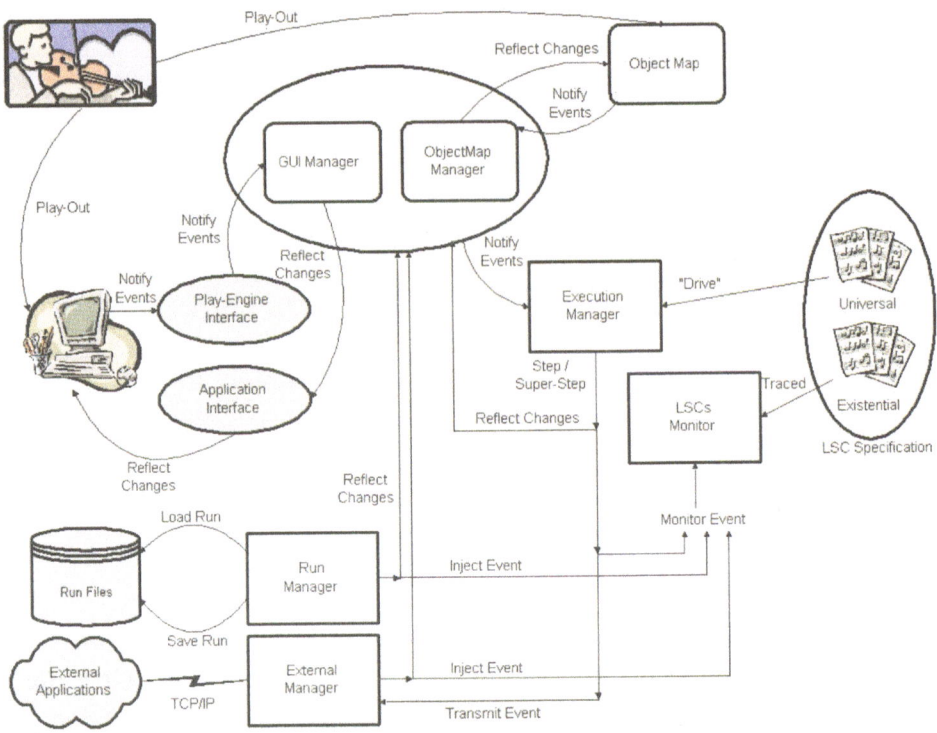

Fig. 19.3. The play-out process

reach the *GUI Manager* or the *ObjectMap Manager*. In play-out, the module that 'listens' to the events is not the *Sequence Manager* but, rather, the *Execution Manager*, which is the module responsible for executing LSC specifications.

When the *Execution Manager* receives a user event, it performs a *step* with the event and then performs a *super-step*. During the super-step, the *Execution Manager* tracks the universal LSCs in the specification and generates events as dictated by their bodies. Every such event is executed by calling *step* again. When an event is executed using *step*, the *GUI Manager* and the *ObjectMap Manager* are instructed to reflect the changes caused by the event in the GUI application and in the object map, respectively. In addition, the event is sent to another module, the *LSCs Monitor*, which is responsible for monitoring existential (and universal) LSCs that the user asked to be traced. The *LSCs Monitor* does not affect the application but only indicates the progress of execution in the traced LSCs. This is done by applying the procedure *Monitor Event* to the event to be monitored.

19.4 Recording Runs and Connecting External Applications

As an LSC specification is executed, the generated sequence of events can be recorded and saved into *Run Files*. These files can also be produced manually or by any other model or implementation, and either way they can then be loaded and replayed. Thus, a system model or an implementation can be instrumented to record the events generated as it runs, and these recorded runs can then be loaded into the Play-Engine and replayed there to check whether the system satisfies the specification.

The module responsible for recording and replaying runs is called the *Run Manager*. When a run is replayed, the *Run Manager* injects the events one after the other into the *LSCs Monitor*, so that they can affect the traced LSCs, and at the same time it instructs the GUI application and the object map to reflect the changes in the values of properties, as indicated by the injected events.

The Play-Engine is able to do more than just test an LSC specification with respect to prerecorded runs. It can also receive events online from external models or implementations via a TCP/IP connection. The module responsible for receiving such events and injecting them into the execution mechanism is the *External Manager*. The *External Manager* can also be used to transmit events along a communication line as they are being generated by the *Execution Manager*.

This functionality of receiving and transmitting events through communication lines can be used, among other things, to connect two Play-Engines. In Chap. 14 we showed how component-based specifications can be developed using external objects to represent elements that are external to the currently specified system or component. After preparing two such 'complementary' specifications for two related parts of a system, we can connect two Play-Engines and have each of them execute one part of the specification. In this configuration, incoming events serve as inputs from external sources, while messages that are sent to external objects are actually sent along the communication line, feeding the other executed specification. For a discussion of a more general approach for connecting multiple Play-Engines, see Sect. 21.5.

19.5 Additional Play-Engine Features

We have implemented several features in the Play-Engine that are not crucial to its main functionality, but which nevertheless make the system more convenient and useful. Some of the features were mentioned here and there in previous chapters, and some were not. This section provides brief descriptions of them all.

Run-time information – The Play-Engine can be asked to reflect its current mode by coloring the background of the work area with different light hues. If this option is chosen then, when playing in, the work area is colored light green, when specifying forbidden elements it is colored light red, and when playing out it is colored light blue.

During play-out, the user is often interested in the values of various elements in the charts. By pointing to an element, the Play-Engine shows a tool tip with the relevant information. When pointing to assignments or messages, the variables used are shown with their values (if they are bound). When pointing to a condition, the participating objects are highlighted in the GUI application or object map, and for each object its constraints are shown in a separate tool tip. Moreover, the condition is evaluated anew whenever the pointing occurs, and its current value is shown in a separate tool tip.

When pointing to an assignment, the Play-Engine connects the assignment with a thin purple line to all the conditions that directly involve the assignment's variable. Similarly, when pointing to a condition, lines are drawn to all the assignments that have a variable to which the condition refers.

Lines are also drawn between forbidden elements and their scopes.

Notes – LSCs can sometimes be quite complicated. The Play-Engine allows the user to attach *notes* to charts and point from the notes to the elements in the chart that are of interest. The user may write a short description that will appear in the note, and may also give a longer, more detailed description that will be displayed as a tooltip when the mouse is located over the note (see Fig. 19.4). A note can include pointers to websites that will open up when clicked. This has been found useful in the C. elegans application of the Play-Engine (see Chap. 18) to point to pdf files of scientific articles that are relevant to the part of the chart in question.

Jump starts – Users often describe different scenarios, assuming different initial system configurations. The Play-Engine allows the setting up of *Jump Starts*. A Jump Start is a set of object properties associated with initial values, and is used to represent initial configurations. Any such configuration can then be reached with a single mouse click. A jump start can be defined to reflect the system's state at any given moment during play-in or play-out; i.e., at the user's request the engine will query all the objects for the current values of their properties, and will create an appropriate jump start from those values.

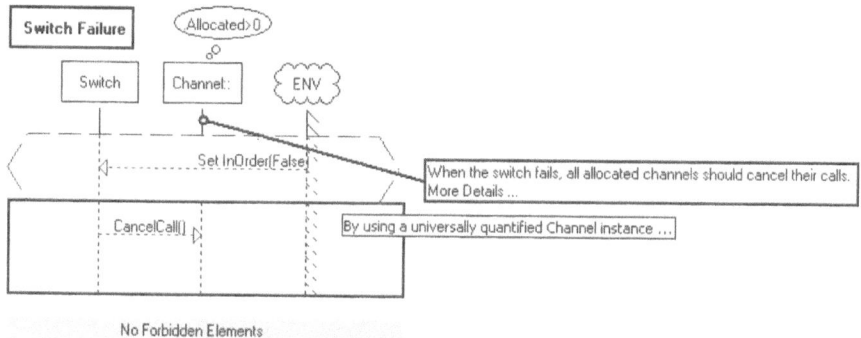

Fig. 19.4. Attaching a note to an LSC

Breakpoints – When debugging a large specification, we often run through a scenario and at some point want to examine the situation more closely. The Play-Engine enables the setting of breakpoints on messages, conditions and assignments. When a breakpoint is reached during execution, the engine moves into *step* mode, thus letting the user examine the system configuration and the currently active charts in a step-by-step fashion.

Statistics – The Play-Engine provides various statistics, including information about the size of the specification (e.g., number of use cases and LSCs) and the number of different LSC constructs used in it (e.g., total number of messages, conditions, loops, etc.). It also produces on-the-fly information about the length of super-steps carried out and the number of simultaneously active LSC live copies.

Controlling the execution – As we know, a specification will typically consist of many LSCs. While preparing for playing out, the user can decide which of the universal LSCs will participate in the execution and which of the universal and existential LSCs will be merely traced. Moreover, some of the charts can be set up to participate in the execution but without being shown when activated. This feature is useful for small trivial charts that are opened many times during execution. The user may also instruct the Play-Engine not to show any charts during play-out. Using this feature, and minimizing the Play-Engine's own window, gives the feeling of working with a truly independent application.

20. A Play-Engine Aware GUI Editor

This chapter describes GUIEdit, a rather rudimentary editor we have built to help the user construct GUI applications that can be used with the Play-Engine.

20.1 Who Needs a GUI Editor?

The Play-Engine in its current guise does not support the process of building a GUI application as the front end to a desired system model. The main reason is the fact that we did not want to restrict the methodology or the tool to work with a specific technology for building user interfaces, since such technologies constantly evolve, providing increasingly faster ways of constructing ever nicer-looking applications.

Several skills are required of a user faced with the task of constructing a nontrivial GUI application to work with the Play-Engine:

- The GUI application must be written in some convenient programming language, in which the user must be able to program.
- Each GUI application must implement an application interface that we call *IUserApp*. It consists of all the procedures and functions that may be called by the Play-Engine to obtain information from the application (e.g., values of properties, values of implemented functions applied to specified values, etc.), or to instruct the application to perform changes (e.g., set new values for properties, highlight objects, etc.). *IUserApp* is a COM (Component Object Model) interface, which is described in detail in Appendix D. To implement this interface, the user again has to be familiar with a programming language that supports COM.
- The structure of the system model (i.e., the types, objects, properties, functions, etc.) should be given in a separate file (see Appendix B) in XML format. To create such a file, the user should be familiar with XML.

Although these skills are not beyond reach, and can be expected of most programmers, we would not like to limit the use of the Play-Engine to people with such skills. Moreover, even for the more skilled user, the task of constructing such an application entails a large amount of tedious work, involving little creativity or imagination, and is bound to be error-prone.

To tackle these problems, and to show that the task of constructing GUI applications for the Play-Engine can be carried out by most end-users, we have developed **GUIEdit**, an editor with which one can relatively easily build GUI applications that are 'aware' of the Play-Engine. This means that they can provide all the information required by the Play-Engine, and can interact with it as needed. Moreover, as we argue in Sect. 20.5, this shows that standard commercially available software for building GUIs can be easily adapted to do the same.

20.2 GUIEdit in Visual Basic

GUIEdit was developed as an *Add-On* to the Visual Basic 6.0 development environment. Having no aspirations to compete with existing GUI builders, we have chosen Visual Basic as the basis for GUIEdit, for the following reasons:

- Visual Basic provides a friendly and powerful environment for creating forms and putting controls onto them. It provides many libraries of ready-to-use standard controls, such as buttons, text boxes, sliders, lists, etc.
- Using Visual Basic, one can create custom controls of various shapes, providing different required functionality, and can then easily load them into the Visual Basic environment, where they can be used just like any other standard controls.
- Visual Basic inherently supports COM. Every class can be automatically referred to as a COM object and no complicated programming is required (in contrast to Visual C++, for example).

Having Visual Basic as our underlying foundation, the GUIEdit Add-On can be loaded from the Visual Basic standard menu bar and can then be used as if it were an integral part of the environment itself. The interface of GUIEdit is really just a small toolbar, as shown in Fig. 20.1.

20.3 What Does GUIEdit Do?

The process of constructing a GUI application with GUIEdit consists of the following steps, in which the numbers in parentheses refer to the buttons in Fig. 20.1.

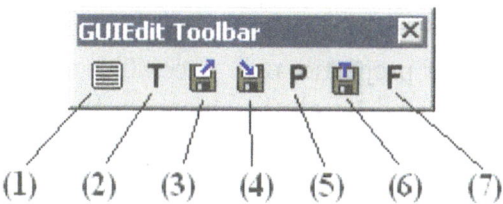

Fig. 20.1. The GUIEdit toolbar

Build GUI representation of the system – The graphical representation of the system is built with the standard tools of Visual Basic. The user creates forms, drags controls from the controls toolbox and drops them onto the forms. When developing a Visual Basic project, the next step would have been to associate code with the different controls, describing their behavior and reactions to different events. In our case, no such programming is needed.

Define application types – All object properties are based on application types. Therefore, before we can define the system objects and their properties we should specify the various types in the application domain. GUIEdit allows us to define types by clicking the *Types* button (number (2) in Fig. 20.1) and then filling in the type's details. GUIEdit also allows us to load *type libraries*, which contain one or more types in an XML format. The user can load type libraries by clicking the *Load Type Libraries* button (6) and then selecting the files to be loaded.

Define objects and properties – The main step in working with GUIEdit is defining the system's objects and their properties. This step consists of going through the graphical objects and defining those that will be used as system objects,[1] to be recognized by the Play-Engine. This is done by clicking an object and then clicking the *Properties* button on the GUIEdit toolbar (5). In response, an object dialog opens, in which the user may give the object a name and define its properties with all of their attributes. An object property can be defined as being *standard*, meaning that it maps directly to a property of the Visual Basic control (e.g., a display object that is based on a *label* control can have a color property that maps directly to the *BackgroundColor* property of the label control). Later, when the code is generated, GUIEdit knows that it should reflect the changes in object properties by applying the corresponding changes to the Visual Basic properties of the underlying controls.

---

[1] Not all visual objects must be declared as system objects. One can certainly add objects that have no functionality, but give a more realistic nature to the graphical representation of the system.

Visual Basic allows us to create arrays of controls. GUIEdit recognizes such arrays and enables the user to give each object a different name but to specify the set of properties only once. This set of properties is then automatically replicated for all the objects in the array. Later, when the GUI application is loaded into the Play-Engine, the natural thing would be to create a class based on one of these objects and to associate all of them with this class.

Load implemented functions – Implemented functions are used by the Play-Engine during the specification and execution processes, and should be implemented by the GUI application. This, of course, cannot be done automatically, since such functions are domain-dependent. One way of implementing them would be to simply write their code after all the other code is automatically generated by GUIEdit. This would result in a process that is not fully automatic and which cannot be conducted totally by an end-user. We therefore propose a different approach.

Implemented functions are written in *function libraries*. A function library is an XML file that contains all the function information that should be exported to the Play-Engine. In addition, the XML file contains the name of a Visual Basic module in which the functions are actually implemented. This way, the task of developing function libraries can be given to expert programmers, and these libraries can then be used by people who want to build GUIs but have no programming skills.

The Play-Engine allows the user to load function libraries by clicking the *Load Function Library* button (7).

Generate application description file – When a GUI application is loaded into the Play-Engine, the first thing the engine does is read its description file. This file contains all the information the Play-Engine needs to know about the application. The application description file is generated automatically by GUIEdit using the *Save to XML* button (4).

Generate code – The final step in creating a GUI application with GUIEdit is automatic code generation. By clicking the *Generate Code* button (1), GUIEdit generates all the code that is needed for the GUI application to interact with the Play-Engine. This includes the data structures for storing property values, the procedures and functions required by the *IUserApp* interface, the code that will notify the Play-Engine as events occur, and more.

GUIEdit also generates *hook procedures* for the user to fill in when a certain behavior should be overridden or redefined. For example, suppose there is an object that is rendered using different bitmaps according to its state — say, on or off. The code for associating correctly the bitmaps with the states cannot be generated automatically. GUIEdit therefore creates a procedure that is automatically called when the state is changed. All the user has to do is endow this procedure with the details for correctly displaying the bitmaps.

At the end of this step, the user has a working Visual Basic project, which is compiled and linked like any other Visual Basic project, resulting in a dll file that can be loaded by the Play-Engine.

Refine the application – Constructing a GUI application can be an iterative process, which will usually be interleaved with the process of specifying the system's behavior. When the user wishes to modify the GUI application by adding properties to existing objects, adding new objects, adding types or functions, etc., he/she will have to first open the Visual Basic project. To load the Play-Engine information that is relevant to that project, the user clicks the *Load XML File* button (3). He/she then selects the file that was saved earlier and the information is loaded and associated with the Visual Basic controls. The user may then continue to modify the application, save it again and generate the new code.

20.4 Incorporating Custom Controls

Since GUIEdit is based on Visual Basic, it can utilize the capability of Visual Basic to incorporate user-defined custom controls. To enable the construction of rich and nice-looking GUI applications, expert programmers and graphic designers can create custom controls for specific purposes, with specific functionality. Custom controls can export their properties as standard Visual Basic properties and encapsulate the code needed to graphically render the various property values.

Building such libraries of controls has obvious benefits in developing reusable components. It also the following advantage: since all the properties are exported as standard Visual Basic properties, end-users can use the controls within GUIEdit without having to worry about implementing any hook procedures. Indeed, almost all of the GUI applications described in this book were built with GUIEdit using various kinds of controls (e.g., the switch and light in the calculator, the thermometers in the bakery panel, the phones in the NetPhone application, etc.).

20.5 GUIEdit As a Proof of Concept

We developed GUIEdit with two objectives in mind. The first, the one this chapter concentrated on, was to make our life, and the life of our users, easier, by enabling us and them to create different examples and modify them very quickly. The other objective, which is of broader interest, was to prove that the concept of a GUI builder with inherent capabilities for interacting with the Play-Engine, is indeed feasible. After demonstrating this concept with GUIEdit, it is clear that any visual programming environment (e.g., Delphi, Visual Studio, Java Swing, etc.) and any product for building rich graphical interfaces (e.g., Altia FacePlate, e-SIM Rapid, Macromedia Flash, etc.) can be easily modified to contain the GUIEdit capabilities, so that applications built with these environments will be able to interact seamlessly with the Play-Engine.

This concept leads to a new possible development process for various kinds of systems. The user first builds the graphical user interface with tools that specialize in doing just that. Then the graphical user interface is loaded into the Play-Engine, where its behavior is played in, resulting in LSCs. These two components, i.e., the GUI application and the LSC specification, can then be executed in tandem by the play-out part of the Play-Engine, which acts as a **universal reactive system**, running a particular 'program'. Obviously, each of the two components — the GUI application and the LSC behavior — can be changed separately, thus adding a measure of flexibility and independence to the process.

20.6 Bibliographic Notes

Microsoft Visual Basic [116] is an integrated development environment (IDE) that uses the BASIC programming language. The Component Object Model (COM) [24] is a software architecture that allows applications to be built up from binary software components. COM is the underlying architecture that forms the foundation for Microsoft's higher-level software services.

Borland Delphi [30] is a visual IDE, which uses Object Pascal as its programming language. Swing is a graphical user interface (GUI) component kit, part of the Java Foundation Classes (JFC) integrated into Java 2 platform, Standard Edition (J2SE). Swing provides a complete set of user-interface elements written in the Java programming language.

Macromedia Flash [36] is software for the creation and implementation of vector-based interactive animations and rich graphical interfaces. Altia FacePlate [2] and e-SIM Rapid [35] are powerful environments for rapid development of Human-Machine Interface (HMI) prototypes.

The Extensible Markup Language (XML) [122] is the universal format for structured documents and data on the Web.

A detailed description of how to use GUIEdit and how to build custom controls that can be used within GUIEdit appears in the *Play-Engine User's Guide* [50].

21. Future Research Directions

The play-in/play-out methodology is very new. The first ideas for play-in were conceived of only in 1998, around the time that the first version of the LSCs paper [27] was being written. While we do feel that our work, including its implementation in the form of the Play-Engine, has matured enough to be deserving of a detailed book-length treatment, there are still many issues that have not been dealt with yet at all, and others that require considerable further investigation before they can be finalized. Thus, we regard our work as still being a research-level effort, with much remaining to be done.

In this chapter, we give a short overview of some of the topics that have not yet found their way into the Play-Engine. For some of these we only mention the problems, but for others we share our thoughts regarding the way they should be resolved. Indeed, some of them are being investigated and implemented even as we write. We have only included topics that we feel are truly important, and which have the potential to significantly increase the power and appeal of the entire approach.

21.1 Object Refinement and Composition

In Chap. 14, we introduced internal, non-GUI objects, and discussed their importance in specifying system behavior. However, anyone who has been involved in complex system development recognizes the need for a hierarchy of structural elements, and here this would translate into the need for a hierarchy of objects. Accordingly, as the design becomes more detailed, we want to be able to carry out downward and upward enrichment of the object hierarchy, by allowing the designer to refine objects into sets of sub-objects and to compose sets of objects into compound objects, respectively. Thus, we want mechanisms for **object refinement** and **object composition**, both of which have to be dealt with in terms of structure and behavior.

As for the structure, we would like to have user-friendly methods for refining an abstract object into actual sub-objects and for composing several 'real' objects into one high-level object. A main issue that has to be resolved is whether the high-level object will be an actual object in its own right, or only an abstract container that is totally defined by its sub-objects. The main difference is whether the high-level object can have properties and methods of its own that can be changed and invoked (respectively) directly, or whether the properties and methods of the high-level object are only a facade for those of its sub-objects.

In the first approach, there need not be a direct linkage between the interface (properties and methods) of the high-level object and the interfaces of its sub-objects. Thus, there cannot be an automatic transformation between an LSC consisting of the high-level object and another consisting only of its sub-objects. In the second approach, the high-level object is but an abstract container, and refinement and composition should be consistent across the levels of the hierarchy. This means that a high-level object should provide an interface that is consistent with the interfaces of its sub-objects, so that when a property of the high-level object is changed or one of its methods is invoked, these can be directly mapped to the corresponding property or method of the appropriate sub-object, and vice versa. In this case, an automatic transformation between abstract and detailed LSCs *is* possible.

Note that there is no loss of generality in choosing the second approach, since we can always add a 'controller' object, which would contain the main logic of the high-level object and would interact with the other sub-objects and the object's environment. As a matter of fact, real-world composed objects are usually implemented that way. Indeed, we feel that the second approach for defining object hierarchies is more suitable in the context of the LSC language and the play-in/play-out approach, enabling more rigorous and semantically meaningful relations between abstract and detailed LSCs.

So much for the structural aspects of refinement and composition. The behavioral aspects are far more complicated. They involve the use of the appropriate level of detail in inter-object behavior, while preserving the meaning of such behavior under the refinement and composition operations. Thus, after defining the desired hierarchy of objects and sub-objects, we would like to be able to automatically transform an LSC containing a high-level object into an equivalent LSC containing the concrete sub-objects, by preserving the property changes and the method calls using the mapping between the object interfaces. The natural next step after carrying out such a transformation would usually be to add the interaction between the sub-objects (should we call it *sub-interaction?*) so that the desired behavior of the high-level object is achieved in full.

All this is not at all straightforward. Here is one example of why. With refinement and composition, several LSCs of varying levels of detail may be active simultaneously, yet they must be executed by the play-out mechanism in a synchronized manner. Thus, if some LSC $L1$ contains a message M going into a high-level object O, and another LSC $L2$ contains the same message M going into O's sub-object $O1$, then the two messages should be propagated simultaneously. Things get even more complicated when taking conditions into account. Consider an LSC $L1$ containing a condition that refers to two properties $P1$ and $P2$ of a high-level object O, and a more detailed LSC $L2$ containing the same condition, but this time the condition refers to sub-objects (since $P1$ can be a property of sub-object $O1$ and $P2$ a property of sub-object $O2$). Now, suppose that the two LSCs are active simultaneously, the condition in $L1$ is enabled and that in $L2$ is not, since $O2$ has not yet reached it. Should the condition in $L1$ be evaluated and propagated, or should it wait for the equivalent, more detailed condition to become enabled too?

These kinds of synchronization issues between high-level and detailed LSCs that describe consistent behavior arise in many other cases. Careful thought must be given to all of them, and rules and mechanisms should be defined and implemented to enable the most natural execution of an LSC specification consisting of LSCs with different levels of detail.

21.2 Object Model Diagrams, Inheritance and Interfaces

In Chap. 15, we showed how classes can be used to specify general scenarios that are not limited to concrete objects. We have also shown how symbolic instances can be bound to concrete objects using general binding expressions. One of the most natural ways to refer to concrete objects in the OO world is to use **navigation expressions**, which can be built up from specific relationships (associations) specified to exist between objects. We would thus like to extend the Play-Engine's object map to support the full features of object model diagrams, which enable graphical specification of associations between objects. We would then use the resulting navigation expressions (e.g., Phone.Channel(3)) to create statically defined binding expressions in a more intuitive manner.

Object model diagrams also support the specification of **class inheritance**, which we have not dealt with in our work yet either. Thus, they can be used to model class hierarchies that involve both inheritance and composition. Once we are able to incorporate class inheritance into our methodology and tool, a symbolic instance would be able to represent any class in the class hierarchy, and it would be able to bind in runtime to any concrete object that is an instance of that class or of some other class that inherits from it.

Since at present the Play-Engine supports only a flat one-level organization of classes, each class is associated with a set of properties and methods and all of its instance objects share these same sets. When introducing class inheritance, the Play-Engine must be modified so that in general a class inherits the properties and methods from its base class, but can also be endowed with additional properties and methods of its own, and can also override the inherited ones.

Another issue that will have to be considered is the way symbolic instances are played in. Currently, the user plays in scenarios using one of the concrete objects, and after the scenario is completed, the instance is declared as symbolic. Since we still have a one-level class hierarchy, determining the class that is represented by the symbolic instance is straightforward. Given a multilevel hierarchy of classes, the user would have to specify which class is intended. It may be the class of which the object in question is an instance, or any class from which that class (even indirectly) inherits. However, since each class can contain new properties and methods, we must make sure during play-in that the class to be represented by the symbolic instance supports all the properties and methods that are used in the particular LSC at hand. Clearly, there are a number of ways to enforce this.

The problem of handling different objects using different views (e.g., considering telephones, televisions and VCRs as all being electronic devices) can be solved not only by class inheritance but also by using **interfaces**. In the context of the Play-Engine, an interface is simply a set of properties and methods. Given a set of interfaces, each object can be defined as implementing one or more of the interfaces. In a way, using interfaces is more powerful than using simple class inheritance (i.e., with multiple inheritance being forbidden), since an object can implement multiple interfaces, thus providing different views of its functionality. Using interfaces, the same instance can implement the interface for a telephone, for an electronic device, and for a machine with a mouthpiece. The play-in process could still be conducted as is, but at the end, when the user declares an instance as being symbolic, he/she would have to choose the interface that is to be represented by the instance. Again, the Play-Engine would have to verify that candidate interfaces have all the properties and methods that were used in the LSC at hand.

21.3 Dynamic Creation and Destruction of Objects

The use of classes via symbolic instances allows us to specify general behavior for an a priori unknown number of actual object instances. We can thus specify parameterized systems, in which the number of objects is fixed but unknown. In principle, this should also allow the specification of behavior for systems with a dynamically varying number of objects, but we have not yet extended our work to support **dynamic creation and destruction** of objects.[1]

Several problems must be resolved in order to extend the Play-Engine along these lines. We limit the discussion to the creation and destruction of internal objects, since we would like to assume that GUI objects are present from the start and do not get destroyed during execution.

First, we must provide a setup for initializing classes, so that they start out with some number of initial instances, perhaps zero. Second, for those classes that start out with no live instances, we have to find a convenient way of starting the play-in process despite this fact. This could be done by displaying classes in the object model diagram and allowing play-in from there as with internal objects, even though these classes are still empty.

Creating an object during system execution would consist of clicking the class and selecting the act of object creation. A new object should be created and placed in the object model diagram, so that it can be used during play-in. Obviously, the life cycle of an object need not necessarily begin and end in a single chart, which means that we must find a way to identify the object in the different LSCs. This issue is non-trivial, and should be subject to further research. One direction, which we think may be suitable, is to index objects according to their order of creation (e.g., Phone(5) is the phone that was created fifth), and use the indexing for identification. During play-in, when an object is dynamically destroyed, it should be removed from the object model diagram, so the current state of the system will be correctly depicted. This imposes a difficulty in modifying a chart that was played in earlier, since the object no longer shows up.

21.4 Structured Properties and Types

In the current implementation of the Play-Engine, each object is associated with a set of properties. There is no structure to the properties, and they all reside on a single level. It could be useful to allow the organization of properties into a hierarchy, so that if there is a large number of them, they could be accessed in a more convenient and intuitive manner.

Some of the properties are based on enumeration types, each of which is defined by a set of values, and these values do not form a hierarchy either. As opposed to arranging properties in a hierarchy, which is purely cosmetic, we would like to arrange type values into a hierarchy that imposes a semantic relation between them. The semantics would be that a property can be

---

[1] Although the Play-Engine does not support dynamic creation and destruction of objects, it can be used to monitor systems that do support these features.

specified to have some high-level value, meaning that the actual value could be any sub-value thereof.

Arranging values of a type in a hierarchy is like having super-states and sub-states in statecharts. For example, the status of a system can be defined over a 'flat' type, consisting of the values { *Open, Initializing, Ready, Closed*}. It could also be defined over a hierarchy of values that has *Open* and *Closed* on the top level and *Initializing* and *Ready* as sub-values of *Open*. As in statecharts, this is not merely cosmetic, but has semantic significance that makes a difference in the dynamics of executing the model. Using this hierarchy, one could specify a condition that says *S is Open*, and the condition will hold if *S* evaluates to *Open, Initializing* or *Ready*. Note that saying *S is Open* here really means that we do not know or care about the exact value, but only about the more abstract one, and play-out would have to be able to deal with this too. This feature has already been defined, and is currently being implemented in the Play-Engine.

A related issue has to do with **compound types**. In the current implementation of the Play-Engine, all the properties and variables are arranged around basic types (i.e., enumerations, strings or discrete ranges). We would like to have compound types and arrays, just like in most programming languages. An array would contain a fixed number of values from a given type and a compound type would contain several fields, each based on some type, which need not necessarily be the same for all fields. To do this, we would have to modify the play-in and play-out processes by helping the user fill in values for compound types, and by enriching the unification mechanisms to support them.

21.5 Linking Multiple Engines

One of the most important features needed in order to support large-scale use of play-in/play-out and the Play-Engine is the ability to link up several engines, and to link these up also to other, complementary tools. In recent months we have been modifying the Play-Engine along these lines.

In a project called **SEC** (simulation engines coordinator) we are in the midst of defining and implementing a standard interface and an interaction protocol for reactive simulation engines, so that a number of them can be used together, each executing a different part of the system. By and large, every such part considers the other parts to be its environment. Thus, we can use SEC to execute a large system, with various parts specified by different teams, and even systems for which some parts have been implemented or modeled in an intra-object fashion (e.g., using code or statecharts).

Current experimentation with a number of linked Play-Engines playing out a specification together, or with a Play-Engine linked to the Rhapsody tool, are very encouraging.

Part VII

Appendices

A. Formal Semantics of LSCs

This appendix summarizes the combined syntax and operational semantics of the entire LSC language and its extensions. It can be viewed as the grand sum of all the "And a Bit More Formally ..." sections that appear in many of the chapters of the book.

A.1 System Model and Events

Object Systems

An object system $\mathcal{S}ys$ is defined as

$$\mathcal{S}ys = \langle \mathcal{D}, \mathcal{C}, \mathcal{O}, \mathcal{F}, \mathcal{C}lock \rangle$$

where $\mathcal{D}$ is the set of application types (domains), $\mathcal{C}$ is the set of classes, $\mathcal{O}$ is the set of objects, $\mathcal{F}$ is the set of externally implemented functions, and $\mathcal{C}lock$ is the system global clock. We refer to the user of the system as $User$ and to the external environment as Env.

A type $D \in \mathcal{D}$ is simply a finite set of values.

A class C is defined as

$$C = \langle Name, \mathcal{P}, \mathcal{M} \rangle$$

where $Name$ is the class name, $\mathcal{P}$ is the set of class properties, and $\mathcal{M}$ is the set of class methods.

An object O is defined as

$$O = \langle Name, C, \mathcal{PV}, External \rangle$$

where $Name$ is the object's name, C is its class, $\mathcal{PV} : C.\mathcal{P} \rightarrow \bigcup_i D_i$ is a function assigning a value to each of the object's properties, and $External$ indicates whether the object is external to the system. We define the function $class : \mathcal{O} \rightarrow \mathcal{C}$ to map each object to the class it is an instance of. We also use $Value(O.P) = O.\mathcal{PV}(O.C.P)$ to denote the current value of property P in object O.

An object property P is defined as

$$P = \langle Name, D, InOnly, ExtChg, Affects, Sync \rangle$$

where $Name$ is the property name and D is the type it is based on. $InOnly \in \{True, False\}$ indicates whether the property can be changed only by the user, $ExtChg \in \{True, False\}$ indicates whether the property can be changed by the external environment, $Affects \in \{User, Env, Self\}$ indicates the instance to which the message arrow is directed to when the property is changed by the system, and $Sync \in \{True, False\}$ indicates whether the property is synchronous.

An object method M is defined as

$$M = \langle Name(D_1, D_2, \ldots, D_n), Sync \rangle$$

where Name is the method name, $D_i \in \mathcal{D}$ is the type of its ith formal parameter, and $Sync \in \{True, False\}$ indicates whether calling this method is a synchronous operation.

An implemented function is defined as

$$Func = Name : D_1 \times D_2 \times \ldots \times D_n \rightarrow D_F$$

where $Name$ is the function name, $D_i \in \mathcal{D}$ is the type of its ith formal parameter, and $D_F \in \mathcal{D}$ is the type of its returned value.

The clock is an external object with one $Time$ property and one $Tick$ method:

$$Clock.\mathcal{P} = \{Time\}$$
$$Clock.\mathcal{M} = \{Tick\}$$
$$Clock.External = True$$

Messages and Events

Given a system model $\mathcal{S}ys$, we define a system message M_s as

$$M_s = \langle Src, Dst, P, V, f, \lambda_f^F, m, \lambda_m^M, Symbolic \rangle$$

where Src is the object sending the message, Dst is the object receiving the message (which could be the same as Src), $P \in \mathcal{P} \cup \{\perp\}$ is the property changed, V is a variable holding a new value for the property P, $f \in \mathcal{F} \cup \{\perp\}$ is a function describing a new value for P, λ_f^F is a function information structure, $m \in Dst.\mathcal{M} \cup \{\perp\}$ is the method of Dst called by Src, λ_m^M is a method information structure, and $Symbolic$ is a Boolean flag indicating whether the message is symbolic. Each message represents either a property change or a method call:

$$\forall M_s : \quad (M_s.P \neq \bot) \oplus (M_s.m \neq \bot)$$

A *function information* structure λ_f^F is defined for $f \in \mathcal{F} \cup \{\bot\}$ as follows:

$$\lambda_f^F = \begin{cases} (V_1 \in f.D_1, \ldots, V_n \in f.D_n) & \text{if } f \in \mathcal{F} \\ \bot & \text{if } f = \bot \end{cases}$$

A *method information* structure λ_m^M is defined for $m \in \bigcup_{C \in \mathcal{C}} C.\mathcal{M} \cup \{\bot\}$ as follows:

$$\lambda_m^M = \begin{cases} (V_1 \in m.D_1, \ldots, V_n \in m.D_n) & \text{if } m \in \bigcup_{C \in \mathcal{C}} C.\mathcal{M} \\ \bot & \text{if } m = \bot \end{cases}$$

The *message content* Λ of a message M_s is defined as

$$M_s.\Lambda = \begin{cases} M_s.\lambda_f^F & \lambda_f^F \neq \bot \\ M_s.\lambda_m^M & \lambda_m^M \neq \bot \\ M_s.V & \text{otherwise} \end{cases}$$

Definition A.1.1 (synchronous system messages). *A message M_s is synchronous if $M_s.P \neq \bot \wedge M_s.P.Sync = true$ or $M_s.m \neq \bot \wedge M_s.m.Sync = true$. A self message is also synchronous.*

The alphabet of possible messages of $\mathcal{S}ys$, denoted by Σ, is defined as

$$
\begin{aligned}
\Sigma \quad &= \Sigma_{FromUser} \cup \Sigma_{ToUser} \cup \Sigma_{FromEnv} \cup \Sigma_{ToEnv} \cup \Sigma_{Self} \cup \Sigma_{Calls} \\
&\quad \cup \Sigma_{Clock} \\
\Sigma_{FromUser} &= \{M_s \mid Src = User \wedge P \in class(Dst).\mathcal{P}\} \\
\Sigma_{ToUser} &= \{M_s \mid Dst = User \wedge P \in class(Src).\mathcal{P} \wedge P.Affects = User \\
&\quad \wedge P.InOnly = False\} \\
\Sigma_{FromEnv} &= \{M_s \mid Src = Env \wedge P \in class(Dst).\mathcal{P} \wedge P.ExtChg = True \\
&\quad \wedge P.InOnly = False\} \\
\Sigma_{ToEnv} &= \{M_s \mid Dst = Env \wedge P \in class(Src).\mathcal{P} \wedge P.Affects = Env \\
&\quad \wedge P.InOnly = False\} \\
\Sigma_{Self} &= \{M_s \mid Dst = Src \wedge P \in class(Src).\mathcal{P} \wedge P.Affects = Self \\
&\quad \wedge P.InOnly = False\} \\
\Sigma_{Calls} &= \{M_s \mid Dst, Src \in \mathcal{O} \wedge m \in class(Dst).\mathcal{M}\} \\
\Sigma_{Clock} &= \{M_s \mid Dst = Src = Clock \wedge m = Tick\}
\end{aligned}
$$

The set of *system events*, $\mathcal{E}$, is defined as

$$
\begin{aligned}
\mathcal{E} = \ &((\Sigma_{FromUser} \cup \Sigma_{ToUser} \cup \Sigma_{FromEnv} \cup \Sigma_{ToEnv} \cup \Sigma_{Calls}) \times \{Send, Recv\}) \\
&\cup ((\Sigma_{Self} \cup \Sigma_{Clock}) \times \{Send\})
\end{aligned}
$$

A.2 LSC Specification

LSC Constructs

An LSC specification for $\mathcal{S}ys$ is defined as the disjoint union

$$\mathcal{S} = \mathcal{S}_{\mathcal{U}} \cup \mathcal{S}_E$$

where $\mathcal{S}_{\mathcal{U}}$ is a set of universal charts and $\mathcal{S}_E$ is a set of existential charts.

An LSC L is defined to be

$$L = \langle I_L, V_L, M_L, [Pch_L], A_L, C_L, SUB_L, ITE_L, LOOP_L, \overline{M}_L, \overline{C}_L, Strict,$$
$$evnt, subchart, temp \rangle$$

where I_L is the set of LSC instances, V_L is the set of variables used in L, M_L is the set of messages in L, Pch_L is the prechart of L (in universal charts), A_L is the set of assignments in L, C_L is the set of conditions in L, SUB_L is the set of subcharts in L, ITE_L is the set of if-then(-else) constructs in L, $LOOP_L$ is the set of loops in L, $\overline{M}_L$ is the set of forbidden messages in L, $\overline{C}_L$ is the set of forbidden conditions in L, $Strict$ is a Boolean flag indicating whether the LSC is strict or tolerant, and $evnt$, $subchart$ and $temp$ are functions that will be discussed shortly.

An instance I is defined as

$$I = \langle \ell, O, C, \psi, Mode, \Phi \rangle$$

where ℓ is the set of instance locations, $O \in \mathcal{O} \cup \{\bot\}$ is the concrete object represented by I ($O = \bot$ if I is symbolic), $C \in \mathcal{C} \cup \{\bot\}$ is the class represented by I ($C = \bot$ if I is not symbolic), $\psi \in \{P \times Oper \times RHS\}$ is the binding expression of I, $Mode \in \{Existential, Universal\}$ is the instance quantification, and Φ is a set of forbidden objects, which the instance is not allowed to bind to.

We denote by l_x^i the xth location of instance I_i, and by $\ell(I) = I.\ell$ the set of locations of instance I. We use $\ell(L)$ as an abbreviation for $\bigcup_{I \in L} \ell(I)$.

We define the function $AppObj$ to map each instance to the object or class it represents

$$AppObj : \bigcup_{L \in \mathcal{S}} I_L \to \mathcal{O} \cup \mathcal{C}$$

and we require that a single object cannot be represented by more than one instance in an LSC:

$$\forall I, I' \in I_L : \ AppObj(I) \in \mathcal{O} \ \Rightarrow \ AppObj(I') \neq AppObj(I)$$

We use the predicate $symbolic(I)$ as an abbreviation for $I.C \neq \perp$. We define the relation $X \preccurlyeq Y$, where $X \in \mathcal{O}$ and $Y \in \mathcal{O} \cup \mathcal{C}$, to denote that either X and Y are the same object, or Y is the class to which X belongs:

$$X \preccurlyeq Y \triangleq (X \in \mathcal{O} \wedge (X = Y \vee class(X) = Y))$$

The relation $\preccurlyeq$ is extended to have instances as arguments in the natural way (i.e., the relation refers to the objects or classes represented by the instances).
    A message $M \in M_L$ is defined as

$$M = \langle I_{Src}, I_{Dst}, M_S \rangle$$

where $I_{Src} \in I_L$ is the instance representing the sender, $I_{Dst} \in I_L$ is the instance representing the receiver, and $M_s \in \Sigma$ is the system message represented by M, so that $M_S.Src \preccurlyeq AppObj(I_{Src}) \wedge M_S.Dst \preccurlyeq AppObj(I_{Dst})$. The message M is synchronous if and only if $M.M_s$ is synchronous.
    A variable $V \in V_L$ is defined as

$$V = \langle D, \omega \rangle$$

where $D \in \mathcal{D}$ is the variable's type, and $\omega \in D \cup \{\perp\}$ is the value assigned to V. For a free variable we have $\omega = \perp$. We shall use simple predicate notation for notions like free and bound, as in $free(x)$.
    An assignment $A \in A_L$ is defined as

$$A = \langle V, I_A, C, P, f, \lambda_f^F, Timed \rangle$$

where V is the assigned-to variable, $I_A \subseteq I_L$ is the set of instances that are synchronized with the assignment, $C \in (\bigcup_{D \in \mathcal{D}} D) \cup \{\perp\}$ is a constant of some type in case the assignment stores a constant and $\perp$ if not, $P \in (\bigcup_{I \in I_A} AppObj(I).P) \cup \{\perp\}$ is the property stored in case this assignment stores a property value and $\perp$ if not, $f \in \mathcal{F} \cup \{\perp\}$ is a function in case the assignment stores some function and $\perp$ if not, λ_f^F is a function information structure in case $f \neq \perp$, and $Timed \in \{True, False\}$ is a flag indicating whether A is a timed assignment. We require that one and only one of the following expressions holds for each assignment:

$$(C \neq \perp),\ (P \neq \perp),\ (f \neq \perp),\ (Timed = true)$$

We say that the *assignment kind* (or simply kind) of A is *constant* if $C \neq \perp$, *property* if $P \neq \perp$, *function* if $\lambda_f^F \neq \perp$, and *time* if $Timed = true$.
    A condition C in an LSC L is defined as

$$C = \langle I_C, \Psi \rangle$$

where $I_C \subseteq I_L$ is the set of instances that are synchronized with the condition and Ψ is the set of basic expressions. A basic expression $\psi \in \Psi$ is defined over the following alphabet:

$$\psi \in \{LHS \times Oper \times RHS\} \cup \{\texttt{TRUE}, \texttt{FALSE}, \texttt{SELECT(P)}, \perp\}$$
$$\cup \ \{Time \times Oper \times V_L \times RHS\}$$

where

$$LHS \in \{O.P \mid O \in \mathcal{O}, P \in O.\mathcal{P}\} \cup V_L$$
$$Oper \in \{=, <, \leq, >, \geq, \neq\}$$
$$RHS \in (\bigcup_{D \in \mathcal{D}} D) \cup V_L \cup \{(f, \lambda_f^F) \mid f \in \mathcal{F}\}$$

The first kind of expression is used to constrain a property or a variable, using some comparison operator, with a constant value, another variable or with a function. The second kind of expression consists of the reserved words (SYNC is considered as a synonym for TRUE), the SELECT statement with probability P, and free expressions (all free expressions are reduced to $\perp$). The third kind of basic expression is timing constraints, which constrain the current time with respect to a time value stored in some variable and a delay that can be a constant value, another variable or a function. We denote by $value(\psi)$ the result of evaluating ψ in the natural way. If $\psi = SELECT(P)$, a Boolean value is chosen randomly with probability P for true, and if $\psi = \perp$ the user is prompted for a value. In case ψ is a time constraint, $value(\psi)$ is computed by evaluating ψ in the natural way where $Time$ is replaced by the current value of $Clock.Time$. The value of a condition C is defined as:

$$value(C) = \bigwedge_{\psi \in \Psi} value(\psi)$$

SUB_L is the set of subcharts in L. Every LSC construct can be contained in at most one subchart. The function $subchart$ returns for each construct the subchart to which it belongs (if there is no such subchart the function returns $\perp$). The domain of $subchart$ includes SUB_L, thus enabling nested subcharts:

$$subchart : M_L \cup A_L \cup C_L \cup SUB_L \rightarrow SUB_L \cup \{\perp\}$$

The set of instances, I_{Sub}, participating in a subchart Sub is defined as the set of all instances that are involved in some activity in Sub:

$$I_{Sub} = \{I \in I_L \mid \exists M \in M_L \ \text{s.t.} \ (subchart(M) = Sub$$
$$\wedge \ (I = M.I_{Src} \vee I = M.I_{Dst}))$$
$$\vee \ \exists A \in A_L \ \text{s.t.} \ (subchart(A) = Sub \wedge I \in I_A)$$
$$\vee \ \exists C \in C_L \ \text{s.t.} \ (subchart(C) = Sub \wedge I \in I_C)$$
$$\vee \ \exists Sub' \in SUB_L \ \text{s.t.} \ subchart(Sub') = Sub \wedge I \in I_{Sub'}\}$$

An if-then-else construct ITE in L is defined as

$$ITE = \langle I_{ITE}, C, Sub_T, Sub_E \rangle$$

where $I_{ITE} = I_C \cup I_{Sub_T} \cup I_{Sub_E}$ is the set of instances participating in the if-then-else construct, C is the main condition of the if-then-else construct, $Sub_T \in SUB_L$ is the subchart containing the 'then' part, and $Sub_E \in SUB_L \cup \{\bot\}$ is the subchart containing the 'else' part (if there is no such part, $Sub_E = \bot$).

A loop construct $Loop$ in L is defined as

$$Loop = \langle Kind, \mu, Sub \rangle$$

where $Kind \in \{Fixed, Unbound, Dynamic\}$ is the loop's kind, $\mu \in \mathbb{N} \cup \{\infty\}$ is the loop's number of iterations, and $Sub \in SUB_L$ is the subchart containing the loop events to be iterated. We denote by $I_{Loop} = I_{Sub}$ the set of instances participating in the loop.

A forbidden message $\bar{M} \in \overline{M}_L$ is defined as

$$\bar{M} = \langle M, Level, Scope \rangle$$

where M is an LSC message, $Level \in \{Message, Objects, All\}$ is the *generality level* of the forbidden message, and $Scope \in \{LSC, Pre, Main\} \cup SUB_L$ is the forbidden scope restricted by the message.

A forbidden condition $\bar{C} \in \overline{C}_L$ is a pair

$$\bar{C} = \langle C, Scope \rangle$$

where C is an LSC condition and $Scope$ is defined as above.

The temperature function $temp$ assigns temperatures to some of the LSC constructs:

$$temp : \ell(L) \cup M_L \cup C_L \cup \overline{M}_L \cup \overline{C}_L \to \{hot, cold\}$$

Locations and Events

We denote by E_L the set of *LSC events* in L:

$E_L =$

$\quad (\{m \in M_L \mid m.M_s \in \Sigma_{FromUser} \cup \Sigma_{ToUser} \cup \Sigma_{FromEnv} \cup \Sigma_{ToEnv} \cup \Sigma_{Calls}\}$

$\quad\quad \times \{Send, Recv\})$

$\quad \cup (\{m \in M_L \mid m.M_s \in \Sigma_{Self} \cup \Sigma_{Clock}\} \times \{Send\})$

$\quad \cup (Pch_L \times \{Start, End\}) \cup \{Completed\}$

$\quad \cup \{perform(A) \mid A \in A_L\} \cup \{eval(C) \mid C \in C_L\}$

$\quad \cup (SUB_L \times \{Start, End\}) \cup \{branch(ITE) \mid ITE \in ITE_L\}$

$\quad \cup (LOOP_L \times \{Start, End\})$

$\quad \cup \{skip(Loop) \mid Loop \in LOOP_L \wedge loop.Kind = Dynamic\}$

$\quad \cup \{bind(I) \mid I \in I_L \wedge symbolic(I)\}$

$\quad \cup \{evalf(\bar{C}) \mid \bar{C} \in \overline{C}_L\}$

The virtual event (ITE, End) is defined as:

$$(ITE, End) \triangleq \begin{cases} (ITE.Sub_E, End) & ITE.Sub_E \neq \bot \\ (ITE.Sub_T, End) & ITE.Sub_E = \bot \end{cases}$$

Events that match system events are called *visible events* while events that are internal to an LSC are called *hidden events*.

The function $evnt : \ell(L) \rightarrow E_L$ maps a location to the event it is associated with. Its inverse, $loc : E_L \rightarrow 2^{\ell(L)} = evnt^{-1}$, maps an event to the set of locations associated with it.

The function *subchart* is extended to events and to instance locations in the natural way. We also use the notation $e \in Sub$ as an equivalent to $subchart(e) = Sub$.

There is one point to be clarified regarding the relation between system events and LSC events. A system event e_s is defined over the set $\Sigma \times \{Send, Recv\}$. When such an event is generated by the system, it has to be matched with LSC events that are defined over the set $M_L \times \{Send, Recv\}$. As we shall see later, we also want to be able to match two LSC events (usually in different charts). We use the expression $e = \langle m, t \rangle$ both for system events and for LSC visible events. Note that in the first case $m \in \Sigma$ and in the second $m \in M_L$. In both cases $t \in \{Send, Recv\}$.

The Partial Order of an LSC

Every LSC induces a partial order among locations, which is the central aspect in determining the order of execution.

Definition A.2.1 (affecting a variable). *An LSC message $M \in M_L$ affects a variable X if $M.M_s.V = X \vee X \in M.M_s.\lambda_m^M$. An assignment $A \in A_L$ affects a variable X if $A.V = X$.*

Definition A.2.2 (using a variable). *An LSC message $M \in M_L$ uses a variable X if $X \in M.M_s.\lambda_f^F$. An assignment $A \in A_L$ uses a variable X if $X \in A.\lambda_f^F$.*

A condition basic expression ψ uses a variable X if at least one of the following holds:

1. *$\psi.LHS \in V_L$ and $\psi.LHS = X$.*
2. *$\psi.RHS \in V_L$ and $\psi.RHS = X$.*
3. *$\psi.RHS = (f, \lambda_f^F)$ and $X \in \lambda_f^F$.*

A condition C uses a variable X if one of its basic expressions uses it.

The notions of affecting and using a variable are extended to LSC events and locations in the natural way.

We say that l_x^i is the *first* location in L to affect the variable X if it affects X, and for any other location l_y^j that affects X either $l_x^i <_L l_y^j$ or $l_x^i <_V l_y^j$ (where $<_V$ is the vertical order in L). The predicate $first(l, X)$ is true iff l is the first location that affects X.

The partial order $\leq_L$, induced by a chart L, is obtained by the following relations:

Instance line - The locations along a single instance line are ordered top-down, beginning with the prechart start and ending with the chart end. Thus, things higher up are carried out earlier:

$$x < y \Rightarrow l_x^i <_L l_y^i$$

Send-Receive - For an asynchronous message $m \in M_L$, the location of the $\langle m, Send \rangle$ event precedes the location of the $\langle m, Recv \rangle$ event. Thus, an asynchronous message is sent before it is received. For synchronous messages, the two events take place simultaneously:

$$\forall m \in M_L :$$
$$(async(m) \Rightarrow loc(\langle m, Send \rangle) <_L loc(\langle m, Recv \rangle))$$
$$\wedge \; (sync(m) \Rightarrow loc(\langle m, Send \rangle) =_L loc(\langle m, Recv \rangle))$$

Prechart - All the instances participating in the prechart are synchronized at the beginning of the prechart and at its end.

$$\forall l_x^i, l_y^j \in loc((Pch, Start)) : l_x^i =_L l_y^j$$
$$\forall l_x^i, l_y^j \in loc((Pch, End)) : l_x^i =_L l_y^j$$

Chart completion - In order for a chart to complete, all the instances must reach their final location.

$$\forall l_x^i, l_y^j \in FinalLocations(L) : l_x^i =_L l_y^j$$

Variables - The first location that affects a variable precedes all other locations that affect or use the variable.

$$\forall l, l' \in \ell(L) : first(l, X) \wedge (affects(l', X) \vee uses(l', X)) \Rightarrow l <_L l'$$

Synchronize at assignments - All the instances that participate in an assignment are synchronized there.

$$\forall A \in A_L, \; \forall l_x^i, l_y^j \in loc(A) : \; l_x^i =_L l_y^j$$

Synchronize at conditions - All the instances that participate in a condition are synchronized there.

$$\forall C \in C_L, \; \forall l_x^i, l_y^j \in loc(C) : \; l_x^i =_L l_y^j$$

Synchronize at subcharts - All the instances that participate in a subchart are synchronized at its start and at its end.

$$\forall Sub \in SUB_L \; \forall l_x^i, l_y^j \in loc((Sub, Start)) : l_x^i =_L l_y^j$$
$$\forall l_x^i, l_y^j \in loc((Sub, End)) : l_x^i =_L l_y^j$$

If-then-else branch - All the events in an if-then-else construct may be carried out only after the main condition has been evaluated and one of the 'then' or 'else' branches has been selected.

$$\forall ITE \in ITE_L \; \forall e \in ITE.Sub_T \cup ITE.Sub_E : branch(ITE) <_L e$$

Disconnect If and Else - Events in 'then' subcharts should not be considered as preceding events in 'else' subcharts.

$$\forall ITE \in ITE_L, \forall l_x^i, l_y^i \; s.t. \; l_x^i \in ITE.Sub_T \wedge l_y^i \in ITE.Sub_E : l_x^i \nless_L l_y^i$$

We extend the partial order $\leq_L$ to events in the following way:

$$e' <_L e \; if \; \exists l \in loc(e), \exists l' \in loc(e') \; s.t. \; l' <_L l$$

A.3 Operational Semantics

Copies, Cuts and Events

Definition A.3.1 (LSC legal cut). *An LSC cut of L is a tuple of locations mapping every instance of L to one of its possible locations.*

$$Cut_L \in \prod_{I \in I_L} \ell(I)$$

A set of locations S is down-closed if

$$l_x^i \in S \Rightarrow \forall y \leq x,\ l_y^i \in S$$

The down-closure of an LSC cut C, denoted by $\downarrow C$, is the minimal down-closed set that contains C.

An LSC legal cut C is an LSC cut that satisfies:

$$\forall l \in C,\ \forall l' \leq_L l : l' \in\ \downarrow C$$

The top-line of a down-closed set S, denoted by $\uparrow S$, is a set of locations obtained by:

$$l_x^i \in\ \uparrow S \iff l_x^i \in S \wedge \not\exists l_y^i \in S \text{ s.t. } y > x$$

We denote by $Cut(I)$ the location of instance I in Cut.

The following utility functions dealing with cuts are used as we continue:

- The function $InitialCut(L)$ returns a legal cut of L containing the initial location for each instance.
- The function $BeginMainCut(L)$ returns the cut containing for each instance the location associated with the beginning of the main chart.
- The function $AdvanceCut(C, e) = \uparrow (\downarrow C \cup loc(e))$ is defined for a legal cut C and an event e that is enabled with respect to C, and returns a legal cut that is the result of advancing the cut C beyond e.

Definition A.3.2 (temperature of a cut). *The temperature of a cut is hot if at least one of the instances is in a hot location and is cold otherwise. We use $temp(C)$ to denote the temperature of cut C.*

Definition A.3.3 (LSC live copy). *Given an LSC L, a live copy of L, denoted by C^L, is defined as*

$$C^L = \langle LSC, Mode, Cut \rangle$$

where LSC is a copy of the original chart, $Mode \in \{PreActive, Active, Check\}$ is the execution mode of this copy, and Cut is some legal cut of L representing the current location of the instances of L in this particular copy.

Definition A.3.4 (minimal event in a chart). *A visible event e is minimal in a chart L if there is no visible event e' in L such that $e' <_L e$.*

Definition A.3.5 (enabled event). *An event e is enabled with respect to a cut C if* $\uparrow(\downarrow C \cup loc(e))$ *is a legal cut. That is, if the location in C of every instance participating in the event e is the one exactly prior to e, and there is no* $e' <_L e$ *that is not already in the down-closure of C.*

- *If* $e = \langle m, Send \rangle$, *m is synchronous and* $e' = \langle m, Recv \rangle$, *we require also that* $\downarrow C \cup loc(e) \cup loc(e')$ *is down-closed, thus making sure that a synchronous message will not be sent unless it can be received.*
- *If* $e = eval(C), temp(C) = hot$ *and* $FALSE \notin C.\Psi$, *we require also that* $value(C) = true$.

Definition A.3.6 (reachable event). *A visible event e is reachable from a cut C if:*

1. *The event e is enabled with respect to C, or*
2. *There exists an enabled hidden event* e' *such that e is reachable from the cut* $C' = AdvanceCut(C, e')$, *or*
3. *There exists an enabled dynamic loop, Loop, such that e is reachable from the cut* $C' = AdvanceCut(C, (Loop, End))$, *or*
4. *There exists an enabled dynamic loop, Loop, such that* $(Loop, End)$ *is currently enabled from C, and e is reachable from the cut* $C' = AdvanceCut(C, (Loop, Start))$.

Definition A.3.7 (violating event). *An event e violates a chart L in a cut C if* $L.Strict = True$ *and* $e \in M_L \times \{Send, Recv\}$ *but e is not enabled with respect to C.*

Unification

Definition A.3.8 (variable unification). *Two variables X and Y are positively-unifiable if* $X.\omega = Y.\omega \vee free(X) \vee free(Y)$. *X and Y are negatively-unifiable if* $X.\omega = Y.\omega \neq \bot$.

Definition A.3.9 (function unification). *Two function information structures* λ_f^F *and* λ_g^F *are unifiable (both positively and negatively) if* $f(\lambda_f^F) = g(\lambda_g^F)$ *(where* $f(\lambda_f^F)$ *is the value of f applied to the actual parameters in* λ_f^F*).*

Definition A.3.10 (variable-function unification). *A variable X and a function information structure* λ_f^F *are positively-unifiable if* $X.\omega = f(\lambda_f^F) \vee free(X)$. *X and* λ_f^F *are negatively-unifiable if* $X.\omega = f(\lambda_f^F)$.

Definition A.3.11 (method unification). *Two method information structures* $\lambda_{m_1}^M$ *and* $\lambda_{m_2}^M$ *are Q-unifiable (where Q is 'positively' or 'negatively') if:*

$$m_1 = m_2$$
$$\wedge\ \forall i\ \lambda_{m_1}^M.V_i\ \text{and}\ \lambda_{m_2}^M.V_i\ \text{are } Q\text{-unifiable.}$$

Definition A.3.12 (message unification). *Two system messages*
$M_s = \langle Src, Dst, P, V, f, \lambda_f^F, m, \lambda_m^M, Symbolic\rangle$ *and*
$M'_s = \langle Src', Dst', P', V', f', \lambda_{f'}^F, m', \lambda_{m'}^M, Symbolic'\rangle$ *are Q-unifiable (where*
Q is 'positively' or 'negatively') if they represent the same property or method
$P = P' \wedge m = m'$ and their contents are Q-unifiable. In case $m = m' = Tick$,
M_s and M'_s are only positively-unifiable.

Definition A.3.13 (event unification).

1. *A system event $e_s = \langle m_s, t\rangle$ and an LSC event $e_l = \langle m_l, t'\rangle$ with $t, t' \in$*
   $\{Send, Recv\}$ are Q-unifiable (where Q is 'positively' or 'negatively') if:
   a) *$t = t'$.*
   b) *$m_l.M_s$ and m_s are Q-unifiable.*
   c) *$m_s.Src \preccurlyeq m_l.I_{Src} \wedge m_s.Src \notin m_l.I_{Src}.\Phi$.*
   d) *$m_s.Dst \preccurlyeq m_l.I_{Dst} \wedge m_s.Dst \notin m_l.I_{Dst}.\Phi$.*
2. *Two LSC events $e = \langle m, t\rangle$ and $e' = \langle m', t'\rangle$ with $t, t' \in \{Send, Recv\}$ are*
   Q-unifiable if $t = t'$, $m.M_s$ and $m'.M_s$ are Q-unifiable, and

$$((m.I_{Src} \preccurlyeq m'.I_{Src}\ \wedge\ AppObj(m.I_{Src}) \notin m'.I_{Src}.\Phi)$$
$$\vee\ (m'.I_{Src} \preccurlyeq m.I_{Src}\ \wedge\ AppObj(m'.I_{Src}) \notin m.I_{Src}.\Phi))$$

$$\text{and}$$

$$((m.I_{Dst} \preccurlyeq m'.I_{Dst}\ \wedge\ AppObj(m.I_{Dst}) \notin m'.I_{Dst}.\Phi)$$
$$\vee\ (m'.I_{Dst} \preccurlyeq m.I_{Dst}\ \wedge\ AppObj(m'.I_{Dst}) \notin m.I_{Dst}.\Phi))$$

When we use the term unification without specifying whether it is positive
or negative, it should be read as positive unification.

As events occur in the system, LSC events are checked to see if they
can be unified, and, if so, their variables are actually bound to new values
according to the unification process. In the following we describe the different
procedures used in the unification process.

If the two variables to be unified are free, no binding occurs and the two
variables are connected in a connection set:

Connect(X, Y, Context)

1. Create a connected pair in the context:

$$S \leftarrow \{X, Y\}; \quad Context \leftarrow Context \cup \{S\}$$

2. If X or Y are already connected, join the sets:

if $\exists S_X \in Context$, s.t. $X \in S_X$, then $S \leftarrow S \cup S_X$;

$$Context \leftarrow Context \setminus \{S_X\}$$

if $\exists S_Y \in Context$, s.t. $Y \in S_Y$, then $S \leftarrow S \cup S_Y$;

$$Context \leftarrow Context \setminus \{S_Y\}$$

Binding a variable in $Context$ with a given value entails binding all the variables in its connection set:

Bind(X, Val, Context)

1. Let S_X be the set in $Context$ s.t. $X \in S_X$.
2. Assign values to all variables in the set:

$$\forall U \in S_X, U.\omega \leftarrow Val$$

$$Context \leftarrow Context \setminus \{S_X\}$$

Variables are therefore unified as follows:

Unify(X, Y, Context)

1. If $X.\omega = \bot \wedge Y.\omega \neq \bot$ then $X.\omega \leftarrow Y.\omega$.
2. If $X.\omega \neq \bot \wedge Y.\omega = \bot$ then $Y.\omega \leftarrow X.\omega$.
3. If $X.\omega = \bot \wedge Y.\omega = \bot$ then $Connect(X, Y, Context)$.
4. If $X.\omega \neq \bot$ then $Bind(X, X.\omega, Context)$.
5. If $Y.\omega \neq \bot$ then $Bind(Y, Y.\omega, Context)$.

A variable and a function information structure are unified as follows:

Unify(X, λ_f^F, Context)

1. If $X.\omega = f(\lambda_f^F)$ then return.
2. $X.\omega \leftarrow f(\lambda_f^F)$.
3. $Bind(X, X.\omega, Context)$.

And two method information structures are unified as follows:

Unify(λ_m^M, $\lambda_m^{M'}$, Context)

1. For $i = 1, \ldots, n$:
    a) Unify($\lambda_m^M.V_i$, $\lambda_m^{M'}.V_i$, Context).

For two unifiable messages, we use $Unify(M, M', Context)$ as an abbreviation to $Unify(M.\Lambda, M'.\Lambda, Context)$. Next, we show how two LSC events are unified:

Unify(e, e', Context)

1. Unify($e.m$, $e'.m'$, Context).
2. If $symbolic(e.m.I_{Src}) \wedge e'.m'.I_{Src} \preccurlyeq e.m.I_{Src}$ then bind the symbolic instance with the concrete object:
    a) $e.m.I_{Src}.O \leftarrow e'.m'.I_{Src}.O$.
    b) $e.m.I_{Src}.C \leftarrow \bot$.
3. If $symbolic(e'.m'.I_{Src}) \wedge e.m.I_{Src} \preccurlyeq e'.m'.I_{Src}$ then bind the symbolic instance with the concrete object:
    a) $e'.m'.I_{Src}.O \leftarrow e.m.I_{Src}.O$.
    b) $e'.m'.I_{Src}.C \leftarrow \bot$.
4. If $symbolic(e.m.I_{Dst}) \wedge e'.m'.I_{Dst} \preccurlyeq e.m.I_{Dst}$ then bind the symbolic instance with the concrete object:
    a) $e.m.I_{Dst}.O \leftarrow e'.m'.I_{Dst}.O$.
    b) $e.m.I_{Dst}.C \leftarrow \bot$.
5. If $symbolic(e'.m'.I_{Dst}) \wedge e.m.I_{Dst} \preccurlyeq e'.m'.I_{Dst}$ then bind the symbolic instance with the concrete object:
    a) $e'.m'.I_Dst.O \leftarrow e.m.I_{Dst}.O$.
    b) $e'.m'.I_{Dst}.C \leftarrow \bot$.

A system event $e_s = \langle m_s, t \rangle$ and an LSC event $e_l = \langle m_l, t \rangle$ are also unified according to these same lines, except that the system event is guaranteed to have concrete objects as the sender and receiver of the message:

Unify(e_s, e_l, Context)

1. Unify($e_s.m_s$, $e_l.m_l$, Context).
2. If $symbolic(e_l.m_l.I_{Src}) \wedge e_s.m_s.Src \preccurlyeq e_l.m_l.I_{Src}$ then bind the symbolic instance with the concrete object:
    a) $e_l.m_l.I_{Src}.O \leftarrow e_s.m_s.Src$.
    b) $e_l.m_l.I_{Src}.C \leftarrow \bot$.
3. If $symbolic(e_l.m_l.I_{Dst}) \wedge e_s.m_s.Dst \preccurlyeq e_l.m_l.I_{Dst}$ then bind the symbolic instance with the concrete object:
    a) $e_l.m_l.I_{Dst}.O \leftarrow e_s.m_s.Dst$.
    b) $e_l.m_l.I_{Dst}.C \leftarrow \bot$.

A different kind of unification is used when trying to match events with forbidden messages.

Definition A.3.14 (forbidden message unification). *A system message* M_s *and a forbidden message* $\bar{M}$ *are unifiable if one of the following holds:*

1. $\bar{M}.Level = All.$
2. $\bar{M}.Level = Objects$ *and* $M_s.Src \preccurlyeq \bar{M}.M.I_{Src} \wedge M_s.Dst \preccurlyeq \bar{M}.M.I_{Dst}.$
3. $\bar{M}.Level = Message$ *and* M_s *and* $\bar{M}.M$ *are positively-unifiable.*

Checking for unification of an *LSC message* M_l with a forbidden message $\bar{M}$ is defined similarly, with $M_s.Src$ and $M_s.Dst$ replaced by $M_l.I_{Src}$ and $M_l.I_{Dst}$, respectively.

Definition A.3.15 (active scope). *A scope* $S \in \{LSC, Pre, Main\} \cup SUB_L$ *is active in an LSC live copy* C^L *if one of the following holds:*

1. $S = LSC.$
2. $S = Pre$ *and* $C^L.Mode = PreActive.$
3. $S = Main$ *and* $C^L.Mode \in \{Active, Check\}.$
4. $S \in SUB_L$ *and* $\forall I \in I_S, loc((S, Start)) <_L C^L.Cut(I) <_L loc((S, End)).$

We use the predicate notation $active(S)$ to indicate that a scope S is active.

Definition A.3.16 (hot-forbidden event). *An event* e *is hot-forbidden in a chart* L *being in a cut* C *if* e *is not enabled with respect to* C *and one of the following holds:*

- $\exists \bar{M} \in \bar{M}_L$ *s.t.* $active(\bar{M}.Scope) \wedge temp(\bar{M}) = hot \wedge Unifiable(e.M, \bar{M}).$
- $e.M.P \neq \bot$ *(i.e.,* e *represents a change of property value) and* $\exists \bar{C} \in \bar{C}_L$ *s.t.* $temp(\bar{C}) = hot \wedge active(\bar{C})$ *and* $\bar{C}$ *will become true if the current value of* P *is replaced with the value in* $e.M.$

Definition A.3.17 (cold-forbidden event). *An event* e *is cold-forbidden in a chart* L *being in a cut* C *if* e *is not enabled with respect to* C *and* $\exists \bar{M} \in \bar{M}_L$ *s.t.* $active(\bar{M}.Scope) \wedge temp(\bar{M}) = cold \wedge Unifiable(e.M, \bar{M}).$

Since the same event can cause the violation of more than one forbidden message or more than one forbidden condition, we define the function $dominant(S)$, which gets a set of forbidden messages and returns one of the dominant messages in the set. A hot message is more dominant than a cold one, and a cold message with a scope containing the scope of another cold message is more dominant than the message whose scope is contained.

---

dominant(S)

1. If $\exists \bar{M} \in S$ s.t. $temp(\bar{M}) = hot$ then return $\bar{M}$.
2. If all messages are cold then
   a) Set $\bar{M}$ to be any message in S.
   b) $S \leftarrow S \setminus \{\bar{M}\}$.
   c) While $S \neq \emptyset$ do
      i. Choose a message $\bar{M}' \in S$.
      ii. $S \leftarrow S \setminus \{\bar{M}'\}$.
      iii. If $\bar{M}.Scope \subset \bar{M}'.Scope$ then set $\bar{M} \leftarrow \bar{M}'$.
   d) Return $\bar{M}$.

The function *dominant* is defined in the same way for sets of forbidden conditions.

The Transition System

The operational semantics is given as a transition system

$$Sem(\mathcal{S}) = \langle \mathcal{V}, V_0, \mathcal{S}_D, \mathcal{S}_M, \Delta[\mathcal{S}_O, \mathcal{S}_C] \rangle$$

where $\mathcal{V}$ is the set of possible configurations (states) of $Sem(\mathcal{S})$, V_0 is the initial configuration, $\mathcal{S}_D \subseteq \mathcal{S}_\mathcal{U}$ is the set of driving LSCs, $\mathcal{S}_M \subseteq \mathcal{S}_\mathcal{U} \cup \mathcal{S}_E$ is the set of monitored LSCs, and $\Delta \subseteq \mathcal{V} \times (\mathcal{E} \cup \bigcup_{L \in \mathcal{S}} E_L) \times \mathcal{V}$ is the set of allowed transitions. We require that $\mathcal{S}_D \cap \mathcal{S}_M = \emptyset$.

A state $V \in \mathcal{V}$ is defined as

$$V = \langle \mathcal{RL}, \mathcal{ML}, Violating \rangle$$

where $\mathcal{RL}$ is a set of live copies of 'driving' LSCs, $\mathcal{ML}$ is a set of live copies of monitored LSCs, and *Violating* indicates by *True* or *False* whether the state is a violating one.

The initial configuration contains no copies of driving LSCs and no copies of monitored LSCs, and is defined as:

$$V_0 = \langle \emptyset, \emptyset, False \rangle$$

The transition relation Δ is parameterized with two sets. The first set $\mathcal{S}_O$ is the set of original LSCs to which Δ should be applied. The second set $\mathcal{S}_C$ is the set of live copies that currently exist. This set contains only copies of LSCs from $\mathcal{S}_O$. The two sets are instantiated with either $(\mathcal{S}_D, \mathcal{RL})$ or $(\mathcal{S}_M, \mathcal{ML})$. The 'standard' part of the semantics, i.e., the part that enables a system to be tested and verified against an LSC specification, is achieved by setting $\mathcal{S}_M = \mathcal{S}$ and $\mathcal{S}_D = \emptyset$.

We describe Δ as a set of rules to be applied to its set parameters and to *Violating* with respect to a given event e. Since the set parameters are instantiated also by $\mathcal{RL}$ and $\mathcal{ML}$, which are taken from a state V, the result of applying Δ is a new state V' consisting of the modified components. Given an event, all the applicable rules are applied before the next event is considered. Also, Δ handles *hidden events* with higher priority than *visible events*. Therefore, in order for a visible event to be handled, all hidden events must be processed first. Other than that, the semantics imposes no order on the particular event to be processed, and is thus nondeterministic:

- If $e = \langle M, t \rangle$ *(where $t \in \{Send, Recv\}$)* then:
  1. If $e.M.m = Tick$ then set $Clock.Time \leftarrow Clock.Time + 1$.
  2. Set $Context \leftarrow \emptyset$.
  3. If $\exists C^L \in \mathcal{S}_C$ and $\exists \bar{M} \in C^L.LSC.\overline{M}_L$, such that $e.M$ and $\bar{M}$ are unifiable and $active(\bar{M}.Scope)$, and there is no enabled event e' positively level$_2$-unifiable with e, then:
     a) Set $S \leftarrow \{\bar{M} \in C^L.LSC.\overline{M}_L | Unifiable(e.M, \bar{M}) \wedge active(\bar{M}.Scope)\}$.
     b) Set $\bar{M} \leftarrow dominant(S)$.
     c) If $temp(\bar{M}) = hot$ then
        i. Set $\mathcal{S}_C \leftarrow \mathcal{S}_C \setminus \{C^L\}$.
        ii. Set $Violating \leftarrow True$.
     d) If $temp(\bar{M}) = cold$ then
        i. If $\bar{M}.Scope \in \{LSC, Pre, Main\}$ then set $\mathcal{S}_C \leftarrow \mathcal{S}_C \setminus \{C^L\}$.
        ii. If $\bar{M}.Scope = Sub \in SUB_L$ then set

        $$C^L.Cut \leftarrow AdvanceCut(C^L.Cut, (Sub, End))$$

  4. If $\exists C^L \in \mathcal{S}_C$ and $\exists e' \in C^L.LSC$, such that e and e' are negatively level$_2$-unifiable and e' violates C^L, then:
     a) Set $\mathcal{S}_C \leftarrow \mathcal{S}_C \setminus \{C^L\}$.
     b) If $temp(C^L.Cut) = hot$, set $Violating \leftarrow True$.
     c) If $symbolic(e'.M.I_{Src})$ or $symbolic(e'.M.I_{Dst})$ then create an identical copy C'^L of C^L, set $\mathcal{S}_C \leftarrow \mathcal{S}_C \cup \{C'^L\}$, and in the copy set
        $$e'.M.I_{Src}.\Phi \leftarrow e'.M.I_{Src}.\Phi \cup \{e.M.Src\} \quad \text{if } symbolic(e'.M.I_{Src})$$
        $$e'.M.I_{Dst}.\Phi \leftarrow e'.M.I_{Dst}.\Phi \cup \{e.M.Dst\} \quad \text{if } symbolic(e'.M.I_{Dst})$$
  5. For every universal LSC $L \in \mathcal{S}_O$ which has an event e', positively level$_2$-unifiable with e, as a minimal event in its prechart, create a copy of L, C^L, and set $\mathcal{S}_C \leftarrow \mathcal{S}_C \cup \{C^L\}$. Set $C^L.Mode = PreActive$ and set its cut by $C^L.Cut \leftarrow AdvanceCut(InitialCut(L), \langle Pch_L, Start \rangle)$. Unify the variables of e and e', by $Unify(e, e', Context)$. For each hidden event $e'' <_L e'$, apply $\Delta(e'')$.

6. For every existential LSC $L \in \mathcal{S}_O$ which has an event e', positively level$_2$-unifiable with e, as a minimal event in the chart body, create a copy of L, C^L, and set $\mathcal{S}_C \leftarrow \mathcal{S}_C \cup \{C^L\}$. Set $C^L.Mode = Check$, and set its cut to the beginning of the chart by $C^L.Cut \leftarrow BeginMainCut(C^L.LSC)$. Unify the variables of e and e', by $Unify(e, e', Context)$. For each hidden event $e'' <_L e'$, apply $\Delta(e'')$.

7. For every copy $C^L \in \mathcal{S}_C$ that has a reachable event e' positively level$_2$-unifiable with e:
   a) If $symbolic(e'.M.I_{Src})$ or $symbolic(e'.M.I_{Dst})$ then create an identical copy of C^L, C'^L, set $\mathcal{S}_C \leftarrow \mathcal{S}_C \cup \{C'^L\}$, and in the copy set
   $$e'.M.I_{Src}.\Phi \leftarrow e'.M.I_{Src}.\Phi \cup \{e.m.Src\} \quad \text{if } symbolic(e'.M.I_{Src})$$
   $$e'.M.I_{Dst}.\Phi \leftarrow e'.M.I_{Dst}.\Phi \cup \{e.m.Dst\} \quad \text{if } symbolic(e'.M.I_{Dst})$$
   b) Set $C^L.Cut \leftarrow AdvanceCut(C^L.Cut, e')$.
   c) If $e' = \langle M, Send \rangle$, M is synchronous and $e'' = \langle M, Recv \rangle$, set $C^L.Cut \leftarrow AdvanceCut(C^L.Cut, e'')$.
   d) Unify the events e and e', $Unify(e, e', Context)$.
   e) For each hidden event $e'' <_L e'$, apply $\Delta(e'')$.
- If $e = Completed(C^L)$ for some $C^L \in \mathcal{S}_C$ then set $\mathcal{S}_C \leftarrow \mathcal{S}_C \setminus \{C^L\}$.
- If $e = \langle Pch_L, End \rangle$ for some $C^L \in \mathcal{S}_C$, then set $C^L.Cut \leftarrow BeginMainCut(C^L.LSC)$ and $C^L.Mode \leftarrow Active$.
- If $e = perform(A)$ for some $A \in A_L$ s.t. $C^L \in \mathcal{S}_C$, then set $C^L.Cut \leftarrow AdvanceCut(C^L.Cut, e)$ and set

$$A.V \leftarrow \begin{cases} A.C & \text{if } A.Type = constant \\ Value(A.P) & \text{if } A.Type = property \\ A.f(A.\lambda_f^F) & \text{if } A.Type = function \\ Clock.Time & \text{if } A.Type = time \end{cases}$$

- If $e = eval(C)$ for some $C \in C^L$ s.t. $C^L \in \mathcal{S}_C$ then
  1. If $value(C) = true$ then set $C^L.Cut \leftarrow AdvanceCut(C^L.Cut, e)$.
  2. If $value(C) = false$ then
     a) If $subchart(C) \in \{ITE.Sub_T, ITE.Sub_E\}$ for some ITE then

     $$set\ C^L.Cut \leftarrow AdvanceCut(C^L.Cut, (ITE, End))$$

     b) If $subchart(C) = Sub \in SUB_L$ then

     $$set\ C^L.Cut \leftarrow AdvanceCut(C^L.Cut, (Sub, End))$$

     c) If $subchart(C) = \bot$ then set $\mathcal{S}_C \leftarrow \mathcal{S}_C \setminus \{C^L\}$.
     d) If $temp(C) = hot$ then set $Violating \leftarrow True$.
- If $e = branch(ITE)$ for some $ITE \in C^L$ s.t. $C^L \in \mathcal{S}_C$ then

1. If $value(ITE.C) = true$ then set
   $C^L.Cut \leftarrow AdvanceCut(C^L.Cut, (ITE.Sub_T, Start))$.
2. If $value(ITE.C) = false$ then

$$set \; C^L.Cut \leftarrow \begin{cases} AdvanceCut(C^L.Cut, (ITE.Sub_E, Start)) & \text{if } ITE.Sub_E \neq \perp \\ AdvanceCut(C^L.Cut, (ITE.Sub_T, End)) & \text{if } ITE.Sub_E = \perp \end{cases}$$

- If $e = (ITE.Sub_T, End)$ for some $ITE \in C^L$ s.t. $C^L \in \mathcal{S}_C$ then

  $$set \; C^L.Cut \leftarrow AdvanceCut(C^L.Cut, (ITE, End))$$

- If $e = (ITE.Sub_E, End)$ for some $ITE \in C^L$ s.t. $C^L \in \mathcal{S}_C$ then

  $$set \; C^L.Cut \leftarrow AdvanceCut(C^L.Cut, (ITE.Sub_E, End))$$

- If $e = (Sub, End)$ for some $Sub \in C^L$ s.t. $C^L \in \mathcal{S}_C$ then

  $$set \; C^L.Cut \leftarrow AdvanceCut(C^L.Cut, (Sub, End))$$

- If $e = skip(Loop)$ for some $Loop \in C^L$ s.t. $C^L \in \mathcal{S}_C$ then

  $$set \; C^L.Cut \leftarrow AdvanceCut(C^L.Cut, (Loop, End))$$

- If $e = (Loop, Start)$ for some $Loop \in C^L$ s.t. $C^L \in \mathcal{S}_C$ then

  $$set \; C^L.Cut \leftarrow AdvanceCut(C^L.Cut, (Loop, Start))$$

  For every variable $V \in V_L$ that is used in $Loop$ for the first time, set $V.\omega \leftarrow \perp$.
- If $e = (Loop, End)$ for some $Loop \in C^L$ s.t. $C^L \in \mathcal{S}_C$ and $Loop.Kind \neq Dynamic$ then
  1. Set $\mu \leftarrow \mu - 1$.
  2. If $\mu > 0$ then

     $$set \; C^L.Cut \leftarrow AdvanceCut(C^L.Cut, (Loop, Start))$$

     For every variable $V \in V_L$ that is used in $Loop$ for the first time, set $V.\omega \leftarrow \perp$.
  3. If $\mu = 0$ then

     $$set \; C^L.Cut \leftarrow AdvanceCut(C^L.Cut, (Loop, End))$$

- If $e = bind(I)$ for some symbolic instance $I \in C^L$ s.t. $C^L \in \mathcal{S}_C$, then:
  1. $S \leftarrow \{O \in \mathcal{O} \mid O \preccurlyeq I, O \text{ satisfies } I.\psi \text{ and } \nexists I' \in C^L \text{ s.t. } I'.O = O\}$.
  2. If $S = \emptyset$ then $\mathcal{S}_C \leftarrow \mathcal{S}_C \setminus \{C^L\}$.

3. If $I.Mode = Existential$ then
   a) Set $I.O = O$, for some $O \in S$.
   b) Set $I.C = \bot$.
4. If $I.Mode = Universal$ then perform the following for every $O \in S$:
   a) Create an identical copy C'^L of C^L.
   b) Set $\mathcal{S}_C \leftarrow \mathcal{S}_C \cup \{C'^L\}$.
   c) Set $I.O = O$.
   d) Set $I.C = \bot$.
   Finally, set $\mathcal{S}_C \leftarrow \mathcal{S}_C \setminus \{C^L\}$.
- If $e = evalf(\bar{C})$ for some $\bar{C} \in C^L$ s.t. $C^L \in \mathcal{S}_C$, then (it is guaranteed that $value(\bar{C}) = true$)
1. If $temp(\bar{C}) = hot$ then
   a) Set $\mathcal{S}_C \leftarrow \mathcal{S}_C \setminus \{C^L\}$.
   b) Set $Violating \leftarrow True$.
2. If $temp(\bar{C}) = cold$ then
   a) If $\bar{C}.Scope \in \{LSC, Pre, Main\}$ then set $\mathcal{S}_C \leftarrow \mathcal{S}_C \setminus \{C^L\}$.
   b) If $\bar{C}.Scope = Sub \in SUB_L$ then set

$$C^L.Cut \leftarrow AdvanceCut(C^L.Cut, (Sub, End))$$

Using Δ for Testing Systems

Definition A.3.18 (violating transition). *A transition in Δ is violating if it sets Violating to false.*

Definition A.3.19 (run/trace). *A run or trace is a sequence of visible events.*

Definition A.3.20 (consistent run). *A run R is consistent with an LSC specification S if, starting from V_0, the rules of Δ can be applied to the events in R and to the hidden events generated between them, without reaching a violating transition.*

Definition A.3.21 (consistent system). *A system Sys is consistent with an LSC specification S if all the runs of Sys are consistent with the specification, and for every existential LSC $L \in \mathcal{S}_E$, there exists a run that satisfies L.*

If a sequence of visible events is monitored against an LSC specification, the events are sent one by one to the procedure *monitor-event*. The input to *monitor-event* is a single event, and after monitoring this event the procedure advances all the hidden events until there are no hidden events enabled:

---

monitor-event(ev)

1. Apply $\Delta[\mathcal{S}_M, \mathcal{ML}](ev)$.
2. Compute the set of forbidden conditions:

$$Forbidden \leftarrow \bigcup_{C^L \in \mathcal{ML}} \{\bar{C} \in \overline{C}_L | \; active(\bar{C}.Scope) \wedge value(\bar{C}.C) = true\}$$

3. If $Forbidden \neq \emptyset$ then
   a) $\bar{C} \leftarrow dominant(Forbidden)$.
   b) Apply $\Delta[\mathcal{S}_M, \mathcal{ML}](evalf(\bar{C}))$.
   c) Go back to 2.
4. compute the set of enabled events:

$$Enabled \leftarrow \bigcup_{C^L \in \mathcal{ML}} \{e \in E_L | enabled(e)\}$$

$$Waiting \leftarrow \bigcup_{C^L \in \mathcal{ML}} \{e | e = branch(ITE)\}$$

$$\cup \bigcup_{C^L \in \mathcal{ML}} \{e | e = (Loop, End) \wedge Loop.Kind = Dynamic\}$$

$$Enabled \leftarrow Enabled \setminus Waiting$$

5. If there is a *hidden* enabled event $e \in Enabled$, then
   a) Apply $\Delta[\mathcal{S}_M, \mathcal{ML}](e)$.
   b) Go back to 2.
6. Terminate monitor-event.

Using Δ for Executing Specifications

One of the main purposes of the Play-Engine is to execute the specification directly. The engine's execution mechanism works in phases of *step* and *super-step*. The input to a *step* is a system event e. The procedure for a step phase consists of applying the transition relation onto the event e and, if the event represents a property change, changing the state of the system model according to the new value in the message:

---

step(e)

1. Apply $\Delta[\mathcal{S}_D, \mathcal{RL}](e)$.
2. If $e.M.P \neq \bot$ then change the property value according to the value in the message:

   a)
   $$O \leftarrow \begin{cases} e.M.Src \text{ if } M \in \Sigma_{ToUser} \cup \Sigma_{ToEnv} \\ e.M.Dst \text{ otherwise} \end{cases}$$

   b) $P \leftarrow e.M.P$.

   c)
   $$Value(O.P) \leftarrow \begin{cases} e.M.f(e.M.\lambda_f^F) \text{ if } e.M.f \neq \bot \\ e.M.V.\omega \qquad \text{otherwise} \end{cases}$$

3. monitor-event(e).

Step also calls monitor-event, so that while some LSCs are used to drive model execution other LSCs can be monitored.

In the *super-step* phase, the Play-Engine continuously executes the steps associated with internal events, i.e., those that do not originate with the user, the environment, the $Clock$ or with external objects, until it reaches a 'stable' state where no further such events can be carried out. We define

$$External = \{\bigcup_{L \in \mathcal{S}} \langle m, Send \rangle | m.M_s.Src.External = true\}$$

and a super-step phase is then given as:

---

super-step

1. Compute the set of forbidden conditions:

$$Forbidden \leftarrow \bigcup_{C^L \in \mathcal{RL}} \{\bar{C} \in \overline{C}_L \mid active(\bar{C}.Scope) \wedge value(\bar{C}.C) = true\}$$

2. If $Forbidden \neq \emptyset$ then
   a) $\bar{C} \leftarrow dominant(Forbidden)$.
   b) Apply $\Delta[\mathcal{S}_C, \mathcal{RL}](evalf(\bar{C}))$.
   c) Go back to 1.
3. Compute the set of enabled events:

$$Enabled \leftarrow \bigcup_{C^L \in \mathcal{RL}} \{e \in E_L \mid enabled(e)\}$$

$$Waiting \leftarrow \bigcup_{\substack{C^L \in \mathcal{RL}, \\ C^L.Mode = PreActive}} \{e \mid e = branch(ITE)\}$$

$$Enabled \leftarrow Enabled \setminus (External \cup Waiting)$$

4. If there is a *hidden* enabled event $e \in Enabled$, then
   a) Apply $\Delta[\mathcal{S}_C, \mathcal{RL}](e)$.
   b) Go back to 1.
5. If there is a *visible* enabled event $e \in Enabled$, such that e does not violate and is neither hot-forbidden nor cold-forbidden in any copy which is either in *active* or *preactive* mode, then
   a) *step(e)*.
   b) Go back to 1.
6. If there is a *visible* enabled event $e \in Enabled$, such that e does not violate and is neither hot-forbidden nor cold-forbidden in any copy which is in *active* mode, then
   a) *step(e)*.
   b) Go back to 1.
7. If there is a *visible* enabled event $e \in Enabled$, such that e does not violate and is not hot-forbidden in any copy which is in *active* mode with a hot cut, then
   a) *step(e)*.
   b) Go back to 1.
8. Terminate super-step.

B. XML Description of a GUI Application

The GUI application is described using an XML file. If GUIEdit is used (see Chap. 20), then this file is generated as an outcome of the GUI-building activity. In this appendix, we describe the required structure of this XML file and explain each of the fields. The XML structure is tree-like.

⋆ **Application** – The root element of the XML file.

   ⊙ **Types** – A root node for the application types.
     • **Type** – A single type.
       – **ID (Integer)** – A unique ID for each type. Begins with 1 and is continuously incremented.
       – **Name (String)** – The type name.
       – **Description (String)** – The type description.
       – **Symbolic (True/False)** – Indicates whether the type is symbolic. That is, whether, if used in a symbolic message, values of this type can be interchanged.
       – **Kind (Enum/Range/String)** – The kind of the type. Enum stands for a list of values. Range stands for a discrete range going from a minimal value to a maximal value in steps of a given delta. String represents different strings characterized by a given length.
       – **Values** – The root node of an Enum type's possible values.
         • **Val (String)** – One value of an enumeration.
       – **MinValue (Real)** – The minimal value in a Range type.
       – **MaxValue (Real)** – The maximal value in a Range type.
       – **Delta (Real)** – The delta step in a Range type.
       – **Length (Integer)** – The length of allowed strings in a String type.
   ⊙ **GUIObjects** – A root node for the GUI objects.
     • **GUIObject** – A single GUI object.
       – **ID (Integer)** – A unique ID for the object. Begins with 1 and is continuously incremented.
       – **Name (String)** – The object's name.
       – **Kind (GUI_In/Internal/App_Class)** – The object's kind. Should always be GUI_In. The other two types are for the Play-Engine's internal use.

- **Layout** – A root node for the object's layout.
  - **Top (Integer)** – The top coordinate of the object.
  - **Left (Integer)** – The left coordinate of the object.
  - **Width (Integer)** – The width of the object.
  - **Height (Integer)** – The height of the object.
- **Properties** – The root node for the object's properties.
  - **Property** – A single property.
    - **ID (Integer)** – A unique ID for the property. Begins with 1 (separated for each object) and is continuously incremented.
    - **Name (String)** – The property name.
    - **Type (String)** – The name of the type upon which the property is based. The type must be one of the types defined earlier in the types section.
    - **Prefix (String)** – A verb that can be used to denote the action of setting a value to this property (e.g., Set, Change, Turn, Click, etc.).
    - **Affects (Self/User/Env)** – Shows where the message arrow in the LSC leads to when the property is changed.
    - **InOnly (True/False)** – Indicates whether this property can be changed only by a user action (e.g., clicking a button).
    - **Default (True/False)** – Indicates whether the property is a default property, i.e., whether we can omit its name when referring to it in the object's context.
    - **Synchronous (True/False)** – Indicates whether the messages generated when the property is changed are synchronous.
    - **CanBeChangedExternally (True/False)** – Indicates whether this property can be changed by the external environment.
- ⊙ **Implemented Functions** – The root node for functions that are implemented within the GUI application. Every such function must be backed up by a function in the code.
- **ImplementedFunction** – A single implemented function.
  - **ID (Integer)** – A unique ID for the function. Begins with 1 and is continuously incremented.
  - **Name (String)** – The function's name.
  - **Description (String)** – The function's description.
  - **BinaryOp (True / False)** – Indicates whether the function is a binary operation (e.g., $+$, $-$, etc.). Binary operations are written as $Arg_1 \ op \ Arg_2$ instead of $op(Arg_1, Arg_2)$.
  - **ReturnType (String)** – The name of the type returned by the function. The type must be one of the types defined earlier in the types section.

Params – A root node for the function's formal parameters. Each function can have up to five parameters.

- **Param** – A single parameter.
  - **ParamName (String)** – The parameter's name.
  - **ParamType (String)** – The name of the parameter's type. The type must be one of the types defined earlier in the types section.

C. The Play-Engine Interface

This appendix describes *IPlayEngine*, an interface implemented by the Play-Engine and used by GUI applications to interact with it. The IPlayEngine interface is installed as part of the Play-Engine installation, in the form of a COM (Component Object Model) component with the file name EngineLib.dll.

The IPlayEngine interface has three methods:

ObjectClicked(ObjID: Integer) – The GUI application should call this method whenever a GUI object is clicked. The *ObjID* parameter should contain the ID of the clicked object.

ObjectChanged(ObjID: Integer, PropID: Integer, strValue: String) – The GUI application should call this method whenever a property of some object is changed (e.g., clicking a switch to on, moving a slider, writing text in a text box, etc.). *ObjID* should contain the ID of the object, *PropID* the ID of the modified property, and *strValue* the new value of the property.

ObjectRightClicked(ObjID: Integer) – The GUI application should call this method whenever a GUI object is right-clicked. The *ObjID* parameter should contain the ID of the right-clicked object.

C.1 Visual Basic Code

Here is the Visual Basic code for the IPlayEngine interface:

Public Sub ObjectClicked(ByVal ObjID As Integer)
End Sub
Public Sub ObjectChanged(ByVal ObjID As Integer, PropID As Integer, strValue As String)
End Sub
Public Sub ObjectRightClicked(ByVal ObjID As Integer)
End Sub

D. The GUI Application Interface

This appendix describes *IUserApp*, an interface that should be implemented by any GUI application wishing to interact with the Play-Engine. This interface is used by the Play-Engine to interact with the GUI application. The IUserApp interface is installed as part of the Play-Engine installation in the form of a COM (Component Object Model) component with the file name UserAppLib.dll.

The IUserApp interface has the following methods:

ShowGUI () – The Play-Engine calls this method to display the GUI application.

HideGUI () – The Play-Engine calls this method to hide the GUI application (this only hides the display; it does not unload or free the application).

GetAppDataXMLFile () : String – This function returns the name of the XML file that contains the application description (see Appendix B).

InfoMode (InInfoMode: Boolean) – This method is currently not in use. When implementing this interface, this method should be left empty.

SetGUIObject (ObjID: Integer, PropID: Integer, sValue: String) – The Play-Engine calls this method in order to set some property of some object to some new value. *ObjID* contains the object ID, *PropID* contains the property ID, and *sValue* contains the property's new value.

GetGUIValue (ObjID: Integer, PropID: Integer) : String – This function returns the current value of some object's property. *ObjID* contains the object's ID and, *PropID* contains the property's ID.

PlayEngine (Engine: IPlayEngine) – This property is used by the Play-Engine in order to register itself within the GUI application. Upon loading the GUI application, this method is called. The GUI application is expected to keep a reference (pointer) to this particular calling engine and to use it to interact later with the Play-Engine.

HighlightObject(ObjID: Integer) – The Play-Engine calls this method in order to highlight an object in the application (usually by circling it in red, but this is application-dependent). *ObjID* contains the ID of the object to be highlighted.

ClearObject(ObjID: Integer) – The Play-Engine calls this method in order to remove the highlight from an object in the application. *ObjID* contains the ID of the object to be de-highlighted.

GetObjectPosition(ObjID: Integer, Left: Integer reference, Top: Integer reference) – The Play-Engine calls this method in order to get the top and left coordinates of an object. *ObjID* contains the object's ID. The returned values should be placed in *Left* and *Top*, respectively.

GetObjectLayout(ObjID: Integer, Left: Integer reference, Top: Integer reference, Width: Integer reference, Height: Integer reference) – The Play-Engine calls this method in order to get the layout information for an object. *ObjID* contains the object's ID. The layout values should be placed in *Left*, *Top*, *Width* and *Height*, respectively.

TerminateGUI () – The Play-Engine calls this method just before it terminates, thus giving the GUI application a chance to free memory and conduct all the actions needed for clean termination.

ApplyFunction(XMLFuncData: String) : String – This function is used by the Play-Engine in order to compute the value of an implemented function applied to given parameter values. *XMLFuncData* is a string that contains an XML description of the function to be applied. Its XML structure is as follows:

- **Function_Info** – The function information node
  - **Func_Name (String)** – The name of the implemented function. One of the functions that were declared in the implemented functions section in the application XML description file.
  - **Param1 (String)** – The value of parameter 1.
  - **Param2 (String)** – The value of parameter 2.
  - **Param3 (String)** – The value of parameter 3.
  - **Param4 (String)** – The value of parameter 4.
  - **Param5 (String)** – The value of parameter 5.

If there are fewer than five[1] parameters, only the relevant number of parameters is given in the string.

D.1 Visual Basic Code

Here is the Visual Basic code for the IUserApp interface:
Public Sub HideGUI()
End Sub

---

[1] In the current implementation, there is a technical bound of up to five parameters. This bound can be easily increased or avoided.

```
Public Sub ShowGUI()
End Sub
Public Function ApplyFunction(XMLFuncData As String) As String
End Function
Public Property Get AppDataXMLFile() As String
End Property
Public Property Let InfoMode(InInfoMode As Boolean)
End Property
Public Sub SetGUIObject(ObjID As Integer, PropID As Integer, sValue As
          String)
End Sub
Public Function GetGUIValue(ObjID As Integer, PropID As Integer) As
          String
End Function
Public Property Let PlayEngine(Engine As IplayEngine)
End Property
Public Sub HighlightObject(ObjID As Integer)
End Sub
Public Sub ClearObject(ObjID As Integer)
End Sub
Public Sub GetObjectPosition(ObjID As Integer, ByRef Left As Integer,
          ByRef Top As Integer)
End Sub
Public Sub GetObjectLayout(ObjID As Integer, ByRef Left As Integer,
          ByRef Top As Integer, ByRef Width As Integer, ByRef Height
          As Integer)
End Sub
Public Sub TerminateGUI()
End Sub
```

E. The Structure of a (Recorded) Run

A recorded run of the Play-Engine is saved as an XML file, which can later be loaded and replayed. This appendix provides information on the structure of such an XML file and explains each of its fields. Knowing the structure of a run can be very useful if one wishes to create a run, either manually or by using another tool, and then load it into the Play-Engine. Runs can therefore be generated by actual applications, by implementation tools, by conventional intra-object models, and so on.

⋆ **Run** – The root element of the Run XML file.

- **ID (Integer)** – The ID of the run.
- **Name (String)** – The name of the run.
- **RunEvents** – The root node for the events in the run.
  - **RunEvent** – A single run event.
    - **ID (Integer)** – A unique ID for each event. Starts from 1 and is continuously incremented.
    - **Value (String)** – If the event corresponds to a property change, then the new property value is given here (for example, Off). If the event corresponds to a method call between objects, the full string that describes the method call is written here (for example, SetState(Off), Method1(X1,X2), and so on).
    - **EventKind (Send/Recv)** – Indicates whether this is a send event or a receive event. For synchronous messages and for self-messages, only the Send event is specified in the run.
    - **FromObjID (Integer)** – The ID of the object sending the message. This is the object ID that is specified in the application description file.
    - **ToObjID (Integer)** – The ID of the object receiving the message. This is the object ID that is specified in the application description file. In the case of a self-message, ToObjID is the same as FromObjID.
    - **ToProperty (Integer)** – The ID of the property that was changed. This is specified only if the parent run event describes a property value change, and is the ID associated with this property in the application description file.

- **Method (Integer)** – The ID of the method that was called. This should be specified only if the parent run event describes a method call, and is the ID associated with this method in the application description file.
- **Param1 (String)** – The value of parameter 1.
- **Param2 (String)** – The value of parameter 2.
- **Param3 (String)** – The value of parameter 3.
- **Param4 (String)** – The value of parameter 4.
- **Param5 (String)** – The value of parameter 5.
  Parameter values are given only in the case of a method call. When there are fewer than five parameters, only the relevant number of parameters is given.

References

1. M. Abadi, L. Lamport, and P. Wolper. Realizable and Unrealizable Concurrent Program Specifications. In *Proc. 16th Int. Colloq. Aut. Lang. Prog.*, vol. 372, *Lecture Notes in Computer Science*, pp. 1–17. Springer-Verlag, 1989.
2. Altia Design & Altia FacePlate. Web page http://www.altia.com.
3. R. Alur. Timed Automata. In *11th Int. Conf. on Computer-Aided Verification*, vol. 1633, *Lecture Notes in Computer Science*, pp. 8–22. Springer-Verlag, 1999.
4. R. Alur and D.L. Dill. A Theory of Timed Automata. *Theoretical Computer Science*, 126:183–235, 1994.
5. R. Alur, K. Etessami, and M. Yannakakis. Inference of Message Sequence Charts. In *Proc. 22nd Int. Conf. on Software Engineering (ICSE'00)*, Limerick, Ireland, June 2000.
6. R. Alur and T.A. Henzinger. Logics and Models of Real Time: a Survey. *In Real-Time: Theory in Practice, REX Workshop*, vol. 600, *Lecture Notes in Computer Science*, pp. 74-106. Springer-Verlag, 1991.
7. R. Alur and T.A. Henzinger. A Really Temporal Logic. In *Proc. 30th Annual Symp. on Foundations of Computer Science (FOCS'89)*, pp. 164–169. IEEE Computer Society Press, 1989.
8. R. Alur and T.A. Henzinger. Real-Time System = Discrete System + Clock Variables. *Software Tools for Technology Transfer*, 1:86–109, 1997.
9. R. Alur, G.J. Holzmann, and D. Peled. An Analyzer for Message Sequence Charts. *Software Concepts and Tools*, 17(2):70–77, 1996.
10. R. Alur and M. Yannakakis. Model Checking of Message Sequence Charts. In *Proc. 10th Int. Conf. on Concurrency Theory (CONCUR'99)*, Eindhoven, The Netherlands, August 1999.
11. D. Amyot and A. Eberlein. An Evaluation of Scenario Notations for Telecommunication Systems Development. In *Int. Conf. on Telecommunication Systems*, Dallas, TX, 2001.
12. K. Apt. *Verification of Sequential and Concurrent Programs*. Springer-Verlag, 2nd edition, 1997.
13. H. Ben-Abdallah and S. Leue. Timing Constraints in Message Sequence Chart Specifications. In *Proc. 10th Int. Conf. on Formal Description Techniques FORTE/PSTV'97*, Osaka, Japan, November 1997. Chapman & Hall.
14. G. Berry and G. Gonthier. The Esterel Synchronous Programming Language: Design, Semantics, Implementation. *Sci. Comput. Program.*, 19:87–152, 1992.
15. A.W. Biermann and R. Krishnaswamy. Constructing Programs from Example Computations. *IEEE Trans. Softw. Eng.*, SE-2:141–153, 1976.
16. G. Booch. *Object-Oriented Analysis and Design with Applications*. Addison-Wesley, 1994.
17. G. Booch, J. Rumbaugh, and I. Jacobson. *Unified Modeling Language for Object-Oriented Development (Version 0.91 Addendum)*. RATIONAL Software Corporation, 1996.
18. M. Broy and I. Krüger. Interaction Interfaces – Towards a Scientific Foundation of a Methodological Usage of Message Sequence Charts. In J. Staples, M.G.

Hinchey, Shaoying Liu Hinchey, and Shaoying Liu (ed.), *Formal Engineering Methods* (*ICFEM'98*), pp. 2–15. IEEE Computer Society, 1998.

19. F. Buschmann, R. Maunier, H. Rohnert, P. Sommerald, and M. Stal. *A System of Patterns. Pattern-Oriented Software Architecture.* Wiley, 1996.

20. A.K. Chandra and P.M. Merlin. Optimal Implementation of Conjunctive Queries in Relational Databases. In *Proc. 9th ACM Symp. on the Theory of Computing*, pp. 77–90, 1977.

21. P.P. Chen. The Entity-Relationship Model: Toward a Unified View of Data. *ACM Trans. on Database Systems*, 1:9–36, 1976.

22. E.M. Clarke, O. Grumberg, and D. Peled. *Model Checking.* MIT Press, 2000.

23. A. Colmeraurer, H. Kanoui, P. Roussel, and R. Pasero. *Un système de communication homme-machine en francais.* Technical Report, Group de Recherche en Intelligence Artificielle, Univ. d'Aix-Marseille, 1973.

24. Microsoft COM. Web page: http://www.microsoft.com/com.

25. L. Constantine and E. Yourdon. *Structured Design.* Prentice-Hall, 1979.

26. S. Cook and J. Daniels. *Designing Object Systems: Object-Oriented Modeling with Syntropy.* Prentice-Hall, 1994.

27. W. Damm and D. Harel. LSCs: Breathing Life into Message Sequence Charts. *Formal Methods in System Design*, 19(1), 2001. Preliminary version in *Proc. 3rd IFIP Int. Conf. on Formal Methods for Open Object-Based Distributed Systems* (*FMOODS'99*), pp. 293–312, P. Ciancarini, A. Fantechi and R. Gorrieri, (eds.), Kluwer, 1999.

28. W. Damm, B. Josko, and R. Schlör. Specification and Verification of VHDL-Based System-Level Hardware Designs. In E. Börger (ed), *Specification and Validation Methods*, pp. 331–410. Oxford University Press, 1995.

29. W. Damm and J. Klose. Verification of a Radio-Based Signalling System Using the STATEMATE Verification Environment. *Formal Methods in System Design*, 19(2):121–141, 2001.

30. Borland Delphi. Web page http://www.borland.com/delphi/.

31. T. DeMarco. *Structured Analysis and System Specification.* Yourdon Press, 1978.

32. L.K. Dillon, G.Kutty, L.E. Moser, P.M. Melliar-Smith, and Y.S. Ramakrishna. A Graphical Interval Logic for Specifying Concurrent Systems. *ACM Trans. on Soft. Eng. and Meth.*, Vol 3(2), pp. 131–165, 1994.

33. R.G. Dromey. Genetic Software Engineering. *Manuscript*, 2001.

34. E.A. Emerson and E.M. Clarke. Using Branching Time Temporal Logic to Synthesize Synchronization Skeletons. *Science of Computer Programming*, 2:241–266, 1982.

35. e-SIM Rapid. Web page http://www.e-sim.com/home/.

36. Macromedia Flash. Web page http://www.macromedia.com/software/flash/.

37. R.W. Floyd. Assigning Meanings to Programs. In *Proc. Symp. on Applied Math.*, vol. 19: Mathematical Aspects of Computer Science, pp. 19–32. American Mathematical Society, 1967.

38. I. Greenwald. Development of the vulva. In: D.L. Riddle, , T. Blumenthal, B.J. Meyer, and J.R. Priess (eds.) *C. elegans* vol. II pp. 519–541. Cold Spring Harbor Laboratory Press, 1997.

39. R. Grosu, I. Krüger, and T. Stauner. Hybrid Sequence Charts. Tech. Report TUM-I9914, Technical University of Munich, 1999.

40. E.L. Gunter, A. Muscholl, and D. Peled. Compositional Message Sequence Charts. In *Tools and Algorithms for Construction and Analysis of Systems*, vol. 2031 of *Lecture Notes in Computer Science* pp. 496–511. Springer-Verlag, 2001.

41. N. Halbwachs, P. Caspi, P. Raymond, and D. Pilaud. The Synchronous Data-Flow Programming Language LUSTRE. *Proc. IEEE*, 79(9):1305–1320, September 1991.

42. D. Harel. Statecharts: A Visual Formalism for Complex Systems. *Sci. Comput. Prog.*, pp. 231–274, 1987. (Preliminary version: Tech. Report CS84-05, The Weizmann Institute of Science, Rehovot, Israel, February 1984.)

43. D. Harel. From Play-In Scenarios to Code: An Achievable Dream. *IEEE Computer*, pp. 53–60, January 2001.

44. D. Harel and E. Gery. Executable Object Modeling with Statecharts. *IEEE Computer*, pp. 31–42, 1997.

45. D. Harel and Y. Koren. Drawing Graphs with Non-uniform Vertices. In *Proc. Working Conf. on Advanced Visual Interfaces (AVI'02)*, pp. 157–166. ACM Press, 2002.

46. D. Harel and H. Kugler. Synthesizing State-Based Object Systems from LSC Specifications. *Int. J. of Foundations of Computer Science (IJFCS)*, 13(1):5–51, Febuary 2002. (Also, *Proc. 5th Int. Conf. on Implementation and Application of Automata (CIAA 2000)*, July 2000, vol. 2088, *Lecture Notes in Computer Science*. Springer-Verlag, 2000.)

47. D. Harel, H. Kugler, R. Marelly, and A. Pnueli. Smart Play-Out of Behavioral Requirements. In *Proc. 4th Int. Conf. on Formal Methods in Computer-Aided Design (FMCAD'02), Portland, USA*, 2002. Also available as Tech. Report MCS02-08, The Weizmann Institute of Science, 2002.

48. D. Harel, H. Lachover, A. Naamad, A. Pnueli, M. Politi, R. Sherman, A. Shtull-Trauring, and M. Trakhtenbrot. STATEMATE: A Working Environment for the Development of Complex Reactive Systems. *IEEE Trans. Soft. Eng.*, 16:403–414, 1990. (Preliminary version in *Proc. 10th Int. Conf. Soft. Eng. pp. 396–406*. IEEE Press, 1988).

49. D. Harel and R. Marelly. Specifying and Executing Behavioral Requirements: The Play-In/Play-Out Approach. *Software and System Modeling (SoSyM)*, to appear, 2003.

50. D. Harel and R. Marelly. *Play-Engine User's Guide*. 3rd edition, 2002.

51. D. Harel and R. Marelly. Playing with Time: On the Specification and Execution of Time-Enriched LSCs. In *Proc. 10th IEEE/ACM Int. Symp. on Modeling, Analysis and Simulation of Computer and Telecommunication Systems (MASCOTS'02)*, Fort Worth, Texas, 2002.

52. D. Harel and A. Pnueli. On the Development of Reactive Systems. In K. R. Apt, (ed.), *Logics and Models of Concurrent Systems*, NATO ASI Series, Vol. F-13, pp. 477–498. Springer-Verlag, 1985. 1985.

53. D. Harel and M. Politi. *Modeling Reactive Systems with Statecharts: The STATEMATE Approach*. McGraw-Hill, 1998. Early version titled *The Languages of STATEMATE*, Technical Report, I-Logix, Inc., Andover, MA (250 pp.), 1991.

54. D. Hatley and I. Pirbhai. *Strategies for Real-Time System Specification*. Dorset House, 1987.

55. C. Heitmeyer, J. Kirby, B. Labaw, and R. Bharadwaj. SCR*: A Toolset for Specifying and Analyzing Software Requirements. In A.J. Hu and M.Y. Vardi (eds.), *Int. Conf. on Computer Aided Verification (CAV'98)*, vol. 1427 of *Lecture Notes in Computer Science*, pp. 5–51. Springer-Verlag, 1998.

56. J.G. Henriksen, M. Mukund, K. Narayan Kumar, and P.S. Thiagarajan. On Message Sequence Graphs and Finitely Generated Regular MSC Languages. In *Proc. 27th Int. Colloq. on Automata Languages and Programming (ICALP'2000)*, Geneva, Switzerland, 2000, vol. 1853 of *Lecture Notes in Computer Science*. Springer-Verlag.

57. J.G. Henriksen, M. Mukund, K. Narayan Kumar, and P.S. Thiagarajan. Regular Collections of Message Sequence Charts. In *Proc. of the 25th Int. Symp. on Mathematical Foundations of Computer Science (MFCS'2000)*, vol. 1893 of *Lecture Notes in Computer Science*, Bratislava, Slovakia, 2000. Springer-Verlag.

58. C.A.R. Hoare. An Axiomatic Basis for Computer Programming. *Comm. Assoc. Comput. Mach.*, 12(10):576–583, 1969.

59. C.A.R. Hoare. Communicating Sequential Processes. *Comm. Assoc. Comput. Mach.*, 21:666–677, 1978.

60. I-Logix, Inc. Products Web page. http://www.ilogix.com/fs_prod.htm.

61. American National Standards Institute. Reference Manual for the ADA Programming Language. February 1983. ANSI/MIL-STD 1815A. Also published by Springer-Verlag as vol. 155 of Lecture Notes in Computer Science.

62. I. Jacobson. *Object-Oriented Software Engineering: A Use Case Driven Approach*. Addison-Wesley, 1992.

63. N. Kam, D. Harel, H. Kugler, R. Marelly, A. Pnueli, E.J.A. Hubbard, and M.J. Stern. Formal Modeling of C. elegans Development: A Scenario-Based Approach. In *Proc. Int. Workshop on Computational Methods in Systems Biology (CMSB 2003)*. Kluwer, February 2003.

64. J. Klose and B. Westphal. Relating LSC Specifications to UML Models. In *Proc. 2nd Int. Workshop on Integration of Specification Techniques for Applications in Engineering (INT 2002), Grenoble, France*, 2002.

65. J. Klose and H. Wittke. An Automata Based Interpretation of Live Sequence Charts. In *Proc. 7th Intl. Conf. on Tools and Algorithms for the Construction and Analysis of Systems (TACAS'01)*, 2001.

66. K. Koskimies and E. Makinen. Automatic Synthesis of State Machines from Trace Diagrams. *Software — Practice and Experience*, 24(7):643–658, 1994.

67. K. Koskimies, T. Mannisto, T. Systa, and J. Tuomi. SCED: A Tool for Dynamic Modeling of Object Systems. Tech. Report A-1996-4, University of Tampere, July 1996.

68. K. Koskimies, T. Systa, J. Tuomi, and T. Mannisto. Automated Support for Modeling OO Software. *IEEE Software*, 15(1):87–94, 1988.

69. R.A. Kowalski. Predicate Logic as a Programming Language. *Information Processing'74, pp. 569–574*. North-Holland, 1974.

70. R. Koymans, J. Vytopil, and W.-P. de Roever. Real-Time Programming and Asynchronous Message Passing. In *Proc. 2nd Annual Symp. on Principles of Distributed Computing*, pp. 187–197. ACM Press, 1983.

71. I. Krueger. *Distributed System Design with Message Sequence Charts*. Ph.D. Thesis, Department of Informatics, Technical University of Munich, 2000.

72. I. Kruger, R. Grosu, P. Scholz, and M. Broy. From MSCs to Statecharts. In *Proc. DIPES'98*. Kluwer, 1999.

73. O. Kupferman and M.Y. Vardi. Synthesis with Incomplete Information. In *2nd Int. Conf. on Temporal Logic*, pp. 91–106, Manchester, July 1997.

74. L. Lamport. Time, Clocks, and the Ordering of Events in a Distributed System. *Communications of the ACM*, Vol 21(7), pp. 558–565, 1978.

75. L. Lamport. The Temporal Logic of Actions. *ACM Trans. on Prog. Lang. and Sys.*, Vol 16(3), pp. 872–923, 1994.

76. M. Lettrari and J. Klose. Scenario-Based Monitoring and Testing of Real-Time UML Models. In *4th Int. Conf. on the Unified Modeling Language, Toronto*, October 2001.

77. S. Leue, L. Mehrmann, and M. Rezai. Synthesizing ROOM Models from Message Sequence Chart Specifications. Tech. Report 98-06, University of Waterloo, April 1998.

78. M. Broy, C. Hofmann, I. Krüger, and M. Schmidt. A Graphical Description Technique for Communication in Software Architectures. Tech. Report TUM-I9705, Technical University of Munich, 1997.

79. P.W. Sternberg and M. Wang. Pattern Formation During C. elegans Vulval Induction. *Curr. Top. Dev. Biol.*, 51:189–220, 2001.

80. J. Magee and J. Kramer. *Concurrency - State Models & Java Programs*. Wiley, 1999.

81. J. Magee, N. Pryce, D. Giannakopoulou, and J. Kramer. Graphical Animation of Behavior Models. *22nd Int. Conf. on Soft. Eng. (ICSE'00), Limeric, Ireland*, 2000.

82. Z. Manna and A. Pnueli. *The Temporal Logic of Reactive and Concurrent Systems: Specification*. Springer-Verlag, 1992.

83. Z. Manna and R.J. Waldinger. A Deductive Approach to Program Synthesis. *ACM Trans. on Programming Languages and Systems*, 2:90–121, 1980.

84. R. Marelly, D. Harel, and H. Kugler. Multiple Instances and Symbolic Variables in Executable Sequence Charts. In *Proc. 17th Ann. ACM Conf. on Object-Oriented Programming, Systems, Languages and Applications (OOPSLA'02), Seattle, WA*, 2002.

85. S. Mauw and M.A. Reniers. Refinement in Interworkings. In U. Montanari and V. Sassone (eds.), *CONCUR'96*, vol. 1119 of *Lecture Notes in Computer Science*, pp. 671–686. Springer, 1996.

86. N. Meng-Siew. Reasoning with Timing Constraints in Message Sequence Charts. Master's Thesis, University of Stirling, UK, August 1993.

87. B. Meyer. *Eiffel: The Language*. Prentice-Hall, 1992.

88. R. Milner. *A Calculus of Communicating Systems*, vol. 92 of *Lecture Notes in Computer Science*. Springer-Verlag, 1980.

89. B. Moszkowski. A Temporal Logic for Multi-level Reasoning about Hardware. *IEEE Computer*, 18:10–19, 1985.

90. B. Moszkowski. *Executing Temporal Logic Programs*. Cambridge University Press, Cambridge, UK, 1986.

91. ITU-TS Recommendation Z.120 (11/99): MSC 2000. ITU-TS, Geneva, 1999.

92. A. Pnueli. The Temporal Semantics of Concurrent Programs. *Theoretical Computer Science*, 13:1–20, 1981.

93. A. Pnueli. *Applications of Temporal Logic to the Specification and Verification of Reactive Systems: A Survey of Current Trends*. In de Bakker et al. (eds.), *Current Trends in Concurrency*, vol. 224 of *Lecture Notes in Computer Science*, pp. 510–584. Springer-Verlag, 1986.

94. A. Pnueli and W.-P. de Roever. Rendez-vous with Ada: A Proof Theoretical View. In Proc. SIGPLAN AdaTEC Conf. on Ada, pp. 129–137. ACM Press, 1982.

95. A. Pnueli and E. Harel. Applications of Temporal Logic to the Specification of Real-Time Systems. In M. Joseph (ed.), Formal Techniques in Real-Time and Fault-Tolerant Systems, vol. 331 of Lecture Notes in Computer Science, pp. 84–98. Springer-Verlag, 1988.

96. A. Pnueli and R. Rosner. On the Synthesis of an Asynchronous Reactive Module. In *Proc. 16th Int. Colloq. Aut. Lang. Prog.*, vol. 372 of *Lecture Notes in Computer Science*, pp. 652–671. Springer-Verlag, 1989.

97. A. Pnueli and R. Rosner. Distributed Reactive Systems Are Hard To Synthesize. In *Proc. 31th IEEE Symp. Found. of Comp. Sci.*, pp. 746–757, 1990.

98. A. Pnueli and R. Rosner. On the Synthesis of a Reactive Module. In *Proc. 16th ACM Symp. on Principles of Programming Languages*, pp. 179–190, Austin, TX, January 1989.

99. N. Pryce and J. Magee. SceneBeans: A Component-Based Animation Framework for Java. http://www-dse.doc.ic.ac.uk/Software/SceneBeans/.

100. Rational, Inc. Web page http://www.rational.com.

101. W. Reisig. *Petri Nets: An Introduction*. Springer-Verlag, 1985.

102. M.A. Reniers. *Message Sequence Charts. Syntax and Semantics*. Ph.D. Thesis, Eindhoven University of Technology, 1999.

103. J.A. Robinson. *Logic: Form and Function*, Chap. 11, pp. 182–198. North-Holland, 1979.

104. A. Roychoudhury and P.S. Thiagarajan. Interface Modeling with Cyclic Transaction Processes. In *Formal Methods at the Crossroads: From Panacea to Foundation Support, 10th Anniversary Colloq. of UNU/IIST*, Lisbon, Portugal, 2002, *Lecture Notes in Computer Science*, Springer-Verlag, to appear.

105. J. Rumbaugh, M. Blaha, W. Premerlani, F. Eddy, and W. Lorensen. *Object-Oriented Modeling and Design*. Prentice-Hall, 1991.

106. J. Rumbaugh, I. Jacobson, and G. Booch. *The Unified Modeling Language Reference Manual*. Addison-Wesley, 1999.

107. S. Bornot and J. Sifakis. An Algebraic Framework for Urgency. *Information and Computation*, 163:172–202, 2000.

108. R. Schlor and W. Damm. Specification and Verification of System-Level Hardware Designs using Timing Diagram. In *Proc. European Conf. on Design Automation*, Paris, France, 1993, pp. 518–524. IEEE Computer Society Press.

109. R. Schlör, B. Josko, and D. Werth. Using a Visual Formalism for Design Verification in Industrial Environments. In T. Margaria, B. Steffenan, R. Rückert, and J. Posegga (eds.), *Services and Visualization: Towards User-Friendly Design, ACoS'98*,

VISUAL'98, AIN'97, Selected Papers, vol. 1385 of *Lecture Notes in Computer Science*, pp. 208–221. Springer-Verlag, 1998.

110. SDL: ITU-T Recommendation Z.100, Languages for Telecommunications Applications: Specification and Description Language, Geneva, 1999.

111. B. Selic, G. Gullekson, and P. Ward. *Real-Time Object-Oriented Modeling*. Wiley, 1994.

112. J. Sifakis. Modeling Real-Time Systems – Challenges and Work Directions. In *EM-SOFT01, Tahoe City, CA, USA*, October 2001, vol. 2211 of *Lecture Notes in Computer Science*, Springer-Verlag.

113. J. Suzuki and Y. Yamamoto. Extending UML for Modelling Reflective Software Components. In R. France and B. Rumpe (eds.), *UML'99 — the Unified Modeling Language. Beyond the Standard. 2nd Int. Conf.*, Fort Collins, CO, USA, 1999, vol. 1723 of *Lecture Notes in Computer Science*, pp. 220–235. Springer-Verlag, 1999.

114. S. Uchitel, J. Kramer, and J. Magee. Detecting Implied Scenarios in Message Sequence Chart Specifications. In *9th European Software Engineering Conferece and 9th ACM SIGSOFT Int. Symp. on the Foundations of Software Engineering (ESEC/FSE'01). Vienna, Austria.*, September 2001.

115. Documentation of the Unified Modeling Language (UML), available from the Object Management Group (OMG). http://www.omg.org.

116. Microsoft Visual Basic. Web page http://msdn.microsoft.com/vbasic/.

117. P. Ward and S. Mellor. *Structured Development for Real-Time Systems*, vol. 1–3. Yourdon Press, 1985.

118. D.H.D. Warren. Implementing Prolog – Compiling Logic Programs (1 and 2). DAI Research Reports 39 and 40, University of Edinburgh, 1977.

119. J. Whittle and J. Schumann. Generating Statechart Designs from Scenarios. In *22nd Int. Conf. on Software Engineering (ICSE 2000)*, pp. 314–323. ACM Press, 2000.

120. R.J. Wieringa. *Design Methods for Reactive Systems: Yourdon, Statemate, and the UML*. Morgan Kaufmann, 2002.

121. H. Wong-Toi and D.L. Dill. Synthesizing Processes and Schedulers from Temporal Specifications. In *Computer-Aided Verification '90*, DIMACS Series in Discrete Mathematics and Theoretical Computer Science, vol. 3, pp. 177–186, 1991.

122. Web page http://www.xml.com.

123. ITU-TS Recommendation Z.120: Message Sequence Chart (MSC). ITU-TS, Geneva, 1996.

124. ITU-TS Recommendation Z.120: Message Sequence Chart (MSC) — Annex B: Algebraic Semantics of Message Sequence Charts. ITU-TS, Geneva, 1995.

Index